Antisemitism, Christian Ambivalence, and the Holocaust

Antisemitism, Christian Ambivalence, and the Holocaust

EDITED BY

Kevin P. Spicer, C.S.C.

Indiana University Press

BLOOMINGTON AND INDIANAPOLIS

*Published in association with the
United States Holocaust Memorial Museum
Washington, D.C.*

This book is a publication of

Indiana University Press
601 North Morton Street
Bloomington, IN 47404-3797 USA

http://iupress.indiana.edu

Telephone orders   800-842-6796
Fax orders   812-855-7931
Orders by e-mail   iuporder@indiana.edu

© 2007 by Indiana University Press

Library of Congress Cataloging-in-Publication Data
Antisemitism, Christian ambivalence, and the Holocaust / edited by Kevin P.
Spicer.
p. cm.
The scholars whose essays appear in this volume met at the Center for
Advanced Holocaust Studies of the United States Holocaust Memorial
Museum in the summer of 2004 for a workshop about the Holocaust and
antisemitism in Christian Europe"—Preface.
Includes bibliographical references and index.
ISBN-13: 978-0-253-34873-9 (cloth : alk. paper)
ISBN-10: 0-253-34873-0 (cloth : alk. paper) 1. Antisemitism—Europe—
History—Congresses. 2. Antisemitism—Germany—History—Congresses.
3. Holocaust, Jewish (1939–1945)—Moral and ethical aspects—Congresses.
4. Holocaust, Jewish (1939–1945)—Germany—Congresses. 5. Christianity and
antisemitism. 6. National socialism—Germany. I. Spicer, Kevin P., date
II. Center for Advanced Holocaust Studies.
DS146.E85A577 2007
940.53'18—dc22
                                                              2006033233

1 2 3 4 5   12 11 10 09 08 07

In memory of
Monsignor Bernhard Lichtenberg
(1875–1943)

CONTENTS

PREFACE

KEVIN P. SPICER

The scholars whose essays appear in this volume met at the Center for Advanced Holocaust Studies of the United States Holocaust Memorial Museum in the summer of 2004 for a workshop about the Holocaust and antisemitism in Christian Europe. Our goal was to examine how the legacy of antisemitism within the Christian churches limited the ability of their clergy and laity to critique National Socialism as evil and unequivocally condemn it.

The Center's workshops provide a unique experience for researchers to gather together outside the confines of their regular college or university milieu and to devote two weeks solely to examining a shared interest. Before the workshop began, each participant prepared an original essay based on primary source material, which we shared with one another. Over the course of the two weeks, we devoted approximately two and a half hours to in-depth discussion of the content of each paper. At the end of our time together, each of us agreed to revise his or her paper for publication. The essays in this volume are the product of this introspective process.

The contributors to this volume agree that the study of the historical and theological basis for antisemitism remains paramount today, as the recent controversy over Mel Gibson's film *The Passion of the Christ* made clear.[1] It is the responsibility of contemporary scholarship to inform present and future generations of students, scholars, and the broader population about antisemitism's subtleties and intrinsic evils. Through their research, responsible historians and theologians encourage the Christian churches to continue to observe carefully the roles that antisemitism has played and continues to play in their history, theology, and liturgical worship. Although an ever-growing body of literature deals with the study of antisemitism, scholars of Christian and Jewish studies have, until recently, kept a strict but misleading separation between Nazi "racial antisemitism" and "Christian antisemitism."[2]

More than twenty years ago, Ulrich von Hehl, an historian of German Catholicism, publicly lamented that historians and theologians had not worked together to study how the churches had responded to National Socialism. Hehl argued that it was very difficult for younger historians to interpret authentically the experience of the Christian churches under National Socialism because of their lack of "lived understanding." He also criticized the perceived need on the part of younger historians to pass judgment upon Christianity without an essential understanding of the theology of this period.[3] Since the early 1980s, historians and theologians have made increasing and earnest efforts to address antisemitism in the churches. Normally, these discussions have taken place in individual sessions at conferences dedicated to the study of the Holocaust in general or, alternatively, in conferences dedicated to the study of the 1933–1945 German *Kirchenkampf* (church struggle). Few, if any, conferences have specifically brought together historians and theologians to discuss antisemitism.[4] Consequently, our workshop sought to address this void by gathering scholars of German, Danish, Polish, and Romanian history alongside scholars of Judaism and Christianity. Our goal was to examine specifically the role antisemitism played in the Christian response to National Socialism.

The contributions in this volume reference the familial relations between Jews and Christians and the matter of crucifixion and the Jews in the New Testament period itself; interwar Polish and German Christian theology and the civil struggle in Spain; German-Christian theological views and their application through the war; wartime Christian and antisemitic attitudes in Romania and Denmark; and postwar Christian theological developments in occupied Germany and in the Holy See. Though these essays raise a multitude of issues, one in particular stands out: the Christian failure to understand and acknowledge Judaism on its own terms. Ever since Jesus of Nazareth walked this earth, his followers have professed to live his teaching of love of neighbor. Unfortunately, Christians have often failed to embrace the fullness of this teaching.[5] This was especially true under National Socialism. Nevertheless, some Christians were open to providing *caritas,* or charity, to Jews in need. Still, these acts of kindness did not mean that individual Christians truly viewed Jews as equals or fully acknowledged their religious and cultural heritage as legitimate. For Christians, there was still the desire, or even the command, to proselytize and bring Jews "into the fold." Unfortunately, similar initiatives today persist in most Christian denominations. In addition, few Christian denominations, if any, have fully recognized the salvific nature of the original and everlasting covenant made between Abraham and Yahweh.

Though the churches have advanced substantially in their understanding of their relationship to Jews and Judaism, there is still a long way to go. Declarations such as *Dominus Iesus* from the Holy See's Congregation for the Doctrine of the Faith, which fail to acknowledge this unique relationship, only perpetuate the teaching of a triumphant Christianity.[6] In turn, Judaism is then easily relegated to second-place status beneath Christianity, thereby creating an atmosphere for antisemitism to thrive. For antisemitism is still quite present in Christianity: in its Scripture, in its worship, and in its everyday rhetoric. We hope that the essays in this volume serve to raise the reader's awareness of Christianity's role in the propagation and spread of antisemitism.

So many individuals contributed to the success of our workshop and of this volume. In particular, in the name of all the contributors, I would like to offer special words of gratitude to Paul A. Shapiro, Director of the Center for Advanced Holocaust Studies, United States Holocaust Memorial Museum; Robert Ehrenreich, Director of University Programs for the Center; Benton Arnovitz, Director of Academic Publications for the Center; Ann Millin, special assistant to the Center's director; Suzanne Brown-Fleming, senior program officer for the Center's University Programs; Aleisa Fishman, editorial coordinator for the Center's Academic Publications; Martin Dean, an applied research scholar of the Center; and Eric Brinkert, a Center intern; all of whom contributed their many talents and gifts to make our time at the museum enjoyable and extremely productive. The original workshop was also made possible by the generosity of the Cannon Hottberger Fund. I completed the editing of this volume while a fellow of the Center. During this time, my colleagues there were extremely generous with their time and insights. In particular, I would like to thank Victoria Barnett, Diana Dimitru, Judith Gerson, Daniel Magilow, Jürgen Matthäus, Lisa Yavnai, and Lisa Zaid. In addition, I would like to express my appreciation to the administration of Stonehill College, especially Mark Cregan, C.S.C., Esq., President; Katie Conboy, Vice-President for Academic Affairs; Karen Talentino, Dean of Faculty; and Nancy Dunsing, Assistant to the Vice-President for Academic Affairs, for their continued support of my research and writing. Last, but never least, I would like to acknowledge especially my confreres in the Eastern Province of the Congregation of Holy Cross and my parents, John and Gloria Spicer, whose concern and support strengthen me in my ministry and academic endeavors.

NOTES

1. For a summary of recent debate on *The Passion,* see Peter J. Boyer, "The Jesus War: Mel Gibson's Obsession," *New Yorker,* September 15, 2003, 58–71. For critical essays on the film and its theological implications, see Daniel Burston and Rebecca I. Denova, eds., *Passionate Dialogues: Critical Perspectives on Mel Gibson's* The Passion of the Christ (Pittsburgh: Mise, 2005); Paula Fredriksen, ed., *On* The Passion of the Christ: *Exploring the Issues Raised by the Controversial Movie* (Berkeley: University of California Press, 2006); *Perspectives on* The Passion of the Christ: *Religious Thinkers and Writers Explore the Issues Raised by the Controversial Movie* (New York: Miramax Books, 2004).

2. Works on antisemitism by theologians include: Judith H. Banki and John T. Pawlikowski, O.S.M., eds., *Ethics in the Shadow of the Holocaust: Christian and Jewish Perspectives* (Franklin, Wisc.: Sheed and Ward, 2001); Gregory Baum, *Is the New Testament Antisemitic? A Re-evaluation of the New Testament* (Glen Rock, N.J.: Paulist Press, 1965); Gregory Baum, *Christian Theology after Auschwitz* (London: Council of Christians and Jews, 1976); Edward H. Flannery, *The Anguish of the Jews: Twenty-Three Centuries of Antisemitism,* rev. (New York: Paulist Press, 1985); Franklin H. Littell, *The Crucifixion of the Jews,* reprint (Macon, Ga.: Mercer University Press, 1986); Rosemary Radford Ruether, *Faith and Fratricide: The Theological Roots of Antisemitism,* reprint (Eugene, Ore.: Wipf and Stock, 1997). Studies on antisemitism by historians include: Doris L. Bergen, "Catholics, Protestants, and Antisemitism in Nazi Germany," *Central European History* 27 (1994): 329–48; Olaf Blaschke, *Katholizismus und Antisemitismus im Deutschen Kaiserreich,* 2nd rev. ed. (Göttingen: Vandenhoeck and Ruprecht, 1999); Hermann Greive, *Theologie und Ideologie. Katholizismus und Judentum in Deutschland und Österreich 1918–1935* (Heidelberg: Lambert Schneider, 1969); Christhard Hoffmann, Werner Bergmann, and Helmut Walser Smith, eds., *Exclusionary Violence: Antisemitic Riots in Modern Germany History* (Ann Arbor: University of Michigan Press, 2002); Heinz Hürten, *Deutsche Katholiken 1918 bis 1945* (Paderborn: Ferdinand Schöningh, 1992), 425–40; David I. Kertzer, *The Popes Against the Jews: The Vatican's Role in the Rise of Modern Anti-Semitism* (New York: Knopf, 2001); Helmut Walser Smith, *The Butcher's Tale: Murder and Antisemitism in a German Town* (New York: Norton, 2002); Uriel Tal, *Christians and Jews in Germany: Religion, Politics, and Ideology in the Second Reich, 1870–1914,* trans. Noah Jonathan Jacobs (Ithaca, N.Y.: Cornell University Press, 1975).

3. Ulrich von Hehl, "Kirche und Nationalsozialismus: Ein Forschungsbericht," in *Kirche im Nationalsozialismus* (Stuttgart: Geschichtsverein der Diözese Rottenburg, 1984), 11.

4. One notable exception was the September 1999 conference, "Christian Life and Thought: Responses to Totalitarianism and Authoritarianism in the Twentieth Century," organized by Donald Dietrich at Boston College in Chestnut Hill, Massachusetts. For selected papers from this conference see Donald J. Dietrich, ed., *Christian Responses to the Holocaust: Moral and Ethical Issue.* (Syracuse, N.Y.: Syracuse University Press, 2003).

5. For a discussion of the Catholic Church's teaching of love of neighbor in Germany under the Third Reich, see Kevin P. Spicer, *Resisting the Third Reich: The Catholic Clergy in Hitler's Berlin* (DeKalb: Northern Illinois University Press, 2004), 128–33.

6. "Dominus Iesus," *Origins* 30, no. 14 (2000): 209–19.

INTRODUCTION:
LOVE THY NEIGHBOR?

JOHN T. PAWLIKOWSKI AND KEVIN P. SPICER

For many years, Father Heinrich Weber labored as the *Caritas* (Catholic Charities) director in the diocese of Münster. His coworkers remember him as a kind, gentle man, who had great compassion for the poor and oppressed. In 1935, the University of Breslau offered him an opportunity to share his wealth of pastoral experience with seminarians from Berlin and Breslau by becoming a professor of pastoral theology.[1] Weber happily accepted this opportunity, especially the chance to influence the ministerial approach of these future priests. At the same time, Weber realized that the German government under National Socialism would provide him with great challenges in his attempt to teach students about Christian compassion and charity in ministry. Similarly, Weber also knew that he had Father Felix Haase, a member of the Nazi Party and dean of the Faculty of Theology at the university, constantly watching to ensure that he did not teach anything contrary to the spirit of the new German state.[2] Therefore, he refined the way he presented the traditional Christian commands to love God and neighbor.

In 1938, Weber published his lectures on this subject as *The Essence of Charity.* According to Weber, "every person, even foreigners, indeed even enemies of the *Volk*[3] fall under the concept of neighbor." He referred his readers to the parable of the Good Samaritan as an example of this teaching.[4] Weber further explained that "our neighbors include not only blood relations or friends, but every person who suffers, whether a Samaritan or a pagan or a Jew. The command of Christ to love neighbor" superseded "all personal, societal, national, and religious barriers" and required that one must be willing to sacrifice one's own bodily well-being for the salvation of one's neighbor.[5] However, Weber tempered this bold statement by emphasizing that a Catholic should "never place his own salvation in jeopardy in order to love neighbor."[6] Instead of discussing how concretely to show one's love for a neighbor, Weber continued to qualify his interpretation by making distinctions in the definition of who is neighbor. Weber stated that though each person was our neighbor, "not everyone" was our "neighbor to the same degree."[7] He argued that "the union of blood, of family, of tribal identity and of membership in a race, the union of a household, the union of the same homeland and of friendship, the union of the same faith and the same culture" established and gave rise "to narrower and closer partnerships."[8]

In his interpretation of Christ's command to love neighbor, Weber made concessions and stated preferences as to whom should primarily benefit from the teaching. One can almost see Professor Weber at a chalkboard drawing circles around circles to differentiate between the "degrees" of neighbor. In contrast, when one turns to the biblical text, the commandment is clear and void of any preferentialism: "One of the scribes came near and heard them disputing with one another, and seeing that he [Jesus] answered them well, he asked him, 'Which commandment is the first of all?' Jesus answered, 'The first is, 'Hear O Israel: the Lord our God, the Lord is one; you shall love the Lord your God with all your heart, and with all your soul, and with all your mind, and with all your strength.' The second is this, 'You shall love your neighbor as yourself.' There is no other commandment greater than these'" (Mk 12:28–31).[9] In the Gospel of John, Jesus goes even further when he teaches his disciples: "This is my commandment that you love one another as I have loved you. No one has greater love than this, to lay down one's life for one's friends. You are my friends if you do what I command you" (Jn 15:12–14).

Unfortunately, all too often in history, Christians have chosen to ignore these great commandments or to interpret them according to their own worldview. The history of Jewish-Christian encounters over the centuries is no exception. This history is filled with lies, hatred, persecution, violence, and murder. While there were always Christians willing to reach out to Jews by offering charity in the form of material goods when the dominant Christian society restricted, oppressed, and persecuted them, seldom would the same Christians embrace the fullness of Jesus' commandments and place themselves in complete solidarity with Jews to the point of risking their own lives. Under National Socialism, Christians did not change this pattern of behavior.

There are many factors that account for why more Christians did not resist the persecution and murder of European Jews during the Holocaust. It is not possible here to review all of these complex factors. In addition, many responses had nothing to do with religion or hatred of Jews, but instead centered around questions of self-preservation and fear of reprisal. Many Christians who lived under National Socialism have admitted in interviews that they simply were not ready to spend torturous years in prison or even become martyrs in order to help Jews. Nevertheless, behind the operating mindset of Europe's Christians, whether articulated or not, existed centuries of official teaching of the Christian churches, which portrayed Jews as the Other. This mindset identified Jews as the people who rejected Christ and crucified him. The Gospels, especially John, recorded and proclaimed this image. Through their sermons and writings, the early Church Fathers reinforced this teaching. And this teaching stuck and became an accepted fact for the Christian churches. As a German Catholic woman who lived through Hitler's Germany testified, it was not necessary for her religion teachers even to emphasize the deicide charge, because it was something that every Catholic knew and believed to be true.[10]

To assess how Christianity responded to the question of loving neighbor in 1920s–1940s Europe, the authors in this collection examine the churches from the perspective of both the leadership (local, national, and universal level) and the laity in four areas: Christian theology, clerical pastoral practice, Jewish-Catholic dialogue, and popular perceptions Jews and Christians share of one another.

In the section exploring "Theological Antisemitism," Thorsten Wagner, Anna Łysiak, Robert Krieg, and Donald Dietrich reveal the ties between historical anti-Judaism and modern antisemitism within the theology of Europe's Lutheran and Catholic churches. These authors recognize that the churches often made distinctions between Christian anti-Judaism and racial antisemitism. Commonly, the churches viewed anti-Judaism as religiously and theologically driven and stemming from the Christian belief that Christianity has superseded Judaism and made it a fossilized relic. At times, the churches also generally acknowledged that anti-Judaism has led to teaching contempt for Jews and to violence against them because of their so-called stubborn rejection of Jesus as the Messiah. In turn, they welcomed Jews who converted into the Christian community. In contrast, the churches understood antisemitism as a condemnation of Jews because of their "inferior" race and tied this to the development of nineteenth-century racial science. Despite these distinctions, at the root of hatred of Jews in all its various forms was the initial Christian portrayal of Jews as the Other who crucified Christ. Christians reinforced this notion by easily turning to Scripture and reading, "Then the people [Jews] as a whole answered, 'His blood be on us and on our children!'" (Mt 27:25). Therefore, in their contributions, Wagner, Łysiak,

Krieg, and Dietrich reveal the integral connection between anti-Judaism and antisemitism in the theology of the Lutheran and Catholic churches.

Specifically, in his essay, Thorsten Wagner probes the actions of the Lutheran Church in Denmark beyond the generalizations about the heroic posture of the Danes. While in no way wishing to undermine the recognition Denmark truly deserves for its rescue efforts on behalf of its Jewish community, Wagner shows the actual story to be considerably more complex than the prevailing image of Denmark during World War II, especially in reference to the predominant Lutheran Church. Wagner offers a comprehensive analysis of how the majority Lutheran population in Denmark viewed Jews and Judaism. He finds that their outlook was not entirely positive and, in fact, not all that different from stereotypes of Jews and Judaism prevalent among the peoples of other European countries at the time. In addition, Danish Lutheranism never halted its campaign to missionize Jews. Fundamentally, Danish Lutheranism exhibited considerable contempt for Judaism as a religion, whether in its ancient forms or in its more modern guise. Judaism was dubbed a ridiculous and pitiful legalism, and Danish theologians and pastors spoke out strongly against what they regarded as perverse Jewish support for modern liberalism and capitalism. According to Wagner, the classic anti-Jewish stereotypes were clearly present within the Danish Lutheran community. Then why, Wagner correctly asks, did classical Christian anti-Judaism in Denmark not translate into church support for Nazi racial antisemitism as it did in so many other European countries? Wagner believes the answer lies in the emergence of a challenge to the Danish nation as to whether it would collaborate or resist. It chose the latter and thus rescue of Danish Jews became an immediate imperative.

Anna Łysiak builds upon similar theological themes in her essay on Catholic theologians' perceptions of Jews in prewar Poland. Łysiak persuasively establishes a significant link between Catholic leaders' concepts about Jews and Judaism and their views of the Church's missionary nature that obliged it to pursue the conversion of Jews. She shows how even those scholars considered experts on Judaism, such as Stanisław Trzeciak and Jozef Kruszyński, debased Judaism, particularly in its modern forms. Łysiak also reveals that there were other voices in the Polish Catholic Church that sought a reevaluation of the Church's relationship with Judaism. In Warsaw and several other dioceses in Poland, Catholics founded chapters of the *Amici Israel* (Friends of Israel) organization. Cardinal Kakowski and several other bishops supported these endeavors. *Amici Israel* published a bulletin, *Pax Super Israel.* That bulletin championed the overall goals of the organization in Poland, such as the cessation of the deicide accusation against Jews, the removal of negative terms about Jews in the Christian liturgy, and the elimination of all antisemitic language in general. Prior to the Second World War, this certainly represented a promising movement in Poland. Regrettably, in March 1928, the Vatican's Congregation of the Holy Office decreed the dissolution of the organization throughout Europe on the grounds that its perspectives were not in keeping with the spirit of the Church, the teachings of the Church Fathers, and the Catholic liturgy.

Likewise, in their articles, Robert Krieg and Donald Dietrich show how the views of prominent Christian theologians affected Christian consciousness in Germany prior to and during the period of the Third Reich. In turn, they establish an unquestionable link between Nazism and Christian descriptions of Jews and Judaism over the centuries. There is little doubt that those negative descriptions provided a fertile seedbed for Christian acquiescence to and even outright endorsement of Nazi ideology, on both the popular and scholarly levels and within all the major branches of Christianity. Their combined research demonstrates a significant influence on Catholic self-identity during this critical period in German history. While neither would argue that such theological perspectives were the sole influence on Catholic behavior at the time, their work definitely establishes that such theological views had a significant influence on Catholic reaction to the Nazi onslaught against Jews. In so doing, they help to undercut any thesis that Nazi antisemitism was exclusively a neo-pagan phenomenon; rather, it also found its roots in theological anti-Judaism and antisemitism.

With the theological connection between Christian anti-Judaism and antisemitism established, the next section, "Christian Clergy and the Extreme Right Wing," shows how some members of the Catholic and Orthodox clergy embraced this theological antisemitism and made it a concrete part of their pastoral ministry and ecclesiastical outlook. In his piece, Kevin Spicer reveals how Father Dr. Phillip Haeuser embraced the most negative elements of his Church's anti-Jewish teaching, coupled them with modern antisemitism, and used this to agitate for National Socialism. This essay continues his work on "brown priests"—Catholic clergymen who publicly embraced National Socialism. While they were much smaller a number than the "German Christian" pastors in the Evangelical Lutheran Church, the brown priests' lives and choices, along with their interaction with their Church superiors, offer a unique and unflattering portrait of Church acceptance of antisemitism. In turn, the preaching and writings of the brown priests show how they translated traditional Christian hostility for Jews into overt support for Nazism. Spicer also reveals that the brown priests encountered opposition from German Catholic bishops. Yet the bishops regularly centered on a priest's failure to obey episcopal commands, rather than on his antisemitism.

Similarly, in her contribution on the Spanish Civil War and the German Catholic hierarchy, Beth A. Griech-Polelle reveals how the bishops' myopic social vision enabled them to share goals similar to those of National Socialism. Reminiscent of the domino theory with regard to Vietnam in the sixties, a strong belief among European Catholics held that if Spain fell to the communists, the rest of western Europe might follow. Many feared this would end Catholicism's influence in Europe. Certainly, Spanish communists did not treat Catholic leaders and Catholic institutions in Spain well. The Catholic leadership's stance during the Spanish Civil War galvanized Catholic attitudes in both Europe and America and, in turn, strengthened support for fascist alternatives, including the Nazi version of fascism, among Catholics. Since antisemitic rhetoric portrayed Jews as supporters of communism, this only added to anti-Jewish sentiment. As a result and in reaction to the communist effort to take over Catholic Spain, Catholics increasingly supported the cause of the extreme right.

Support of the extreme right was not limited to Catholics alone. In his analysis of the causal relationship between Romanian antisemitism and the teachings of the Romanian Orthodox Church, Paul Shapiro unmasks the practical aspects of this linkage by examining the active involvement of churchmen in the notorious Iron Guard. The spiritual mentors for the Iron Guard included prominent Orthodox religious scholars such as Mircea Eliade, who after fleeing the country taught at the University of Chicago. Shapiro's chapter also addresses Orthodox Christianity's role in the Holocaust, an under-researched area in comparison to the role of Protestantism and Catholicism during this time frame.

In the next section, "Postwar Jewish-Christian Encounters," Matthew Hockenos and Elias Füllenbach examine how the Christian churches attempted to reinterpret their relationship with Jews after the Holocaust. Their articles show that the reality of the Holocaust forced Christians to see Jews as their neighbors. Both Hockenos and Füllenbach demonstrate that there was clearly ecclesiastical pressure placed upon individuals such as Gertrud Luckner to desist in their efforts to generate a wholesale review of Christian attitudes toward Jews and Judaism in light of the

Holocaust. As Hockenos writes in his essay on the proselytization of Jews in postwar Germany, "recognition by Protestant clergymen of the need for a fundamental transformation of the Church's relationship to Jews and its understanding of Judaism was slow and halting." Nevertheless, Füllenbach shows that while there is certainly more than adequate room for criticism of the churches as institutions and individuals, the picture is not totally slanted toward the negative. In this immediate postwar era, individuals planted seeds that would mature in the 1960s within the churches in the form of official statements that spoke of Jews and Judaism in a positive light, the most influential of them being chapter four of the Second Vatican Council's Declaration on Non-Christian Religions (*Nostra Aetate*). Nevertheless, one must recognize that there is still much to do before the churches can fully free themselves of antisemitism.

Finally, in the section "Viewing Each Other," Gershon Greenberg, Suzanne Brown-Fleming, and Richard Steigmann-Gall show how far both Christians and Jews still need to journey in order to embrace each other authentically as neighbor. In his essay, Gershon Greenberg examines how Orthodox Jews responded to the Holocaust theologically. He finds not one single understanding, but rather two major trends. The unitive held that Christianity shared Judaism's God, morality, and Scripture. The unitive concept also maintained that Christianity was compromised by a latent paganism and consequently had the potential for an extreme hatred of Jews. Thus for Jewish religious thinkers such as Yehuydah Layb Gerst of Łódź, Poland, Christianity's involvement with Nazism was a matter of paganism's cooption of the Christian religion. A more dominant view within the orthodox Jewish community, which Greenberg labels as dualistic, viewed Christianity as profane and in opposition to the sacred reality of Jews. In this dualism, Christianity represented the profane and Judaism the sacred.

In her piece, Suzanne Brown-Fleming extends Greenberg's analysis by studying the experience of Rabbi Philip Bernstein, an advisor on Jewish affairs to General Joseph T. McNarney of the United States occupation forces. Brown-Fleming reveals how very different Bernstein's observations on postwar Germany and the treatment of war criminals were from those of Catholic counterpart Cardinal Aloisius Muench, who cared for Catholic displaced persons. These two radically different observations portray the profound gap between the Jewish and the Christian experiences under National Socialism. These different experiences also shed light on the difference between their views on postwar Germany.

In conclusion, Richard Steigmann-Gall shows the distance that the churches must overcome before truly comprehending the depth of anti-semitism still present within their traditions. As a concrete example, he speaks of Rabbi A. James Rudin's refusal to add his name to the important September 2000 Jewish document on Christianity, *Dabru Emet*, despite his central decades-long role in promoting enhanced Jewish-Christian understanding. Rudin objected to the first sentence of point five of the document, which read, "Nazism was not a Christian phenomenon."[11] While the subsequent sentence does connect Nazism with traditional Christian support of antisemitism, the first sentence's apparent endorsement of the interpretation of Nazism as essentially a pagan philosophy opposed to all forms of religion concerned Rudin. His objection has raised an important issue. There is a disturbing tendency in some Christian circles to label Nazism equally anti-Christian and anti-Jewish. Certainly, Nazism was fundamentally anti-Christian and did attack the churches; however, it was also clearly willing to use the support of Christians who accepted its ideology. One must resist such a simple equation of Nazism's opposition to both Judaism and Christianity. They were not fully analogous in the minds of the Nazis. To equate them as such often hides a desire to mitigate Christianity's responsibility for the Holocaust. Unfortunately, this approach was visible in Pope Benedict XVI's remarks during his August 2005 visit to a synagogue in Cologne. While one may not fault him for calling Nazism "neo-pagan," this assertion must be accompanied by definite mention of Christian complicity. In recent years, Catholic bishops in France and Germany have made such an acknowledgement in statements on the Church and the Holocaust. Even the 1988 Vatican statement on the Holocaust, *We Remember*, which carried the personal endorsement of Pope John Paul II, made some references to this fact.[12] Steigmann-Gall also shows that many convinced Nazis saw nothing incompatible between National Socialism and Christianity. He offers substantial evidence of Christian influence in the writings and speeches of National Socialists. In light of this evidence, Steigmann-Gall forces Christians to reevaluate their tradition's Scripture and doctrine to see what was and continues to remain present within it that enabled followers of Adolf Hitler to find a connection between Christianity and National Socialism.

Recent events, particularly in Europe, have shown the continuing persistence of antisemitism. If we are to combat its influence we must understand its previous developments. Similarly, Christians of every denomination must learn to embrace the fullness of Christ's greatest commandments to love God and to love neighbor. The essays in this volume bring to the fore dimensions of the failure to put this teaching into practice. Similarly, they detail antisemitism's rise and impact within the religious community at a critical moment in human history. Understanding antisemitism's previous emergence within the Christian churches provides invaluable insights on how we today might resist this ugly reality.

NOTES

1. Specifically, Weber was a professor of *Caritaswissenschaft*, or the art of charity.

2. On May 1, 1933, Hasse joined the NSDAP and became member number 3,523,647. He served as dean of the Faculty of Theology from 1933 to 1945. See U.S. National Archives and Records Administration, College Park, MD, Ortsgruppenkartei RG242-A3340-MFOK-F083; NSDAP Korrespondenz RG242-A3340-PK-D103; and Erich Kleineidam, *Die katholisch-theologisch Fakultät der Universität Breslau 1811–1945* (Cologne: Weinand, 1961), 134–35.

3. *Volk* may be translated as people. However, especially during the Third Reich, the term has racial overtones and connotes blood, soil, and a shared past and future.

4. Heinrich Weber, *Das Wesen der Caritas* (Freiburg: Herder, 1938), 68.

5. Ibid., 146.

6. Ibid., 77.

7. Ibid., 152.

8. Ibid., 155.

9. Also see Mt 22:36–40 and Lk 10:25–28.

10. Kevin P. Spicer, *Resisting the Third Reich* (DeKalb: Northern Illinois University Press, 2004), 123.

11. For the text of *Dabru Emet* and commentary by Jewish and Christian scholars, see Tikva Frymer-Kensky et al., eds. *Christianity in Jewish Terms* (Boulder, Colo.: Westview, 2000).

12. For a wide-ranging discussion of *We Remember*, see Judith H. Banki and John T. Pawlikowski, O.S.M., eds., *Ethics in the Shadow of the Holocaust: Christian and Jewish Perspectives* (Franklin, Wisc.: Sheed and Ward, 2001), 5–227.

Antisemitism, Christian Ambivalence, and the Holocaust

I

Theological Antisemitism

1 Belated Heroism

THE DANISH LUTHERAN CHURCH AND THE JEWS, 1918–1945

THORSTEN WAGNER

A Light in the Darkness?

Compared to most other countries, the Danish-Jewish experience seems to stand out as a remarkable exception in modern European history. Obviously, this perception is intrinsically linked to the unique rescue effort of the Danish people in October 1943, causing Nazi Germany's attempt at rounding up and arresting Danish Jews to fail: only a few hundred Jews ended up being deported to Theresienstadt, and even of these, only about fifty—less than 1 percent of the more than seven thousand Jews living in Denmark at the time—perished.

One may date the origins of the positive image of Danish-Jewish relations back to the seventeenth century, when Glikl von Hameln, a merchant woman from Hamburg-Altona, praised the Danish king as just, pious, and extraordinarily benevolent toward Jews.[1] The only dissertation on Danish-Jewish history published so far, Nathan Bamberger's *Viking Jews*, traced this presumably exceptional phenomenon throughout Modern Danish history and concluded: "In the admirable history of Danish Jewry, one cannot overlook the Danes' strong humanistic values, their sense of decency, and their care for all citizens."[2] Organizations such as "Thanks to Scandinavia" promote the Danish commitment to human dignity and ethical values in World War II as a role model for moral behavior today by stating: "The selfless and heroic effort of the Scandinavian people through the dark days of Nazi Terror is a shining example of humanity and hope for now and tomorrow."[3] In addition, books such as *Moral Courage under Stress* and *The Test of a Democracy* attest to this glorification of the Danish past in a Jewish perspective.[4]

Over the last two decades, in the collective memory of American Jews, Denmark has become the antithesis of a Nazi-dominated Europe bogged down by the collaborators' active complicacy and the bystanders' indifference. Despite this dominating perception of Denmark as a Righteous Nation—even honored as such by Yad Vashem—recent political developments suggest that it may be necessary to take a closer look at these positive portraits of Danish-Jewish relations. In 1999, the nationalist-conservative publishing house Tidehverv, run by Jesper Langballe and Søren Krarup, right-wing theologians and clerics, republished Martin Luther's *On the Jews and Their Lies.* Langballe and Krarup are also both highly influential members of parliament for the Danish People's Party (Dansk Folkeparti), a populist radical right-wing party that constitutes the parliamentary basis of the present center-right government. In the introduction, the editors stress the work's "contemporary relevance" in affirmative terms without any critical commentary, while employing anti-Jewish traditions to legitimize their xenophobic populist agenda. In light of the enduring positive image of Danish-Jewish history, this republication—and even more the fact that it did not provoke any academic protest, let alone public outcry—indicates that this perception deserves more scrutiny.

Recently, however, a series of newspaper articles that focused on Krarup and his anti-Jewish rhetoric sparked public criticism of these tendencies. Repeatedly, Krarup has attempted to exculpate Harald Nielsen, a writer who welcomed Nazi antisemitic legislation and favored the introduction of the Jewish star. Krarup has also sympathized with Nielsen's attack on the Danish-Jewish literary scholar Georg Brandes by stating, "Because of his Jewish blood he felt no reverence towards or intimate connection with the country's past."[5] Krarup reacted to allegations of antisemitism by emphasizing his rejection of racism and racial antisemitism as ideologies incommensurate with a Christian worldview. He also emphasized that his family had fought in the national-conservative resistance against the Nazi occupiers in Denmark. Through his reference to Christian convictions and nationalist orientations, Krarup positioned himself in line with key dimensions of Danish memory culture. To many observers, the most salient event in the history of the Jews of Denmark was their successful attempt to escape the Nazi roundup action of October 1943. As hundreds of non-Jewish Danes assisted them, this rescue operation over the Øresund added to the triumphalist narrative of successful integration that dominates the perception of Danish-Jewish history. This narrative, augmented by the sense of gratitude displayed by many Danish Jews for the rejection of antisemitism, has helped to view Danish Jews as the exceptional case of the European-Jewish experience. Danish Lutheran clergy played a key role in these rescue activities. Pastors warned Jews of the imminent danger of deportation, offered them hiding places, and facilitated their escape to Sweden. The pastor of Trinitatis Church in central Copenhagen even received the Torah scrolls from the nearby synagogue in *Krystalgade* and hid them in a secret chamber in his church. Even more explicit was the protest pastoral letter initiated by the bishop of Copenhagen, Hans Fuglsang-Damgaard, and signed on September 29, 1943, by all the Danish Lutheran Church bishops. It was an immediate reaction against the roundup of Danish Jews. On the following Sunday, October 3, 1943, Lutheran pastors throughout Denmark read the letter. Repeatedly, reports told of congregants rising from their pews to express their solidarity and support. The pastoral letter boldly stated that was the duty of the Lutheran Church to protest against the persecution of Jews because of Jesus' own Jewish heritage and his command to love your neighbor. The letter also added an additional reason for protest:

> Because [the persecution of Jews] conflict[s] with the understanding of justice rooted in the Danish people and settled through centuries in our Danish Christian culture. Accordingly, it is stated in our constitution that all Danish citizens have an equal right and responsibility towards the law, and they have freedom of religion, and a right to worship God in accordance with their vocation and conscience and so that race or religion can never in itself become the cause of deprivation of anybody's rights, freedom, or property. Irrespective of diverging religious opinions we shall fight for the right of our Jewish brothers and sisters to keep the freedom that we ourselves value more highly than life. The leaders of the Danish Church have a clear understanding of our duty to be law-abiding citizens that do not unreasonably oppose those who execute authority over us, but at the same time we are in our conscience bound to uphold justice and protest against any violation; consequently we shall, if occasion should arise, plainly acknowledge our obligation to obey God more than man.

This unequivocal declaration of solidarity with Denmark's Jews seems to confirm the exceptional status of Danish-Jewish relations. Nevertheless, the case of Krarup alerts us to the fact that the picture is more complex than this episcopal statement indicates. The work of Benjamin Balslev offers a starting point for an investigation of these ambiguities of Christian and clerical thinking about Jews.

The Ambiguities of the Christian Danish Perspective on Jews and Judaism

Benjamin Balslev was pastor at the parish of Soderup, an activist of Mission to Israel (Israelsmissionen), an organization committed to converting Jews, and the author of one of the early popular works on the history of Danish Jewry, *The History of Danish Jews,* published in 1932 in Copenhagen. In 1934, Balslev published an article on the "Race-Struggle in Germany" in the theological journal *Nordisk Missions-Tidsskrift.* Also published separately in the same year, this publication to some degree justified the persecution of Jews. Reports of a Nazi rule of terror did not dissuade Balslev in his beliefs that he developed over the previous two decades. Rather, he argued that there was merely a struggle going on between two peoples: Germans and Jews. Jews, he wrote, had an enormous and destructive influence both morally and economically in Germany. Furthermore, Jews constituted the bulk of an ethnically indigestible anti-Germanism that the Nazis fought to neutralize: "Germany has taken notice of its Jews and its Jewish question to a degree which is unknown to us. . . . While countries such as England and, we could add, Denmark always have had a homogeneous population, Germany has internally suffered from an anti-Germanism, something ethnically indigestible, and among these ranks, Germany's Jews were disproportionally well represented."[6] Such thinking led Balslev to argue that the burning of allegedly morally detrimental books was a meaningful act of self-defense.

While Balslev purported to have the main objective to refute racist antisemitism and to reject racial theories and generalizing accusations against all German Jews, he still presented the ongoing disenfranchisement and persecution of Jews as the battle between two peoples. In Balslev's twisted worldview, one should refute racial antisemitism because it defied conversion, God's solution to the Jewish question. Nevertheless, he held that antisemitic perceptions, attitudes, and practices were legitimate since they constituted Germans' defense against the detrimental influence of Jews on the economy and culture. His argument would then hold true for Denmark if its population were not homogeneous and if its Jewish community were less assimilated and more significant in terms of size and influence. Balslev's point of view implied that, under these circumstances, such a reaction would be meaningful and necessary. Thus, the dream of an ethnically and culturally homogeneous nation proved to be the crucial pitfall of both Danish history and present politics.

Sources and Historiography

In order to understand the historical underpinnings of Danish Lutheran clergy's attitudes toward Jews, one must examine the history of Danish-Jewish relations. In turn, this will provide a basis for an analysis of the dream of a homogeneous nation as it played itself out in the context of Danish clerical discourses and practices from 1918 to 1945. The discussion of these problems is, in contrast to the case of Norway,[7] hampered by the still sizeable lacunae of research in this field. This is even more true in regard to the period's church history. Recent publications are of limited use since they idealize the rejection of antisemitism in regard to clerical attitudes toward Jews.[8] Here, my focus will not be on individual theologians or specific organizations, but rather on the "public sphere" of the church in its declarations, pastoral letters, protests, and written works. Because of this approach of mine, a certain bias in favor of those pastors and scholars who made the church's views heard in public is naturally unavoidable. A lack of sources makes it very difficult to draw any "representative" conclusions on attitudes toward Jews among rank-and-file laymen, be it church members or activists, let alone conclusions regarding the relevance of clerical attitudes for the rescue action itself.

Frequently, scholars, journalists, and other intellectuals have presented "October 1943" as proof of the irrelevance or even absence of anti-Jewish resentment in modern Danish society. Similar to the case of England, antisemitism is understood to be an essentially *un-Danish* phenomenon. The roots of this concept are manifold: Danes are supposedly carrying an innate immunity against Jew-hatred—an immunity that is defined either in an essentialist way, by pointing to the humane and tolerant national character of the Danish people, or in historical terms, by referring to a specifically smooth "Danish Path" into a democratic, pluralistic, modern society. Furthermore, dubbing antisemitism as an import—a German import—without autochthonous roots and traditions, helped to reinforce this notion of immunity.

Finally, reference is often made to the specific nature of the Jewish community in Denmark, its "invisibility," caused by the small number of

Jews and their high degree of acculturation and integration. The successful story of integration and the notion of innate tolerance has contributed to dramatic lacunae of critical research in terms of both Danish-Jewish history and the history of antisemitism in Denmark. There is no need to investigate an issue that is perceived to be nonexistent. Furthermore, the interpretative confinement of the concept of antisemitism as un-Danish has frequently been accompanied by an often implicit comparative perspective that reinforced the notion of immunity. If German racial antisemitism and systematic genocide do not provide the standard of comparison, one may perceive other xenophobic and anti-Jewish stereotypes as marginal. One may dismiss single unequivocal expressions of antisemitism as irrelevant exceptions rather than investigate the origins, traditions, and functions of these concepts and explore the ways in which they have been instrumental in construing individual and collective identities by defining the Jew as "the other."[9]

More recent research pursued by a younger generation of Danish scholars has begun to question the narrative of heroic humanism that would imply an immunity against fascism and antisemitism. Lone Rünitz's investigation of the government's restrictive refugee policy in the interwar period[10] and the Danish Center for Holocaust and Genocide Studies' research project on German and Austrian Jewish immigrants who attempted to seek refuge in Denmark are just two examples of this more critical research.[11] In addition, Michael Mogensen has examined the antisemitic attitudes prevalent among the members of the Danish exilian community in Sweden,[12] and together with Rasmus Kreth, has produced the first thorough research on the rescue operation itself.[13] Mogensen and Kreth have stressed the importance of the Swedes' willingness to help and of the intentional passivity of key German authorities. In addition to this, their research has highlighted the less flattering fact that the much-celebrated Danish fishermen sailing the Jews to the safe shores of Sweden frequently demanded exorbitant payments, which in no way was justifiable by reference to their personal risk and often was legitimized by antisemitic references to Jewish wealth. Furthermore, Sofie Bak has published an introductory survey of the representations of the rescue operation in Danish postwar historiography and memorial culture.[14] In addition, her work on Danish antisemitic movements in the early twentieth century is groundbreaking.[15]

In the framework of these attempts of reevaluation, a more critical view of the policy of collaboration has developed. "Cooperation" that implied the acceptance and implementation of limited discriminatory measures against Danish Jews actually did lead to an offer by the Danish authorities to inter Danish Jews in September 1943 in an attempt to prevent the SS and Gestapo from pursuing a roundup. This contribution is obviously sharing a "revisionist" point of view since it argues that though an aggressive racial antisemitism found only little support in milieus affiliated with the Lutheran Church, negative stereotypes about both Jews and Judaism nevertheless were widespread and constituted core elements of identity formation and group formation in these milieus. This is not to suggest that this ambiguity characteristic of clerical writing on Jewish issues accounts for the impact of antisemitism in Danish society or for the successful rescue of Danish Jews to Sweden.

Previous articles have addressed the often overlooked complexities of the history of Danish-Jewish relations by underlining the need for a critical revision of the existing and often idealizing scholarship.[16] This essay will demonstrate that the problematic and often repeated claim about Denmark being less antisemitic than most other European countries is misleading. The issue at stake is not first and foremost the strength or weakness of Danish antisemitism, but the fact that in Danish Lutheran Church–affiliated contexts, the debate on the status of Jews as part of European culture and society was cast in an antimodernist, anticapitalist, and anticommunist mold. As the internal dynamics of this clerical discourse contributed only marginally to the incremental delegitimization of antisemitism in Denmark, one has to look for other factors to explain the absence of antisemitic persecution in Denmark.[17]

The History of Danish-Jewish Relations

The beginnings of a Jewish presence in the Danish Commonwealth date back to the seventeenth century, when Sephardic Jews in the Duchies of Schleswig and Holstein attained freedom of movement and residence permits for the kingdom. Jews settled in Glückstadt (1620) and Altona (Danish since 1640), and then also in cities in the kingdom. In the course of the eighteenth century, Copenhagen became the primary center of Danish-Jewish cultural and political activities. In 1730, the Jewish community in Copenhagen consisted of approximately 300 members; in 1780 this number had risen to 1,600, which was more than 80 percent of the Jewish population residing in the kingdom and around 2 percent of the capital's inhabitants.

The first Jews to carry on trade in Copenhagen were "Portuguese" Jews, who provided the court with financial services and luxury goods such as jewelry. The "second or third generation" of Iberian émigrés had often migrated to Denmark via Amsterdam and Hamburg-Altona. In the course of the last decades of the seventeenth century, still more Ashkenazi Jews trickled into the kingdom, taking advantage of the generous privileges granted to the Sephardic merchants and bankers. Finally, in 1684, the Danish king legalized their status as a community in Copenhagen by granting them permission to hold public synagogue services in their homes. Due to the small size of their community, the Sephardic immigrants only obtained this status eleven years later. In the course of the following decades, the Ashkenazim soon outnumbered the Portuguese, but the concentration in wholesale and petty trade, commerce, and banking remained overwhelming.[18]

As a somewhat ironic contrast to the recent instrumentalization of the "Late Luther" for present political purposes, the contemporary impact of these writings even in a strongly Lutheran country such as Denmark was extremely limited. The protagonists of the Reformation in Denmark seemed not to see any need to refer to them or to their violent agenda. They did not translate Luther's anti-Jewish works and seldom quoted from them before the 1720s, when they used his writing as arguments against Jews' employing Christian servants. In a similar vein, they did not refer to Eisenmenger's *Jewry Uncovered*—one of the most influential compendia of Christian anti-Jewish tenets published in 1700/ 1710—extensively before the 1770s. Of course, this does not imply that Luther's and Eisenmenger's views were irrelevant in a Danish context; on the contrary, Luther's theological teaching on the Jews, in general, informed most of the important theological works of the seventeenth and eighteenth centuries.

An analysis of published sermons that mention Jews and Judaism points toward the prevalence of patterns and concepts familiar to us from other regions of Europe, which portrayed Jews as living warnings that eternally testified to the victory and truth of the Gospels and as the radical "Other"—an enemy of God and the persecutor of his flock. Similarly, clergymen frequently extended these concepts to encompass Jews as abstract symbols of heresy meant to warn present-day rationalist "heretics." Furthermore, ministers also depicted Jews as morally corrupt and depraved.

In many ways these images relate to the key narrative, the nexus of Jewish disobedience, deicide, and divine punishment—a key narrative strongly rooted in the early Christian and medieval tradition that one could also find in Denmark. Thus, authors transferred this concept of

obduracy and dispersion in reference to Jews even before they actually settled there. Such mentalities informed and inspired theological
works, devotional literature, and paintings and frescos. Nevertheless,
anti-Jewish accusations, as found in Medieval Central Europe, such as
the poisoning of wells, ritual murder, or desecration of the Host, were
not raised in Denmark.

Through these views and images of Jews, influential clergy defined
the character of the Jewish presence in Denmark as deceitful and detrimental. Clergymen perceived Jews as specifically disturbing, though, only
when their growing presence actually became an issue: only when, during
the late seventeenth century, the confessional homogeneity of the population and the hegemony of Lutheranism seemed challenged, did the bishops of Zealand, such as Hans Wandal and Hans Bagger, begin to articulate
their "unease" regarding the growing immigration of Jews and the presumably much too benevolent terms of settlement. This resulted in a
harsh control of immigration, especially of poor Jews, and strict limitations of Jewish involvement in economic life. When the guilds saw their
economic interests endangered, the authorities mostly responded favorably to their protests and curtailed Jewish privileges even further. In
addition, Jews remained barred from Christian schools as well as from
universities and mercantile corporations. Thus, a story of conflict, hatred,
and exclusion grounded in religious legitimization and reinforced by
economic competition was one long-neglected dimension of Christian-
Jewish relations in seventeenth- and eighteenth-century Denmark.

If one views this history in the light of a European comparative
perspective, though, pre-emancipation privileges were more extensive,
and the process of Danish-Jewish acculturation and social integration in
the course of the nineteenth century went smoother, than in many other
countries. Nevertheless, when Danes discussed the status of the Jews in
Danish society in the wake of the state's economic disaster of 1813, not
only did they hold Jews responsible for the bankruptcy, but many authors described Jews as parasitic and alien to the Danish nation. Such
conclusions implicitly defined the Danish nation in religiously Christian
and ethnocentric terms. While Enlightenment figures who had dominated the discourse on the "Jewish question" of earlier decades had
underlined the need for "civic betterment and regeneration," they still
had upheld the basic principle of perfectibility. But with the gradual
marginalization of these positions, the intense public debate of these
years brought attitudes to the fore that presumed the impossibility of
Jews' becoming Danes.[19] In the decades to follow, Romanticist intellec-

tuals rose to become the dominating opinion makers. Thus, it comes as no surprise that the only non-German territory to which the HepHep pogroms of 1819 spread to was Denmark. In the capital as well as in a number of towns in the province, the well-calculated and partly intentionally provoked violence of the alleged "mob" turned against Jews and their property. In 1830, Danes repeated this outbreak of anti-Jewish, anti-emancipationist violence with ideological, political, and economic underpinnings.

In the 1830s and 1840s, the estate assemblies finally discussed the question of complete Jewish emancipation. Many deputies voiced strong opinions against granting further rights to Jews, and rural clerics, often depicted as the avant-garde of democratization and liberal values, rejected Jewish integration and legal equality on a combination of ethnicist and religious grounds: Jews could never become Danes because the core of being Danish was a profession of Christianity, and the essence of being Jewish was to belong to a nation alien to the Danish people.

Protestant Clergy and the Jews in the Nineteenth Century

For the time being, the government made no further progress in terms of Jewish emancipation. In fact, one of the most influential contemporaries, Nicolai Frederik Severin Grundtvig, the poet, politician, and patron saint of a supposedly tolerant and civic version of nationalism and arguably the most important Danish theologian, spoke out publicly against Jewish emancipation on similar ethnicist and religious grounds. In general, Grundtvig had a hard time finding any arguments against further Jewish rights that would not be all too self-contradictory. Nevertheless, he favored a policy that would deny Jews suffrage and prevent their eligibility by prohibiting them land ownership, the prerequisite for all suffrage rights. Furthermore, when Meir Goldschmidt, the illustrious Danish-Jewish writer, participated in the heated debate over Schleswig in 1848–49, Grundtvig denied him the right to contribute to a discussion on an issue of such eminent national importance, since he—being a Jew—was and always would remain a guest in Denmark.[20]

After full emancipation in 1848–49, the successful democratization of Danish society and its economic stability since the second half of the nineteenth century did provide the prerequisites for a society fairly capable of integrating the Jewish community, as well as other immigrant communities. However, this did not imply any kind of immunity against

racism, neither in a historical perspective nor in regard to present problems and debates. It repeatedly became clear that the high degree of
ethnic homogeneity of the Danish population proved to imply its own
trappings: a homogeneity reinforced by the all-but-monopoly of the
Lutheran "state church." Furthermore, traditions of xenophobia and
racism can be traced back to a definition of Danishness that amalgamated ethnic and religious criteria: in this context, Lutheran pastors
had repeatedly provided the key arguments by mobilizing the resistance
against an extension of Jewish rights or even explicitly arguing against
Jewish emancipation on religious grounds. Grundtvig constituted a key
figure in this line of tradition, providing a link between the discourses of
the eighteenth and of the early twentieth centuries. One may view his
ambiguous stand on the issue of inclusion and exclusion as emblematic
of the history of Danish-Jewish relations.

In the late 1870s, Johannes Kok, Nicolai Gottlieb Blædel, Hans Lassen Martensen, Zealand's bishop, and Frederik Nielsen, a professor of
theology, notably all representatives of the church, caused the first post-
emancipation conflicts on the status of Jews in Danish society.[21] Dismissing what has been called "replacement theology" out of hand, in *The Holy
Land and Its Neighboring Countries in Past and Present,* Kok described the
restoration of Israel and the return to Zion drawing close.[22] However, this
in no way prevented him from perpetuating the Augustinian notion that
the humiliated, marginalized Jews would provide the proof of the truth of
the Gospel, nor from attacking observant Judaism in harsh words. Informed by Blædels' *Extended Confirmation Textbook,*[23] he dismissed this
halakhic observance as a set of meaningless rituals, bound together primarily by a vile hatred against Christians and Christianity.

Martensen took this attack one important step further. In his widely
disseminated *Christian Ethics,* he did not display much interest in observant Judaism. His obsession was rather with modern, assimilated, and
emancipated Jews, constituting the primary force undermining the concept of the Christian nation-state. According to Martensen, the Jews
had joined forces with individualistic hedonism, materialistic capitalism,
radical skepticism, and anticlerical liberalism, and now they were taking
the lead in a forceful attempt to destroy the organically grown Christian
state. Martensen's keywords were dissolution and destruction, and the
means for this purpose were supposedly the Jews' influence in the economy, in the press, and in politics. For him, the government had made a
mistake granting emancipation to the Jews, and now the former guests
had turned into despotic rulers. Interestingly enough, in spite of this
vicious attack on the allegedly immense and detrimental power of mod-

ern Jews, Martensen still shared Kok's eschatological hopes for the future. Thus, he argued that the Jews should be stripped of their civic rights, but still be encouraged to retain their ethnic identity in order to be prepared for their wholesale conversion and their function as God's major missionary tool in the Last Days.

Both lines of reasoning had a significant influence on the debates of post-WWI Denmark. As Martensen dismissed traditional Judaism as a set of meaningless rituals, at the same time, he identified an urban, upper-middle-class culture that was hostile to the Christian establishment in the Jewish freethinker Georg Brandes. Thus by bracketing modern Judaism with secular Copenhagen and modern culture, he had linked the crucial topoi of the interwar period.[24]

The Rabbi's Response: Abraham Alexander Wolff

Brandes was not the only individual to react to these anti-Jewish diatribes. Rather, Abraham Alexander Wolff, the long-time chief rabbi of the Jews of Denmark, offered the most elaborate Jewish response. In *The Enemies of the Talmud,* Wolff gave a five-hundred-page rebuttal where he not only distanced himself from Brandes's secular liberalism, but articulated a sharp counterattack on the Lutheran pastors and theologians that in many ways had been inspired by August Rohling's *The Jew of the Talmud.*[25] Wolff refuted the accusation that the Talmud was anti-Christian and established an ethic of double standards. On the contrary, he argued, Christianity should be careful not to find itself in this ethical quandary. Furthermore, Wolff claimed that the attacks against Jews were similar to those voiced against the early Christians by their heathen contemporaries. His response was effective since the debate ended when the pastors and theologians partially revised their publications. Nevertheless, the debate of the 1870s marked a crucial transition period that provided a bridge between the anti-emancipationist concepts of the first half of the nineteenth century and the rearticulation of anti-Jewish stereotyping since the late nineteenth century.

Between Inclusion and Exclusion: Jews in Twentieth-Century Denmark

In the year 1931, fewer than 5,800 Jews lived in Denmark. The majority of them lived in the Danish capital, and more than 60 percent were born in the kingdom.[26] The percentage of mixed marriages was high—almost 45 percent in the decades from 1884 to 1903.[27] In spite of the slow integration of East European Jews who immigrated at the turn of the century, the speed with which the Jews of the kingdom had climbed the social ladder and had gained acceptance was remarkable. In 1931, their average annual income was twice as high as the national average, though with a strong internal differentiation. In addition, since the end of the nineteenth century, Danes perceived Jews of the kingdom increasingly as compatriots.

Nevertheless, the discourse of pastors and theologians on Jews and Judaism followed the general trends in Danish society—a society that turned out not to be immune to anti-Jewish attitudes at all. In contrast to the postwar view of Danish history that portrayed antisemitism as irrelevant, the political and social implications of these attitudes reveal that antisemitism played an important role. This becomes quite clear when we examine the changing images of "the Jew" and their political implications in the course of historical events: from the perception of the Jewish question as being imminent and urgent after World War I, to the reactions to the challenge of Nazi Germany, and finally to the dilemmas of occupation itself.

In the first decades of the twentieth century, Lutheran Church–affiliated authors often pointed to the Jewish question as being pressing and highly problematic. Their views were also shared by nationalist movements reacting to the immigration of Eastern European Jews to Denmark and the alleged participation of a disproportionate number of Jews in the Russian Revolution. After the Nazi rise to power, the refugee problem became an issue in Denmark, as political and economic considerations as well as antisemitic attitudes guided politicians, diplomats, and bureaucrats. For example, the government's memoranda and drafts for its refugee policy often contained anti-Jewish stereotypes. In addition, diplomats as well as police officers regularly voiced harsh anti-Jewish arguments against immigration. In this situation, no critical voice from Lutheran pastors—neither as a reaction to the extremely restrictive refugee policy nor to the public debate about it—was to be heard. Instead, one finds, for example, statements by Lutheran ministers who described *Reichskristallnacht* as the result of a "stupid crime" committed by Herschel Grynszpan. Also among church-affiliated authors, we find the assumption that a higher number of Jews in Denmark, or a higher degree of visibility in Danish society, would create a "Jewish Problem" in Denmark as well.

A longstanding tradition of antimodernism, as well as a strong affiliation with anticommunism, was presumably one of the most important reasons why influential Lutheran Church leaders, such as Christian Bartholdy, pastor and leader of the Pietist *Home Mission,* only belatedly came to reject Nazism, including its antisemitism. The *Kirchenkampf* (church struggle) helped him to hamper his excitement about a new chance for a moral revival in Nazi Germany, and instead to develop an apocalyptic thinking, now interpreting Nazism as the movement of the Antichrist. This reevaluation went hand in hand with a growing awareness that racist ideology would undermine the concept of an end-time conversion of Jews. In the 1930s, though, the willingness to go along with Nazi anti-Jewish measures was quite significant in this milieu.[28]

The Pietists were by far not the slowest to develop a more critical stance. The Grundtvigians displayed a tendency to pragmatism encouraged by their traditional aversion against "intervening in state affairs." This could even imply ridiculing protests against a politics of collaboration that might risk introducing racial legislation against "Jewish pastors" to Denmark. Some Grundtvigians also went as far as stating that the Nazi regime was merely overreacting in a exaggerated way to a Jewish question constituting a real problem for German society. In general, a significant distinction marked the years of occupation leading up to the attempted deportation. While a growing number of pastors publicly attacked anti-Jewish legislation and demanded a radical reaction of the Lutheran Church if it should be introduced in Denmark, the bishops only debated the issue but failed to agree on any public activity.[29]

In the light of these debates, the Lutheran Church's fearless and unequivocal condemnation of the roundup has to be reevaluated. In the 1930s and 1940s, the Jewish issue had primarily been discussed as part of other discourses. To a significant degree, it was not perceived as a problem in its own right that deserved to be addressed on the basis of human rights, but as part of a "missionary discourse" of antimodernism. In the fall of 1943, this *Judenaktion* situated the Jewish issue in a different context. Now it was loaded with a specific national meaning and relevance. In turn, this contributed significantly to the unequivocal and massive protest and the personal involvement of many pastors in the rescue action, even including Bartholdy. This points to a more general problem of postwar evaluation of prewar behavior. Frequently, the massive engagement of conservatives in the resistance caused their earlier involvement in antidemocratic—and for that matter anti-Jewish—activities to be blurred and forgotten.

Predominant Perceptions of Jews in the Danish Church

The traditions outlined here played themselves out in a complex set of notions and attitudes toward Jews and Judaism, which were surprisingly constant over the years. It will become apparent that there was no clear-cut distinction between traditional anti-Judaism and antisemitic stereotyping. Underlying recurrent common denominators were the lack of a distinction between contemporary Jews and Jews of antiquity, the semiracist concepts of Jewish mind or character, and the fundamental dilemma that antisemitism in its explicitly racist variant would question one of the axiomatic implications of these Christian concepts of Jews—the endeavor to convert them to Christianity. This goal was never given up, and excluding Christians of "Jewish origin" was always ruled out. Thus, a racial antisemitism as such was generally rejected out of hand. Nevertheless, Lutheran pastors and theologians never hesitated to emphasize that both the positive and the negative features of the Jewish spirit or character have to be mentioned. The negative traits seemed no less real to them simply because they belonged to the arsenal of antisemitic reasoning.

Lutheran pastors and theologians acknowledged that a bright future awaited the Jewish people as converts, though in a long-term perspective they gave no legitimacy to a continued existence of "this peculiar religion." They recognized that Jews still constituted the Chosen People of God, but they argued that after undergoing a mass conversion at the end time, Jews would have the crucial task to bring the Gospel to the rest of the world. The pastors and theologians accompanied these eschatological considerations with a strong contempt for Judaism as a religion. They labeled it ridiculous and pitiful legalism. In turn, they both condemned and celebrated the social and cultural isolation of traditional Orthodox Judaism as a precondition for the continued existence of the people. However, they disapproved of Reform Judaism as a hybrid phenomenon without religious sincerity and depth, and of assimilation as a cause of a flaw of the character, a moral degeneration. They argued that this deformation was "proven" by listing "Jewish sins" that allegedly resulted from any attempt to assimilate. "Assimilated Jews," they described, tended to oscillate between hypocritical servility and impudent audacity, between sensitive nervousness and obtrusive, pushy vigor, between interference and self-isolation. Assimilation and radical modernism, they stated, had turned Jews into a powerful threat to the indigenous host peoples, their moral survival, and national autonomy. They linked this to speculations on the reasons why antisemitism was weak in Denmark and much stronger in France and Germany. They concluded that in the latter the Jewish communities were more sizable and their power and arrogance had been all the more visible and influential. In this perspective, conflicts caused by antisemitism were seen as acts of Gentile/Christian self-defense, or defined as an even-handed struggle between two equal parties.

Despite these negative descriptions, clerical writers unequivocally praised the moral standards of traditional Judaism, especially its emphasis on the integrity of the home. They especially lauded its emphasis on family values and saw this as a role model for the disintegrating Christian family in modern society. They also argued that the distinctiveness and difference of Jewish existence had to be upheld. Nevertheless, they argued, Jews ought to do this without arrogant self-consciousness and pride. Instead, they should follow the path of Christian humility.[30] As a consequence, emancipation and integration as liberal solutions to the Jewish question were dismissed, as "amalgamation" would not be compatible with the divine intention to make use of the Jews as the primary agents of the coming eschatological drama. But also Zionism was seen in ambivalent terms: it seemed to guarantee the continued existence of the Jewish nation and might be the first step of a spiritual revival, but its secular character and self-assertive "pride" confused and annoyed Christian theologians.

The attitudes and notions discussed above were articulated in the most explicit way in a specific milieu of the Israel Mission, linked to the influential organized Pietism of the Home Mission. But when analyzing other sources, one is surprised to find how many other milieus shared these attitudes as well. Those who articulated these views were not part of a fringe sect, but an established, informed group of writers that a significant segment of church-affiliated individuals read regularly.[31] When one compares these notions with the statements by bishops, scholars, and professors of theology, such as Frederik Nielsen or Frederik Torm, a high degree of consensus becomes obvious. This might not be surprising, since the Mission to Israel constituted almost the only way in which the Danish Lutheran Church engaged Jews directly.

Nevertheless, there were alternative approaches on both sides of spectrum. The pastor Anders Malling, for one, illustrates the potential in this mission milieu for affiliation with Nazi ideology. Malling became a member of the Danish Nazi Party, DNSAP, in the early 1930s and was instrumental in programmatically formulating the party's views concerning the relationship between state and church.[32] While he demonstrated a significant amount of critical distance toward the German role model, he was in no way intent on softening the antisemitic stance, but succeeded in combining *Home Mission* traditions of anti-Judaism with antisemitism.[33]

On the other wing of the theological spectrum and church politics there was Grundtvigianism, providing most of the Folk High Schools and their press with an ideological foundation. Politically, it was a rather broad movement. Nevertheless, it is important to focus on three of its theologians who expressed their views on Christianity and the Jewish question.

In October 1933, in *Dansk Udsyn,* Ulrich Balslev published a detailed analysis of modern Jewish history and antisemitism.[34] He argued that an "external factor" for antisemitism resulted from a need for individuals to place blame on a scapegoat for both economic turmoil and the erosion of a secure social status. The "internal factor" for antisemitism resulted from Danes' characteristic nature. In Germany and in Denmark, Balslev stated, there existed Orthodox Jews and those who identified with the respective nation. Alongside these were assimilated Jews, who were most influential in arts, literature, and politics. Balslev described the latter as rootless and unfettered by national or cultural loyalties. In essence, he argued that these assimilated Jews failed to hold even a general sense of responsibility for the progress of the nation in which they lived. Therefore, these Jews became a great challenge to every society. Despite this obstacle, Danes had a strong sense of inner balance, of national unity, and of forceful ethnic cohesion that enabled them to integrate foreigners and make them fruitful participants in Danish culture. Germany, however, was much more diverse, heterogeneous, and at conflict with itself; therefore, this inner tension transformed into antisemitism. Primarily then, Balslev placed central blame on the non-Jewish Germans and challenged them to overcome their national crisis and integrate Jews into society. One might have hoped for a more unequivocal criticism. Nevertheless, the author did diverge from stating that Nazi anti-Jewish policy was legitimate and a justifiable answer to the so-called Jewish threat.

It is important to note, however, that the new "rules of discourse" did not develop among Danish pastors and theologians before *Reichskristallnacht* and in most cases after the occupation. Before this point, they continued to point to Jews as the cause for anti-Jewish sentiments in

Germany. Even after the occupation, Danish Lutheran pastors and theologians did not give up this perspective entirely, but rather, simply articulated it less explicitly. Their primary focus shifted to a refutation of a radical, aggressive racism and the practice of persecution. Now they described antisemitism as a basically pathological and primarily German phenomenon. In turn, their debates revolved around the issue of racial discrimination in Denmark, which, in essence was a debate on the issue of collaboration versus resistance. One may find a prominent example of this in the writings of the theologian K. E. Løgstrup. In a series of articles from December 1941 to May 1942, published in church periodicals, he attacked hatred of Jews. In his writings, he argued that antisemitism resulted from a psychotic need for a scapegoat; a need that the Danish people ought to be immune to because of their enlightenment and sense of justice. In turn, he called on his compatriots uncompromisingly to reject any German demands for anti-Jewish legislation. Similarly, Halfdan Høgsbro defined racist antisemitism as anti-Christian since Christ and all the apostles and prophets had Jewish blood.

Only a few authors, however, took this critical point of view one crucial step further and argued unequivocally in favor of cultural, religious, and ethnic pluralism. For example, in 1938 and 1939, the theologian F. L. Østrup did this in a series of essays he published in the leading conservative daily, *Berlingske Tidende.* Though much less knowledgeable about Jewish history and religion than Balslev, he still systematically refuted antisemitic charges of deicide and false claims about the Talmud and Jewish support for immorality and the Russian Revolution. He even questioned extreme antisemitic nationalism by arguing that nationalism always needed to be balanced with an element of internationalism. According to Østrup, the Danish Jews provided this international perspective; he wrote: "The physiognomy of Denmark in its totality would be so much more boring, sad and homogeneous without the Jews. . . . What a loss, aesthetically, morally, religiously, yes in all kinds of ways, if the Jews disappeared!"[35] His convincing argument in favor of protecting the unique distinctiveness of Jewish existence in Denmark has to be contrasted with the perceptive patterns outline earlier. Østrup's voice constituted an exception. It was much more common for Lutheran pastors and theologians to embrace antisemitism as part of their worldview that displayed admiration for Nazi Germany or, at least, did not place first priority on the condemnation of its anti-Jewish policy.

The attitudes expressed by Lutheran pastors and theologians were more self-deceptive when writers thought of themselves as being friendly and well-meaning to Jews. They reinforced the importance of such "well-intended" views by the attempt not to be antisemitic, or even to be philosemitic. Writers either held to the notion that there was no breeding ground for antisemitism in Denmark or viewed antisemitism as a danger and saw themselves as combatants of this threat. This self-perception rendered these milieus vulnerable to antisemitic patterns of perception and political thought, and even to Nazi antisemitic policies to some degree. It was only during the occupation that many reversed their views. One may see an example of this in local Lutheran Church publications. From late 1941 to 1943 numerous articles condemned Nazi antisemitism and ruled out any kind of anti-Jewish legislation in Denmark. This campaign, however, was part of a defense for Danish national sovereignty and independence. The article authors now saw the Jews as part of the body politic. Rejecting anti-Jewish measures had become part of a national consensus by which to define the limits of collaboration; it was in no way a defense of the notion of a pluralistic society or universal rights of cultural and ethnic minorities. The attitude of pastors toward Jews and Judaism, even with all of its ambiguities, especially made this fundamental distinction clear. This was the reason why the persistence of anti-Jewish perceptions could exist at the same time alongside a resistance against Nazi persecution and a willingness to be in active solidarity with the Jews in October 1943.

How did Danish Jews react to this problem? Generally speaking, there was a tendency to keep a low profile and to trust the Danish politicians. Nevertheless, in 1936, Rabbi Marcus Melchior articulated the most influential response to antisemitic accusations in a polemical booklet.[36] In the tradition of Wolff, Melchior focused on describing how authors such as Houston Stewart Chamberlain and Alfred Rosenberg had misused the Talmud.

Conclusion

The central question that still lingers is this: why did an aggressive racial antisemitism find almost no support in milieus affiliated with the Danish Lutheran Church? This question is obviously linked to the even more general question: why was antisemitic violence almost absent in Denmark in general? And why did antisemitism never produce an influential political agenda for action nor grow into a powerful political force? To be sure, these questions require complex answers that cannot be restricted to theology, but have to take into account the long-term development of liberal democracy, the fairly stable process of economic modernization, and the traditions of political culture.

In many ways, though, we are only beginning to explore the dissemination and function of antisemitic patterns of perception, interpretation, and behavior in Denmark. More than likely, future studies will be less flattering than the long-cherished self-indulging perceptions of a peaceful and humanistic nation. We know that the weakness of racial antisemitism did not at all prevent anti-Jewish stereotypes from being disseminated and influential even in the face of Nazism. While antisemitism found no home in symbolic politics, legislation, or jurisdiction, it did receive sympathy in regard to administrative practice and political debates. Antisemitic attitudes were in no way delegitimized on a wholesale basis before the German occupation of the country and before the Final Solution began to cast its shadow on Denmark.

The rescue of Danish Jewry in October 1943 notwithstanding, negative perceptions and attitudes toward Jews and Judaism played a conspicuous role in the Danish Lutheran Church–affiliated milieus in the first half of the twentieth century. Danish theologians and clerics contributed significantly to this by relating the reflection on Jewish issues to antipluralist missionary ambitions or antimodernist and anticapitalist discourses. Only when the turn of events forced them to frame these issues in terms of the dilemma of collaboration versus resistance and the specific challenge involved for the church did categories such as the protection of human rights or ethnic and cultural diversity gain ground. Thus, traditions of anti-Judaism and varying modes of consent with modern antisemitic concepts were not delegitimized as such before the occupation and the rescue action—as an act of *national* resistance—enforced a process of rethinking in milieus affiliated with the church. Only then, the episcopal protest against the *Judenaktion* grew into a consensual expression of popular contempt for the occupation regime. In turn, existing anti-Jewish attitudes did not become a hindrance to the national project of protecting the Danish Jews—as Danes—from persecution and death. In February 1942, Halfdan Høgsbro articulated this view so unequivocally in a church newspaper: "We do not step into the breach for the Jews because they are human beings of some special worth, but because they are human beings and because God has commanded us to treat human beings in a humane way."[37]

Even in the second half of the twentieth century, this fundamental ambiguity has not lost its impact on the discourses on Jews and Judaism. In spite of a growing diversification and secularization of society, the antipluralistic dream of an ethnically and culturally homogeneous Danish national community lives on. This becomes visible in both the xenophobic and the Islamophobic character of the immigration and integration debate as well as in an unholy alliance of residual elements of conventional antisemitism and anti-Israel sentiments.

NOTES

1. Alfred Feilchenfeld, ed., *Glückl von Hameln,* reprint (Frankfurt: Athenäum, 1987), 19.

2. Nathan Bamberger, *The Viking Jews: A History of the Jews of Denmark,* 2nd ed. (New York: Soncino, 1990), 16.

3. www.thankstoscandinavia.org.

4. Leo Goldberger, ed., *The Rescue of the Danish Jews: Moral Courage under Stress* (New York: New York University Press, 1987), and Leni Yahil, *The Rescue of Danish Jewry: Test of a Democracy* (Philadelphia: Jewish Publication Society of America, 1969).

5. Søren Krarup, *Harald Nielsen og hans tid* (Copenhagen: Gyldendal, 1960), 101.

6. Benjamin Balslev, *Racekampen i Tyskland* (Copenhagen: Israelsmissionens bogfond, 1934), 16–17.

7. Thanks to the work of Arne Hassing and Torleiv Austad. See Arne Hassing, "The Churches of Norway and the Jews, 1933–1943," *Journal of Ecumenical Studies* 26 (1989): 496–522; Torleiv Austad, "Hebreerbrevet af 1942," *Tidsskrift for teologi og kirke* 86 (1986): 28–54.

8. Erik Thostrup Jacobsen, *Som om intet var hændt* (Odense: Odense University Press, 1991).

9. See Tony Kushner, "Comparing Antisemitisms: A Useful Exercise?" in *Two Nations: British and German Jews in Comparative Perspective,* ed. Michael Brenner, Rainer Liedtke, and David Rechter (Tübingen: M. Siebeck, 1999), 91–109. See also Tony Kushner, *The Persistence of Prejudice: Antisemitism in British Society during the Second World War* (Manchester: Manchester University Press, 1989).

10. Cf. Lone Rünitz, *Danmark og de jødiske flygtninge 1933–1940. En bog om flygtninge og menneskerettigheder* (Copenhagen: Museum Tusculanum, 2000).

11. The results of this research project have recently been published in a series of publications: Lone Rünitz, *Af hensyn til konsekvenserne. Danmark og flygtningespørgsmålet 1933–1940* (Odense: Syddansk Universitetsforlag, 2005); Hans Kirchhoff, *"Et menneske uden pas er ikke noget menneske." Danmark i den internationale flygtningepolitik 1933–1939* (Odense: Syddansk Universitetsforlag, 2005); Cecilia Stokholm Banke, *Demokratiets skyggesigde. Flygtninge og menneskerettigheder. Danmark før Holocaust* (Odense: Syddansk Universitetsforlag, 2005); Vilhjálmur Örn Vilhjálmsson, *Medaljens bagside. Jødiske flygtningeskæbner i Danmark 1933–1945* (Copenhagen: Vandkunsten, 2005).

12. See Michael Mogensen, "Det danske flygtningesamfund i Sverige og 'jødespørgsmålet' 1943–45," in *I tradition og kaos. Festskrift til Henning Poulsen,* ed. Johnny Laursen, et al. (Aarhus: Aarhus University Press, 2000), 150–60.

13. See Rasmus Kreth and Michael Mogensen, *Flugten til Sverige. Aktionen mod de danske jøder oktober 1943* (Copenhagen: Gyldendal, 1995).

14. Sofie L. Bak, *Jødeaktionen oktober 1943. Forestillinger i offentlighed og forskning* (Copenhagen: Museum Tusculanum, 2001).

15. Sofie L. Bak, *Dansk Antisemitisme 1930–1945* (Copenhagen: Aschehoug, 2004). Her findings confirm my research presented in Thorsten Wagner, "Overcoming Prejudice: The Danish Church and the Jews 1918–1945: Stepping into the Breach or Relativizing Antisemitism?" *Kirchliche Zeitgeschichte* 16 (2003): 149–68.

16. See Thorsten Wagner, "Jøder og andre danskere. Den nyere antisemitismeforskning og dens implikationer for dansk historieskrivning," *Scandinavian Jewish Studies/Nordisk Judaistik* 22 (2001): 131–56; Thorsten Wagner, "Ein vergebliches Unterfangen? Der Antisemitismus und das Scheitern des dänischen Nationalsozialismus," in *Vorurteil und Rassenhaß. Antisemitismus in den faschistischen Bewegungen,* ed.Wolfgang Benz, et al. (Berlin: Metropol, 2001), 275–96; Thorsten Wagner, "Fællesskabets nationalisering og jødespørgsmålet i en liberal kultur. Jøderne i Danmark mellem inklusion og eksklusion," in *Folk og fællesskab. Træk af fællesskabstænkningen i mellemkrigstiden,* ed. Uffe Østergaard and Cecilie S. Banke (Århus: Werks, 2001), 47–61.

17. These are some of the issues dealt with in the framework of my dissertation project on the emancipation and acculturation of the Jewish community in Denmark, 1780–1850, in a comparative European perspective.

18. In contrast to the worsening legal status of Jews in Prussia in the course of the eighteenth century, regulations of acceptance are even eased, as are other regulations.

19. Thorsten Wagner, "Juden in Kopenhagen 1780–1820. Studien zu Emanzipation und Akkulturation" (M.A. thesis, Technische Universität Berlin, 1998), 85–99.

20. Thyge V. Kragh, *Grundtvigs syn på Israel* (Copenhagen: Dansk Israelsmission, 1971), 23.

21. See Fredrik Nielsen, *Das moderne Judenthum, seiner Emancipation und Reform entgegen geführt durch die Verdienste Lessings, Moses Mendelssohns und Abraham Geigers. Eine historische Charakteristik,* trans. E. Schumacher (Flensburg: A. Westphalen, 1880).

22. Johannes Kok, *Det hellige Land og dets nabolande i fortid og nutid. Til vejledning og opbyggelse for bibellæsere* (Copenhagen: P. G. Philipsen, 1878).

23. Nicolai Gottlieb Blædel, *Udvidet Confirmations-Underviisning eller evangelisk-luthersk Kirkelære* (Copenhagen: Gyldendal, 1876).

24. It was published in German as well: Hans Lassen Martensen, *Die christliche Ethik,* vol. 2 (Gotha: Besser, 1878), §§ 45–50, especially §48.

25. Abraham Alexander Wolff, *Talmudfjender. Et Genmæle mod de seneste Angreb paa Jøderne og Jødedommen* (Copenhagen: C. A. Reitzel, 1878).

26. See Rünitz, *Danmark og de jødiske flygtninge 1933–1940,* 155.

27. Ibid., 156.

28. Bak, *Dansk Antisemitisme,* 180. Here she observes a development, a change of opinion within the Home Mission with regard to the Jewish question; but as she argues that the Mission's stance became less antisemitic in the course of the late 1930s and especially after the Nazi occupation of Denmark in April 1940, she has a hard time explaining Bartholdy's harsh condemnation of Jews as a modernizing force, assimilatory, denying God's existence and furthering moral decay. They can never become part of the national community and will always remain an alien element and guests. Bartholdy publishes this view at the climax of the Holocaust—summer 1942. On the latter, see Christian Bartholdy, *Lav Os en Gud* (Copenhagen: O. Lohse, 1942).

29. Hal Koch, leader of the Youth Associations, aforementioned Løgstrup, or Johannes Nordentoft.

30. This might be reminiscent of some neo-Augustinian concept, trying to make sense of the continued existence of a religious community that was supposed to vanish after the rise of Christianity.

31. Bak, *Dansk Antisemitisme,* did not investigate other clerical milieus such as Grundtvigianism (p. 42), but focused only on the Home Mission as an example for religious antisemitism. Thus she missed the degree to which many of the concepts presented here were widespread in Danish church-affiliated milieus in general, and tends to belittle the crucial ambiguity of a theologian such as Frederik Torm (p. 353f.). In his *Jødefolket og Verdenshistorien* (Copenhagen: G. E. C. Gad, 1939), Torm sets out to attack antisemitism, though he still criticizes Jews for their tendency to develop a sense of superiority and to abuse their powerful position in modern society (p. 17).

32. I am indebted for Sofie Bak for drawing my attention to the case of Malling.

33. This success constituted a stark contrast to the Norwegian developments, where the adoption of German Nazi antisemitism almost caused a split of the Norwegian National Socialist movement, "Nasjonal Samling." See Hassing, *The Churches of Norway and the Jews.*

34. Ulrich Balslev, "Om jødespørgsmaalet," *Dansk Udsyn* 13 (1933): 428–37.

35. F. L. Østrup, "Symbiose," *Berlingske Tidende* (February 2, 1939).

36. Marcus Melchior, *Man siger, at Jøderne* (Copenhagen: Det Schønbergske Forlag, 1936).

37. Halfdan Høgsbro, "Om Jøderne," *Herstedernes Menigheds-Blad* 12 (February 1943): 1–2.

Rabbinic Judaism in the Writings of Polish Catholic Theologians, 1918–1939

2

Anna Łysiak

In the interwar period, Polish prelates spent a great deal of time discussing Jewish matters. Authors wrote much about the "Jewish Question," including Jews' so-called involvement in capitalism, socialism, liberalism, and revolutions; their anonymous empire aimed against all non-Jews, especially Christians; and their destructive and demoralizing impact on social, political, and cultural life. Both nationalistic and Catholic publications, whether mass-circulated or elite, dealt with this issue by using religious arguments and terminology while also making reference to history, psychology, economics, politics, and culture. Stemming from the value Polish society placed on religion and the Catholic faith, these religious arguments held great significance in Polish society. At the same time, they denigrated the Jewish faith and Polish Jews, for they presented Catholicism as the only true religion and stigmatized Judaism as the root of moral evil.

In this essay, I examine the image of rabbinic and modern Judaism in the most important Polish Catholic periodicals connected with academic centers and seminaries. The editors aimed their articles at the Catholic intelligentsia, both lay and cleric. These journals included *Ateneum Kapłańskie,* a monthly edited by Włocławek Seminary professors, *Gazeta Kościelna,* from the Lwów area, *Głos Kapłański,* a Lublin-based monthly, *Przegląd Biblijny,* published in Kraków, and *Przegląd Katolicki* and *Przegląd Powszechny,* both of which targeted Warsaw. In addition to these journal articles, I will also examine books and brochures by Catholic theologians who were considered experts in Judaism.

The presentation of Judaism in Catholic writings was inseparably linked to the concept of Catholic truth and mission. For instance, the article "The Dogmatic Justification of Missionary Assignments and Obligations" in *Misje Katolickie* discussed the relationship between Catholic truth and God. It claimed that Catholic truth radiated with a spirit of harmony and a compound of multiplicity and singularity, whose source was God. Missionary outreach was understood as part of God's general plan, and God Himself was the center of the mission. The Catholic religion's universality and truth ensured its ability to overcome any national limitations. Despite the differences among people, humanity was one, because it originated in the biblical couple of Adam and Eve. The Church's role, through its missionary outreach, was to bring people closer to divine grace. Although human nature was free and able to accept God's grace freely, to reject this grace would bring certain death and condemnation. Even to despise this fact was to attack God's power over creation and to sin against the Holy Spirit.[1]

The idea of the Church's inherently missionary nature derived from the message of Jesus Christ to proclaim the Gospel to all nations. Its zeal was manifested, among other things, by the widespread theological thought in papal and conciliar documents through the principle *Extra Ecclesiam salus non est*—there is no salvation outside the Church.[2] This principle was often understood literally to mean only a baptized member of the Church could be saved, since the Church alone controlled the means to salvation. However, a few Polish theologians offered contrasting interpretations. For example, in his article, "*Extra Ecclesiam salus non est* in the Light of the Teaching of St. Augustine," Father Jan Czuj examined God's salvific acts in St. Augustine's writings. According to Czuj, salvation outside the Church was possible if the visible means were unavailable. Official doctrine had actually contained this novel understanding since the Council of Trent. Czuj argued that St. Augustine never completely excluded the possibility of salvation outside the Church. Rather, he emphasized the value of faith and love present outside the Church. He claimed that Jesus Christ revealed himself in many different ways to many different people and nations, even before his coming into this world. Czuj maintained that while God never begrudged anyone grace, God did refuse those who were unworthy by their own actions. Nevertheless, he argued that since Jews lived among Christians, they, in turn, could access the visible means of salvation present in the Church. Therefore, Czuj reasoned, a Jew could be saved, even if he maintained his Jewish faith. Still, a Jew had to show his readiness to convert and to be baptized.[3]

Among the writings of Catholic Polish theologians, we find statements referring to the concept of "baptism of desire," using such terms
as "Christian souls" and "Christ souls," in reference to Jews.[4] These theologians wrote about the need for Jews to convert visibly—to break
cleanly with the Jewish environment.[5] Some of the theologians had serious doubts about the authenticity of Jewish conversion. They ascribed
these doubts to Jews' "spiritual blindness" and the "sin of deicide." In
addition, they feared that Judaism and its traditions were too contrary
and hostile to Christianity for many converts to abandon them totally.
Therefore, they suspected some Jewish converts of hidden malevolent
activities against the Church. In the face of these problems, they discussed the issue of mass conversion with great trepidation. They also
commented on the ideas developed in the eleventh chapter of Paul's
Letter to the Romans, which, read literally, stated that Jews would join
the Church in the last days after a period of spiritual renewal and increased religiosity for Christians themselves.[6]

Throughout history, churchmen have attempted to convert Jews,
most often through forceful means. In the publications under discussion, with the exception of the abovementioned issues surrounding conversion, Polish Catholic theologians wrote about groups who prose-
lytized among Jews. At the end of nineteenth century and the beginning
of the twentieth century, churchmen created groups and organizations
that were missionary but that also promoted religious renewal in the
Polish Church's view of Jews and Judaism. The initiators of these movements were often Jewish converts themselves. Theologians wrote about
the most famous and popular religious organizations and associations,
such as the Sisters of Notre Dame de Sion, the Fathers of Notre Dame de
Sion, Pauluswerk (Vienna Pastoral Institute), and the Catholic Guild of
Israel.[7] Among the various groups, Rome especially made note of Amici
Israel—Friends of Israel—and ordered it dissolved.

In 1926, Father Antoine van Asseldonk and Francesca van Leer, a
Jewish convert, founded Amici Israel. They campaigned against the accusation of deicide, the spread of false teachings about Jews and Judaism,
and antisemitism. They advocated speaking about God's love for the
Jewish people, and how it had increased after Christ's resurrection.
Amici Israel also encouraged the introduction of changes to Catholic
liturgy, especially the elimination of any reference to Jewish "perfidy"
during the Good Friday service. Amici Israel initiated a buoyant and
fast-developing movement that included thousands of priests, hundreds
of bishops, and a dozen or so cardinals. In Poland this organization was

canonically established in a few dioceses, such as Warsaw, Łomża, and Siedlce, and promoted by local bishops and Cardinal Aleksander Kakowski. The association's central committee published a bulletin, *Pax Super Israel,* which included the group's main ideas and program. Unfortunately, the spread of these ideas led to the group's eventual prohibition by the Congregation of the Holy Office. On March 25, 1928, the Congregation issued a decree stating that Amici Israel's manner of speaking and acting did not accord with the spirit of the Church, with the thought of the Church Fathers, and with the Catholic liturgy. Pope Pius XI confirmed the Congregation's decision.[8] At the same time, the decree praised the initiatives and activities connected with the conversion of Jews. It emphasized the Church's constant prayer to this end and the Apostolic See's role as protector of Jews from injustice. The decree also condemned antisemitism, which it defined as hatred of Jews, who were once the chosen people. This was the Church's first official condemnation of antisemitism, but paradoxically, it appeared only in the decree that dissolved the organization that also endeavored to oppose it. Though the statement rejected religious prejudice toward Jews, it did not alter the Church's teaching on deicide. Thus, the idea of sinful Jewish people who suffered because they rejected and crucified Christ continued to form the Church's "theology of Judaism."

Polish Catholic theologians considered Amici Israel a powerful and threatening manifestation of "judaization"[9] and beguilement[10] that desired to Judaize the Church and take over society. They argued that was "why the Catholic world welcomed the fact that the Church acted just in time and killed the insatiable wolf of Jewish racism and pan-Semitism, this time clothed in the sheepskin of the Catholic zealot." To them, this group was a manifestation of "false ideology" and "divisive theology."[11] Theologians referred to the official decree and emphasized that they agreed that the association acted contrary to the spirit of the Church.

Despite this development, the end of nineteenth century and the beginning of twentieth century in many European countries was a time of pioneering development of Christian-Jewish dialogue and theological debates in Christianity about Judaism and Israel and in Judaism about Christianity and Jesus Christ.[12] In Poland, however, these developments did not significantly influence Catholicism. For the most part, the commentaries of Polish theologians were highly apologetic in nature and in accordance with official Church teaching. Nevertheless, one may find some traces of this development in reviews, bibliographies, and articles. For example, the reaction to a Jewish study about Jesus, *Jesus of Nazareth* by Joseph Gedaliah Klausner, a professor at Hebrew University, reveals the more critical discussion that took place among Polish Catholic intellectuals. Many welcomed this work with great interest even though it created further controversies between Christians and Jews.

In 1933, in Poland, the Jewish-Polish weekly *Opinia* published sections from Klausner's book. On August 15, the weekly announced the work's publication and printed the first excerpt on August 27. By late September, however, Cardinal Kakowski ordered the banning of the September 22 edition and the confiscation of all earlier editions. Although the book had received positive reviews in papal biblical writings, in Poland it was considered blasphemy and treated as a "Jewish farce."[13] A few Polish theologians did write enthusiastically about the book, especially about its sources and the comparisons between Jewish and Christian ethics. However, they criticized Klausner for referring to the methods of Protestant biblical exegetes and stressed that it revealed a dead ritualism. They often quoted Klausner's statements of radical differences between Christianity and Judaism.[14]

These comments reflected how over 123 years of partitions, wars, conflicts, and statelessness had negatively affected the development of theology in Poland. For example, in 1918 Poland, there were only two theology faculties at state universities. By 1939, the number had increased only to five. It is difficult to compare the level of theological studies in Poland with Western Europe, despite the achievements of some outstanding theologians and scholars.[15] Among the important theologians who wrote about Judaism were Fathers Józef Kruszyński, Stanisław Trzeciak, Witold Gronowski, and Eugeniusz Dąbrowski.

Józef Kruszyński was a biblical scholar, lecturer, prefect, and vice-regent at the Włocławek seminary. From 1925 to 1933, he was rector of the only Catholic University in Poland, established in 1918. He lectured in the Old Testament, the New Testament, Hebrew language, biblical archeology, and the history of comparative religion. For his services to the Church, he received the titles of Honorary Canon of Włocławek Cathedral, Canon of the Włocławek Chapter, Papal Domestic Prelate, and Apostolic Protonotary. During his life, Kruszyński was a prolific writer who authored fifty books and one hundred articles and reviews. He devoted the majority of his works to biblical studies, but he also wrote studies on Jews and Judaism (the majority were anti-Jewish in nature) and published them in the series "In the Domain of Knowing Jews and Judaism."[16]

Stanisław Trzeciak, a theologian and sociologist, wrote apologetically and popularized theology. He studied theology in Przemyśl seminary, and later in Fribourg, Switzerland, Vienna, Rome, Kraków, and Jerusalem. After earning his doctorate in Kraków, in 1907, he was appointed professor at Petersburg Academy. He published works on religion, society, and politics in the time of Jesus. His works on Judaism were most controversial and evoked reactions, polemics, and criticism from Jews.[17]

Witold Gronkowski was a biblical scholar. In 1921, he entered Poznań seminary and studied theology and philosophy there for two years. Afterward, his superiors sent him to Strasbourg. Ordained in 1926, he continued his studies and, in 1930, defended his dissertation in theology on messianism in Ezekiel under L. Dennfeld. His work was well received in Poland and abroad. From 1930 to 1933, he studied at the Pontifical Biblical Institute in Rome. Then from 1933 to 1934, he attended the Biblical School in Jerusalem. In 1934, he began lecturing in Old Testament studies at Poznań Seminary, and in 1936 he was appointed professor ordinarius.[18]

Like Gronkowski, Eugeniusz Dąbrowski was a biblical scholar. He studied at Warsaw seminary and at Warsaw University. Two years after his 1923 ordination, he traveled to Oxford and Cambridge to study English. In the same year, he earned his doctorate from Warsaw University. In 1926, he traveled to Rome and began studies at the Pontifical Biblical Institute. By 1929, he returned to Warsaw and received the appointment as professor of New Testament at Warsaw Seminary.[19]

With the exception of Trzeciak, these priests began their academic careers soon after the First World War. The interwar period in Poland was a time of dynamic development, change, and crises, especially in social-political life, which affected both the Catholic majority and different minorities, among them Jews. The clergy were not only engaged in religious and theological life. They were also involved in social-political activities, many representing right-wing movements, especially these intolerant to national and religious minorities.

Despite this intolerance, Catholic theologians still wrestled with the question of how to define Judaism and how to classify it. They treated biblical Judaism as a part of the history of Christianity. However, they defined the Church as the New Israel and portrayed it as the legitimate and authentic heir to the Old Testament and the Mosaic religion. In 1920, Kruszyński, in *Jews and the Jewish Question,* wrote that Jews did not practice a pure Mosaic religion, but another variety: rabbinic Judaism. He referred to a scholarly division of Judaism into two groups: the

Old Testament, called "Israeli religion," and rabbinic Judaism, called the Jewish religion.[20] In the same publication, he called rabbinic Judaism "a new religion"—"a religion of the Talmud"—created by Jews after the destruction of the Temple and dispersion of Jews.[21] It was characterized by detailed regulations concerning activities of everyday life. A few years later, Kruszyński's statements became more radical. In 1925, in his study of the Talmud, he claimed that modern Judaism had hardly anything in common with the Mosaic religion. He argued that even though Jews followed Moses' laws, they did so in the hate-filled spirit of the Talmud.[22] According to Kruszyński, evidence thereof could be found in Bolshevism, which had its roots in the Talmud.[23]

In 1928, *Ateneum Kapłańskie* published three articles by Szczepan Szydelski in response to a controversial book, *Hellenism and Judaism*, by Tadeusz Zieliński. Zieliński's book sparked heated discussions among Christians and Jews because it posited a unique relationship between the Greek religion and Christianity, excluding Judaism. In his response, Szydelski attempted to show a strong, undeniable, and essential relationship between Judaism and Christianity. He took into serious consideration biblical Judaism's most important features and ideas. He emphasized the Mosaic religion's highly developed ethics, which one could observe especially in the relationship between the Jewish people and God, but also in relationship to others. He stressed the meaning and great importance of religion to Jews and its centrality to their daily lives. He wrote about the Scripture's monotheistic and theocentric character, which manifested Jewish religiosity and showed how Jews praised and glorified God for God's kindness, goodness, and mercy. Szydelski emphasized that only the Jewish Old Testament had prepared for and preceded Christianity, and that Christians accepted the Old Testament as canonical.[24] In the conclusion of his second article, Szydelski posed a question about both the Greek and the Jewish religions: "Which one was alive and which one was dead?" In response, he wrote that the Greek religion had ceased to exist, whereas Jewish religion of the Old Covenant was alive. Further, he explained that Jews kept the religion of the Old Covenant despite the many problems they had faced on the way. In turn, he argued that they had survived as a separate and independent nation thanks to religion.[25] However, the conclusion of the second article was not compatible with the remarks he made in his third and last article on this topic. There, he stressed Christianity's Jewish roots and its victory over the Hellenistic religion in large part due to its Jewish heritage. Yet he also pointed out that the Jewish religion had developed around the Talmud and stood in opposition to Christianity.[26] In addition, he suggested that modern Judaism had broken with biblical Judaism and formed itself contrary to Christianity. Consequently, he argued Christianity became the true bearer of biblical Judaism because it alone carried and spread the values of the Old Testament.

In the same journal, in an article, "About a New Work on Judaism," Julian Unszlicht quoted an opinion of a well-known Jesuit scholar, Father Joseph Bonsirven, who had written much on the unique value of Judaism, but who had also stressed that modern Judaism had no right to receive the same level of respect as biblical Judaism. The reason he gave for such degradation was his conviction about the nature of the Jews who, he argued, were full of sin as a result of their rejection by God for killing Jesus.[27] Dąbrowski shared a similar outlook and claimed that it would be a mistake to ignore the differences between the Old Testament and rabbinical Judaism. In his 1934 article published in *Przegląd Katolicki,* "Reasons for a Negative Attitude of Judaism toward Christianity," Leon Radziejowski referred to Dąbrowski's statements when he argued that modern Judaism had broken from its roots and that, as a result, the ideals of the Old Testament no longer had anything to do with it. He claimed that rabbinic Judaism treated the covenant with God as a trade contract meant to bring Jews worldly and earthly profits. According to Dąbrowski, Judaism should be treated as a pathological manifestation of a religion.[28] Gronkowski called modern Judaism "Talmudism," an heir to Phariseeism and its distortion at the same time. In a series of articles entitled "Talmudism or Christianity," published in 1937 and 1938 in *Miesięcznik Kościelny Archidiecezji Gnieźnieńskiej i Poznańskiej* and in *Ateneum Kapłańskie,* he stressed that Talmudism did not continue the religion of the Old Covenant, but ritually slaughtered it.[29] He stated that Pharisaic Judaism had fought and continued to fight against Christianity with all possible means. He referred to the writing of the world-famous biblical scholar Father Maria Joseph Lagrange, a Dominican, who stated that Talmudic tactics could be summarized in two phrases: to harm Christians as much as possible and to avoid any contact with them.[30] In a 1934 series of articles about ritual slaughter in *Przegląd Katolicki,* Trzeciak also claimed that modern Judaism was not the Mosaic religion, but rather a Talmudic religion that did not follow the Old Testament's rules, regulations, and commandments.[31]

Catholic theologians presented post-biblical Judaism as a false religion that introduced anti-values and immoral ethics through the Talmud. In this way, they identified Judaism as "a religion of hatred" in that it was dead and lacked development due to its break with God and the truth. "Empty" and "brainless" religious rituals marked its practice. For example, in 1936, in an article about the attitude of Judaism toward Christianity, Dąbrowski called Judaism a "Judaistic ideology."[32] In 1939, Gronkowski called it a caricature or imitation religion. Already, in a series of articles entitled "Talmudism or Christianity," Gronkowski had degraded rabbinical practices and described them as imaginary.[33] This line of attack on Judaism became customary in many Catholic theological journals. For example, the editor of *Roczniki Katolickie* called Judaism a "pseudo-religion"[34] At the same time, Kruszyński called Judaism "a religious nationality, a sect"[35] and a "hateful social autonomy."[36] In a 1923 brochure, *A Religion of Modern Jews*, Kruszyński discussed Judaism's Decalogue based upon the popular and non-scholarly writings of Andrzej Niemojewski. In his analysis, he pointed out the ways the commandments could be transgressed within the confines of the Talmud. He suggested that adherents of rabbinic Judaism considered these transgressions as proper and morally good. He gave the examples of receiving baptism without faith, ignoring regulations of the Sabbath, annulling oaths, killing (including handicapped children and Gentiles), and cheating Gentiles.[37] Through such examples, he portrayed the Jewish faith as demonic and antireligious, without any value system.[38]

The Catechism for Converts further discussed the distance between Judaism and Catholicism.[39] In this work, the author treated Judaism as a religion that was lower than and unworthy of comparison to Catholicism. The author argued against granting it equal rights in Poland. Such a victory, he argued, would mean humiliation for the Catholic Church. The key issue here was conversion. One should approach conversion by encouraging Jews to break with the Talmud and to read Scripture independently.[40] No longer would Jewish believers need to read Scripture blindfolded by their religious tradition. Here the author referred to St. Augustine's statement that Jews carried books, but Christians drew faith from them. To foster this development, the *Catechism* recommended the work *Why Jews Become Catholics* by Maria Rosalia Levy. This dictionary-style publication contained fifty biographies and autobiographies of well-known Jewish converts. Other theologians reinforced the need to emphasize conversion. For example, Marian Osowicki, in his article "The Issue of Conversion of Israel," claimed that the sign of the twentieth century would be the conversion of Israel by directing prayer toward the Sacred Heart of Jesus.[41] Not surprisingly, the prayer ends with an antisemitic quotation from the Gospel of Matthew: "His blood be upon us and on our children" (Mt 27:24–25), which Christians had used for centuries to accuse Jews of deicide. Pope Leo XIII had approved the first version of the prayer. However, it was not until 1925 that the Congregation for Divine Worship added the negative biblical phrase.[42]

Polish Catholic theologians also identified Judaism as a messianic religion in which its followers waited in faith for a Messiah. In 1934, Trzeciak addressed this point in his work *Messianism and the Jewish Question.* There he attempted to prove that the Talmud contained information about the Messiah—an image that accorded with the Gospels and the Christian teaching about Jesus Christ. He discussed the concepts of preexistence of the Messiah, of his suffering, satisfaction, and reconciliation, of his salvific death and his glorification, and of his sitting at God's right hand. Trzeciak assured his readers that if Jews had only good will they could recognize the Messiah in Jesus Christ, especially in Talmudic commentaries for Psalms and the prophecies of Isaiah.[43] Trzeciak's approach was not novel. The same method was advocated in the Middle Ages. For centuries, Christians have attempted to use the Talmud to prove the truth of the Catholic faith.

Other theologians, such as Józef Archutowski[44] and Jan Sznurowacki,[45] wrote about how Judaism degraded a Jewish Messiah by portraying him as an earthly warrior and avenger. According to them, this trend suppressed the Messiah's spiritual character. It later dominated Jewish literature and tradition when Jews passed it on through the apocryphal books and the Talmud itself. The image of a Jewish Messiah as a warrior and avenger was common in the writings of Catholic theologians. Trzeciak claimed that Jews believed that the Jewish nation would suffer in exile for its sins, but later God would show God's mercy on them and would take revenge on other nations. Next, God would invoke a world war; then, following a period of horrible suffering and devastation, the Messiah would come. He would call all Jews to the land of Israel, where they would reign. Trzeciak maintained that such an interpretation of messianism was actually a summary of messianic concepts from ancient Jewish literature, the Talmud, and modern theological works. According to him, *The Protocols of the Elders of Zion* best presented Jewish messianic desires.[46] Trzeciak considered messianism as the key to the Jewish question.

In his publications, Trzeciak actually mentioned a pseudo-Messiah, Jakub Lejbowicz Frank, and the Frankist movement in Poland.[47] Trzeciak explained that Orthodox and rabbinical Jews had considered Frank and his movement as heresy and cursed them.[48] But Trzeciak maintained that the disputes between Frank and the rabbis existed only to distract attention from the Jews' main goal: to capture Poland, to establish their kingdom there, and to oppress and exploit the Polish people.[49] Trzeciak called such aspirations "pathological perversion in messianism" and considered them a manifestation of God's curse for their killing the true Messiah.[50]

Theologians aligned Jewish messianism with Jewish political nationalism. They called this messianism "pseudo-messianism," shaped after killing the true Messiah, Jesus.[51] In the 1924 article "Messianic Hopes of Israelis verses Rejection of Jesus," Sznurowacki described the Jewish Messiah as an "earthly avenger," who indulged the Jews' quest for world political power.[52]

Generally, Polish Catholic theologians believed that God's curse for crucifying Jesus weighed heavily on the Jews. In his 1925 passion sermons, Zygmunt Pilch described Jews as a living image of God's anger and wrath. He called the murder of Jesus a psychological and immoral secret of this nation,[53] whose hatred was passed on from generation to generation through property, blood, custom, and false teachings.[54] Unszlicht, however, tried to link deicide to God's will.[55] In 1928, he called Israel "a rebelling slave," but also "an obedient tool" through whom God redeemed the world. Still, God rejected them and sentenced them to "everlasting wandering among nations." Unszlicht defined killing Jesus as a "crime" against which "all the crimes of the world taken together went pale." Yet he stressed that deicide was God's will. In contrast, his fellow theologians did not concentrate on God's will, but on the so-called rebellious and hateful character of murderous Jews.

In their treatment of Judaism as a distorted religion and the antithesis of Christianity, Polish Catholic theologians used both theological and political arguments from medieval writings that presented Jews as the tools of diabolic activities. Kruszyński claimed that a revengeful character of a messiah was an antithesis of Jesus Christ.[56] Stanisław Kowalski developed this idea by discussing the special vocation of Jews whose messianic mission turned into "lust for ruling and exploiting other nations." Further, he argued that Jews lived under the influence of Satan's temptation. Those who did not accept Jesus' teaching were under the influence of the Antichrist. Such influence he saw manifested in Jewish involvement in Masonry, communism, socialism, and liberalism.[57]

The conviction that Jews encoded messianism in social-political movements was widespread in the writings of theologians. Trzeciak even entitled the thirteenth chapter of his work on messianism and Jews as

"Bolshevism as the Fight of Judaism against Christianity."[58] Kruszyński also equated Bolshevism and the Jews and stated that both followed the voice of the Antichrist.[59] However, Kruszyński claimed that the Talmud itself was the source of Bolshevism and the Jews' desire to conquer the world. Other theologians described "modern manifestations of messianism"[60] as natural consequences of distorted Jewish messianic ideas of world domination, which *The Protocols of the Elders of Zion* confirmed. Theologians were aware of the 1933–36 trial in Brno in which the court declared the *Protocols* to be fictional. Still, many Poles accused those judges of partiality and bias;[61] even those who accepted the verdict still perceived truth in the *Protocols.*[62]

Polish Catholic theologians also defined Judaism as a materialistic religion. By this, they meant that material and earthly goods formed the religion's core. Dąbrowski claimed that materialism had begun to dominate Judaism in the times of Jesus. Jesus contradicted this tendency through his teaching about the Kingdom of God that required a purity of heart from its adherents. Thus, Dąbrowski argued that the ideas Jesus proposed were foreign to Judaism.[63]

Theologians often gave examples of Jews' involvement in social and political life as proof that Judaism was a materialistic religion. They considered the *Protocols* as further evidence. They presented Jewish socialists as future capitalists whose condition of being socialists or communists was only a temporary state. In his 1920 article "Revolution, Jews and the Sacred Books," Jan Urban claimed that the same tendencies formed a Jewish capitalist and a Jewish revolutionist.[64] Two main commands of "distorted Judaism" were to look for paradise here on earth and to conquer the world economically. Jews were to fulfill these commands whether they practiced their religion faithfully or not. Urban claimed that the fact that Jews were situated on different steps of "a social ladder" was not contradictory in Judaism since everything in it emerged from a materialistic spirit. He admitted that a poor communist Jew supported social justice, but when the same individual became rich, he switched and supported capitalism.[65] In the article "Socialism and Judaism," Urban characterized socialism as a well-organized and institutionalized materialistic religion with a canon of sacred books by Lassalle, Marx, and Engels. The doctrine of socialism was materialism. Urban compared debates and commentaries present in socialistic books and programs to Gemara and Mishnah.[66]

For his part, Unszlicht claimed that socialism could also develop without Jews, but would never be so momentous. According to him, a

Jew was simply a more natural representative of socialism than any-body else. When he remarked on the de-Christianization of laborers, he stressed the growth of the cult of synagogue. For him, socialism and Judaism became inseparable, since one hurried to help the other in the case of the slightest danger.[67] Presenting Judaism as a materialistic reli-gion was closely connected with the idea of false Jewish messianism. In his publications, Trzeciak attempted to prove that extreme socialism and communism were based on Jewish law aimed at destroying Christian civilization. He argued that Marx, as a descendant of Jewish rabbis and product of Jewish materialism, had used a Jewish-influenced exegesis to analyze politics and economics. In turn, he viewed socialism as an ex-pression of Jewish messianic hope, whereby Jews destroyed other nations by causing their inner decay through promoting class struggle.[68]

Polish Catholic theologians did not analyze Jews and Judaism only politically. They also attempted to examine the tenets of the Jewish faith and cultural life, particularly Jewish marriage and pedagogical practices. They regularly based their writings on previous scholars' work and of-fered little new research or thought. For example, Józef Dajczak, used the publications of Paul Billerbeck and Herman Strack as a basis for his writing on the use of the Talmud as a commentary for New Testament.[69] And Tomasz Wąsik used the well-known works of Karl August Wunsche and A. Eberharter to write about the fall of Adam and Eve in the Jewish tradition.[70] Roman Konecki even based his work on Jewish homiletic theory and the synagogue on lectures by Rabbi Manuel Joel.[71]

Polish Catholic theologians wrote about Jewish doctrines and re-ligious practices in a superficial way. Their work discussed Jewish under-standings of God, prayer, and Sabbath; however, they concentrated their commentary on what they considered to be negative aspects of this "apparent religion" and its "dead rituals" and "formalism." They espe-cially focused on the Talmud, and emphasized its so-called double ethics and presentation of ritual slaughter.

Polish Catholic theologians did admit that the Talmud was an im-portant religious code and called it "a monument of morality," "a spiri-tual food for Jews," and "an encyclopaedia of Jewish wisdom." Some even discussed its genesis and history, especially how its teachings became normative for Jews. Still, the theologians also applied many negative labels. They maligned the Talmud as "a book of hatred," "a liquid of manure," "a code for thieves," "a poison," "an immoral book," "an an-tithesis of Christianity," "a root of all evil," "an ungodly book of Phari-sees," "a dump in which God's laws are buried," "an anti-social book that divides people in the world and teaches hatred," "one great lie," "a work of Satan's perversity," "a racist book," and "a root of monstrous and inhuman teaching."[72]

Polish academics considered Kruszyński and Trzeciak experts on the Talmud. Catholic publications frequently referred to their works. Kruszyński viewed hatred of Christians and Christianity as a basic characteristic of the Talmud.[73] He claimed that the authors of the Talmud elevated hatred to "the level of moral perfection," because Jews by their "hateful" interpretation of the Old Testament "introduced hatred as an obligation for believers," which they aimed at destroying Christianity.[74]

Polish Catholic theologians referred often to the Talmud in their writings, but failed to show any depth of understanding for it. They especially wrote about the Talmud's "double ethics" that separated Jews from non-Jews. The concept of "double ethics" led theologians to comment on a "double psyche" of Jews and a "double life" in which Jews often engaged themselves in contradictory political, social, cultural, and religious practices. These theologians also viewed Jewish ethics as a tool to degrade Gentiles, to weaken their moral standards, to strip their culture of meaning and to force them into slavery. In turn, they interpreted any Jewish activities that advocated freedom, human rights, equality, solidarity, or goodness as a conspiracy to exploit and to dominate Gentiles. In his publications, Kruszyński stated that Talmudic ethics encouraged Jews to cheat Gentiles in order to gain riches. Furthermore, in his 1925 work, *Why Do I Speak against Jews?* Kruszyński spent a significant amount of space attacking the Talmud. He argued that it commanded Jews to reject traditional ethics and the truth altogether.[75] Theologians, such as Kruszyński, feared that "double ethics" would result in a poor religious education for Jewish children and instill in them an "ominous seed of hatred" toward Christianity.[76]

In 1939, F. Mączyński made similar comments in a review on a recent work on Israel. He wrote that a Talmudic-based morality taught Jews to forever seek profits for themselves and to separate themselves from Christians. In addition, he argued that the Talmud encouraged Jewish believers to a fanatical hatred toward anything and everything that was not Jewish. It thereby fueled a fanatical pride of the Jewish soul. Mączyński claimed that this teaching resulted in "a hereditary load" that forced and pushed Jews into revolutionary movements. He perceived them as driven by "an extreme utilitarianism."[77] In his earlier publications, Kruszyński had reinforced Mączyński's interpretation by arguing that the Talmud did contain positive messages about altruistic love and love of a neighbor, but it was rare[78] since it excluded even "hostile altruism" toward Christians.[79]

Polish Catholic theologians also attacked the Talmud as a work that mocked the Catholic sacraments. To this end, they argued that the Talmud allowed Jews to be baptized without embracing the Catholic faith. For example, in a 1937 article in *Roczniki Katolickie,* an unnamed author argued that the Talmud led to perversion of Jews by inverting ideas to give them an opposite meaning. The author accused Jews of degrading the spiritual, supernatural, and holy character of baptism for pure business purposes. This is why, the author argued, Jews form their entire lives around their business ventures.[80] In turn, the Talmud allowed this idolatry by presenting Catholicism, in the sacrament of baptism, as idolatrous.[81]

Some theologians claimed that ambiguity and contradictions in the Talmud were apparent and even purposeful in order to hide secret information in code. In his article about *The Protocols of the Elders of Zion,* Ignacy Charszewski called the Talmud "a secret book" full of contradictions to confuse those who would like to explore "the Talmudic secrets." He was sure that a reader needed a special key to decipher its language. Charszewski stated that Hebrew was good for conspiracy and coding since it did not have vowels, which made hiding ideas easier.[82] Kruszyński also described the language of the Talmud as rich in metaphors, secrets, mysticism, illogical statements, and complexity that served to hide its contents from Christians and other strangers.[83]

Besides these general statements and remarks concerning the Talmud, Trzeciak tried to be more specific by referring to and quoting Talmudic tractates in his publications. He assumed that all the regulations written in the Talmud were valid. He also ignored the Talmud's complex debates on the different regulations and cases. Instead, he had the habit of taking sentences completely out of context and mixing them together while totally ignoring their historical context. He wrote that the regulations on Gentiles were impure, demonic, and discriminatory. He repeated typical and traditional charges against the Talmud by stating that it described Gentiles as animals, dogs, donkeys, and cattle and as nonhuman.

In 1935, Trzeciak also discussed Jewish ritual slaughter in a series of articles entitled "Ritual Slaughter in the Light of the Bible and the Talmud."[84] These publications contain the essence of his disputes with Jews. In the articles, he discussed the origin of ritual slaughter, its religious significance, and humanitarian issues. He hoped his articles would lead to a complete ban on a ritual slaughter in Poland. Trzeciak attempted to prove that this practice had no biblical roots and had been based solely on the Talmud, which he believed had little in common with the Mosaic religion. He claimed that ritual slaughter was not a religious practice and argued against it or any other religious privileges for ritual slaughterers. He called this custom "a monstrosity of the twentieth century."[85] In 1936, the Board of the Association of Rabbis took its concerns to the Sejm Administrative Council Committee of the Polish parliament. This committee declared that Trzeciak's writings were pseudo-scholarly and described him as fully ignorant of Jewish religious practices. Furthermore, it declared that his commentaries were false and that his writing revealed he knew neither Hebrew nor Aramaic. Though Trzeciak refused to discuss these findings, he admitted that, in his writing, he had referred not to original texts but to commentaries by Jewish authors: Lazarus Goldschmidt's *The Babylonian Talmud*, Pereferkowicz's *Mishnah Talmud and Tosefta*, and George Loewe's *Shulkhan Arukh*.[86] He also refused the rabbinical board's request that he translate one page of the Talmud. Despite this development, his position did not change among those Catholics who continued to consider him an expert on Judaism and the Talmud. As a result of his writing, however, in 1936, the government did pass a law that instituted quotas on ritual slaughter. In 1937 and again in 1938, the Polish government considered a ban on ritual slaughter. Finally, in 1939, the Sejm enacted a bill that prohibited ritual slaughter beginning in 1942.[87] This law concerned the Jewish community greatly, and soon thereafter its leading figures published brochures that explained the origin and religious meaning of ritual slaughter in an attempt to convince Christians about its humanitarianism.[88]

In some publications, Polish Catholic theologians attempted to explain their reasons for writing about Jews. They especially centered on Paul's Letter to the Romans, in which he expressed compassion and concern toward Jews. Despite this positive note, most theologians primarily focused on God's rejection of the Jews, which they admitted was temporary until the last days, when everyone in the world would become a member of the Catholic Church. Still, other theologians stressed the need to understand Jews and Judaism in order to carry out more successfully the work of conversion. Some of them even considered themselves followers of a Christ who they believed was sent into the world in order to fight against Jews in a struggle for good and truth. These theologians who treated Judaism as a threat for Christians and the Polish state wrote about Jews as if in self-defense and in an effort to make Catholic Poles aware of Jews' so-called hidden and visible dangers. However, a few of the theologians revealed a genuine desire to understand Judaism. Normally, the writings of these latter theologians lacked propaganda and contained little negative assessment of Jews and the Jewish faith.

In 1930, *Przegląd Powszechny* published a summary of an article by the French rabbi and historian M. Liber. Liber discussed Judaism as both a religion and a nationality. He pointed out false interpretations of Judaism, which presented it as a religion of hatred and revenge, and showed that, in fact, it was a religion of justice, love, and respect. Similarly, he characterized Judaism as a religion open to numerous interpretations of Scripture and of ritual. Liber emphasized his belief that Jews could cooperate with Gentiles to develop human civilization primarily because Judaism had always promoted unity of humankind, love of a neighbor, social justice, and world peace. Liber was sure that Judaism could propagate these essential ideas among all the nations.[89]

Similar in character was a 1930 review article in *Ateneum Kapłańskie* by Unszlicht. Unszlicht discussed the book *On the Ruins of the Temple* by the French Jesuit Joseph Bonsirven. He wrote about the beauty of the Jewish liturgy and customs as significant elements for Jewish identity. He stressed a strong relationship between God the Father and the Jewish people. He presented God in Judaism as just and merciful, and Jews as a missionary and priestly people who were obliged to be more holy than other peoples. He stressed that the Torah and the Talmud were at the heart of this religion. Similarly, he discussed what Judaism taught about the Messiah—a king and ruler who would establish a kingdom with a capital in Zion and who would bring together all dispersed Jews there. However, he departed from his positive presentation of Judaism when he interjected negative comments, such as "derailed messianism," "narrow particularism," "Jewish pride," "dirt in the Talmud," "Jewish perfidy," and "a deicide race."[90]

In 1932, Father Dajczak published a series of articles about the Talmud as a commentary on the New Testament. These publications were inspired by modern biblical research, especially by the works of Billerbeck and Strack. Unfortunately, Dajczak began his commentary with negative remarks about the Talmud. He called it the most clumsy and least absorbing book in the world. He also cited an opinion of biblical scholars that the Talmud was not a treasure of wisdom and truth, but a book of immorality and nonsense that contained valueless discussions and deliberations. Still, Dajczak assured his readers that in the Talmud they could find a lot of beautiful and valuable thoughts, especially those about the period when Christ lived. More specifically, he commented on the "right to revenge." He wrote that the Talmud taught that it would be better to be prosecuted than to prosecute. But it also taught that everyone had the right to self-defense. In turn, the teachings of Christ could be understood in this same spirit since Christ did not preclude the right of individuals to protect themselves or their personal belongings. In the Talmud, Dajczak searched for information that would help him to understand other teachings of Christ. For example, allowing someone to slap you on your right cheek, not on the left one. In the Talmud, he found a note that the act of slapping a right cheek with a back of a hand was a greater insult and humiliation than the left one. He also searched for a context to understand better other biblical phrases and situations, such as a needle eye, proclaiming on rooftops, the number thirty (silver coins), mercy, martyrdom, miracles, healing with saliva, burial customs, and pilgrimages.[91]

Among those who attempted to evaluate Judaism fairly was an exceptional figure, Tadeusz Zaderecki. Often called the "Christian defender of the Talmud," Zaderecki endured harsh criticism from Polish Catholic theologians, especially Gronkowski and Trzeciak. Zaderecki wrote about the great and unique value of the Talmud. In his critique, he detailed the mistakes and utter ignorance of his fellow theologians, paying special attention to the publications of Trzeciak, Kruszyński, and Charszewski. He accused them of unreliability and plagiarism, especially from the discredited works of August Rohling and Justyn Bonawentura Pranajtis. He also encouraged other scholars to study the Talmud without bias and to focus particularly on the question of what the Talmud and the Gospels shared in common. His articles did not find a home in traditional Catholic journals, but in the Jewish periodical *Chwila*.[92] Jews respected him and called him "an excellent Christian Talmudist."

Conclusion

In interwar Poland, Catholics judged theological works primarily based upon the reputation of the authors. Kruszyński, Trzeciak, Gronkowski, Dąbrowski would be rated among the most prominent authors. They were very popular among both academics and ordinary Catholics and were well known as experts on Judaism and the Jewish question. Despite their popularity, these theologians failed to adopt exegetical methodology. If they used any specific approach to their studies, one might identify it as dogmatic. The circular method attempted to understand and prove dogma primarily by using the existing dogma itself. Nevertheless, Gronkowski and Kruszyński did write about Jewish methods of Scripture interpretation. Through this they showed their general awareness of different approaches one may take to understand the Jewish texts. Despite this insight, they still assessed them negatively. They remained resolute in their refusal to consult with Jewish scholars in order to gain a deeper and authentic understanding of the Jewish tradition. Instead, they relied on discredited publications and often used their sources out of context. In essence, they showed little or no respect for their source material. And though these theologians tended to omit and ignore the essence of Judaism and its main concepts, historical context, and evolution, they often did the same in their discussion of the Gospels and other books of Scripture in their publication on Jews and Judaism. They regularly quoted selectively and out of context to support their negative portrayal of Judaism. They especially liked to emphasize the hypocrisy of the Pharisees as a main trait of Jewish rabbis. Unfortunately, they chose not to gaze into a mirror and see the hypocrisy of their own false interpretations.

NOTES

1. Anonymous, "Dogmatyczne uzasadnienie zadań i obowiązków misyjnych," *Misje Katolickie* 37 (1918): 219.

2. This principle in a rigorist form was present in papal and conciliar documents from the fifth to fifteenth centuries. The principle expressed the idea and conviction that Catholicism was the only true religion and the Church was the only "ark of salvation," outside which people were lost. In 1442, the Council of Florence affirmed the most rigorist understanding of the principle. However, a century later, the Council of Trent approved the doctrine of "baptism of desire," and it was solemnly declared that those outside the Church could also be saved. Later documents cautiously confirmed it. See Jacques Depuis, *Chrześcijaństwo i religie. Od konfrontacji do dialogu* (Kraków: Wydawnictwo WAM, 2003), 31–99.

3. Jan Czuj, "*Extra Ecclesiam salus non est* w świetle nauki św. Augustyna," *Przegląd Teologiczny* 3 (1922): 205–15. According to Jacques Depuis, St. Augustine claimed that if the Gospel had not been preached to some people or peoples, it was because God had foreseen that they would be unworthy of it (since they would have rejected it) even if it had been preached to them. See Jacques Depuis, *Toward a Christian Theology of Religious Pluralism* (Maryknoll, N.Y.: Orbis Books, 1997), 91.

4. According to Jacques Depuis, St. Augustine was convinced that if Jews did not have faith in Jesus and were not baptized, they would not be saved, because they had access to the Gospel. He maintained that they should blame only themselves for this, because they did not join the Church by their own will, where salvation was

waiting for them. See Jacques Depuis, *Toward a Christian Theology of Religious Pluralism*, 90–91.

5. Mateusz Jeż, "Chrzcić Żydów, czy nie chrzcić," *Gazeta Kościelna* 31 (1924): 179–80; Mateusz Jeż, "Jak nawracać Żydów?" *Gazeta Kościelna* 41 (1934): 495–96; Julian Unszlicht, "W sprawie nawracania Żydów," *Homo Dei* 4 (1935): 112–16; Nikodem Cieszyński, "Crux apostolatus," *Roczniki Katolickie* 14 (1937): 184–98. *Roczniki Katolickie* was published by Nikodem Cieszyński. Although Cieszyński's name did not appear as the author of the articles cited in the essay, he was identified in the interwar press as the author. For example the article "Złudy i zawody" published in *Roczniki Katolickie* in 1929 was also published in *Gazeta Kościelna* under the title "Izrael współczesny a katolicyzm" and signed with his name. See Nikodem Cieszyński, "Izrael współczesny a katolicyzm," *Gazeta Kościelna* 36 (1929): 137–38; Konwertyta (Pseudonym), "Konwertyta w sprawie żydowskiej," *Przegląd Powszechny* 55 (1938): 23–35; Witold Gronkowski, "Chrzest Żydów w świetle nauki Kościoła," *Ateneum Kapłańskie* 31 (1939): 435–38; Nikodem Cieszyński "Jak się bronić przeciwko judaizmowi," *Roczniki Katolickie* 16 (1939): 194–205.

6. Sprawa żydowska w świetle nauki katolickiej," trans. A. Zagierski, *Pro Christo* 2 (1926): 576–85, and Marian Osowicki, "Sprawa nawrócenia Izraela," *Pro Christo* 2 (1926): 853–69.

7. Nikodem Cieszyński, "Crux apostolatus," *Roczniki Katolickie* 14 (1937): 186–87; Mateusz Jeż, "Jak nawracać Żydów?," *Gazeta Kościelna* 41 (1934): 496; Henryk Weryński, "Jedna strona kwestii żydowskiej," *Gazeta Kościelna* 41 (1934): 203; Nikodem Cieszyński, "Jak się bronić przeciwko judaizmowi," *Roczniki Katolickie* 16 (1939): 202; J. K., "Módlmy się za wiarołomne żydostwo," *Misje Katolickie* 53 (1934): 5–9.

8. See Grzegorz Ignatowski, *Kościoły wobec przejawów antysemityzmu* (Łódź: Archidiecezjalne Wydanictwo Łódzkie, 1999), 15–18; Ronald Modras, *The Catholic Church and Antisemitism Poland, 1933–1939* (N.Y.: Harwood Academic Publishers, 1994), 317.

9. Julian Unszlicht, "Z powodu nowego dzieła o judaizmie," *Ateneum Kapłańskie* 16 (1930): 266.

10. Marian Wiśniewski, "Krótka historia 'Przyjaciół Izraela,'" *Pro Christo* 6 (1930): 70.

11. Ibid.

12. In the Catholic world one could mention the works of Leon Bloy, Joseph Bonsirven, Charles Journet, Maria Joseph Lagrange, Jacques Maritain. Additionally, a significant dispute took place in 1916 between the philosophers Eugen Rosenstock-Heussy and Franz Rosenzweig. They discussed the legal aspect of Judaism and the spiritual aspect of Christianity. Rosenzweig stressed a false image of Jews and Judaism, emphasized Christian's negative intentions, and raised doubts about the legitimacy and truthfulness of Christian dogma. Deep interpretation and symbols marked this dispute.

13. Publishers' note, "Konfiskata 9 numerów 'Opinji' oraz dzieła prof. J. Klausnera p.t. 'Jezus z Nazaretu,'" *Opinia* 38 (1933): 1.

14. This commentary may be found in Eugeniusz Dąbrowski, "Chrystus w literaturze żydowskiej," *Przegląd Katolicki* 71 (1933): 711–13; Witold Gronkowski, "Miesięcznik Kościelny Archidiecezji Gnieźnieńskiej i Poznańskiej," *Talmudyzm czy chrześcijaństwo* 52 (1937): 68–74. J.K., "Módlmy się i za wiarołomne żydostwo," *Misje Katolickie* 53 (1934): 5–9; Leon Radziejowski, "Judaizm wobec chrześcijaństwa," *Przegląd Katolicki* 72 (1934): 767–69; Julian Unszlicht, "Z powodu nowego dzieła o judaizmie," *Ateneum Kapłańskie* 16 (1930): 255–67; Julian Unszlicht, "Rabin Klausner o Chrystusie," *Gazeta Kościelna* 43 (1936): 262–63.

15. *Dzieje teologii katolickiej w Polsce. Wiek XIX i XX,* 1 and 2, ed. Marian Rechowicz (Lublin: Towarzystwo Naukowe KUL, 1976).

16. Józef Kruszyński left an unpublished manuscript, *My Memoirs.* Now located in the seminary library in Włocławek, it examines Jews and the "Jewish question," and thereby offers an insight to understand the origin of Józef Kruszyński's anti-Jewish publications. On this point, see Stanisław Librowski, "Kruszyński Józef," in *Polski Słownik Biograficzny* 15, ed. Władysław Konopczyński (Kraków: Polska Akademia Umiejętności, 1975), 442, and see Kazimierz Rulka, "Kruszyński Józef," in *Słownik Polskich Teologów Katolickich* 6, ed. Ludwik Grzebień (Warszawa: Akademia Teologii Katolickiej, 1983), 215–22.

17. On Stanisław Trzeciak, see *Słownik Polskich Teologów Katolickich* 7, 327.

18. On his life and publications, see *Słownik Polskich Teologów Katolickich* 5, 521.

19. On Eugeniusz Dąbrowski, see *Słownik Polskich Teologów Katolickich* 5, 283.

20. Józef Kruszyński, *Żydzi i kwestia żydowska* (Włocławek: Wydawnictwo Księgarni Powszechnej i Drukarni Diecezjalnej we Włocławku, 1920), 13.

21. Ibid., 129–30.

22. Józef Kruszyński, *Talmud co zawiera i co naucza* (Lublin: Drukarnia Udziałowa Lublin, 1925), 50.

23. Ibid., 56.

24. Szczepan Szydelski, "Religia helleńska, Stary Testament i chrześcijaństwo," *Ateneum Kapłańskie* 14 (1928): 1–16, 105–35, 227–47.

25. Ibid., 135.

26. Ibid., 246.

27. Julian Unszlicht, "Z powodu nowego dzieła o judaizmie," *Ateneum Kapłańskie* 16 (1930): 267.

28. Leon Radziejowski, "Judaizm wobec chrześcijaństwa," *Przegląd Katolicki* 72 (1934): 768.

29. Witold Gronkowski, "Talmudyzm czy chrześcijaństwo," *Miesięcznik Kościelny Archidiecezji Gnieźnieńskiej i Poznańskiej* 53 (1938): 223; Witold Gronkowski, review of "*Talmud w ogniu wieków,*" *Ateneum Kapłańskie* 22 (1936): 413.

30. Witold Gronkowski, review of "*Talmud w ogniu wieków,*" *Ateneum Kapłańskie* 22 (1936): 413.

31. Stanisław Trzeciak, "Ubój rytualny w świetle Biblii i Talmudu," *Przegląd Katolicki* 73 (1935): 270–71, 299–300, 318–20, 363–65.

32. Eugeniusz Dąbrowski, "Jeszcze o stosunku judaizmu do chrześcijaństwa," *Głos Kapłański* 10 (1936): 473.

33. Witold Gronkowski, "Talmudyzm czy chrześcijaństwo," *Miesięcznik Kościelny Archidiecezji Gnieźnieńskiej i Poznańskiej* 52 (1937): 389.

34. Nikodem Cieszyński, "Judaizm, jednym z największych niebezpieczeństw," *Roczniki Katolickie* 16 (1939): 186.

35. Ibid.

36. Józef Kruszyński, *Rola światowa żydostwa* (Włocławek: Wydawnictwo Księgarni Powszechnej i Drukarni Diecezjalnej we Włocławku, 1923), 27.

37. Józef Kruszyński, *Religia Żydów spółczesnych* (Włocławek: Wydawnictwo Księgarni Powszechnej i Drukarni Diecezjalnej we Włocławku, 1923), 30–33.

38. Józef Kruszyński, *Talmud co zawiera i co naucza,* 49.

39. W. Danek, *Katechizm dla konwertytów według dziełka ks. Dr. E. Huszara* (Kraków: Wydawnictwo Apostolstwa Modlitwy, 1939), 6. The full title states that W. Danek based his catechism on the work of Father Dr. E. Huszar.

40. X. J. Cavatier, "O nawrócenie Żydów we Francji," *Gazeta Kościelna* 27 (1920): 76–77; Franciszek Pistol, "W kwestii nawrócenia Żydów słów kilka," *Gazeta*

Kościelna 32 (1925): 19–20; Witold Gronkowski, "Chrzest Żydów w świetle nauki Kościoła," *Ateneum Kapłańskie* 31 (1939): 436–38. In 1929 and in 1930, a Jewish-Polish convert, Gabriel Jehuda Ibn Ezra, published reviews and commentary in *Chrześcijańskiego Żyda wspomnienia, łzy i myśli.* On this point, see Stanisław Solarz "Krok naprzód do rozwiązania kwestii żydowskiej," *Ateneum Kapłańskie* 21 (1935): 82; Nikodem Cieszyński, "Crux apostolatus," *Roczniki Katolickie* 14 (1937): 196–97; Adam Gyurkovich, "Pax super Israel," *Gazeta Kościelna* 36 (1929): 481–82; Ceka (Pseudonym), review of *Chrześcijańskiego Żyda wspomnienia, łzy i myśli* in *Ateneum Kapłańskie* 15 (1929): 517–18. In 1930, Józef Kruszyński also discussed Ezra's work in his article "Problem katolicyzmu wśród Żydów," *Przegląd Katolicki* 68 (1930): 33–34.

41. Marian Osowicki, "Sprawa nawrócenia Izraela," *Pro Christo* 2 (1926): 864.

42. Ibid.

43. Stanisław Trzeciak, *Mesjanizm a kwestia żydowska* (Warszawa: Przegląd Katolicki, 1934): 14–24.

44. Józef Archutowski, review of *Herold Chrystusa na tle epoki, Przegląd Biblijny* 1 (1937): 196.

45. Jan Sznurowacki, "Nadzieje mesjanistyczne Izraelitów a odrzucenie Jezusa Chrystusa," *Przegląd Homiletyczny* 2 (1924): 28.

46. See Stanisław Trzeciak, *Mesjanizm a kwestia żydowska* (Warszawa: Przegląd Katolicki, 1934); Stanisław Trzeciak, *Program światowej polityki żydowskiej* (Warszawa: Gebethner i Wolff, 1936).

47. On Frank and his followers see *Polski Słownik Judaistyczny. Dzieje, kultura, religia, ludzie* 1, ed. Zofia Borzymińska and Rafał Żebrowski (Warszawa: Prószyński i S-ka, 2003), 439–40 and Jan Doktór, *Śladami Mesjasza Apostaty. żydowskie ruchy mesjańskie w XVII i XVIII w. a problem konwersji* (Wrocław: Wydawnictwo Leopoldinum Fundacji dla Uniwersytetu Wrocławskiego, 1998).

48. Stanisław Trzeciak, *Mesjanizm a kwestia żydowska*, 96.

49. Ibid., 98.

50. Ibid., 129–30.

51. On this question, see Jan Sznurowacki, "Nadzieje mesjanistyczne Izraelitów a odrzucenie Jezusa Chrystusa," *Przegląd Homiletyczny* 2 (1924): 22–29; Zygmunt Pilch, *Odrzucenie Mesjasza jako następstwo grzechów narody żydowskiego* (Kielce: Wydawnictwo Przeglądu Homelitycznego, 1925); Marian Wiśniewski, "Lud Jezusa," *Pro Christo* 1 (1925): 1–12; Julian Unszlicht, "Z powodu nowego dzieła o judaizmie," *Ateneum Kapłańskie* 16 (1930): 255–67; Ignacy Charszewski, "*Protokoły Mędrców Syjonu* znów aktualne," *Pro Christo* 10 (1934): 882–93; Stanisław Kowalski, "Posłannictwo i tragedia narodu żydowskiego," *Ruch Katolicki* 6 (1936): 312–16.

52. Jan Sznurowacki, "Nadzieje mesjanistyczne Izraelitów a odrzucenie Jezusa Chrystusa," *Przegląd Homiletyczny* 2 (1924): 28.

53. Zygmunt Pilch, *Odrzucenie Mesjasza jako następstwo grzechów narodu żydowskiego*, 5.

54. Ibid., 7.

55. Julian Unszlicht, "Ku czci Dziewicy Izraela," *Pro Christo* 10 (1928): 742.

56. Józef Kruszyński, *Polityka żydowska* (Włocławek: Wydawnictwo Księgarni Powszechnej i Drukarni Diecezjalnej we Włocławku, 1921), 8.

57. Stanisław Kowalski, "Posłannictwo i tragedia narodu żydowskiego," *Ruch Katolicki* 6 (1936): 313.

58. Stanisław Trzeciak, *Mesjanizm a kwestia żydowska*, 209–16.

59. Józef Kruszyński, *Niebezpieczeństwo żydowskie* (Włocławek: Wydawnictwo Księgarni Powszechnej i Drukarni Diecezjalnej we Włocławku, 1923), 33.

60. On the modern manifestations of messianism see Julian Unszlicht, "W

sprawie nawracania Żydów," *Homo Dei* 4 (1935): 112; Jan Archita, "Ks. Eugeniusz Dąbrowski: *Chrystianizm a judaizm*," *Pro Christo* 12 (1936): 43; Nikodem Cieszyński, "Mesjanizm i rewolucjonizm," *Roczniki Katolickie* 14 (1937): 171–81; Nikodem Cieszyński, "Judaizm, jednym z największych niebezpieczeństw," *Roczniki Katolickie* 16 (1939): 190–92.

61. Józef Białasiewicz, Światowa polityka żydowska," *Przegląd Katolicki* 74 (1936): 341.

62. Piotr Stach, "Mesjanizm a kwestia żydowska," *Gazeta Kościelna* 40 (1934): 562; Ignacy Charszewski, "*Protokoły Mędrców Syjonu* znów aktualne," *Pro Christo* 10 (1934): 884.

63. Leon Radziejowski, "Judaizm wobec chrześcijaństwa," *Przegląd Katolicki* 72 (1934): 769.

64. Jan Urban, "Rewolucja, Żydzi i księgi święte," *Przegląd Powszechny* 37 (1920): 102.

65. Ibid., 106.

66. Jan Urban, "Socjalizm jako religia," *Przegląd Powszechny* 38 (1921): 5–18

67. Julian Unszlicht, "Ku czci Dziewicy Izraela," *Pro Christo* 10 (1928): 742.

68. Staniław Trzeciak, *Mesjanizm a kwestia żydowska*, 162.

69. Józef Dajczak, "Talmud, jako komentarz do Pism św. Nowego Zakonu," *Gazeta Kościelna* 39 (1932): 256–57, 266–68; Józef Dajczak, "Fragmenty Ewangelii według św. Łukasza w świetle Talmudu," *Gazeta Kościelna* 39 (1932): 292–94; Józef Dajczak, "Fragmenty Ewangelii według św. Mateusza w świetle Talmudu," *Gazeta Kościelna* 39 (1932): 303–306, 316–18, 338–40; Józef Dajczak, "Fragmenty Ewangelii według św. Marka, Łukasza, Jana i Dziejów Ap. w świetle Talmudu," *Gazeta Kościelna* 39 (1932): 398–401, 410–13, 434–37; Witold Gronkowski, "Talmudyzm czy chrześcijaństwo," *Miesięcznik Kościelny Archidiecezji Gnieźnieńskiej i Poznańskiej* 52 (1937): 68–74, 207–15, 287–96, 387–97; Witold Gronkowski, *Miesięcznik Kościelny Archidiecezji Gnieźnieńskiej i Poznańskiej* 53 (1938): 97–103, 223–28.

70. Tomasz Wąsik, "Żydowskie i mahometańskie podania o stworzeniu i upadku pierwszych ludzi," *Miesięcznik Katechetyczny i Wychowawczy* 15 (1926): 235–50.

71. Roman Konecki, "Z homiletyki żydowskiej," *Przegląd Homiletyczny* 2 (1924): 29–34

72. See Józef Dajczak, "Talmud, jako komentarz do Pism św. Nowego Zakonu," *Gazeta Kościelna* 39 (1932): 256–57, 266–68; Józef Dajczak, "Fragmenty Ewangelii według św. Łukasza," *Gazeta Kościelna* 39 (1932): 292–94; Józef Dajczak, "Fragmenty Ewangelii według św. Mateusza," *Gazeta Kościelna* 39 (1932): 303–306, 316–18, 338–40; Józef Dajczak, "Fragmenty Ewangelii według św. Marka, Łukasza, Jana," *Gazeta Kościelna* 39 (1932): 398–401, 410–13, 434–37; Witold Gronkowski, "Talmudyzm czy chrześcijaństwo,," *Miesięcznik Kościelny* 52 (1937): 68–74, 207–15, 287–96, 387–97; Witold Gronkowski, *Miesięcznik Kościelny* 53 (1938): 97–103, 223–28; Józef Kruszyński, *Talmud co zawiera i co naucza* (Lublin: Drukarnia Udziałowa Lublin, 1925); Józef Kruszyński, *Żydzi a kwestia żydowska* (Włocławek: Wydawnictwo Księgarni Powszechnej i Drukarni Diecezjalnej we Włocławku, 1920); Józef Kruszyński, *Żydzi a Polska* (Poznań: Drukarnia Robotników Chrześcijańskich T.A., 1921), Józef Kruszyński, *Religia Żydów spółczesnych* (Włocławek: Wydawnictwo Księgarni Powszechnej i Drukarni Diecezjalnej we Włocławku, 1923); Józef Kruszyński, *Niebezpieczeństwo żydowskie* (Włocławek: Wydawnictwo Księgarni Powszechnej i Drukarni Diecezjalnej we Włocławku, 1923); Józef Kruszyński, *Antysemityzm-antyjudaizm-antygoizm* (Włocławek: Wydawnictwo Księgarni Powszechnej i Drukarni Diecezjalnej we Włocławku, 1924); Józef Kruszyński, *Żydzi a świat chrześcijański*

(Włocławek: Wydawnictwo Księgarni Powszechnej i Drukarni Diecezjalnej we Włocławku, 1924).

73. Józef Kruszyński, *Talmud co zawiera i co naucza*, 70.

74. Józef Kruszyński, *Żydzi, a świat chrześcijański*, 12.

75. Józef Kruszyński, *Dlaczego występuje przeciwko Żydom?* (Kielce: Towarzystwo Rozwój, 1923), 36.

76. Nikodem Cieszyński, "Złudy i zawody," *Roczniki Katolickie* 7 (1929), 198.

77. F. Mączyński, review of "H. de Vries de Heekelingen, *Izrael, jego przeszłość i przyszłość*," *Ateneum Kapłańskie* 31 (1939): 514.

78. Józef Kruszyński, *Polityka żydowska*, 16.

79. Józef Kruszyński, *Talmud co zawiera i co naucza*, 25.

80. Nikodem Cieszyński, "Crux apostolatus," *Roczniki Katolickie* 14 (1937): 191.

81. Ibid., 191–92.

82. Ignacy Charszewski, "*Protokoły Mędrców Syjonu* znów aktualne," *Pro Christo* 10 (1934): 891.

83. Józef Kruszyński, *Polityka żydowska*, 10; Józef Kruszyński, *Talmud co zawiera i co naucza*, 12, 55, 60.

84. Stanisław Trzeciak, "Ubój rytualny w świetle Biblii i Talmudu," *Przegląd Katolicki* 73 (1935): 270–71, 299–300, 318–20, 363–65.

85. Ibid.

86. Anonymous, "Proces Żydów z ks. Stanisław Trzeciakiem," *Przegląd Katolicki* 74 (1936): 186. George Loewe was a Jewish convert.

87. *Polski Słownik Judaistyczny. Dzieje, kultura, religia, ludzie* 2, ed. Zofia Borzymińska and Rafał Żebrowski, 755–56.

88. Gadejla Rozenman, rabin Gminy Wyznaniowej Żydowskiej w Białymstoku, *Zagadnienie uboju rytualnego. Odpowiedź Ks. Dr. Staniławowi Trzeciakowi* (Białystok: n.p., 1936); Asz Nahum, Rabin Gminy Wyznaniowej Żydowskiej w Częstochowie, *W obronie uboju rytualnego* (Częstochowa: Gmina Wyznaniowa Żydowska 1936).

89. Anonymous, "Żyd o religijnem odrodzeniu Żydów i ich światowej misji," *Przegląd Powszechny* 47 (1930): 217–26.

90. Julian Unszlicht, "Z powodu nowego dzieła o judaizmie," *Ateneum Kapłańskie* 16 (1930): 255–67.

91. Józef Dajczak, "Talmud, jako komentarz do Pism św. Nowego Zakonu," *Gazeta Kościelna* 39 (1932): 256–57, 266–68; Józef Dajczak, "Fragmenty Ewangelii według św. Łukasza," *Gazeta Kościelna* 39 (1932): 292–94; Józef Dajczak, "Fragmenty Ewangelii według św. Mateusza," *Gazeta Kościelna* 39 (1932): 303–306, 316–18, 338–40; Józef Dajczak, "Fragmenty Ewangelii według św. Marka, Łukasza, Jana," *Gazeta Kościelna* 39 (1932): 398–401, 410–13, 434–37.

92. Tadeusz Zaderecki, *O Żydach, bolszewji, "mordzie rytualnym"* (Lwów: n.p., 1934); Tadeusz Zaderecki, *Z Biblia i Talmudem w walce*, (Lwów: n.p., 1936); Tadeusz Zaderecki, *Talmud w ogniu wieków* (Warszawa: Księgarnia F. Hoesicka, 1936); Tadeusz Zaderecki, *Tajemna wiedza żydowska* (Lwów: "Cofim" Żydowskie Towarzystwo Wydawnicze); Tadeusz Zaderecki, *Tajemnice alfabetu hebrajskiego* (Warszawa: Pum Beditha, 1939).

German Catholic Views of
3 Jesus and Judaism, 1918–1945

ROBERT A. KRIEG

The Second Vatican Council endorsed a change in the Catholic Church's self-understanding and its stance toward the world and other religions. When Pope John XXIII convoked the council on December 25, 1961, he opened the way for both the end of the hegemony of the notion of the Church as a "perfect society," that is, as a self-sufficient, juridical institution, and also the end of the Church's negative attitude toward modernity and non-Christian beliefs. The Council then proceeded in *Lumen Gentium,* the Constitution on the Church, to declare that the Church is "a sacrament—a sign and instrument, that is, of communion with God and of the unity of the entire human race."[1] It also explained that the Church is the people of God and only secondarily an institution. Moreover, the council took a constructive stance toward the world, especially as it acknowledged contemporary society's merits as well as its dilemmas in *Gaudium et Spes,* the Pastoral Constitution on the Church in the Modern World. Further, it conveyed respect for other religions in *Nostra Aetate,* the Declaration on the Relation of the Church to Non-Christian Religions. The Council declared: "Let Christians, while witnessing to their own faith and way of life, acknowledge, preserve and encourage the spiritual and moral truths found among non-Christians, together with their social life and culture."[2] It added that the Church "deplores all hatreds, persecutions, displays of antisemitism leveled at any time or from any source against the Jews."[3] When Pope Paul VI closed the council on December 7, 1965, he envisioned the Church witnessing to the coming God's reign and working with other religions for "the progress of peoples."[4] Vatican II was surely an extraordinary turning point in the life of the Catholic Church.

Since the Second Vatican Council, the Catholic Church has shown a new respect for Judaism.[5] During his long pontificate, Pope John Paul II engaged in a significant dialogue with the Jewish people: going to Auschwitz in 1979, praying at Rome's chief synagogue in 1986, meeting with Jewish leaders from Poland and the United States in 1987, endorsing the "Fundamental Agreement" between the Vatican and Israel in 1994, and visiting Israel in 2000. Nevertheless, pre–Vatican II attitudes about Jews and Judaism still exist among Catholics, even among ecclesiastical officials. Their hold on people became evident in 2003 as some Catholics gave unqualified praise to Mel Gibson's movie *The Passion of the Christ*. If the movie's viewers fully understood and accepted the Church's conciliar and post-conciliar teachings against antisemitism, they would have objected to the movie's implicitly negative depiction of Jews and Judaism.[6] Unfortunately, pre-conciliar ideas and biases have persisted, often on an unconscious level. It is necessary, therefore, that efforts be made to uncover and uproot antisemitism in Catholicism not only for the sake of Jews, but also for the well-being of Catholics.[7]

This essay is meant to contribute to the realization of the Second Vatican Council's vision by highlighting the religious antisemitism, also called anti-Judaism, contained in German Catholic books about Jesus that appeared between the two world wars.[8] Beginning in 1918, Catholicism flourished in Germany as people sought healing from the devastation of the Great War and a strengthening of the moral and spiritual foundation of their lives in the increasingly secular German society. Amid this religious awakening, some Catholic theologians chose to reflect on the content of Christian belief by making use of contemporary thought on personal existence (existentialism) and of Catholics' new interest in the Bible. Working apart from the Neo-Scholasticism that had dominated Catholic theology, some innovative scholars highlighted "the essence" of Christian faith by writing books on the message and ministry of Jesus Christ. As part of this endeavor, Bernhard Bartmann, Karl Adam, and Romano Guardini reflected in their respective books on Jesus' life, death, and resurrection as recounted in the Gospels. Because they appealed to a sense of Jesus' life as narrated in the Gospels, they conveyed an understanding of Jesus as a person, and thus directed attention to the living, transcendent reality at the heart or "essence" of Christian faith. With this accomplishment, Bartmann, Adam, and Guardini contributed to the renewal of Catholicism. At the same time, however, these theologians hurt Catholicism because in their renderings of the Gospels they repeated and even amplified the Gospels' anti-Jewish biases. In other words, these relatively progressive theologians fueled religious antisemitism at the very time that Adolf Hitler was preaching racial antisemitism.[9]

German Catholic Theology, 1918–1945

Neo-Scholasticism entailed the retrieval from the 1860s to the 1960s of the philosophy and theology that emerged in Europe's medieval and baroque universities.[10] In reaction to the Enlightenment's emphasis upon autonomous human reason and its suspicion of civil and religious authority as well as tradition, Catholic scholars from the mid-nineteenth century until the mid-twentieth century tried to reiterate the wisdom of Anselm, Bonaventure, Thomas Aquinas, Duns Scotus, Cajetan, and Francisco Suarez, and in this endeavor they relied on the deductive theological method developed by Melchior Cano and Dionysius Petavius. They assumed that the only valid religious questions were the classical ones addressed by the medieval and baroque theologians. Therefore, they did not directly address the questions emerging in the Church's life, for example, questions concerning the relationship between Jesus Christ and Judaism, and between Jesus Christ and the dignity of every human being.

Neo-Scholasticism dominated Catholic philosophy and theology for a century in part because it provided a technical language, precise definitions of key concepts, and a coherent body of thought, and also because it became the Church's official form of thought, backed by papal authority. Indeed, during the pontificate of Pope Pius X, the Vatican's Holy Office readily excommunicated philosophers and theologians who set aside Neo-Scholasticism and recast the truths of Christian faith in the categories of a contemporary philosophy such as German Idealism. Also, the Holy Office placed these scholars' writings on the Index of Forbidden Books. The Vatican's juridical imposition of Neo-Scholasticism on Catholic philosophy and theology continued during the papacies of Benedict XV, Pius XI, and Pius XII, though it was less stringently enforced than it had been under Pope Pius X.

German Catholic theologians from the mid-1800s into the mid-1900s were trained in Neo-Scholasticism. Since all Catholic theologians were priests, they had been required by the Vatican to study in the seminary the neoscholastic theological manuals written by scholars such as Christian Pesch and Hermann Dieckmann. At the same time, however, because many Catholic theologians became professors at German universities, they had the academic freedom to read the growing number of critical studies on the history of Western thought, especially on the development of Christian doctrine. In light of this new historical consciousness, German Catholic theologians became increasingly aware of Neo-Scholasticism's inability to recognize human historicity, and some of them dared to work outside Neo-Scholasticism, especially after the First World War, when Catholicism flourished in Germany.[11] As German Catholics experienced democracy for the first time in the Weimar Republic, they also participated in the liturgical renewal of their parishes, the blossoming of youth associations, the emergence of study groups on the Bible, and the outreach led by the Kolping Society to the poor, the homeless, and the unemployed. Noting this new vitality among Catholics, Romano Guardini observed in 1922: "A religious dynamism of immeasurable importance has commenced: the Church is awaking in people's souls."[12] One specific manifestation of this spiritual and intellectual vitality occurred in Christology. Theologians generated new literature—apart from the neoscholastic categories—on the life and mission of Jesus Christ. In doing so, they were influenced by at least three religious factors.[13]

First, Pope Pius XI gave a fresh impulse to Christology by issuing two encyclicals concerning the Church in relation to Jesus Christ. On the day of his papal coronation on February 12, 1922, he took as his motto "Christ's peace in Christ's kingdom," thereby conveying that the Church should work in the world to establish the *pax Christi*. Ten months later, on December 23, 1922, he issued his encyclical *Ubi Arcano Dei*, in which he urged all Christians—laity as well as clergy—to devote themselves to bringing Christ into the world. With this message, he provided an ecclesiastical basis for the "lay apostolate" promoted by Joseph Cardijn and the Catholic Action movement. Convinced that the greatest threats to Christ in the world were secularism and communism, Pius XI established the Feast of Christ the King by issuing his encyclical *Quas Primas* on December 11, 1925. This feast was intended to anticipate the day when all peoples would acknowledge Jesus Christ as the divine sovereign whom all nations and their governments must worship and obey. The pope's recurring emphasis on the Church's relationship with Jesus Christ reminded Catholics in general and theologians in particular of the centrality of Jesus Christ in Christian belief.

Second, the biblical movement of the early 1900s made a strong impact on German Catholicism, which had previously associated the reading of the Bible with Martin Luther and Protestantism. After World War I, Catholics purchased pocket Bibles written in German, and they read these Bibles at Mass while the priest at the altar silently read biblical texts in Latin. Further, searching for divine words of comfort and hope, people did what they had previously linked with Protestantism: they gathered in their parishes and their youth groups to discuss the Bible, especially the New Testament. They wanted to know the living Christ. They received instructions on the Bible from pastors who drew on the Catholic biblical commentaries that began appearing in Germany at the turn of the century. These commentaries were the fruit of biblical research that had been stimulated by Pope Leo XIII's encyclical *Providentissimus Deus,* which urged Catholic scholars to undertake new studies of the Bible and the ancient world. Although scholars such as Pierre Lagrange, O.P., Joseph Sickenberger, and J. B. Goettsberger were hindered by Pope Pius X's condemnation of "modernism" in 1907, they quietly persisted in their exegetical work, and they eventually experienced a slight lessening of censorship under popes Benedict XV, Pius XI, and Pius XII. Nevertheless, Catholic biblical scholars, unlike their Protestant counterparts, were not permitted to employ fully the critical methods of source criticism and form criticism. Because the Catholic biblical scholars were not allowed to study and assess the insights about the Bible afforded by these critical methods, neither they nor Catholic theologians were able to incorporate many these biblical insights into their reflections on Jesus Christ. In other words, still relying on a predominantly precritical approach to the Bible, most Catholic scholars continued to read the Gospels as literal descriptions of Jesus' words and deeds.

A third factor that influenced German Catholic theologians between the wars was the conflict within Protestantism between "liberal theology" and "dialectical theology." In 1906, with the publication of the book *The Quest of the Historical Jesus,* Albert Schweitzer had challenged the validity and religious significance of efforts to use critical historiography to construct a biography of Jesus of Nazareth. This refutation of the "original" or "liberal" quest of the historical Jesus set the stage within Protestantism for the emergence of "neo-orthodox" theology. In 1919, Karl Barth published his study *The Epistle to the Romans,* which highlights St. Paul's witness to the living word of God. A conflict ensued between the proponents of "the Jesus of history" and the advocates of "the Christ of faith." This controversy manifested itself during the 1920s in the heated exchange of letters between the senior theologian-historian Adolf von Harnack and the young theologian Karl Barth.

German Catholic theologians followed the Protestant controversy concerning the Jesus of history and the Christ of faith. Most of them shared Schweitzer's and Barth's skepticism concerning the theological value of historical-critical studies of the Bible. They also knew that the Vatican's Holy Office had no tolerance for anything resembling a liberal quest for Jesus. They knew the story of Joseph Wittig, professor of Catholic theology at the University of Breslau. In 1922, Wittig published in the journal *Hochland* an essay entitled "The Redeemed," in which he gave a historical-critical reconstruction of Jesus' life and message.[14] The essay immediately received sharp criticism from Vatican officials, German bishops, and respected theologians such as Engelbert Krebs. On July 29, 1925, the Holy Office placed Wittig's essay on the Index of Forbidden Books, and, one year later, it excommunicated Wittig. Dismissed from his professorship at the University of Breslau, Wittig enlarged "The Redeemed" into his book *Jesus' Life in Palestine.* Through the efforts of Wittig's wife, Anka Wittig, the theologian was readmitted into the Catholic Church in 1945, and he died four years later. In light of what happened to Wittig, German Catholic theologians did not explicitly use either historical-critical methods or the results of these methods in their work, not even in their books on Jesus.

These three aspects of theology during the 1920s and 1930s are important because, as we shall see, they fostered, or at least did not hinder, religious antisemitism in theologians' writings about Jesus Christ. We will return to these elements after analyzing Bernhard Bartmann's *Jesus Christ, Our Savior and King* (1929), Karl Adam's *The Son of God* (1933), and Romano Guardini's *The Lord* (1937).

Bernhard Bartmann on Jesus Christ as King

Bernhard Bartmann was a professor of Catholic dogmatic theology at Paderborn's theological Hochschule, die Bischöfliche Akademie, from 1898 until his death in 1938.[15] After completing in 1897 his monograph on the notion of justification in the thought of St. Paul and St. James, Bartmann wrote approximately eighteen books that united the study of the Bible and dogmatic theology. In 1911, he published his two-volume *Manual of Dogmatic Theology,* which was the most commonly used text in Catholic dogmatic theology in German seminaries during the early 1900s.[16] In this work, Bartmann slightly modified the neoscholastic form by reviewing how doctrine originated in the Bible and in the history of theology. *Manual of Dogmatic Theology* appeared in its eighth and last edition in 1932, and was respected not only by Catholic scholars but also by Protestant theologians such as Karl Barth, who regarded it as representative of Catholic theology.[17]

Bernhard Bartmann moved from his systematic theological overview of Christian belief, *Manual of Dogmatic Theology,* to his in-depth reflection on the mystery of Jesus Christ in 1929 when he published *Jesus Christ, Our Savior and King.*[18] As Bartmann explains in the book's foreword, he intended this study on Christ to enhance the message of Pope Pius XI's encyclical *Quas Primas* on the universal kingship of Christ. Given his aim, he concluded the book with his reflections on Jesus Christ as the *Rex gloriae,* the king of glory. Because monarchies had governed the German states from their beginning until November 8, 1918, Bartmann was able to anchor his thought on Christ as king in his own life of fifty-nine years in a German monarchy. In *Jesus Christ* he conveyed a positive view of monarchical rule, perhaps because he wrote this book while Germans were finding their first experience of democracy in the Weimar Republic to be tumultuous.

As the book's title declares, Bartmann presented Jesus Christ as the individual who from the outset of his life was the world's savior and king. Christ's regal identity threatened King Herod the Great, who tried to have Jesus killed in Bethlehem. After Herod himself died, Jesus' parents resided in Nazareth, where Jesus grew up. In his public ministry, Jesus emerged as a singular figure, indeed a kingly figure, but one who did not fit what the Jewish people expected of the anointed one, the Messiah. In his preaching and by his actions, Jesus witnessed to the coming of a transcendent kingdom, a divine polity not of this world. Pope Pius XI rightly acknowledged that Jesus Christ is the king of all creation, the One whom all authorities should obey. Through their spirituality and devotions, Germany's Christians have enriched the understanding of Christ as king by highlighting that Christ rules from the cross. "The suffering Christ supercedes the triumphant Christ. . . . God governs from the wood of the cross."[19] This understanding of Jesus Christ has a direct bearing on the Christian life. "Catholic Christians resolve all of the issues at the start, in the middle, and at the end of their lives in light of the suffering Christ and the triumphant Christ."[20]

Jesus Christ was an innovative work for its day because it did not follow the conventional form of the theological manuals, not even of Bartmann's own *Manual of Dogmatic Theology.* Bartmann's Jesus book does not comprise propositions or assertions of doctrinal truths concerning Jesus Christ. Rather, it is a narrative. Whereas propositions implicitly convey the understanding of Jesus Christ as an idea or abstract principle, a narrative presents Jesus Christ as a person, a unique individual in history. Moreover, unlike a theological manual in which biblical words or phrases function as proof texts, *Jesus Christ* cites biblical passages at length as it follows the story of Jesus as told in the Gospels. By recalling Jesus' sayings and his parables, it conveys Jesus' voice. In sum, given its narrative form and its reliance on biblical testimony, Bartmann's book communicates a sense of Jesus Christ as a person, and in doing so, it contributed to the renewal of Catholic Christology.

Jesus Christ also had, however, a negative impact on Catholic thought because it manifests an anti-Jewish bias. Bartmann recalled that the Hebrew prophets such as Jeremiah, Ezekiel, and Malachi had criticized Israel's religious authorities and their abuse of rituals and laws. "The prophets are sharp critics of the Jewish practice of the [Mosaic] Law, not of the Law itself. Their critique was amplified by John the Baptist, Jesus, and Paul who declared that the whole Law was invalidated by the coming of Christ."[21] According to Bartmann, the Jewish people became increasingly rigid in their religious practices after the Babylonian exile and, as a result, had distanced themselves from God:

> The old prophetic spirit found no home in the new Israel which then became known as the Jewish people. And Yahweh no longer sent new prophets to his people. Jews were now enthusiastically devoted to the interpretation and exercise of the Law. Through the activities of the rabbinical students and their masters, the Law's scope became ever greater and its legal basis more intricate and difficult. One no longer considered the Torah itself because it stood behind a thick barrier [of regulations] which was meant to protect the authentic Torah. A true teacher of the law had to know how to distinguish and assess no less than 613 great and small regulations. In the study of the Law, rabbinical students were led by their masters, some of whom were regarded with great respect. The synagogues, which had sprung up throughout the land after the Babylonian exile, were special places in which the Law found its cultivation. The synagogues darkened the radiance of the Temple.[22]

Bartmann argued that the Jewish development of monotheism had prepared the way for the coming of the Messiah, and that Jesus himself presupposed Jewish monotheism in his ministry. But Jewish belief in one

God was eclipsed by the Pharisees' emphasis on individual piety, the Sadducees' dominating authority, the people's materialistic exercise of religious belief (for example, in the commerce associated with Jerusalem's temple sacrifices), and the expectation of a political messiah.[23] Given this blurring of monotheism, Jesus increasingly stood apart from the Judaism of his day. He stressed that true worship depends not on its place, such as Jerusalem, but on whether it is undertaken "in spirit and in truth" (John 4:23). Jesus initially held that "salvation is from the Jews" (John 4:22).[24] But after three years of ministry, "when Jesus looked back over his travels and thought about the results of his work, he saw that his success was shamefully small."[25] The Jewish authorities had resisted Jesus and his message, and had ultimately rejected him. Further, the ordinary people to whom he had ministered were "changeable, thoughtless, and dull." Jesus had called for repentance, and "Israel had answered no."[26] As Jesus grasped the situation, he "spoke a definite and sharp judgment over the unwillingness of the Jews. He taught that their unwillingness had become an inability. Jerusalem had not wanted salvation, and it was no longer able to receive it. Israel now lacked God's grace, for God no longer gave it to Israel." Jesus had declared that no one could come to him unless the Father drew the person to Jesus (John 9:44), and God had stopped trying to draw the Jewish people to Jesus. St. Augustine later observed, "'Peccatum poena peccati'; the mis-use of grace is punished by the withdrawal of grace."[27] Such was the case with the Jews: because they had rejected Jesus, they no longer enjoyed God's favor. In sum, according to Bartmann, Israel's covenant with God had come to an end. This claim manifests the religious antisemitism of *Jesus Christ*.

After writing *Jesus Christ*, Bernhard Bartmann published books on purgatory, divine providence, and redemption in Jesus Christ. He also wrote two short books in which he argued for an accommodation between Christian belief and National Socialism. In *Positive Christianity in the Catholic View*, which appeared in December 1934, Bartmann corrected Nazi misrepresentations of Christian belief and upheld the primary tenets of Christian belief, all of which opposed Nazi neo-paganism. At the same time, he also distanced Christian faith from its Jewish origins. For example, he claimed:

> The old covenant is pre-Christian and based on a lesser kind of divine revelation. It had value and significance only in the pre-Christian era, but it relinquished these with the coming of Christ. All of the great mysteries of our sacred religion are revealed in the New Testament. . . .

The entire old covenant possessed only a preparatory and thus provisional significance and reached its definitive end with the revelation of Jesus Christ and the establishment of the Church by Christ.[28]

In January 1938, Bartmann reiterated his anti-Jewish attitude in his book *The Opposition of Belief between Judaism and Christianity,* which he wrote in reaction to German Jewish scholars, such as Martin Buber, Hans Joachim Schoeps, and Ludwig Elias Seidemann, whose books highlighted the family resemblances between Jewish belief and Christian belief. According to Bartmann, the Jewish and Christian faiths are wholly distinct. Again dismissing the sacred character of the Hebrew Scriptures, he asserted that the Old Testament communicates divine "inspiration" but not divine "revelation." In his view, Jesus himself lost respect for the Hebrew Scriptures. "With Christ, the old covenant attained its fullness and reached its end. . . . In his action as in his teaching, Jesus gradually distanced himself from the old covenant."[29]

Karl Adam on Jesus Christ as God's Son

Karl Adam was professor of Catholic dogmatic theology at the University of Tübingen from 1919 until 1947, when he retired as professor emeritus.[30] One of Adam's winning traits was his humanness: he included humor in his lectures as well as in his ordinary conversations, and, although German academics regarded all Bavarians as peasants, Adam kept his Bavarian accent, even in his public speaking. Further, Adam possessed the gift of being able to explain complex ideas in clear, engaging words. Drawing on this talent, he recast Church teachings into a contemporary language that drew on the Romanticism of Goethe, Nietzsche, and Rilke and also on the *Lebensphilosophie* (existentialism) that influenced German culture throughout the early 1900s. In 1923, Karl Adam made a major contribution to the Church's self-understanding with the publication of his book *The Spirit of Catholicism,* which, inspired by the work of Johann Adam Möhler, presents the Church primarily as a mystical community, as the body of Christ (1 Cor 12:27), and only secondarily as a *societas perfecta.* This presentation on the Church immediately appealed to Catholics around the world, and *The Spirit of Catholicism* was eventually translated into at least twelve languages, including Chinese and Japanese. This book contributed to the renewal of Catholic ecclesiology and thus helped prepare the way for the Second Vatican Council.

Karl Adam's emphasis on the notion of community led him, however, to seek an accommodation between the Catholic Church and Hitler's government. On the one hand, he opposed the Nazi movement, even refusing to give the Nazi salutation. Yet, on the other hand, Adam called for cooperation between the Catholic Church and the Nazi state in the summer of 1933 after the German bishops dropped their bans against Catholic membership in the National Socialist party. Given this public stance, he stood among the Catholic "bridge-builders" of 1933.[31] But in January 1934, Adam gave a public address at a Catholic youth rally in Stuttgart in which he sharply criticized Nazi neo-paganism. As a consequence, he was barred by Nazi officials from teaching at the University of Tübingen until he promised to refrain from commenting on National Socialism and the Third Reich.

In his book *The Son of God*, which appeared in 1933, Adam presented Jesus as the new Adam, the God-man who established a new human community living in union with God. The Gospels attest, Adam said, to God's entering into the heart of human life through the self-emptying of the divine word in Jesus Christ (Phil 2:6–11). According to Adam, "the great wonder" of the Christian message concerns "not only a lifting up of humanity to the heights of the divine reality . . . but above all a descent of divinity, of the divine word into the state of a slave, into mere humanity."[32] Unlike the first Adam, Jesus Christ lived in full obedience to the Father, and through his life, death, and resurrection brought about "the new man."[33] Now, through the Holy Spirit and the Church, God invites all people to participate in Christ's new humanity so that they may become God's sons and daughters.

The Son of God was one of the first attempts by a Catholic theologian to undertake a Christology "from below," that is, by stressing Jesus' humanity as the starting point for Jesus' movement to God. This book stands in the trajectory associated with theologians of ancient Antioch such as Theodore of Mopsuestia, Nestorius, and John of Antioch. Similar to their writings, it possesses the strength of upholding the humanity of Jesus Christ but also the weakness of leaving ambiguous Christ's personal unity, the "hypostatic union" of his human and divine "natures."[34] Another weakness of the book is its reliance on images and phrases drawn from the German nationalist, or *Volk*, movement. According to Adam, Jesus possessed the physical stature and stamina of Friedrich Nietzsche's *Übermensch* and hence was not unlike Hitler's ideal German male.[35]

Moreover, *The Son of God* is flawed in its presentation of Jews and Judaism. According to Adam, the Jewish authorities and ordinary Jews of the first century valued "the externals" of their religion. They held "a cold rigid belief" in the law of Talon.[36] Jesus engaged in a "struggle against the Pharisees, those 'whited sepulchres,' representative of the spurious, the finical, the purely exterior and the narrow in religion and life."[37] Jesus saw that the Pharisees and Sadducees had lost sight of genuine religious belief: they wanted to increase their wealth, form a Jewish nation, and build up their own egos. In Adam's words:

> In the majority of the Pharisees and Sadducees, those typical representatives of the property-owning ruling classes of his country, Jesus met with the devastating consequences of the service of mammon in a terrible form. What separated them from him and from the Kingdom of God was their hard self-seeking and arrogance, which put even their most prized possession, the birthright of the Israelite to be numbered among the people of the Covenant and of the seed of Abraham, in the service of their nationalistic egoism and fanaticism, and which, by a thousand man-made regulations and prohibitions, made religion so exterior a thing and so difficult to follow (cf. Matthew 23:4), that it had become a matter for the rich alone, and all the small fry and the poor, who lacked the money and the time to fulfill all the obligations laid upon them, were summarily discredited as notorious sinners.[38]

Following the example of their official leaders, ordinary Jews held a "materialistic view" of God's kingdom. Referring to Jesus, Adam claimed that "his gospel of the kingdom bears a thoroughly ethical and religious stamp in marked contrast to the conception of the kingdom of God then current among Jews, who in speaking of it reveled in the representation of the sensible goods and felicities of that kingdom."[39] Further, the Jewish people envisioned the Messiah bringing about "a restoration of the glories of the kingdom of David."[40] For this reason, Jesus' talk of God's kingdom "stands in the most direct contrast with what the Jews of his time, under the spur of their selfish nationalist instincts, believed and hoped of their expected Messiah."[41] Given his account of Judaism in the first century, Adam wondered how the Jewish people could have given birth to Jesus. "Again, how could there have emerged from a world which was falling to ruins—a world of ossified belief in the letter, of a narrow minded caste-spirit and materialistic piety, a world of skepticism, doubt and libertarianism—a human nature so incomparably pure, so God-united and holy and gracious, so inwardly detached and free and genuine as his?"[42]

The theologian acknowledged that Jews had prepared the way for the coming of the Messiah by rightly developing their monotheism with its hope in a coming Messiah. "It is clear that this question and this possibility can grow only out of monotheistic soil, that is to say, out of Jewish conceptions alone."[43] It is also the case that Jesus clearly stood within the line of the prophets of the Old Testament.[44] Like them, he sharply criticized the Jewish authorities. "As for the polemics against the scribes and Pharisees, against the ruling caste, against the teachers of Israel, and the judgments pronounced on them, [the parables] are down-right feverish in their flaming indignation."[45] At the same time, Jesus obeyed the Jewish laws. Indeed, he "acquiesced in the old Mosaic dis-positions and regulations: the temple, the services in the synagogue, fasting, circumcision, and the rest."[46] Moreover, Jesus "knows that the new man whom he is going to bring into being, that 'the new testament in his blood,' will and must create for itself a special kind of corporate body. Hence it is that he speaks of the Church which at a future time he will build upon the rock of Peter (Matthew 16:18). . . . Nothing was farther from his thoughts than a rigid, lifeless form of public worship laden with regulations."[47] In light of his stress upon the interior character of religious belief, Jesus "purifies the Old Testament teaching of all that is exterior, formalistic, legalistic, in particular of those ceremonial non-essentials."[48] In sum, according to Adam, while Judaism stresses the exterior aspect of religious belief, Christianity emphasizes the interior character of relating to God.

Karl Adam's *The Son of God* stands out in the history of Catholic theology. On the one hand, this book is noteworthy because of its em-phasis on Jesus Christ as a full human being. On the other hand, it also deserves criticism because of its religious antisemitism. This book was not, however, Adam's only publication with a bias against Jews and Juda-ism. In 1943, hence ten years after the appearance of *The Son of God*, Adam communicated his anti-Judaism in his essay "Jesus, the Christ, and We Germans." Still intent on building a bridge between the Catholic Church and the Third Reich, the theologian argued that Germans could attain their full stature only if they and their government embraced Christian belief. This national commitment to Jesus Christ would re-quire, Adam insisted, a profound respect for the Hebrew Scriptures and Jewish belief. It would not entail, however, the adoption of the "negative traits" possessed by Jews because Jesus himself did not have these per-sonal characteristics. The Catholic Church's doctrine on the immaculate conception of the Blessed Mother—that is, the teaching that Mary was conceived without original sin—concretely means that Mary was born without original sin and hence without Jews' unpleasant qualities.[49]

It is not clear whether Karl Adam ever became aware of his religious

antisemitism or even acknowledged his mistake of seeking an accommodation between the Catholic Church and the Nazi state. After the
defeat of the Third Reich and the disclosures of Hitler's death camps, the
theologian did not make any public comments on the nation's twelve
years under the Führer. In 1946, he became active in the ecumenical
movement *Una Sancta* that flourished in postwar Germany, and in 1947
he retired as a professor emeritus from the University of Tübingen.
During the next seven years he fashioned his lectures in Christology into
his book *The Christ of Faith*, which gives a clear synthesis of the Church's
teachings on Jesus Christ beginning with the New Testament and ending
with the theology of his day. This book omits the depiction of Jews and
Judaism that is contained in *The Son of God*. As Adam's health deteriorated, he withdrew from public life, and he died at the age of eighty.

Romano Guardini on Jesus Christ as Lord

Romano Guardini was professor for "philosophy of religion
and the Catholic world-view" at the University of Berlin when Hitler became Germany's chancellor on January 30, 1933.[50] Having accepted the
teaching position in 1923, he had become a widely respected lecturer
at the university. Among the students who were deeply influenced by
Guardini's Berlin lectures were the philosopher Hannah Arendt and the
theologian Hans Urs von Balthasar. Guardini was a Christian humanist,
a Renaissance thinker. Born in Verona and growing up in Mainz, he
prized Europe's world-class literature such as the writings of Dante,
Hölderlin, and Rilke. Further, he deliberately worked in the intellectual
orientation of Neoplatonism and German phenomenology, especially
the thought of Max Scheler, and, from this perspective, he was intent on
shedding light on the underlying structures and dynamics of human life.
Taking a phenomenological or descriptive-analytical approach to worship, Guardini published his book *The Spirit of the Liturgy* in 1919 and
immediately gained international recognition, including praise from
Martin Buber. Throughout the 1920s and into the 1930s, Guardini wrote
books and articles on the literary masterpieces of Dante, Dostoyevsky,
and Rilke, and also on the Church's worship, devotions, and prayer.
Loathing National Socialism, Guardini avoided political topics after Hitler came to power. Nevertheless, in 1935, he published an essay, "The
Savior," implicitly condemning National Socialism as a form of the idolatry. Again relying on a phenomenological method, he argued that whenever people have regarded their national leader as a divine figure, they

have brought ill upon themselves. Guardini insisted that only belief in Jesus Christ, the true savior, can free people as individuals and as a nation to pursue their well-being. The essay's political critique did not elude Nazi leaders, and the Reich minister of education dismissed Guardini from his professorship in 1939.[51]

After writing "The Savior" and prior to his firing, Guardini set out to help Germans identify their authentic savior. Over two years, he gave a series of sermons on the person and work of Jesus Christ as conveyed in the Gospels, especially the Gospel of John, and, in 1937, he published them in the book *The Lord.* According to Guardini, Jesus Christ is "the word made flesh" (Jn 1:14). He is the divine Logos who has entered into history and has revealed who God is and what God intends for human beings. Having suffered rejection and death on the cross, Christ returned in glory to the Father (Jn 17:5). Now, the risen Christ is contemporaneous with every age; in every era and every land, Christ stands before all people and asks for a decision. "Do we accept him, once and for all, as our ultimate authority in everything, or do we rely solely on our own judgment?"[52] If we rely on ourselves, we shall eventually hand ourselves over to an individual or power that will enslave us. If we acknowledge the living Christ, we will move toward personal individuation and genuine freedom.

Inspired and guided by John's Gospel, *The Lord* conveys a Christology "from above."[53] It stands in the theological trajectory associated with ancient Alexandria's scholars such as Cyril of Alexandria. In stressing that Jesus Christ is the incarnation of God's Son, *The Lord* expresses the Alexandrian emphasis on the Logos as the unifying personal center of Jesus Christ. Given this perspective on Christ, *The Lord* possesses the merit of accentuating the absolute uniqueness of Jesus Christ. Unlike anyone else in history, Jesus Christ as the incarnate divine word is worthy of our absolute trust, which therefore we should not give to any human authority, regardless of the individual's civil, ecclesiastical, or institutional office. However it accentuates the divine singularity of Jesus Christ, *The Lord* loses sight of Jesus' humanity. Jesus Christ is the one not like us; he is the one "from above" who calls us out of this world. Along with this shortcoming, the book possesses another: religious antisemitism.

Guardini's *The Lord* conveys an anti-Jewish bias. While it asserts that God chose the Jews or Hebrews, beginning with Abraham and Sarah, to play a singular role in world history, it also declares that this chosen people failed to live up to God's calling. God sent Moses to establish the

Mosaic covenant between God and Israel so that the Jews would mature into a people prepared to accept the fullness of God's revelation in the Messiah, the Christ. By doing so, they would undo what had occurred when Adam and Eve turned away from God at the dawn of time. But, as the Gospels attest, the people of Israel failed to welcome the Messiah. In Guardini's words: "The failure of the Jewish people to accept Christ was the second Fall, the import of which can be fully grasped only in connection with the first."[54] The Jewish people had become so preoccupied with the details of the Mosaic Law that they were no longer receptive to the truth.[55] "It was through the Law that Israel established for herself a unique place in history; but it was also the Law which so hardened her, that when at last he whom she had been taught to expect arrived, she denied him."[56] Referring to the Jews of Jesus' day, Guardini writes:

> They have hardened their hearts against God; have lost interest their old eagerness to hear and obey his voice. . . . Temple observances set a man apart for God. The process was formally prescribed, regulated down to the most minute detail. The result was a welter of rules and rites expressive of deep wisdom and insight into human nature, . . . However, when we realize that not only the general welfare, but also eternal salvation depended upon strict observance, that failure to fulfill the Law meant banishment from the community and the wrath of God, it makes one's blood run cold to read the interminable list of commandments.[57]

Further, *The Lord* places responsibility for Jesus' crucifixion on the Jewish people. It insists that Jesus' suffering and death would not have occurred if Jesus' Jewish contemporaries had come to believe in Jesus and his message. The "Judaic crisis" occurred when Jesus brought his message to Jerusalem (Jn 7) during the Feast of Tabernacles.[58] "But the Jewish people did not believe. They did not change their hearts, so the kingdom did not come as it was to have come."[59] Reiterating this point, Guardini writes that near the end of his life "Jesus' words have grown increasingly grave, but they are not accepted. It is clear that the responsible groups not only reject them, but also desire to destroy Jesus. This [rejection was] humanity's crime (the second fall half-way through history, as the first was the prelude to history), which Christ's love was to transform to the perfect sacrifice that insured salvation."[60] The rejection of Jesus by the Jews "is humanity's second great test and failure—brought about by a specific people at a specific time, but because of our solidarity

with all human existence, also to our woe."[61] As a result of the Jews'
refusal to accept Jesus as the Messiah, God saw that the world's salvation
in Jesus Christ could come about only in a violent manner. "The essential
decision has already fallen. Salvation must now be realized differently; no
longer through the meeting of gospel and faith, of unlimited divine
generosity with pure human acceptance; no longer through the evident
arrival of the kingdom and the renewal of history; now the Father's will
demands the ultimate sacrifice of his Son."[62] Because the Jewish people
never accepted Jesus as the Messiah, they frustrated God's initial plan and
brought about the death of God's Son. It was through his suffering,
death, and resurrection that Jesus Christ established the new chosen
people, the new Israel.[63]

According to Guardini, the Jews' rejection of Jesus as the Messiah led
not only to Jesus' death but also to the emptying of the Mosaic Law's
meaning and value. God's preparation of the Jewish people for the Messiah through the Mosaic covenant ended in "failure." Guardini asks:
"Has then the Law vanished? The old Law certainly. With Christ's coming its whole sense is lost, and St. Paul saw to it that it was eradicated
from the Christian conscience. . . . The history of the Mosaic Law is a
terrible warning. What had come, a holy thing, from God, was turned
into an instrument of disaster. The moment definite revelation, the positive ordering of existence by God is believed, this possibility presents
itself. It is good for the believer to know this, so that, as a member of the
second covenant, he may be spared the fate of the first."[64] If Christians
wish to avoid God's wrath, they must remember how God punished the
Jewish people:

> Moses had to carry the entire nation on his shoulders. He was, neces-
> sarily, the most patient of men. Sometimes it is as though he has to bear
> the additional weight of God's wrath; when, for example, the Almighty
> loses patience and says to Moses: Let me destroy them! But the leader of
> this blind, unmanageable people stands his ground, even when the
> blows rain upon him from both sides. . . . How obdurate this people
> was, is best shown by God's own appraisal of them: not one of those
> who had left Egypt as an adult was deemed worthy to behold the
> promised land; not one of them was deemed fit for pioneer life.[65]

Guardini maintains that when Christians look at the Jews of the first
century, they should see a sinful people, a people who turned away
from God and hid behind their religious laws and institutions. Guardini
writes:

The Jewish people, the Pharisees and Scribes and high priests, how "grown up" they are! The whole heritage of sin with its harshness and distortion looms at us. How old they are! Their memory reaches back more than one and a half millennia, back to Abraham—a historical consciousness not many nations can boast. Their wisdom is both a divine gift and fruit of long human experience; knowledge, cleverness, correctness. They examine, weigh, differentiate, doubt; and when the Promised One comes and prophecy is fulfilled, their long history about to be crowned, they cling to the past with its human traditions, entrench themselves behind the Law and the temple, are sly, hard, blind— and their great hour passes them by. God's messiah must perish at the hands of those who "protect" his law. From his blood springs young Christianity, and Judaism remains prisoner of its hope in the coming of One who has already come.[66]

Soon after its publication in 1937, *The Lord* became a best seller in Germany. It nurtured its readers to resist National Socialism, to center their lives on the living Christ, not on the Führer. During the war, it was taken to bomb shelters and read there by individuals or small groups, and after the war it became a best seller among Christians around the world. Although Guardini never revised the book, it eventually caused him distress as he himself became aware of its anti-Jewish prejudice.

After the fall of the Third Reich and the public revelation of Auschwitz, Guardini sought to remedy his attitudes about Jews and Judaism. As professor for Catholic thought at the University of Tübingen from 1945 until 1947 and then at University of Munich from 1947 until 1963, Guardini resumed lecturing and writing on a wide range of secular and religious topics. In all that he said, he avoided negative characterizations of Jews and Judaism. Further, he publicly supported Konrad Adenauer's efforts in the late 1940s and early 1950s to ensure that West Germany would provide restitution to Jewish survivors. On May 23, 1952, Guardini gave a public lecture at the University of Tübingen in which he declared that the German people needed to assume responsibility for what had happened at Auschwitz and seek reconciliation with the Jewish people.[67] Soon after giving the lecture, Guardini sent a copy of it to the Jewish philosopher of religion Martin Buber in Jerusalem. Guardini and Buber had exchanged letters in the early 1920s when Buber was residing in Frankfurt am Main. At that time, Buber initiated and sustained the communication between the two scholars. During the Third Reich, Guardini and Buber had lost contact with one another. In the autumn of

1952, Buber was deeply moved both by what Guardini said in his lecture at the University of Tübingen and also by Guardini's initiative in sending the lecture to him. Because of Guardini's gesture, Buber felt a renewed tie to Germany and henceforth accepted invitations to give lectures there. Guardini and Buber remained in communication throughout the 1950s, and on the occasion of Buber's eighty-fifth birthday on February 8, 1963, Guardini made a substantial donation to the State of Israel for the Martin Buber Forest.[68]

Theological Factors Contributing to Antisemitism

Each of the three books reviewed above advanced the renewal of Catholic theology, and yet each of them also imparted religious antisemitism. Bartmann's *Jesus Christ, Our Savior and King* showed that the doctrine of Chalcedon refers not to an obscure metaphysical principle but to an actual person. But it simultaneously asserted that Jesus had distanced himself from the Hebrew Scriptures. Adam's *The Son of God* accentuated the humanity of Jesus Christ, which had been eclipsed by Neo-Scholasticism's emphasis upon Christ's divinity. It presented Jews, however, as a materialistic, self-aggrandizing people. Finally, Guardini's *The Lord* shed light on the utter singularity of Jesus Christ, and yet it declared that Jews remained closed to God's revelation and hence were responsible for Jesus' crucifixion.

How did it come about that three groundbreaking theological books of the 1920s and 1930s were tainted by anti-Judaism? More specifically, what theological factors fueled this prejudice against Jews and Judaism, and are these factors valid today in Catholic theology? Four theological elements deserve consideration: the notion of supersessionism, the reliance on precritical interpretations of the Bible, the rejection of historical reconstructions of Jesus' ministry and Jewish world, and the disavowal of religious freedom. Each of these factors is no longer accepted by the Catholic Church.

First, supersessionism holds that God's covenant in Jesus Christ has superseded God's earlier covenants with the Jews—the covenants with Abraham, Moses, and David. As a consequence, God has abolished the earlier covenants and withdrawn his favor from the Jewish people. Lacking God's blessing, the Jewish people no longer have a religious raison d'être. This view is, however, no longer valid. Vatican II's *Nostra Aetate* teaches that, according to St. Paul and hence the Church, "the Jews remain very dear to God, for the sake of the patriarchs, since God does not take back the gifts he bestowed or the choice he made." It adds that "the Jews should not be spoken of as rejected or accursed as if this followed from holy scripture."[69] This recognition of the eternal character of God's covenant with the Jewish people is reiterated in the *Catechism of the Catholic Church*, which appeared in 1994. Concerning "the relationship of the Church with the Jewish people," it states: "When she delves into her own mystery, the Church, the People of God in the New Covenant, discovers her link with the Jewish people, 'the first to hear the Word of God' [according to the Good Friday prayers in the *Roman Missal*]. . . . To the Jews 'belong the sonship, the glory, the covenants, the giving of the law, the worship, and the promises; to them belong the patriarchs, and of their race, according to the flesh, is the Christ' [Rom 9:4–5], 'for the gifts and the call of God are irrevocable' [Rom 11:29]."[70] In sum, supersessionism can no longer validly shape a Catholic theologian's view of Judaism.

Second, a precritical approach to the Bible directed Catholic theologians to read each scriptural text with no regard for a text's time and place of composition, origins, literary genre, underlying intentions, and later phases of editing. Because Bartmann, Adam, and Guardini viewed the Gospels as eyewitness, literal accounts of Jesus' words and deeds, they failed to appreciate how the Gospels were the literary outgrowth of preexisting sources, and of materials that had been orally passed on in specific literary forms. Further, they overlooked the fact that each Gospel conveys a distinct literary portrait of Jesus Christ, determined by each evangelist's Christology. For this reason, each Gospel's literary and theological integrity is violated when the four biblical accounts are amalgamated into one, as has occurred in Mel Gibson's *The Passion of the Christ*.[71] Finally, because Bartmann, Adam, and Guardini engaged in precritical readings of the Gospels, they did not detect the anti-Jewish prejudices of the evangelists, especially of Matthew and John. As a result, each of the theologians incorporated the early Church's religious antisemitism into his presentation of Jesus' view of first-century Judaism.

Today, a precritical interpretation of the Bible is not valid within Catholicism. It was set aside beginning on September 30, 1943, when Pope Pius XII issued his encyclical *Divino Afflante Spiritu*, giving permission for the limited use of historical-critical methods in biblical hermeneutics. In 1964, the Pontifical Biblical Commission issued its instruction "The Historical Truth of the Gospels," acknowledging the presence of "three stages of tradition" within the Gospels: the preaching and ministry of Jesus (circa CE 27–30), the oral preaching and teaching of the post-

Easter communities (CE 30–100), and the evangelists' editing of the traditions that they received into the Gospels (CE 70–100). In April 1993, the Pontifical Biblical Commission endorsed the use of historical-critical methods in its instruction "Interpretation of the Bible in the Church," and in May 2002, it issued its instruction "The Jewish People and Their Sacred Scriptures in the Christian Bible" on Christian respect for the Jewish interpretation of the Hebrew Scriptures.

Third, the Church's rejection of historical-critical reconstructions of Jesus' ministry and Jewish world meant that theologians were not able to test out their depictions of Jesus and his Jewish contemporaries in relation to religiously neutral, historical studies. The original or liberal quest for the historical Jesus had troubled Catholic officials and theologians in part because it was indirectly meant to erode Christian doctrines concerning Jesus Christ, especially the doctrine of Chalcedon. When constrained to choose between Harnack's Jesus of history and Barth's Christ of faith, Catholic leaders opted for the latter and saw little or no theological significance in historical-critical research concerning Jesus of Nazareth. As a result, they failed to see that first-century Judaism was marked by diversity and internal conflicts, that the Sadducees were the group primarily responsible for Jesus' death, and that Pilate was ultimately culpable for Jesus' crucifixion because he chose to execute a purported "king of the Jews" in order to maintain the *pax Romana* in the Holy Land.

Catholic leaders and theologians today acknowledge the theological importance of historical-critical research into Jesus' life and times. They agree with Cardinal Walter Kasper's view that the Christian faith and theology "has in the earthly Jesus, as he is made accessible to us through historical research, a relatively autonomous criterion, a once-and-for all yardstick by which it must continually measure itself."[72] In September 1980, the Vatican's International Theological Commission declared: "The great value of scholarly inquiries on the Jesus of history is beyond doubt. Inquiries of this sort are particularly important for fundamental theology, and in exchanges with non-believers." Since the Second Vatican Council, Catholic biblical scholars and historians increasingly have used historical-critical methods to shed light on the Jewishness of Jesus and also on first-century Judaism, and Catholic theologians have allowed the results of these historical-critical investigations to shape their Christologies.[73]

One specific misrepresentation of Jews and Judaism deserves comment. Bartmann, Adam, and Guardini overstated the difference between the legalism of first-century Judaism, on the one hand, and Jesus' opposition to Jewish legalism and the Pharisees, on the other hand, in part because each of them judged that Jesus' teachings were not adequately conveyed in the Catholic Church's ecclesiastical legalism and bureaucracy.[74] Throughout the early twentieth century, relatively progressive theologians challenged the Church's preoccupation with canon law and juridical procedures by first sketching an implicit resemblance between ancient Judaism and contemporary Catholicism, and second depicting Jesus Christ as a sharp critic of religious legalism. The harsh words by Bartmann, Adam, and Guardini about the Pharisees and their purported obsession with external religious observance were aimed in fact at the Catholic Curia. These polemics could not have occurred if the theologians were required to meet the standards of historical accuracy about first-century Judaism. Today, scholarship is correcting theologians' misrepresentations of the Pharisees.[75]

Fourth and finally, the Catholic Church's disavowal of the principle of religious freedom in a nation-state influenced how the Catholic theologians of the 1920s and 1930s viewed first-century Jews' expectations for a political Messiah. Starting in the 1800s, the Church taught that, because "error has no rights," any religious belief other than Catholicism had no right to exist. In civil terms, this rejection of religious toleration meant that, according to papal teachings, a state should provide legal protection to the Catholic Church but not to other religious bodies. In the twentieth century, the Church's intolerance of other religions manifested itself in the civil laws of Italy under Mussolini, of Portugal under Salazar, and of Spain under Franco. As ecclesiastical officials and Catholic political leaders upheld the ideal of a Catholic nation-state, Catholic theologians brought this outlook to their presentations on Judaism in the Roman empire. Bartmann, Adam, and Guardini conveyed no empathy for the first-century Jewish expectation that the Messiah would bring about Israel's political and religious freedom. Implicitly building on the notion of supersessionism, they judged that, with the coming of Jesus Christ, Judaism had lost its right to exist in the Roman empire as well as its aspiration to regain the political autonomy it attained with King David.

One of the most significant decisions of the Second Vatican Council was its adoption on December 7, 1965, of *Dignitatis Humanae,* the Declaration on Religious Liberty. In a reversal of Pope Pius IX's "Syllabus of Errors" (1864), the Council declared that "the human person has a right to religious freedom. . . . This right of the human person to religious freedom must be given such recognition in the constitutional order of society as will make it a civil right."[76] In light of this acknowledgement of the principle of religious freedom, theologians must respect Jews' valid concern for their civil rights and the civil protection of Judaism. Scholars must also respect Judaism's commitment to an autonomous Jewish nation-state, such as the State of Israel.

The four theological factors that contributed to the anti-Jewish bias in Catholic views of on Jesus and Judaism in the early twentieth century no longer have the backing of the Church's official teachings. The notion of supersessionism, a precritical reading of the Bible, a disregard of historical-critical studies, and a disavowal of religious freedom are not accepted today in mainstream Catholicism. The theological ideas that undergirded religious antisemitism in the nineteenth and twentieth centuries have lost their legitimacy. Nevertheless, as Catholics' positive reception of *The Passion of the Christ* has exhibited, the advances in the Church's teachings have not yet made an impact on all Catholics, not even on all ecclesiastical officials. Although forty years have passed since Pope Paul VI closed the Second Vatican Council, the council's vision and theological changes still await their full realization in the Church. In particular, given the influence that Mel Gibson's movie about Jesus has had upon its viewers' imaginations and attitudes, the Church's leaders and theologians must urgently rededicate themselves to implementing the renewal and reforms begun by Pope John XXIII, Pope Paul VI, and Vatican II, especially those teachings that acknowledge God's eternal covenant with Judaism and the sacred dignity of the Jewish people.

NOTES

1. Second Vatican Council, *Lumen Gentium,* ch. 1, art. 1, in *Vatican Council II,* ed. Austin Flannery, O.P. (Northport, N.Y.: Costello, 1996), 1.

2. Second Vatican Council, *Nostra Aetate,* art. 2, in *Vatican Council II,* 571.

3. Ibid., art. 4, p. 573.

4. Paul VI used this phrase at the outset of his encyclical *Populorum Progressio* (1967).

5. On the relationship between Catholicism and Judaism, see Mary C. Boys, *Has God Only One Blessing?* (New York: Paulist, 2000); Avery Dulles and Leon Klenicki, *The Holocaust, Never To Be Forgotten* (New York: Paulist, 2001); Eugene J. Fisher, *Faith without Prejudice,* rev. ed. (New York: Crossroad, 1993); Hans Küng, *Judaism,* trans. John Bowden (New York: Continuum, 1992); Richard P. McBrien, *The Popes and the Jews* (San Francisco: SWIG Judaic Studies Program, University of San Fran-

cisco, 2003); John Pawlikowski, "*We Remember:* Looking Back, Looking Ahead," *Month* 33 (January 2000): 3–8; idem, *Jesus and the Theology of Israel* (Wilmington, Del.: Michael Glazier, 1989).

6. On antisemitism in *The Passion of the Christ,* see Philip Cunningham, "A Dangerous Fiction: 'The Passion of the Christ' and Post-conciliar Catholic Teaching," *America* 191 (April 5, 2004): 8–11; Eugene J. Fisher, "The Bible, the Jews and the Passion," *America* 191 (February 16, 2004): 7–9.

7. On antisemitism in pre-conciliar Catholicism, see Olaf Blaschke and Aram Mattioli, eds., *Katholischer Antisemitismus im 19. Jahrhundert* (Zürich: Orell Füssli, 2000).

8. This essays builds on Robert A. Krieg, *Catholic Theologians in Nazi Germany* (New York: Continuum, 2004); Kevin P. Spicer, *Resisting the Third Reich* (DeKalb: Northern Illinois University Press, 2004); Donald J. Dietrich, ed., *Christian Responses to the Holocaust* (Syracuse, N.Y.: Syracuse University Press, 2003); idem, *Catholic Citizens in the Third Reich* (New Brunswick, N.J.: Transaction Books, 1988).

9. This essay evolved out of discussions in 1996 with Susannah Heschel and Michael A. Signer. The author is grateful to these scholars for their questions about pre-conciliar Catholicism as well as for their relevant scholarship, including: Susannah Heschel, *Abraham Geiger and the Jewish Jesus* (Chicago: University of Chicago Press, 1998); Michael A. Signer, ed., *Memory and History in Christianity and Judaism* (Notre Dame, Ind.: University of Notre Dame, 2001); idem, "The Rift That Binds: Hermeneutical Approaches to the Jewish-Christian Relationship," in *Ecumenism,* ed. Lawrence S. Cunningham (Notre Dame, Ind.: University of Notre Dame Press, 1998), 95–115.

10. See Benedict M. Ashley, "Neo-Scholasticism," in *The HarperCollins Encyclopedia of Catholicism,* ed. Richard P. McBrien (San Francisco: HarperCollins, 1995), 911; Francis Schüssler Fiorenza, "Systematic Theology: Task and Methods," in *Systematic Theology,* ed. F. S. Fiorenza and John P. Galvin, vol. 1 (Minneapolis: Fortress, 1991), 27–35; Gerald A. McCool, *Catholic Theology in the Nineteenth Century* (New York: Seabury, 1977).

11. See Étienne Fouilloux, "Die Kultur des katholischen Kirche," in *Erster und Zweiter Krieg: Demokratien und Totalitäre Systeme, 1914–1958,* ed. Kurt Meier (Herder: Freiberg, 1992), 175–215; Erwin Iserloh, "Movements within the Church and Their Spirituality," in *History of the Church,* vol. 10: *The Church in the Modern Age,* ed. Hubert Jedin et al., trans. Anselm Biggs (New York: Crossroad, 1981), 299–335.

12. Romano Guardini, *Vom Sinn der Kirche, und Die Kirche des Herrn* (Mainz: Matthias Grünewald, 1990), 19; idem, *The Church and the Catholic, and The Spirit of the Liturgy,* trans. Ada Lane (New York: Sheed and Ward, 1935), 11.

13. See Leo Scheffczyk, "Main Lines of the Development of Theology between World War I and Vatican II," in *History of the Church,* vol. 10, 260–98; Roger Aubert, "Die Theologie während der ersten Hälfte des 20. Jahrhunderts," in *Bilanz der Theologie im 20. Jahrhundert,* vol. 2, ed. Herbert Vorgrimler and Robert Vander Gucht (Freiburg: Herder, 1969), 7–70; Adolf Kolping, *Katholische Theologie* (Bremen: Carl Schünemann, 1964), 62–126.

14. Joseph Wittig, "Die Erlösten," *Hochland* 19, part 2 (1922): 1–24; Wittig, *Leben Jesu in Palästina* (Munich: Kempten, 1925, 1927). See Otto Weiss, *Der Modernismus in Deutschland* (Regensburg: Friedrich Pustet, 1995), 514–26.

15. See *Biographisch-Bibliographisches Kirchenlexikon,* vol. 1, ed. Friedrich Wilhelm Bautz (Hamm: Traugott Bautz, 1975), 397–98; Eduard Stakemeier, "Bernhard Bartmann," *Theologie und Glaube* 44 (1954): 81–113.

16. Remigius Bäumer, "Bartmann, Bernhard," in *Lexikon für Theologie und Kirche*, 2nd ed., vol. 2 (Freiburg: Herder, 1958), 16.

17. Gisbert Greshake, "Bartmann, Bernhard," in *Lexikon für Theologie und Kirche*, 3rd ed., vol. 2 (Freiburg: Herder, 1994), 47.

18. Bernhard Bartmann, *Jesus Christus, unser Heiland und König* (Paderborn: Bonifacius, 1929).

19. Ibid., 645.

20. Ibid., 646.

21. Ibid., 648n24.

22. Ibid., 31.

23. Ibid., 31–33.

24. Ibid., 128–29.

25. Ibid., 465.

26. Ibid., 466.

27. Ibid., 467.

28. Bernhard Bartmann, *Positives Christentum in katholischer Wesensschau* (Paderborn: Bonifacius, 1934), 4–5.

29. Bernhard Bartmann, *Der Glaubensgegensatz zwischen Judentum und Christentum* (Paderborn: Bonifacius, 1938), 71.

30. See Krieg, *Catholic Theologians in Nazi Germany*, 83–106; idem, *Karl Adam: Catholicism in German Culture* (Notre Dame, Ind.: University of Notre Dame Press, 1992), and Lucia Scherzberg, *Kirchenreform mit Hilfe des Nationalsozialismus* (Darmstadt: Wissenschaftliche Buchgesellschaft, 2001).

31. See Heinz Hürten, *Deutsche Katholiken* (Paderborn: Ferdinand Schöningh, 1992), 214–30.

32. Karl Adam, *Jesus Christus*, 2nd ed. (Augsburg: Haas und Grabherr, 1933), 10. See also Adam, *The Son of God*, trans. Philip Hereford (New York: Sheed and Ward, 1940), 1.

33. Adam, *The Son of God*, 118.

34. See Alois Grillmeier, "The Figure of Christ in Catholic Theology Today," in *Theology Today*, vol. 1: *The Renewal of Dogma*, ed. Johannes Feiner et al., trans. P. White and R. Kelly (Milwaukee: Bruce, 1965), 82n16.

35. See Hans Kreidler, "Karl Adam und Nationalsozialismus," *Rottenburger Jahrbuch für Kirchengeschichte* 2 (1983): 129–40.

36. Adam, *The Son of God*, 151.

37. Ibid., 97.

38. Ibid., 128–29.

39. Ibid., 159–60.

40. Ibid., 177.

41. Ibid., 178.

42. Ibid., 183.

43. Ibid., 185.

44. Ibid.

45. Ibid., 101.

46. Ibid., 117.

47. Ibid., 118.

48. Ibid., 147.

49. Karl Adam, "Jesus, der Christus, und Wir Deutsche," Part 3, *Wissenschaft und Weisheit* 11 (1944): 21.

50. See Robert A. Krieg, *Romano Guardini: Spiritual Writings* (Maryknoll, N.Y.: Orbis Books, 2005), 19–46; Krieg, *Catholic Theologians in Nazi Germany*, 107–30; Krieg, *Romano Guardini: A Precursor of Vatican II* (Notre Dame, Ind.: University of

Notre Dame Press, 1997); Josef Kreiml, *Die Selbstoffenbarung Gottes in Jesus Christus* (Regensburg: S. Roderer, 2001).

51. See Romano Guardini, *Berichte über mein Leben* (Düsseldorf: Patmos, 1984), 52–53.

52. Romano Guardini, *Der Herr* (Mainz: Matthias Grünewald, 1997), 129. See Guardini, *The Lord,* trans. Elinor Castendyk Briefs (Chicago: Henry Regnery, 1954), 116.

53. Arno Schilson, *Perspektiven theologischer Erneuerung* (Düsseldorf: Patmos, 1986), 82–157.

54. Guardini, *The Lord,* 98.

55. Ibid., 103.

56. Ibid., 215.

57. Ibid., 166.

58. Ibid., 139.

59. Ibid., 40.

60. Ibid., 150.

61. Ibid., 346.

62. Ibid., 210.

63. Ibid., 241.

64. Ibid., 170.

65. Ibid., 246.

66. Ibid., 268.

67. Romano Guardini, *Verantwortung: Gedanken zur jüdischen Frage* (Munich: Kösel, 1952).

68. See Robert A. Krieg, "To *Nostra Aetate:* Martin Buber and Romano Guardini," in *Lessons and Legacies,* vol. 4, ed. Larry V. Thompson (Evanston, Ill.: Northwestern University Press, 2003), 81–100; Krieg, "Martin Buber and Romano Guardini," in *Humanity at the Limits,* ed. Michael A. Signer (Bloomington: Indiana University Press, 2000), 138–47.

69. Second Vatican Council, *Nostra Aetate,* art. 4, p. 573.

70. John Paul II, *Catechism of the Catholic Church* (Liguori, Mo.: Liguori Publications, 1994), #839, 222–23.

71. The selection and arrangement of biblical materials in Gibson's *The Passion of the Christ* has been influenced by *The Dolorous Passion of Our Lord Jesus Christ,* which was written by the German mystic Anne Catherine Emmerich in 1833.

72. Walter Kasper, *Jesus the Christ,* trans. V. Green (New York: Paulist, 1976), 35.

73. See Daniel J. Harrington, "The Jewishness of Jesus: Facing Some Problems," in *Jesus' Jewishness,* ed. James H. Charlesworth (New York: Crossroad, 1991), 124–36; Monika Hellwig, "The Re-Emergence of the Human Jesus," *Theological Studies* 50 (1989): 466–80.

74. The author is grateful to John P. Meier for proposing that pre-conciliar theologians' criticisms of the Curia and ecclesiastical legalism may have influenced their depictions of the Pharisees and first-century Judaism. For an analysis of how a similar process occurred among Protestant scholars from the late 1800s into the mid-1900s, see Roland Deines, *Die Pharisäer* (Tübingen: Mohr Siebeck, 1997).

75. John P. Meier, *The Marginal Jew,* vol. 3: *Companions and Competitors* (New York: Doubleday, 2001); Anthony J. Saldarini, *Pharisees, Scribes and Sadducees in Palestinian Society: A Sociological Approach* (Wilmington, Del.: Michael Glazier, 1988).

76. Second Vatican Council, *Dignitatis Humanae,* art. 2, in *Vatican Council II,* 552–53.

Catholic Theology and the
4 Challenge of Nazism

Donald J. Dietrich

Vatican II's foundational document was *Lumen Gentium*. This description of the role of the Church was informed by a biblically and historically rooted ecclesiology as well as by an experientially subjective anthropology. This statement helped nurture the Church's assault on antisemitism in *Nostra Aetate* and supported its engagement in the contemporary human rights dialogue. The foundations for the theological and moral initiatives that led to the renewal that characterized Vatican II were partially established during the wartime period in Germany. In this metamorphosis, German theologians, along with their contemporaries in France, played leading roles as they began to reflect on a Catholic ecclesiology and anthropology, which have offered an envisioned "model" of the Church that has been found useful in helping the faithful engage the political and intellectual culture of the last seven decades.

In 1927, Otto Dibelius, a well-known Protestant theologian, prophesized that the twentieth century would be "the century of the Church." Treatises on the Church had appeared sporadically since the fourteenth century, but ecclesiology was slow to assume the central position in Catholic theology that it has enjoyed since the nineteenth century. The nineteenth century Tübingen School, that is, Drey, Möhler, Staudenmaier, and Kuhn, began to formulate an organic and historical model of the Church as a society that was seen as the way to understand the relationship between the Church and its tradition.[1] This "living" model of a historically changing tradition and Church would embed itself into the twentieth-century discourse as theologians were pressured increasingly to engage secular culture. Theologians from Germany as well as France committed theology to a dynamic and historically driven ecclesiological paradigm. Their contributions were nurtured by German Reform Catholicism and the French concern with the organic development of Catholic tradition. This culture helped support the paradigmatic change in the Church's ecclesiology in *Lumen Gentium.*

Until Vatican II, the dominant neoscholastic manuals of ecclesiology took their cue from the older works of the neoscholastic model that held that the Church of Christ, which was defined as a legalistic and juridical society, essentially constituted the kingdom of God in its present form. This Church was from its origin, the neoscholastics asserted, a hierarchal society, not a democratic or participatory one. The foundation for this approach was based on the conviction that historically Peter had received from Christ a primacy that included jurisdiction. The pope was viewed as the successor of Peter, and the Roman Catholic Church was in essence seen as the true and legitimate Church of Jesus. Generally speaking, the traditional Latin neoscholastic manuals showed a predilection for juridical and abstract categories with little possibility for development that would resonate with historical movements. Christ was viewed as the founder of the Church, a "perfect society," in which the officeholders had jurisdiction over the members. The pope was depicted as the ruler of this society. The bishops derived their jurisdiction from the pope, and the functional attributes of the Church were studied under the aegis of the powers of order and jurisdiction.[2] But perspectives, as a glance at the theological culture of the era indicates, were changing.

In 1941, Charles Journet had explicated a descending ecclesiology that was rooted in statements of dogma rather than in experiential data and that was designed along traditional lines resting on a deductive rather than an inductive methodology. Unlike the manualists, however, Journet tentatively introduced an organic framework to counter the strict juridical approach. In his opinion, the Church was to be seen as an organism of love, having charity as its "created soul." From his perspective, the Church itself was sinless, since sin was viewed as that which separates a member from the body. Among the weaknesses embedded in Journet's ecclesiology was his lack of empathy with empirical and historical data. He scarcely used biblical texts except as "proof texts," and he did not allow history to speak for itself. In his favor, at least from current

perspectives, was the fact that he developed some provocative ecumenical reflections by considering that dissident Christians in good faith were
capable of being affiliated with the "Church" in varied ways.[3]

During the 1940s, Catholic theologians in France, who were sensitive to the historicist twentieth-century culture, produced notable studies nurtured by the ecclesiology of the Fathers. Closely connected with
this return to the patristic sources was the revival of the theology of the
Mystical Body. The historical studies of Emile Mersch, for example,
furthered this development. Dissatisfied with the scholastic tendency to
explore the relationship of Christ to the Church in the philosophical
terms of principal and instrumental causality, Mersch more intensely
focused on the Eastern patristic tradition that stressed the organic union
between the head and the members of a body. From this perspective, the
living Church could be seen as an extension of Christ, who continually
had acted upon it from within as an enlivening force rather than as an
external efficient cause. Reflections on the Church as a Mystical Body
made it possible for Pius XII to produce his 1943 encyclical, the most
comprehensive official Catholic pronouncement on the Church prior to
Vatican II, yet one that dampened any real ecumenical spirit. Drawing on
the first schema of Vatican I and on the viewpoints of Leo XIII, this
encyclical did not repudiate previous Church teachings, but rather attempted to advance beyond the juridical ecclesiologies so prominent in
the neoscholastic manuals and to capitalize on the wealth of insights
emerging from patristic scholars. Pius XII pointed out that the union
between Christ and the Church, while more than moral or juridical, did
not eliminate the distinction between Christ and the members of the
Body; mystical did not mean invisible. The Church as a body was visible,
a concept that opposed Mersch as well as Thomas Aquinas.[4]

For many, *Mystici Corporis* was an important statement of the
Church's essence, since the pope taught that the Mystical Body was physically identical with the Roman Catholic Church; he subsequently reaffirmed this assertion against dissenters in *Humani Generis* (1950). According to the position of Pius XII, only those in the Roman Catholic
Church could be considered as fully members of the mystical body.
Christians not united to the visible structure of the Roman Catholic Church by the bonds of professed faith, sacraments, and obedience
could not be completely in communion with Christ. It was possible,
nevertheless, for non-Catholic Christians to be united to a limited degree
to the Body. If they were living in grace and were in good faith related to
Christ, even though in error, they could be attached unsuspectingly

through their desire and resolution to do God's will to the Mystical Body. Not surprisingly, such a conceptual viewpoint sparked an intense discussion in Catholic theological circles. Without explicitly dissenting, many theologians were understandably dissatisfied with centering salvation solely in the Catholic Church. The result of the conversation among canon lawyers, ecumenists, and theologians finally would lead Cardinal Augustin Bea on the eve of Vatican II to propose a doctrine of Christian membership in God's community that diverged from *Mystici Corporis*.[5] Virtually nothing, however, was said about non-Christians until Vatican II.

The discussions that occurred before and after the promulgation of *Mystici Corporis* in 1943 initiated the shaping of an ecclesiology that could respond more aggressively to the needs of the Church. Yves Congar, for example, dismissed this encyclical and mentioned favorably the critique by Erich Przywara, a German theologian, of "a tendency to a certain vague romanticism, a tendency to conceive the Mystical Body simply as the domain of grace, a tendency to see the consequent aberration of imagining a permanent physical presence of Christ in each Christian." Despite such criticism, Przywara also wrote that the encyclical did at least avoid two extremes: the Church as a mystical milieu and the Church as a rational or legal institution. The authentic Church, many felt, had to seek in a dialectic of history the ability to overcome both the one-sidedness of a Church of immanent life and a Church solely shaped by law and authority. This envisioned new Church model would have to have four modalities: (1) the collective person receiving the presence of the Trinity; (2) the body of Christ; (3) an organization of visible offices; and (4) a Christian spiritual company of individual members, "who are formed by the church and who enter into the world, a church of sent laity, a church of people and of the world."[6] The return to the sources that had brought about the rise of Mystical Body theology contained a dynamism that also uncovered a diversity of historical images that would be crucial to the renewed ecclesiology that served to enliven wartime and postwar Catholic theology and would lead to Vatican II. Theologians, for example, began to look more closely at the patristic concept of "the People of God."[7]

In the years between *Mystici Corporis* and Vatican II, Yves Congar, whose seminal ideas were already present in his 1937 work *Divided Christendom: A Catholic Study of the Problems of Reunion*, was one of the most influential ecclesiologists in the Church. His description of "Catholic unity" in this volume made an authentic space for the creative contributions of diverse cultures and was a prophetic anticipation of the teaching of Vatican II. Congar inserted these seminal ideas into his later works. Through the corpus of his works runs the consistent theme of the Church as essentially constituted by Christ, the founder. In his view, Christ still animates the Church and freely acts through it. From below, however, the institutional Church had to be seen as constituted by fallible and sinful human beings and so always in need of reform.[8] Congar and others reappropriated for ecclesiology the experiences of the Fathers and others in the first millennium, when the Church had not yet been able to exercise its full dominance. Especially in the pre-Constantinian Church, Congar and his contemporaries began to excavate an intense spirituality, a prayerful listening to Jesus, and an openness to conversion and reform. In the Church of the second millennium, Congar discerned a shift that had a profound impact, since the Church began unrelentingly to focus on power and domination. He recognized that this shift was an understandable reaction to a series of threats including the Protestant Reformation and the growth of secularist states. In his study of the Pauline metaphor of the body of Christ, Congar found the central meaning of the Church to lie not simply in its visibility as an organic being, but rather also in its unity encompassing plurality, similar to the way in which the early Church appealed to the diverse populations of the Roman Empire. The Church became for them a "living" community in spirit, an ecclesiology that stressed *communio.* Along with this focus on the "people of God," there also took shape a more collegial model relating the bishops to the universal Church. The papacy was to be reconceived as a ministry of service, not domination, embedded within the Episcopal College. The powers of the bishops as pastors were linked less directly to the canonical responsibilities of the Pope and more immediately to the charism conferred in ordination. Even the laity was perceived as having a call to the apostolate, which was rooted in faith, through the sacraments, rather than connected primarily to a mandate from the hierarchy. These insights reminded many of the theologians of this generation that Christians and the institutional Church itself were still groping within the darkness of history. Their efforts ultimately would yield a more modest ecclesiology that could encourage an ongoing critical stance toward the actions of the institutional Church as it developed. Viewed historically, the interrupted work of Vatican I was now in the process of being completed.[9]

This "sea change" in ecclesiology was formulated comprehensively by Congar and supported by German theologians of this era who contributed to reshaping the previously dominant neoscholastic milieu into one that resonated more solidly with contemporary needs. Since the nineteenth century, the Tübingen School had helped nourish a Catholic tradition in Germany that was more sensitive to biblical and historical studies, and, given the stresses and strains of living in the brutalizing milieu of the Third Reich, theologians reflected on the identity of their Church, that is, its ecclesiology. They began transforming the manner in which the institution would respond to historical issues. Such theologians as Grosche and Koster, although not as prominent as Congar, were influential in the developing German tradition that helped change the ecclesiological milieu of the universal Church. During the dark days of the war, they struggled to move the Church into the public sphere where it could more meaningfully respond to the challenges of the era. These theologians failed to respond to the virulent antisemitism of the Nazi leaders, but they did critique the psychological issues of categorization and marginalization within their ecclesial, and by implication political, community, which helped pave the way for a more ecumenical theology. They critiqued the exclusivistic dynamics that made Catholic and Nazi antisemitism possible, as well as the structural causes of the anomie experienced in modern societies.

When Hitler came to power in 1933, Robert Grosche outlined his views sketching how a Catholic-National Socialist accommodation could occur. He theologically organized his reflections around the concept of a *Reichstheologie,* which was historically useful in fusing a conservative, if not reactionary, Christianity to the secular order. In 1933–34, he published several articles centering on the theme of establishing a foundation for Christian politics that could be utilized by German Catholics in the Third Reich.[10] His views on adaptation can be criticized, but from a different perspective they can also be seen as asserting that the Church had a necessary public role.

Grosche embraced the antiliberal tradition thriving in conservative Europe, which maintained that the Enlightenment Project had failed, since it had tried organizing European states and societies in a way that ignored the historical traditions peculiar to European peoples and cultures. Catholicism had, he asserted, been the principal supporter of the antimodernist tradition that derived its nourishment from the historically fashioned concept of the *Reich Gottes,* a conceptual model explicated in the Middle Ages, but destroyed ideologically by post-1789 modernizing states. The *Reich Gottes* (Kingdom of God), he maintained, was originally and theologically a Christian eschatological term and one of the central lynchpins that organized the Christian tradition. Essentially, this *Reich* was a historical as well as an eschatological goal that was seen as the ongoing fulfillment of God's plan. From the secular perspective, the *Reich* was to connect Charlemagne, the Holy Roman Empire, Bismarck, and now Hitler. Grosche tentatively questioned, of course, whether the Nazi state could really qualify as the next step toward the realization of the theological concept of the *Reich*, but cautiously offered an affirmative answer to the question. He formulated his argument around an incarnational theology. Here Jesus Christ had been proclaimed as one person with a divine and a human nature, which are neither totally separated nor totally mixed. Grosche combined this doctrine of the two natures of Christ with a theology of history, in which humanity had a beginning and moved toward an end. Grosche concluded that spiritual impulses must always precede and anticipate secular events. It seemed necessary, therefore, to reflect more extensively on church history in order to understand the contingent developments of his era. Christian history seemed, he felt, to be moving toward its appointed end with the establishment of the Third Reich. The principle of authority in both the Church and the state, he asserted, had to take precedence over any kind of freedom of speech and voting, that is, liberal democracy, which would divide humans in society rather than help them form an organic unity.[11]

Grosche asserted that he had found the needed evidence that the eschatological "*Reich*" of Christianity was emerging in Germany through the Nazi movement. The foundation for this political *Reich* appeared to be embodied in the *Führerprinzip* (National Socialist leadership principle), the organic German community, and the emergence of a realized corporate political theory that reflected the medieval ideal. He wrote convincingly that if ever there were to be an authentic Christian *Reich*, it could exist only under the dominion of Germany, the only state that had already demonstrated its essential historical identity with the theologically conceptual *Reich* that had helped power European political history since the medieval era. He felt that the Third Reich could become the embodied spiritual *Reich*, but that it had to be blessed by the Church. The task for Catholics, therefore, was to advance the realization of the spiritual *Reich* through their assistance to the Nazi leaders. Only in its relation to the Christian concept of *Reich* could the Nazi state become truly Christian and so fulfill God's plan.[12] In essence both the Church and the state had to cooperate for God's kingdom to emerge. As the Nazis showed their true colors, he saw this attempted metamorphosis fail and so countered this disappointment by developing an ecclesiology not dependent on *Reichstheologie.*

The attempt to adapt Christianity to the Nazi *weltanschauung* can be seen from hindsight as a dangerous move, since it tended to favor those solutions that ultimately could have introduced an insidious corruption that would have reduced the Christian faith to a role supportive of racism. Catholic theologians such as Grosche initially tried to reconcile Nazi ideology, even though a pseudo-religion, with their Christian faith.[13] By naturalizing theological doctrine, they hoped to achieve a political accommodation with the new regime, but Grosche saw that he had jeopardized the transcendent foundation as well as the historical development of his faith.[14] Like so many other theologians, Grosche became less exuberant as the Nazis began to "coordinate" German society. Retreating from politics, Grosche felt it more useful to address the theological issue of reshaping the clearly outdated neoscholastic ecclesiology that could not adequately engage his culture.

Grosche produced his work on the "pilgrim Church" as the war commenced. The study courageously incorporated the ideas enlivening his culture, which could prove useful for both Nazi ideologues and Catholic theologians. His earlier Catholic theology and Nazi ideology reflected the dominant romantic and antimodernist strains of the era, but seemed to lack a much needed critical dimension. Both Grosche and his contemporary, Karl Adam, failed to see the dangers inherent in the Nazi perspective that was nourished in the contemporary German culture that historically had been infused with romantic and organic intellectual motifs. Both theologians contributed significant insights to Catholic theology, and both illustrate the pitfalls into which theologians could fall unless critical safeguards were built into theological systematizations. It was in his second attempt to formulate a relevant ecclesiology that Grosche abandoned his earlier adaptational strategy.[15]

Grosche's contributions to the development of a more viable ecclesiology resonated with the modern needs that he observed. Following in the steps of his predecessors in the Tübingen School, he began by attacking the abstract conceptualism of the Enlightenment that had for many replaced the living God of Christianity. In response to the Enlightenment, the nineteenth-century Tübingen theologians had insisted that ideas nurtured in historical cultures shaped actions, and they condemned the abstract reason of the Enlightenment that seemed to ignore organic, living cultures and traditions. History for the Tübingen theologians was the discipline responsible for recounting the forward movement of the idea that was eschatologically to fulfill humanity's mission. Grosche also adopted Heidegger's stress on the existential historicity that had influenced Romano Guardini as well. History was the battleground where unfree nature was liberated as humans developed, where free will would reign, and where the present exists not as the entirety, but rather as the process rooted in the past and living toward the future.[16]

In Grosche's opinion the Church had successfully preserved the proper meaning of God's revelation through its historical and ongoing tradition and sacraments, which communicated grace to men and women throughout history. The Church's positive theology, therefore, had to be bound to the incarnate and historical Jesus. Grosche very carefully connected the historical person of Christ to the living revelation that was continually being reappropriated within the organic community of the Church.[17] The essence of Christianity was grounded in the historical acts of Jesus on the cross and risen from the dead. Grosche's stress on historicity and development set the stage for his theological analysis of the "pilgrim" Church, an ecclesiology that could have better responded to the needs of the Church in this dark era than did the adaptation of so many German bishops and the prudence of Pius XII.

For Grosche, the religious challenge facing Christians at the time was to understand the essence and the reality of the Church seen as both a cultural and a countercultural force. He envisioned the Church as the institution that was to funnel God's transcendent revelation to men and women living in history. In launching his analysis, Grosche paid tribute to Hermann Schell's Reform Catholicism, which intimately connected the Church as a historical phenomenon and the transcendent Christian faith still unfolding. For Grosche, to understand Christianity meant to connect the Church, its traditions, and its developments. Theologians, particularly in France and Germany by the 1930s and '40s, had developed a record of opposing the post-Tridentine, polemical, and juridical concepts of the Church, which historically had been formulated as a reaction to the Reformers' concept of the invisible Church. Grosche and others of his generation sketched out an ecclesiology that carefully was imbued with the original Christian experiences and their ongoing significance. This more experiential Church concept in Grosche's work can be attributed to the earlier work of Johann Adam Möhler and Matthias Joseph Scheeben.[18] Grosche lived at a time when a new vision of the

Church was sorely needed, and he began to organize earlier "pieces of ecclesiology" into a system that responded to his own perceived needs.

For the Möhler of *Einheit,* the Church was the embodiment of the spirit of Christ, and the hierarchy gained its strength from the soul of the community. Accordingly, canon law was to be conceived as the legally embodied love of the community. Scheeben was interested in the supernatural life of the Church, where the institution was viewed more as a mystery. From such a derivation, he connected the sacramental and jurisdictional responsibilities of the Church. Even though the bishops in Vatican I had organized the constitution of the Church around an exclusivistic ecclesiology, they had ceased stressing the post-Tridentine juridical concept that presumed the Church as solely an institution. Unfortunately, due to the Franco-Prussian War, only the infallibility schema with its juridical component was authorized at Vatican I, and so it appeared that Catholic doctrine stemmed from papal authority embodied in the Petrine office. The already prepared and more broadly inclusive ecclesiological schema, never discussed, would have muted such a rigid and sterile hierarchical position. The defensive posture of the post-Vatican I Church overlooked the fact that papal infallibility, designed to protect the Church against exterior threats, could really be properly appreciated and found useful only if it were rooted in the interior life of the Church, which, to some, seemed to be captured in a "mystical body of Christ" model, but could also be recovered in a historically and organically grounded model.[19]

This mystical body of Christ model, according to Grosche, can be found in its rudimentary form in St. Paul, the early Church Fathers, and the major Scholastic theologians. Grosche reminded his readers that the Church itself never officially settled on one defined identity for itself, but had generally preferred a flexibility that could respond to ecclesial needs. At least up through the Middle Ages, the centrality of the institutional Church in Christian life, in fact, seemed to eliminate the need for any ecclesiology that was theologically defined. The Church was to prepare *das Reich Gottes* and had its own institutional responsibilities. Paul, however, had written about the new Adam as Christ, as the head of the Church (Eph 5:23). This organic Pauline concept, Grosche felt, was most welcome after the nightmare of the sterile individualism that seemed to be the essence of the Enlightenment project. In Grosche's opinion, Karl Adam, situated in the romantic tradition common to both Nazism and Catholicism, had very properly constructed an ecclesiological model that asserted that the mystery of the incarnation had mandated that the

Church was to be seen as an organic community. Adam's adaptational approach, of course, had its problems, since it stimulated him to positively engage Nazism.[20]

In Grosche's organic and historically developing model, the institutional Church does not stand between God and humanity. It is not an institutionalized absolute, since its very reason for existence is tied to Christ and to Christians in a living community. The Church exists through Christ and in Christ. This Church cannot be understood empirically through sociology, but rather can be comprehended only Christologically. As a community (*Gemeinschaft*), this Church is grounded in Christ and realized sacramentally through its works. Christ, in whom the fullness of holiness dwells, is the head of this Church, and the incarnation as the objective entrance of Jesus into history repudiates, for example, the early Möhler, whose romantic idealism tended to value subjective impulses rather than Scripture and tradition, which could serve as a more objective foundation. The visibility of the Church is based on the historical incarnation.[21]

Because the Church historically functions in the world and tries to Christianize the world, it cannot be studied ahistorically. The world of history cannot be subordinated to an abstract and juridical ecclesiology. In the patristic period, the position that the Church and Caesar had their own responsibilities had been articulated. Christ, not the Church, rules both the Church and the secular world, and the process of relating both spheres enlivens history. Presumably, the laity in their work are morally to condition their environment, which means, of course, that they cannot be totally dominated by the Church or by the state. The incarnation also protects the temporal world and gives it a unique dignity.[22] Grosche was clearing a path into the discipline of political theology, which would later be followed more avidly by such theologians as Johannes Metz.

Grosche insisted on the unity of the Church, which was to include the pope, the bishops with their responsibilities as the successors of the apostles, priests, and the laity. Such a unity was not devised to annihilate the multiplicity of peoples, but was to serve as a reminder that there was one human race, to which all historical peoples belonged. Grace—and here he warned that the concept can be misused as it was by theologians hoping to positively relate Nazism and Catholicism—does not destroy nature, but presupposes it as part of God's eschatological goal. No ethnic or racial group, therefore, could validly claim preeminence in the Church. All in the Church are equal in spirit. They all should have an equal place in the eyes of the institutional leaders, particularly the Vicar of Christ.[23] The reality of the Church is found in its historical response to human questions. This Church constitutes the constant proclamation of the kingdom of God and probably should not be seen as the Church of the resurrected Christ (a type of completion), but rather should be perceived as the bride of Christ, who now and in the future awaits the return of her bridegroom. The latter image would better support an ongoing process.

In his work, Grosche had to deal with the *Reich Gottes* theology that had earlier influenced him and that was so popular at the time. From a proleptic standpoint Grosche insisted that the Church is not yet the Kingdom of God. In Grosche's view, the Kingdom of God has "broken into" this world through Jesus Christ. This kingdom is here on earth in the Church, but is veiled as Christ was before his resurrection. The Church has the responsibility to establish the path that would lead to the kingdom. Thus, the Kingdom of God was a proleptic mystery (Mk 4:11) and was, as Jesus said, a mustard seed that would mature. Conceptually, the Kingdom of God could be seen as grace and as living in the past, in the present, and in the future. The eternal Kingdom of God now subsists in the Church, which is on the way, but has not yet reached God as an "*ecclesia gloriosa.*" This Church on earth is a Church of sinners, and its members daily need forgiveness. This Church is a "pilgrim Church," a people of God, wandering in darkness, but guided by the light of faith. On this earth the Church does not embody glory, but rather the cross as Christians move toward their destinations.[24] Grosche offered an ecclesiology navigating historical developments and one in which Christians could freely determine how the Church will exist as it persists in fulfilling its mission. This Church is the people of God working in concrete history and is sinful, even in need of reform. Grosche, of course, was not alone in his reflections on the Church and its meaning.

In 1940, less adaptational in spirit than was Grosche, Dominikus Koster published *The Development of Ecclesiology,* the result of twelve years of discerning the meaning of the Church as an institution in the modern world. Koster viewed the Church as the *Volk Gottes,* the people of God, continuously gaining in spiritual consciousness through its own self-understanding. Such a Church could also be viewed as an organic entity, reflecting the values of his contemporary political and biological culture, but also as an institution that had to be critically evaluated to avoid marginalizing tactics. How could a community be organic and not marginalize? In light of Nazi racial politics, this was an important question that Koster did not adequately handle. Such an organic approach could also sublimate Christ as God into the Church as it changed in history, and so could also introduce potential problems. Koster's work, however, did reinforce the perception that an organic Church community was continuously being historically shaped. A *communio* model could, Koster felt, oppose the instrumentalist practices of the Church itself.[25] His project, then, was to develop a theology that balanced the individual and the community within a theology that stressed Christology and ecclesiology.

Koster could not support an ecclesiology that took the "body of Christ" as its model, since such a move would mean utilizing only a partial theological insight that was not scripturally based. An authentic ecclesiology had to reflect that the Church was not just a collection of discrete individuals belonging to a specific category, but really was an organic whole, within which persons could spiritually thrive. Such a valid ecclesiology should offer an inclusive worldview, into which the Church and world could fit. The metaphor "body of Christ" would not suffice, because it was only a metaphorical description of the instrumentalist institution and did not reveal its essence as the ongoing historical message of Jesus and the Christian community to the world.[26] The metaphor was too static and itself glossed over some real issues of marginalization.

Koster recognized that any vibrant theological perspective had to be rooted in the faith milieu of the specific historical period to which it belonged. Living in a specific culture, people ask questions that make sense to them and can formulate solutions to the issues that are of concern. The Church had to respect this normal human mode of operation. Theologians have an obligation, he maintained, to formulate meaningful theologies. Each generation, therefore, has to reflect anew on what it means to speak of the Church as a living community. Out of the community's enlivened faith, the *sensus fidei* (sense of faith) then has to delineate an ecclesiology that responds to what Vatican II would later refer to as the "signs of the times."[27]

Koster saw the "body of Christ" as too supernatural an entity that could not be the foundational basis for an ecclesiology interacting with the historical milieu. The living Church was to be the subject of each generation's ecclesiology, and the Church's meaning could be grasped only through its concrete historical teachings, which could not be adequately captured fully by some abstract concept. The fact that Paul and Augustine liked the metaphor of the body of Christ did not mean, he maintained, that the ecclesiological question had been resolved for all time, since each of these men had his own reasons for utilizing what to them was a very comforting metaphor. Paul was negotiating the issue of how Jews and Christians were related in his culture. Jews, of course, had historically insisted that they were the people of God. Paul wanted to connect this view, said Koster, to the Christian insistence on salvation through Jesus. Paul stressed, therefore, the collective *Volk*. Paul selected his reference point to accord with his agenda that the human species, even before the incarnation, had always been in some way connected to Christ. It was the new *Volk Gottes* that was now to be seen as the true Israel. Within this context, Paul talked about the Church as the body of Christ uniting Jews and Gentiles. Unfortunately, Paul was advancing a supersessionist theology to deal with his Christian contemporaries and was thinking in terms of the collectivistic notion of salvation so alive in the Hebrew Bible, which he saw completed in the New Testament. Thus, Paul insists that God has proclaimed "the people of God" in such a way that it could encompass the individual as person before and after the resurrection of Jesus. Koster also pointed out that Augustine and Thomas used the body metaphor to deal with their theological concerns, none of which seemed to yield an enduring and satisfactory ecclesiology that could respond to historical change and meet the needs of people in all times and places.[28]

Theologians, Koster insisted, have to respond to the valid questions of their eras, but they also have to reflect as part of the tradition of their Church. Reappropriating past viewpoints, theologians are charged with responding to the challenges of the present. Each theologian, therefore, has to be sensitive to the unfolding of the faith-life within the Church and to the contributions of each era to the whole living Church. This unfolding life of the Church articulates what faith means to Christians over the centuries. Koster was convinced that the living faith powering the Church was being continually shaped as Christians in each age engaged their culture on a daily basis. The consciousness of this faith would provide the indispensable overview of how past Christians have addressed their concerns. The community of the Church is unquestionably present in each generation existentially, but is also continually being reshaped anew. It is freshly and completely experienced and valued, especially when it has been threatened. Living in Nazi Germany with the irrational paganism of its ideology, Koster was aware of the threat to his spiritual community. Somehow Christians had to respond to this new threat from Bonhoeffer's subsequently developed perspective of "a world come of age."[29] Theologians in every age have a responsibility, Koster maintained, to delineate the relationship of the individual person belonging to the living Church and to realize that there continually exists a tension between the community and the individual person in the Church as well as in the secular culture. How is such a tension to be mediated?

In Koster's view, membership in Christ as the incarnate word is to be distinguished from membership in the Church. All members of the Church are attached to Christ, but the reverse is not necessarily so. Those faithful to God are not limited to explicit or implicit membership in the Catholic Church. For Koster the self-understanding of the Church could correctly be encapsulated in the notion of "the people of God." This image with all of its diverse connotations was rooted in the patristic era. The "people of God" model, moreover, would suggest that the inclusion was due to God, not due to institutional membership. Subsequently, this would prove to be a fruitful way to look at the Church. The notion of the *Volk Gottes* also could use the notion of a *Gemeinschaft*, so popular in German theology for nearly a century and a half. In this model, the Church institutionally and as one of its functions could order the actions of the people in each local community. But the *Gemeinschaft* model has ecumenical overtones that proved important in the reflections leading to Vatican II. Such an approach would root the Church in the biblical traditions originating in Israel and continuing through Christ. It would not take its forms and functions from the history of institutional religion, sociology, and politics. The "people of God" model would form the presupposition, the basis, the framework, and the norm for understanding all the spiritual and temporal activities of God's active life with his people in all their diversities. "The people of God" is the way to envision the living God acting among men and women. God interacting with the *Volk Gottes* exists historically, that is, phenomenologically. Koster was focusing on an ecclesiology appropriate for his Church, but once the jump was made from a dominating, juridical, hierarchical institution to the more fruitful metaphor of a "people of God," the implication for spiritual life proved groundbreaking, as Vatican II would show. He used the *communio* model to describe the Church, but his successors could extend the inclusiveness of the model as they discerned more clearly its implications in the light of the Genesis statements concerning humans as the images of God. As a caution, it has to be remembered that Koster did not use his "people of God" metaphor in the amplified fashion of those fathers at Vatican II. He was not explicitly concerned with the diversity of peoples, cultures, and religion. But he did create an opening to change the more exclusive Catholic milieu.[30]

This community is a union that is more than just biological in the Nazi sense. Members of the Church, broadly conceived, stand with Christ in an intimate living community. This Church is not just a juridical body, but rather a community, within which persons funnel God's supernatural life into the temporal culture. The Church is not a living body united as a living community with Christ in the same way in which our body is with our soul, but rather exists as the entire human (body and soul) does as it is vivified with God's word. There is a distinction between Christ and his Church. The two are not identical, and so an opening was given by Koster for a more ecumenical theology and a less dominating institutional structure. In this context, describing the Church as the bride of Christ again might be more accurate, since there would be in this relationship a notion of personal distinction and yet simultaneously a connectedness.[31] Such an approach would also allow theologians to continue opening up the significance of the productive tension existing between the individual and the community. The community cannot absorb, and thereby negate, the unique person.

The Church, then, could be seen as God's extended and continuing salvific act just as Israel's becoming the people of God was the initial salvific activity of Yahweh. Koster stressed that Christians have an ongoing task of understanding the God-human relationship. In conclusion, he reminded his readers that the proper departure point for an ecclesiology of the Church was to be objectively grounded in the notion of the People of God, nurtured through Scripture and liturgy. Koster hoped that his historically attuned ecclesiology would become an acceptable theological model for the Church, since his concept was capable of reforming itself in light of the challenges of each era.[32] He ended his work by asserting that social and legal philosophy would have to be included in any culturally sensitive ecclesiology, but should not be central to it. The emergence of this "people of God" ecclesiology was timely, since it stressed the initial need for Jewish and Christian Scripture as the source of the living community, that is, the Church, which could continuously help us understand the human condition, seen in the relationship of God to men and women. As these ecclesiological reflections were taking shape, Karl Rahner was beginning his career as a systematic theologian who would focus on an anthropology that could reinforce the creative ecclesiology that was taking shape.

In 1941, Karl Rahner published *Hearers of the Word: Laying the Foundation for a Philosophy of Religion,* in which he hoped through dialogue to engage contemporary philosophy, theology, and the secular disciplines in general. As early as *Hearers of the Word,* Rahner explicated the basic anthropological approach that would undergird his future work. For him the reality and actuality of Christian revelation is presupposed, and from that point of origin Rahner asks about the subjective, anthropological, and religious-philosophical conditions that can tell us *why* a human being, as knowing and freely acting, is able to have anything to do with "revelation." Such a manner of thinking can be seen as a "transcendental" and existential subjectivity that presupposes the facticity of a historical reality and simultaneously makes an inquiry before the bar of reason into the ground of legitimacy for each particular spiritual being. Rahner's philosophical starting point was intersubjective; each person coexists with God. For Rahner, humans embody a specific condition that includes grace and nature. How can humans come to an understanding of God and themselves? Rahner's proposed solution to this question of the conditions necessary for the possibility of an understanding of revelation is based on his understanding of the transcendental orientation of the human spirit.

Hearers of the Word launched Rahner's theological career in 1941. In *Hearers of the Word,* he tried to show how each human can listen to the word of the Holy Spirit, who has entered history. Rahner launched his theological speculation from an inductive angle rooted in self-consciousness and natural knowledge, not from supernatural theology. Our capacity to hear God's revelation makes fully actualized human beings of us. Revelation itself is a historical process activated by the person in the concrete world as he or she searches for God. How it takes place and what is communicated depend strictly on the unique combination of persons and historical events, in which God's work speaks authentically to humanity. As spirit and nature, the human person is a historical being. Both biologically and spiritually, persons have a developmental history. Clearly, then, God's self-revelation is more than merely making objective what is humanity's subjective state.[33] Here Rahner stood opposed to the German idealism that had so dominated nineteenth-century German culture and to the liberal Protestantism that had organized German Protestant theology from Kant to Ritschl. For Rahner, the person as mystery is needed to explicate transcendent revelation.

From Rahner's perspective, men and women have to listen to history to discern God's word. To be human means to be absolutely open to all being. To be human is to be spirit, that is, to live life while reaching ceaselessly for the absolute being. In Rahner's view, to our fundamental human makeup there intrinsically belongs a connection to the transcendent. Humanity is open to every kind of knowledge and should not restrict the scope of any possible revelation. Human spirit has to be seen as a dynamic movement toward God, the infinite being. By understanding our own finiteness, as part of our cognitive process, we can find access to God's true infinity. Rahner's central point is that as spirits who know God, we stand before God as freely communicating persons. God as a person is related to us as persons in the process of self-disclosure. Humans always stand before God as revelation matures in history.[34] This maturing human transcendence becomes increasingly more intelligible and occurs because of our openness toward God, who acts freely toward us in a way that we cannot discover by ourselves alone. To be a human person is essentially always to be one who listens for the potential revelation of God.

The human person is connected to God's transcendence, that is, to the embodied, normative being, who is God. To be human means to stand in free love before the God of all possible revelation. We can hear God's word, Rahner maintains, as long as we do not narrow the total horizon of our openness toward historical and transcendent being as such.[35] Additionally, God also determines in what way he wants to encounter us, and so we must be sensitive to all avenues that can yield such knowledge. Revelation is a historical event and not encapsulated in abstract theology. Turning toward our history is a dynamic, inner moment for each spiritual nature. The revelation of God and our openness toward all being is necessarily situated within the human history, in which we develop.[36] We are historical, Rahner asserts, insofar as we are the ones who act freely, even in the presence of the transcendent God. Humans have the responsibility to freely realize themselves through their multiplicity of personal experiences. The human as person also opens the transcendent God for others. Such a profound insight lends dignity to each human and emerges at a time in Rahner's own culture when such a perspective was sorely needed.

As an ongoing process, revelation begins and continues in human history. Humans must listen, Rahner asserts, to their own experiences in order to hear God. The human person as a finite spirit stands freely before the God of revelation. But how does the concrete, historical experience of an individual person penetrate to the historical yet transcendent revelatory event? Religiously inclined persons do not understand their pasts in the way professional historians might. Persons of faith grasp the past through their tradition of living faith, in which past and present flow in a continuous stream and help them to understand the unfolding meaning of God.[37] Rahner in this early work only briefly discusses this process of development, but his stress in *Hearers of the Word* on history, freedom, and revelation laid down the guidelines for his future work as he feverishly engaged the kaleidoscopic culture in which he lived. Rahner regarded history as inextricably revealing God's offer of salvation, and the story could end only when God eschatologically unveiled its penultimate meanings. Until the end, history would remain open and in motion. For Rahner, such a view was particularly useful in the twentieth century, in which theologians and others pointedly pegged their insights on a culture shaped by existentialism, phenomenology, personalism, and a transcendent God who freely revealed.

On January 18, 1943, Conrad Gröber, the archbishop of Freiburg, wrote a twenty-one-page letter to the German episcopate. Cardinal Innitzer asked Rahner to respond. In his "Vienna Memorandum" of 1943, Rahner wrote that the past generation had witnessed a period of extraordinary political, social, and cultural upheaval.[38] Gröber vigorously complained about the innovations being proposed in Catholic theology and in the liturgy. Rahner's reflections cover specific problems. What is the role of theology in the revolutionary era, in which he lived? How can issues raised by the Nazis and others of his generation be meaningfully addressed? How is the tradition of the Church to be preserved despite new philosophical and theological approaches? Rahner pointed out that secular controversies were important as theologians tried to clarify and amplify God's words to humans, and he acknowledged how fatal embittered silence could be as he analyzed the state of theology in Germany and France. Along the way, he urged that the Holy Office should not simply issue prohibitions and warnings, but should recognize that even works consigned to the Index authentically addressed the human condition.[39]

As early as this "Vienna Memo," Rahner seemed to recognize that reflecting on needed political, social, and cultural changes was a source of great anxiety for many. How could faith, which seemed to rely on doctrinal continuity, embrace the possibilities of discontinuity and speak to modernity? What was required, he suggested, was a respect for the past as well as a tentative, careful, and open-to-compromise attitude toward contemporary impulses. He set himself to this task. While he did not deny that preparing for the future inevitably would cause certain strains within the Church, he suggested that mutual love could reduce the anxious path forced by change and could also ensure doctrinal credibility. In the context of the changing times, he maintained that the great enemies that could endanger the Church would be a lack of courage and a lack of prudence. In brief, he did not affirm those in his Church who saw the demise of the "Christian West" as a disaster, since faith had a power to enable men and women to adapt to history. The "living" Church had to be guided by its nearly two millennia of tradition.[40] Rahner stressed several themes that would help define Catholic theology for the duration of his career as a major theologian in the Catholic Church. At no time, he asserted, has the Church ever contained the fullness of truth, which is why the concept of the continual reappropriation of past theological insights has such crucial power. No era in the Church could ever be seen as normative. Finally, the Church was to act as a conduit so that the incarnated Jesus could influence the world.[41] These themes launched his career as a systematic theologian.

What began to appear in Rahner's works in the 1940s was the conviction that the effectiveness of the Church in contemporary society as well as its ability to preach and embody the word of God in ways that the twentieth century would not find alienating depended on its willingness to make substantial changes to its theological anthropology. The secular world could no longer be considered only as a hostile place, and the Church ought no longer assume an unflinching defensive posture or, conversely as in the case of Karl Adam, embrace so readily a stance of adaptation to Nazi ideology. What was needed was a new openness, a willingness to engage, and a willingness to take risks in making changes, even when it could not be known with certainty whether such changes were fully reconcilable with tradition.[42] Rahner's theory of the development of dogma, with its emphasis on a change *in*, not *of*, identity, stressed that continuity and discontinuity could be reconciled. Change implied a growth in understanding new formulations for each new age. The impetus for this change came from each person's and the Church's own existence in history. Risks had to be accepted, and the Church had to see itself as "ever reforming."

Reflection on the changing challenges to the Church in the modern world also dominated Rahner's ecclesiological insights, never systematized, in the years after World War II. In response to the sociopolitical shifts in his world, Rahner sought both to identify the resources that would enable the Church to adapt to the rapidly developing problems of postwar Europe as well as the world itself and to consider how the application of theological resources could alter the face that the Church itself presented. Rahner was convinced that the ongoing history of the Church could not be regarded as complete in any specific manifestation of the institution and that the final stage of the world's and the Church's development had not been reached. In brief, Rahner was committed to the idea that the Church was an "open project" guided by the Spirit.[43] In Rahner's opinion, without a spirit of self-criticism, there would be a permanent danger that the Church would succumb to the temptation of institutionalization and be regarded by its leaders as an end in itself. Were this to occur, the Church would cease to change, would lose contact with the surrounding social realities, and would become a conservative power bent on preservation, not change and engagement.

In his postwar career, Karl Rahner wrote extensively about "transcendental existentialism" and "theological anthropology," suggesting that human experience, while finite and limited in many ways, can nevertheless be open to the whole of reality simply because we cannot speak of God except as human beings. Rahner placed at the foundation of his theology the basic human urge to transcend the physical limitations of human nature. Humans are aware of being made for more than they are now or even more that they can ever hope to achieve by their own abilities. Christian revelation supplies this "more," to which human experience points.[44] In the final analysis, Rahner's lifelong concern was to bring out clearly that, even though we are limited and finite, we possess a strong sense of something that is transcendent—something that surpasses our personal and situational limitations. For Rahner, this awareness had considerable theological significance and potential, since it ultimately led to the realization that the Christian concept of God has to be tied to our understanding of the human situation. Rahner thus makes his anthropology of fundamental importance and establishes the discussion of human nature, including the human awareness of transcendent longing, at the very foundation of his work. The human quest for ultimate meaning raises the question of God and is satisfied only when that God is found. Rahner's starting point is anthropocentric, but his intention is theocentric. Men and women as they concretely exist in history continually search for God. An appreciation of historicity, therefore, is crucial for Rahner and those influenced by him.

From Rahner's perspective, human persons as spiritual beings are constituted by their basic and continuous transcendental experience of God. They unrelentingly interpret and express that experience in historical language and acts. Consequently, a historical and categorical objectification of that transcendental experience emerges and develops. This objectification takes place in and through human history and culture and not alongside of history and independent of culture. When this objectification in history and culture entails an explicitly religious interpretation of that transcendental revelatory experience, it becomes what Rahner calls "categorical revelation."[45]

During the Third Reich, no foundational theology of resistance to Nazi brutalization was developed. During those years there was no formalized theological impetus available, upon which a Catholic theory of resistance really could have been constructed, although personal experiences, the historically sensitive ecclesiologies being developed, and the Rahnerian anthropology would ultimately serve to help subsequent Catholic theologians and laity reflect more vigorously on the relationship between theology and politics. Theologians and others began to seek resources outside of Neo-Scholasticism for the intimate and historically conditioned connections that should exist between persons and their community. The contours of such a theology of historical engagement, and by implication resistance, only gradually emerged in response to the unfolding nature of Hitler's regime and the underlying currents of modernity itself, although too late to affect the regime.[46] Among Roman Catholic theologians in post–World War II Germany, Johannes Metz, one of Karl Rahner's most brilliant students, was the first to retrieve explicitly a political dimension of Christian faith and theology.

It is important to realize that the failures in theology and typical sociopolitical reactions to racist antisemitism and political oppression during the Nazi regime were recognized by several German theologians, and their reflections ultimately became influential far beyond Germany in the general discourse prompted in the Catholic Church leading to Vatican II and beyond. Such theologians as Grosche, Koster, and Rahner reflected on their Third Reich experiences and the reform movements stirring in the Catholic Church itself. The actions of countless other Christians, whose insights into the meaning of the Christian faith and whose acts of resistance helped model and open up for the theologians new paths of how theological reflection could be related to Christian praxis, paved the way for a political theology that made historical events the foundation for doing relevant theology.[47]

The Nazi experience taught Christian theologians and ecclesial leaders some valuable lessons. A spiritual (pneumatological) understanding of Christian faith seemed unable to provide the institutional platform needed to identify and resist oppressive political structures and actions. Equally, a predominantly institutional and legal or juridical understanding of Christian faith along the lines of that used to a degree by Pius XII and more totally by his predecessors historically had been unable to set free the spiritual energy needed by individual Christians to undertake for themselves a responsible assessment of both their faith and the political context, in which their faith could support sponsored acts of physical and/or moral resistance. The Third Reich and Communism could not be resisted by abstract neoscholastic theology. Institutional Christian experiences since 1933 have also taught us that secular and conceptualized religious ideology can repress human freedom. The only corrective for the abstractions that typified earlier theological systems seems to be an openness to the meaning of historical events.[48]

Catholicism was not moribund during the Third Reich, but contained the seeds of reform that would lead to the renewal in Vatican II and beyond. Karl Rahner cogently expressed what was being cultivated in German and French circles, when he maintained that what was manifested and officially received at Vatican II was already present in the Catholic Church during the interwar and postwar period. Przywara also asserted that the deepest realities of Catholicism were in fact an authentic fulfillment of modern subjectivity and history.[49] Gradually, a group of German Catholic theologians became sensitive to notions of historical development that yielded an ecclesiology highlighting a "living Church" as well as an anthropology, in which human experiences could help lead to a knowledge of God. Such a historically sensitive theology was needed before Catholics could theologically engage their culture and its world of "marching soldiers."

NOTES

1. Avery Dulles, "A Half Century of Ecclesiology," *Theological Studies* 50 (1989): 419–42; Otto Dibelius, *Das Jahrhundert der Kirche* (Berlin: Furche, 1927); Donald Dietrich, *The Goethezeit and the Metamorphosis of Catholic Theology in the Age of Idealism* (Bern: Peter Long, 1979); Donald Dietrich and Michael Himes, eds., *The Legacy of the Tübingen School: The Relevance of Nineteenth Century Theology for the Twenty-First Century* (New York: Crossroad, 1997): Thomas O'Meara, *Church and Culture: German Catholic Theology, 1860–1914* (Notre Dame, Ind.: University of Notre Dame Press, 1991).

2. Timoteo Zopelena, *De Ecclesia: Pars Apologetica* (Rome: Gregorian University, 1950); Dulles, "Ecclesiology," 420; Francis Sullivan, *De ecclesia: Tracatatus Apologeticus* (Rome: Gregorian University, 1961).

3. Charles Journet, *L'Eglise du Verbe incarné*, 3 vols. (Bruges: Desclée De Brouwer, 1941, 1951, 1969).

4. Dulles, "Ecclesiology," 421–22; Emile Mersch, *Le Corps mystique du Christ: Etudes de théologie historique* (Paris: Desclée De Brouwer, 1933; *Acta Apostolicae Sedis*

35 (July 20, 1943), 193–248; Albert Mitterer, *Geheimnisvoller Leib Christi nach Thomas von Aquin und nach Papst Pius XII* (Vienna: Herold, 1950); Felix Malmberg, *Ein Leib-ein Geist: Vom Mysterium der Kirche* (Freiburg: Herder, 1960).

5. J. Robert Dionne, *The Papacy and Church* (New York: Philosophical Library, 1987), 195–236; Augustine Bea, *The Unity of Christians* (New York: Herder and Herder), 32–34.

6. Thomas F. O'Meara, *Erich Przywara, SJ: His Theology and His World* (Notre Dame, Ind.: University of Notre Dame Press, 2002), 165–66.

7. Thomas Ruster, *Die verlorene Nützlichleit der Religion: Katholizismus und Moderne in der Weimarer Republik* (Paderborn: Ferdinand Schöningh, 1994), 104–106 for material on Grosche's adaptation techniques; Robert Grosche, *Pilgernde Kirche* (Freiburg: Herder, 1938); Mannes Dominkus Koster, *Ekklesiologie im Werden* (Paderborn: Bonifacius, Verlag der Bonifacius-Druckerie, 1940); Ludwig won Hertling, *Communio: Church and Papacy in Early Christianity*, trans. Jared Wickes (Chicago: Loyola University Press, 1972).

8. Yves Congar, *Chétiens désunis: Principes d'un 'oecumenisme' catholique* (Paris: Cerf, 1937); Dulles, "Ecclesiology," 424–29; see also, Dennis Doyle, "Journet, Congar, and the Roots of Communion Ecclesiology," *Theological Studies* 58 (1997): 461–79; Timothy MacDonald, *The Ecclesiology of Yves Congar: Theology in the Service of God's People* (Chicago: Priory, 1968).

9. Dulles, "Ecclesiology," 425–27; Karl Rahner, "Notes on the Lay Apostalate," *Theological Investigations* 2 (1963): 319–52; Hans Urs von Balthasar, *Der Laie und der Ordenstand* (Einsiedeln; Johannes, 1948); Otto Semmelroth, *Die Kirche als Ursakrament* (Freiburg: Herder, 1960); Rudolf Schnackenburg, *Gottes Herrschaft und Reich* (Freiburg: Herder, 1959).

10. Klaus Breuning, *Die Vision des Reiches. Deutscher Katholizismus zwischen Demkcratie und Diktatur (1929–1934)* (Munich: Max Heuber Verlag, 1969), 238–52; Thomas Ruster, "Roman Catholic Theologians and National Socialism: Adaptation to Nazi Ideology," in *Christian Responses to the Holocaust: Moral and Ethical Issues*, ed. Donald Dietrich (Syracuse: Syracuse University Press, 2003), 19–21; Robert Groshe, "Die Grundlagen einer Christlichen Poltik der deutschen Katholiken," *Schildgenossen* 13 (1933): 46–52; Robert Grosche, "Der Kampf um den Reichsgedanken im politisch-sozialen Leben der Gegenwart," *Deutsches Volk* 1 (1933): 91–99; Robert Grosche, "Reich, Staat und Kirche," in *Die Kirche im deutschen Aufbruch*, ed. F. J.Wothe (Bergisch-Gladbach: Heider, 1934), 26–49.

11. Grosche, "Grundlagen," 48; Oded Heilbronner, "The Place of Catholic Historians and Catholic Historiography in Nazi Germany," *History* 88 (2003): 280–92.

12. Grosche, "Kampf," 99.

13. Gary Lease, "*Odd Fellows" in the Politics of Religion: Modernism, National Socialism, and German Judaism* (New York: de Gruyter, 1995).

14. Thomas Ruster, *Der verwechselbarne Gott. Theologie nach Entflechtung von Christentum und Religion* (Freiburg: Herder, 2000).

15. Richard Goritzka, *Der Seelsorger Robert Grosche (1888–1967): Dialogische Pastoral zwischen Ersten Weltkrieg und Zweitem Vatikanischem Konzil* (Würzburg: Echter, 1999).

16. Grosche, *Pilgernde Kirche*, 4, 6.

17. Ibid., 16, 17.

18. Ibid., 23, 24.

19. Ibid., 25–26.

20. Ibid., 26–27, 29; Karl Adam, *Das Wesen des Katholizismus* (Düsseldorf: Patmos, 1934), 49; Robert Krieg, *Karl Adam: Catholicism in German Culture* (Notre

Dame, Ind.: University of Notre Dame Press, 1992); Lucia Scherzberg, *Kirchenreform mit Hilfe des Nationalsozialismus: Karl Adam als Kontextueller Theologe* (Darmstadt: Wissenschaftliche Buchgesellschaft, 2001).

21. Grosche, *Pilgernde Kirche,* 29–36.

22. Ibid., 36–38.

23. Ibid., 38–41.

24. Ibid., 42, 44, 45, 53, 62, 65–70.

25. O'Meara, *Przywara,* 165–72; Mannes Dominikus Koster, *Ekklesiologie im Werden* (Paderborn: Verlag der Bonifacius-Druckerei, 1940), 7, 12–13; for an excellent analysis of "models" of the church, see Avery Dulles, *Models of the Church* (Garden City, N.Y.: Doubleday, 1974).

26. Koster, 14–15, 17, 20.

27. Ibid., 23–24.

28. Ibid., 35–40.

29. Ibid., 89–92.

30. Ibid., 93, 145–47.

31. Ibid., 150–51.

32. Ibid., 151, 154, 156, 158.

33. James Livingston and Francis Schüssler Fiorenza, *Modern Christian Thought,* vol. 2: *The Twentieth Century* (Upper Saddle River, N.J.: Prentice Hall, 2000), 207–208; Karl Rahner, *Foundations of Christian Faith: An Introduction to the Idea of Christianity* (New York: Crossroad, 1982); Karl Rahner, *The Content of Faith: The Best of Karl Rahner's Theological Writings,* ed. Karl Lehman and Albert Raffelt (New York: Crossroad, 1992). Karl Rahner, *Hearer of the Word: Laying the Foundation for a Philosophy of Religion,* trans. Joseph Donceel (New York Continuum, 1994), 6, 7, 19; for the original text see Karl Rahner, *Sämtliche Werke,* vol. 4: *Hörer des Wortes. Schriften zur Religionsphilosophie und zur Grundlegung der Theologie,* ed. Albert Raffelt (Freiburg: Herder, 1997).

34. Rahner, *Hearer,* 21, 41, 53–55, 61–62, 67–71.

35. Ibid., 84, 88.

36. Ibid., 95.

37. Ibid., 136–37, 141–43.

38. Richard Lennan, *The Eclesiology of Karl Rahner* (Oxford: Clarendon Press, 1995), 117; for the Vienna Memo, see Karl Rahner, *Theologische und philophische Zeitfragen im katholischen deutschen Raum (1943),* ed. Hubert Wolf (Ostfildern: Schwabenverlag, 1994); for further background information, see Theodor Maas-Ewerd, "Odo Casel OSB und Karl Rahner SJ: Disput über das Wienen Memorandum, 'Theologische und philosophisches Zeitfragen im katholischen deutschen Raum,'" *Archiv für Liturgiewissenschaft* 28 (1986): 193–234.

39. Herbert Vorgrimmler, *Understanding Karl Rahner: An Introduction to his Life and Thought* (New York: Crossroad, 1986), 48–69.

40. Lennan, 126–27.

41. Rahner, *Zeitfragen,* 87, 136.

42. Lennan, 135, 139.

43. Ibid., 213, 218.

44. Alister McGrath, *Historical Theology: An Introduction to the History of Christian Thought* (Oxford: Blackwell, 1998), 336–37.

45. Livingston, 209–10; Rahner, *Foundations,* 62, 68, 153; Karl Rahner, "Concerning the Relationship between Nature and Grace," *Theological Investigations,* vol. 1 (Baltimore: Helicon, 1961), 309–17.

46. Werner G. Jeanrod, "From Resistance to Liberation Theology: German Theologians and the Non/Resistance to the National Socialist Regime," in *Resistance*

against the Third Reich, 1993–1990, ed. Michael Geyer and John Boyer (Chicago: University of Chicago Press, 1992), 295.

47. Jürgen Habermas, "Israel oder Athen: Wem gehört anamnetische Vernunft? Johann Baptist Metz zur Einheit in der multikulturellen Vielfalt," in *Diagnösisen der Zeit,* ed. Johann Baptist Metz et al. (Düsseldorf: Patmos, 1994), 51–64; Jeanrond, in Geyer and Boyer, 310–11.

48. Walter Kasper, *Theology and Church,* trans. M. Kohl (New York: Crossword, 1989), 65.

49. O'Meara, *Przywara,* 182–83; Kurt Wolf, "Die katholische Kirche-eine societas perfecta'?" *Theologische Quartalschrift* 157 (1977): 107–18.

Christian Clergy
and the Extreme
Right Wing

5 Working for the Führer

FATHER DR. PHILIPP HAEUSER AND THE THIRD REICH

KEVIN P. SPICER

In December 1930, Dr. Philipp Haeuser stood before the Augsburg members of the National Socialist German Workers' Party (NSDAP) and addressed them: "Today the National Socialists of Augsburg celebrate Christmas. That is a fact. Another fact is: a Catholic priest delivers the address at this Christmas celebration upon the special wish of the National Socialists. Both facts are extremely sad—sad for the self-righteous Pharisees."[1] So began the battle of Father Dr. Philipp Haeuser, a priest of the diocese of Augsburg, specifically for the cause of Hitler—a cause he would support until his last breath. No stranger to right-wing politics, Haeuser had been speaking in behalf of what he called the "German Movement"—broadly and loosely encompassing most right-wing and conservative-nationalistic movements and political parties—since the end of the First World War. However, following his 1930 Christmas address and its subsequent publication in January 1931 by Franz Eher, the NSDAP publishing house, Haeuser would be forever linked to the Nazi party.

Haeuser was just one of a small group of priests, approximately two hundred in number, who, against the wishes of their local ordinaries, either joined or embraced the Nazi party.[2] These brown priests—"brown" because of the official color of Nazi uniforms—radically differed from the rest of the clergymen who had initially shared in the first wave of national enthusiasm for Hitler when he came to power as Reich chancellor. Their allegiance also went far beyond the traditional mode of

German nationalism that the majority of Catholic priests continued to profess throughout the Third Reich.

Brown priests are important in any study of Catholic clergy because they appear at times to have worked together and supported one another to promote state and party goals within their parishes and ministries. In contrast to the majority of their fellow priests and bishops, they did not find the *weltanschauung* of the Nazi Party to be in conflict with Catholic teaching. Instead, they eagerly promoted the party's ideological agenda in their writing and preaching by linking traditional Catholic theological antisemitism with National Socialism's extreme nationalism and lethal antisemitism. Thereby, they created a hybrid Catholic theology—an alternate creed—to accommodate their distorted worldview.

Perhaps the best known of the brown priests in Germany during the Third Reich with the possible exception of his colleague and friend, Abbott Alban Schachleiter, O.S.B., Philipp Haeuser worked tirelessly for the cause of Hitler.[3] Haeuser's devotion was so profound that he put aside his academic career as a biblical exegete and systematic theologian, specializing in patristics, to focus his attention solely on Hitler's cause. Like many of his fellow brown priests, he was a staunch nationalist who despised the Versailles Treaty, the Weimar Constitution with its adoption of democracy, and the participation of his Church in politics, specifically in the Catholic-supported Center Party and Bavarian People's Party. Instead, he advocated support for Hitler and the German Movement. Similar to other brown priests, he professed a great disdain for Jews. However, unlike many of them who only expressed their feelings privately, Haeuser made his beliefs known publicly through his speeches and writings. Throughout his life Haeuser detested Jews and supported Hitler's goals and lethal antisemitism through his public efforts on behalf of the Nazi movement.

Origins

Philipp Haeuser was born on April 23, 1876, in Kempten, into a family of devout Catholics.[4] His father, a lawyer and editor of a local newspaper, and his mother, who came from a noble family, raised Philipp and his three sisters and brother strictly in the Catholic faith.[5] Haeuser professed: "Since I was attached with the most sacred reverence to my parents, I was also devoted to my Catholic faith with the same reverence. I would have considered not sincerely belonging to the Catholic Church as a sin against the fourth commandment, as disregard for my parents."[6] A bright youth, Philipp attended the Gymnasium in Kempten and graduated in 1895. His zealous Catholicism led him to believe he was called to become a priest—a decision, he attested, he made himself.

In 1899, Haeuser still trusted the Catholic Church and his superiors enough to follow through on his call to the priesthood and was ordained on July 20, 1899.[7] Originally, he served as an associate pastor in Bertoldshofen; then he became an instructor of religion at the Royal Teacher Training College in Neuburg and, simultaneously, teacher and chaplain to the Catholic students at the neighboring Neuburg Gymnasium.[8]

While engaging in his initial years in pastoral ministry, Haeuser also continued his theological studies independently. He immersed himself in a study of *The Letter of Barnabas*, a late-first-century noncanonical work written by an unknown author.[9] He also submitted his work to Professor Georg Pfeilschifter, a Church historian at the Albert-Ludwig University of Freiburg im Breisgau, who, to Haeuser's surprise, accepted the work as a dissertation. In July 1911, the university awarded Haeuser a doctorate in theology.

Considering his later life choices, it seems prophetic that Haeuser chose *The Letter of Barnabas* as the subject matter for his first published exegetical work. *Barnabas* is a work openly hostile to Judaism, written in a time when the early Christian community was struggling for its existence. From the content of the *Letter,* one might conclude that any exegete would have preferred to address the work's anti-Jewish element. Haeuser, however, spends an inordinate amount of time juxtaposing the author's representation of Christians, who fully understand God's promises, with the author's negative sketch of Jews, who remained blind to the designs of God.[10]

Evidently, the Church hierarchy, represented by Joseph Schnitz, vicar general of the Diocese of Paderborn,[11] in behalf of Bishop Karl Joseph Schulte, did not find anything in conflict with the Church's teaching in Haeuser's interpretation of the *Letter of Barnabas* and offered an imprimatur prior to its publication in 1912. Over time, Haeuser continued to produce similar studies.

In December 1910, after leaving Neuburg and spending time writing in the Benedictine Abbey in Ettal, Haeuser was forced by Bishop Lingg to accept a parish assignment. Lingg challenged Haeuser: "You were prefect in Neuburg for many years, and now you live in Ettal. But I ordained you to be a pastoral minister!" In reply, Haeuser agreed to accept a parish, but still bucked the authority of his bishop by remaining in Ettal through the end of the 1911 winter semester.[12] Finally, on March 13, 1911, Lingg appointed Haeuser pastor of Straßberg, a tiny working-class town about 7.5 miles outside Augsburg.[13] The parish had fewer than six hundred members and was considered ideal by Haeuser, who wished to continue his scholarly pursuits.[14]

During the First World War, Haeuser remained in his parish and continued to serve the people of Straßberg. Along with the majority of Germans, Haeuser experienced the loss of the Great War as devastating. However, even more destructive in Haeuser's mind was the democratic republic that replaced the empire. Haeuser detested the Weimar Republic and the coalition of parties—the Social Democratic Party, the Center Party, and the German Democratic Party—that formed the first Weimar coalition. He considered all of them—including the Catholic-supported Center—as perfect traitors to Germany. In 1919, he even wrote a letter to Bishop Lingg pleading with him not in any way to lend his support to the revolution and to take a harder line against priests who supported the democratic movement.[15]

According to Haeuser, he never desired to be active politically. However, he attributed his change of mind to the looming threat of Marxism, an insertion of left-wing politics into the new government, and his own "enthusiasm" for his "German fatherland." For this reason, he began to speak out about "what was necessary" to solve these perceived ills plaguing Germany in "the smallest, closest circles" in his parish. "Gradually," he attested, "I was invited to collaborate with different patriotic groups."[16] At first this brought him in contact with parties that favored a monarchical restoration, such as the Bavarian Royalist Party and the Bavarian Home and King's League. Thereafter, Haeuser developed interest in the German National People's Party—a nationalistic, conservative party that rejected the Weimar government and defended Junker agrarian concerns—and, finally, the NSDAP.[17]

Haeuser the Antisemite

Haeuser published *Jew and Christian or to Whom Does World Domination Belong?* in December 1922, and shortly thereafter, a condensed and slightly altered piece, "The Jewish Question from the Standpoint of the Church," both of which specifically identified Jews as enemies of Germany.[18] In these writings, Haeuser informed his readers that he was "strongly nationalistically oriented," endeavored "to be a good patriot," and, as a priest, stood "decidedly on the right."[19] Similarly,

Haeuser assured his readers, that he, "in direct contrast to Nietzsche," not only preached "the cross of Christ," but also desired that one bear "a cross for the Lord through sacrifice of the most difficult nature."[20] For Haeuser, this sacrifice entailed naming the Jew as enemy and ultimately accepting the inevitable criticism from "spiteful readers" who would judge his work to be "shameless Jew-baiting! Danger to the German-Jewish Republic!" However, he affirmed that those who "read and reflected quietly on it will have to conclude: a Christian lesson."[21]

Haeuser's articles were far from a Christian lesson, except to show the world how tainted his faith was because of his antisemitism. In both works, Haeuser intertwined traditional religious antisemitism with more modern fallacies concerning Jews. For example, toward the beginning of *Jew and Christian,* he reinterpreted the Good Samaritan story from the New Testament. In this reinterpretation, the Jews did not even have a chance to "reject" Christ, but instead were "rejected" by Christ. According to Haeuser, Jesus valued "not only the Samaritan more highly than the Jew," but even heathens.[22] In "The Jewish Question," Haeuser intensified Christ's rejection of his own people by portraying him as campaigning "against the leaders of the Jewish people, against the scribes, the Jewish preachers, the representatives of the Jewish law, the inhabitants of Jerusalem."[23]

Though Haeuser embraced a religion-based antisemitism stemming from a misinterpretation of the biblical text, in the early 1920s he drew the line and rejected the *völkisch* portrayal of Jesus when he wrote: "That Jesus in the flesh comes from the Jewish people should not be denied. The fairy tale that Jesus was not a Jew but rather of Aryan birth was invented for national, *völkisch* interests."[24] At this point, Haeuser's theological and exegetical training did not allow him to venture into the realm of fantasy. Despite his unwillingness to embrace the *völkisch* theological interpretation of Jesus' origins, Haeuser was more than willing to incorporate modern economic and politically based antisemitism into his argument. Again, he willingly drew on his patristic studies to bolster his argument.

Haeuser did not limit his argument to examples from the patristic world. Rather, he specifically identified Jews as the main force behind the revolution. In "The Jewish Question," he wrote:

> The revolution is largely a work of the Jews. . . . What has been destroyed in terms of the people's strength and assets during the last four years since the revolution, must be credited many times over to the

Jews. The Jew is now definitely master of the world. In economic and political life, the Christian has become his slave. The Jew through his cleverness, his ruthlessness, his—almost exemplary—determination and tenacity has bound almost all nations and governments to slavish obedience.[25]

Haeuser joined his fellow antisemites and blamed the existence of everything he detested on the Jews: the Weimar constitution, democracy, international conferences, separation of church and state, and the banking industry.[26] Ironically, he considered himself a noble, bold prophet, comparing himself with Stephen, the first Christian martyr, who dared to speak the truth and, therefore, "had to pay with his life in the fight against the Jews."[27] Haeuser inferred that he was ready to make the same sacrifice today.

Though Haeuser did not view Jews as Germans, he was unwilling to advocate direct violence against them. In a footnote in *Jew and Christian,* Haeuser clarified: "We struggle against the Jews not to fight them, but, in the final analysis, because we want to win the Jews for the cross."[28] Here, Haeuser spoke in purely Catholic terms, recognizing the sacrament of baptism as effecting a profound religious categorical change in the convert. Similarly, by recognizing this change and viewing the baptized person now as a Christian, Haeuser revealed that he did not embrace a racial antisemitism based upon unchanging blood. In "The Jewish Question," he emphasized this point even further and proclaimed: "The Jews also have the right to life; our Lord God is also the Lord God of the Jews." Nevertheless, Haeuser qualified his tolerance when he wrote: "In questions of national education and national government, in the important life questions of mankind, not the Jews, but the Christians alone have the last word. . . . No mingling of Jewish and Christian spirit!"[29]

Haeuser was not alone in the beliefs that he professed in his work. Before publication, he submitted *Jew and Christian* to the Regensburg chancery, where the work was published and received an imprimatur from Father Dr. Alphons Maria Scheglmann, vicar general of Regensburg. Furthermore, Father Dr. Kiefl, the Regensburg Cathedral rector, wrote a very positive review of the work: "The work is a direct hit from Haeuser's pen. It is not a matter of doubt that the Jewish question, now that the revolution stands undeniably as the work of Jews, has become a burning issue. Haeuser's work is not an antisemitic inflammatory work. . . . The author moves in an entirely new direction. . . . The

presentation is gripping." Still Kiefl recognized that the work was controversial and acknowledged: "With this work, the courageous and un-
daunted author will also come across protest from the compromise-
prone and the pussyfooters."[30]

Links to the NSDAP

Haeuser not only propagated certain key points of the National Socialist *weltanschauung,* but he also had personal connections
with leading members of the NSDAP. Haeuser's own memoirs testify that
he met with Hitler several times in the early 1920s, when the movement
was in its infancy. Several of the brown priests make similar claims. In the
party's infancy and struggle for power, it was not uncommon for Hitler to
accept whatever support he could obtain to spread his message. A Catholic priest who held a very influential position in a parish and town or city
could easily serve the propaganda needs of the party. Naturally, it is
possible that Haeuser exaggerated his significance in his memoirs to
make himself appear more important than in actuality. Still, in 1939 he
claimed he wrote his memoirs, *My German Struggles and Development,*
for Rudolf Hess, deputy to Hitler, as a testimony to his efforts in behalf of
National Socialism.[31] If Haeuser did send Hess a copy, he took a great risk
with possible penalties for fabricating the truth. Even more telling is his
October 17, 1933, letter to Hess in response to an inquiry for advice
on the appointment of a Catholic to the Board of Governors of the
Catholic Nurses' Association of Germany. Evidently, Hess not only served
as Haeuser's main contact with the NSDAP's upper echelon, but also
sought out Haeuser's advice on Church-related issues—at least in the
initial years after Hitler became Reich chancellor. In his response to Hess,
Haeuser wholeheartedly recommended his friend and fellow brown
priest, Josef Roth, for the position. The tone of the letter betrays an
individual who had known the Nazi movement for a long time. Haeuser
wrote: "Since the beginning of the National Socialist movement [Roth]
has been a participant in it and has through speech and writing supported it under great personal sacrifice. I can attest fully to the German
character and the German loyalty of this man, upon whom the Reich
Ministry can rely in any crisis."[32] Similarly, in March 1933, when the
Illustrierter Beobachter, a NSDAP Party newspaper, offered a profile of
priests who had supported the movement, Haeuser was one of the three
priests chosen for this "honor."[33]

Hitler and Christ the Warrior

After Hitler came to power at the end of January 1933, Haeuser continued to offer sermons and speeches throughout the Augsburg diocese. He gradually "refined" his comparison between Christ and Adolf Hitler and emphasized a link between the work of the Church and the goals of National Socialism. In late May 1934, these comparisons were quite evident during an address he gave before the Kaufbeuren local chapter of the National Socialist Women's Organization. Gathering in the city's town hall, the event began when NSDAP member Bruno Lindenmayer introduced Haeuser as "one of the few who has for more than ten years fought in public against the greatest of our enemies, the Jews. Thereby, he has fought one of the most highly controversial problems and thereby he has paved the way for National Socialism."[34]

During his Kaufbeuren talk, Haeuser sounded more like a programmed National Socialist speaker than a Catholic priest. Instead of addressing Church-related issues, he centered directly upon a variety of key political topics for the National Socialists: the League of Nations, the Versailles Treaty, and disarmament. However, rather than encourage humility, peace, and love of neighbor as a way to approach these issues, Haeuser advocated the exact opposite. For example, Haeuser argued that "toward France" we practiced humility, "but this humility is not Christian, rather it is the cowardice of slaves! . . . the words Christ and Christianity have therefore been misused, since Christianity is the foundation of honor and not of cowardice."[35] Harkening back to his earlier speeches and writings, Haeuser here returned to his theme of a triumphant, militant, manly Christianity that chose battle over forgiveness.

In his address, Haeuser also described Christianity as the foundation not only of honor, but also of National Socialism. He exhorted his listeners to challenge the "unsupported claim" that National Socialism was "unchristian." In response, he argued, one should point out that, from the start, National Socialists stood "in a distinctly Christian movement." Then Haeuser portrayed Hitler, the leader of this movement, as the preeminent Christian, with godlike qualities. Indeed, for Haeuser, Hitler was "the great German soul and the shining star in the spiritual heaven of the German Volk. . . . The German people have had enough occasions to learn much about ethics from Hitler. Therefore, it is above all a moral strength that speaks through him. And in him a powerful Christian person has appeared, not a Jew!" Haeuser then proceeded to make "a marvelous comparison . . . between the struggle of Christ and the struggle of

Hitler." Finally, after elevating Hitler to such moral heights, Haeuser boldly stated that anyone who "poisons the German spirit by fighting against Hitler" ultimately committed a sin against Germany and God.[36]

The coverage that Haeuser's speech received in the *Kaufbeurer Nationalzeitung* left out the details concerning his comparison between Christ and Hitler. Possibly, the reporter did not include this comparison that challenged Church doctrine in an effort to protect Haeuser from censure by his ecclesiastical superiors. However, in a July 1936 address that Haeuser gave to a gathering of various NSDAP organizations in Memmingen, he repeated, and perhaps even intensified, this comparison. At the beginning and several times during his speech, however, Haeuser qualified that he was speaking to a closed gathering and that his words should not in any way be reported to the press. According to a letter to the Augsburg Chancery written by Father Joseph Schmid, the pastor of the Catholic Church in Memmingen, who had received numerous reports and complaints about the contents of the speech, Haeuser stated:

> Christ emphasizes the great law of life (I am the bread of life); He leads the struggle against inaction, against the paragraphs of the synagogue —Hitler does the same today. His highest law is life. . . . There was never a person given so great a task as Hitler. Christ had a great task for his time, now Hitler has an equally challenging task for the present. The past political battles are still a little thing compared to the struggle for weltanschauung, which begins now. . . . Christ could not finish his task, he was crucified. Hitler will see the task through. The struggle was suspended for two thousand years, now it is resumed by someone as great as the former. In religious matters, Hitler is authoritative for me.[37]

Only a year earlier, Haeuser had published *The Warrior Jesus: For Searching and Struggling Germans,* in which he portrayed a heroic, militant, aggressive Christ sent to earth by God in order to establish a Church purified of Jewish practices and traditions. According to Haeuser, "Jesus did not desire to establish a new kingdom peacefully based upon Jewish tradition."[38] In his 1936 address, Haeuser made it even clearer that now it was the task of the Catholic Church to take up the mission of the warrior Christ and join Hitler in his battle to rid Germany of any Jewish influence.

Father Schmid's letter to the Augsburg Chancery forced the diocese to respond. The contents of Schmid's report were too astonishing for chancery officials to dismiss easily. However, first they wanted to ensure that his colleague had actually made the statements contained in the letter. Therefore, in their July 22 reply letter to Schmid, they asked him to name three witnesses who would be willing to testify to the accuracy of the letter. In addition, they centered their concern primarily on a few sentences from the report in which he directly contradicted Church doctrine. Namely, they wanted to know if Haeuser had definitely compared Hitler with Christ and stated that the former was "authoritative" for him "in religious matters." Furthermore, an additional sentence that questioned the role and future of the Church in the German state extremely troubled the chancery officials: "The enemy is not communism, not socialism, but a spiritual force that I do not name and that I have thus named after all."[39] By the contents of the report, it appeared that Haeuser had not only supported Hitler in his antisemitic policies, but also indirectly accused his Church of undermining the German state. Nevertheless, it was clear by the tone of the chancery letter to Father Schmid that the diocese was not overly concerned with Haeuser's antisemitism, but more with his statements that questioned the uniqueness of Christ's mission and the actions of the Church in the German state.

On the same day, chancery officials wrote Haeuser a similar letter to the one they wrote Schmid and demanded to know if he made the statements that witnesses had attributed to him. They also emphasized that the contents of Haeuser's speech had caused people to question whether he really was a Catholic priest.[40] Haeuser immediately replied to the accusations by first attempting to discredit the witnesses by maligning them. In particular, he attacked the veracity of a Protestant woman, who, the chancery had informed Haeuser, had stated: "It shows a complete lack of character that this man still eats the bread of his Church."[41] Not content with only discrediting the witnesses, he attempted to force the chancery to recognize his "accomplishments" by reminding them that he "was not a politician, but a priest" who had helped many National Socialists find their way back to Christianity. If this was not enough, he invited the chancery officials to publish their letter that contained their accusations against him in the public press so that the public could "give its opinion on the truth." According to him, he only recognized that "Hitler is an entirely brilliant personality," but at the same time acknowledged that "Jesus is the religious source. Hitler is a human being, Jesus is God. Nevertheless, even though He is God, He did not wish immediately to end the struggle against evil victorious, just in order to give us a chance to continue the struggle. That such truths were completely misrepresented is not my fault but rather the fault of liars."[42] Interestingly enough, nowhere in his rebuttal did Haeuser refute the accusation that he compared Hitler with Christ. Neither were his comments that different from the original words attributed to him in Father Schmid's report. Furthermore, when Haeuser's comments are compared with his writing in *The Warrior Jesus*, it seems more probable that he did make direct comparisons between Jesus and Hitler in his 1936 Memmingen address.[43]

Denazification

On May 14, 1947, Haeuser's actions during the Third Reich finally caught up with him. The Schwabmünchen Denazification Court declared him a Major Offender and assigned him to Group 1 (Criminals) alongside former Gestapo agents, SS members, and the leadership corps of the NSDAP.[44] The judges sentenced him to five years in Regensburg work camp and ordered that he never hold public office, that he lose all legal claims to pensions, and that he lose his eligibility to vote or be involved in politics.[45]

In their six-page decision, the judges concluded that Haeuser had "in extraordinary ways supported the National Socialist tyranny through propaganda . . . [and] exerted his religious influence on Adolf Hitler and the brown movement." They also doubted Haeuser's claim that "he believed Adolf Hitler wanted to keep the peace." Lastly, the court found that his writing, especially *Jew and Christian*, "provided in many sentences the basic slogans for *Der Stürmer*," with its lethal antisemitism.[46]

Even though life in the work camp was difficult for Haeuser, he relished the opportunities and "benefits" that he received while interned. Since the court had designated him a Major Offender, Haeuser was imprisoned with many former SS men.[47] According to Haeuser, these SS men were "pleasant comrades."[48] He even boasted, "in my room there are four comrades—all were in the SS. One left the Catholic Church. Two left the Protestant Church. One is a Protestant. But they all treat me with the highest respect."[49] It seems while imprisoned Haeuser was able to play the role of chaplain to former Nazis—the same role he had alleged to have originally played among National Socialists prior to 1933. For example, in August 1947, Haeuser wrote his friend Oswald boasting about the events surrounding a visit by Paul Althaus, a Protestant theologian who himself had been extremely nationalistic and open to National Socialism in its early years of power. According to Haeuser, Althaus came "to preach Jesus to the wicked Nazis." When the audience started "to growl," Haeuser volunteered to take over the lecture from Althaus and addressed the room "full of prisoners." Although he described his words as "effective," he assured his friend that he "did not commit a folly." Instead, he "merely awakened enthusiasm among [his] comrades." Then he concluded, "Now even more I believe in new tasks for my life."[50] In a separate letter, Haeuser confided that "once free again," he would "again sacrifice for a great religious and German cause."[51]

By spring 1948, Haeuser's health had deteriorated considerably. The administration of the Regensburg camp took mercy upon the priest and released him early after he had served less than one year of his original sentence.[52] In early 1950, the Appeals Court in Munich reviewed Haeuser's denazification trial and determined that the judgment was too severe. Consequently, they reduced his categorization to Group 3, designated Lesser Offenders.[53] This change of status often became protocol after individuals completed their prison term.[54]

To some of his fellow priests and superiors after the war, Haeuser seemed repentant. However, in his private correspondence, specifically in two letters addressed to his close friend and sympathizer August Oswald, and in a written homily for a small group of sisters, Haeuser revealed himself as an individual who stood unaltered in his belief. He suggested this in September 1958, when he wrote to Oswald: "In German enthusiasm, I happily remembered the great German Movement under Hitler, and the struggle for the Volk against the *unvölkisch* enslavement through financial world powers. In religious enthusiasm, I immersed myself, in order to teach, ever more deeply in the great religious movement under Jesus, and in the religious and spiritual struggle against Jewish and ecclesiastic paralysis and spiritual enslavement."[55] He also suggested this in his homily for the Cistercian sisters on Christmas Day 1958, when he portrayed a Haeuser who had never relinquished his image of a militant Christ ready for battle against the so-called Jewish world influence. He preached: "The peaceful joys in the secluded manger in Bethlehem were the preparation for the hard and bloody life struggle of Jesus. The duty and the goal of the incarnation of Jesus was his life struggle, the struggle for the religion of the spirit and the truth against the paralysis of the Jewish Church. In this hard struggle, Jesus fell at Golgotha."[56] Finally, in a January 28, 1959, letter to Oswald, Haeuser proclaimed: "How gladly I would still speak like in the time of Hitler to the large, educated and leading circles. How it stirs me when I think back!"[57]

Conclusion

Demonstrably, Philipp Haeuser is one of the clearest examples of how a "brown" Catholic priest could become a follower of National Socialism. He devoted his entire life and ministry to the cause of Adolf Hitler and the NSDAP. While imprisoned in the Regensburg work camp, Haeuser had plenty of time to reflect on his activities of the previous twenty-five years. Fully unrepentant of his crimes under National Socialism, Haeuser blamed his diocesan superiors for his arrest and imprisonment. Embittered, he wrote his friend Oswald and asked: "Why had Church officials not come after me earlier with canonical punishments?"[58]

Haeuser asked a perfectly valid question, since as late as 1940, four of his fellow priests had given him positive comments in a routine evaluation of his pastoral ministry. However, they did note that his preaching was "ideologically influenced."[59] A year later, upon his early release from prison, he answered his question in an unpublished essay, "The Church and Denazification."[60] In this fifty-two-page essay, Haeuser not only discussed the selections from his writing that the judges in the denazification court used against him in their ruling, but also briefly examined the history of his Church and fellow clergymen under National Socialism. Through specific factual details, Haeuser revealed the complicity of his Church in supporting and abetting the National Socialist Movement. Ultimately, Haeuser asked: "Am I the only one guilty here?"

NOTES

Research for this essay was supported in part by grants from the American Philosophical Society, the Holocaust Educational Fund, the National Endowment for the Humanities, and Stonehill College. I would like to thank Reinhold Lenski, Jutta Blümel, Dr. Franz-Rasso Böck and Anita Mayr for their kindness and helpfulness during my research in Germany. Let me also thank Ilse Andrews, a dear friend, for her generous assistance while writing this essay.

1. Philipp Haeuser, *Kampfgeist gegen Pharisäertum. Nationalsozialistische Weihnachtsrede eines katholischen Geistlichen* (Munich: Franz Eher, 1931), 5.

2. On the figure of approximately 200 priests who either joined or publicly supported the NSDAP, see Frederic Spotts, *The Churches and Politics in Germany* (Middletown, Conn.: Wesleyan University Press, 1973), 109, and Kevin P. Spicer, "Gespaltene Loyalität. 'Braune Priester' im Dritten Reich am Beispiel der Diözese Berlin," *Historisches Jahrbuch* 122 (2002): 287–320.

3. On Schachleiter, see Roman Bleistein, S.J., "Abt Alban Schachlieter, OSB, Zwischen Kirchentreue und Hitlerkult," *Historisches Jahrbuch* 115 (1995): 170–87, and the National Socialist propaganda biography Gildis Engelhard, *Abt Schachleiter der deutsche Kämpfer* (Munich: n.p., 1941).

4. Philipp Haeuser, *Mein deutsches Ringen und Werden* (manuscript, 1936–39), 1, Stadtarchiv Kempten (StA Kempten), Nachlass Haeuser (NL Haeuser). According to Haeuser, he wrote this "more than 300 page account of [his] political and church difficulties and struggles for Rudolf Hess, deputy to the Führer." Haueser to Merkt, November 6, 1939, StA Kempten NL Haeuser.

5. Reinhold Lenski, "Pfarrer Dr. Philipp Haeuser (1876–1960)—ein Kämpfer für den Nationalsozialismus," 1. Lecture delivered at the 14th Scholarly Meeting of Local Historians in the Administrative District of Schwaben, Irsee, November 29–30, 2002.

6. Haeuser, *Mein deutsches Ringen,* 1.

7. Information Card on Haeuser, Archiv des Bistums Augsburg (ABA), Personalakte (PA) 1410 Haeuser.

8. Haeuser, *Mein deutsches Ringen,* 11.

9. The English text of the *Letter of Barnabas* may be found in *The Apostolic Fathers,* trans. and ed. Kirsopp Lake (Cambridge, Mass.: Harvard University Press, 1952), 335–409.

10. Philipp Haeuser, *Der Barnasbrief neu untersucht und neu erklärt* (Paderborn: Ferdinand Schöningh, 1912), see especially 13–16, 27, 91, and 98.

11. In 1930, Paderborn became an archdiocese.

12. Haeuser, *Mein deutsches Ringen,* 29.

13. Information Card on Haeuser, ABA NL Haeuser.

14. In 1933, the parish had 545 members. *Schematismus der Geistlichkeit des Bistums Augsburg für das Jahr 1933.*

15. Haeuser to Lingg, August 5, 1919, ABA PA 1410 Haeuser.

16. Haeuser, *Mein Werden,* 13.

17. For a brief description of the political parties of the Weimar era see Kirk, *The Longman Companion to Nazi Germany,* 16–20. For a discussion on the nature of the DNVP, see Hans Mommsen, *The Rise and Fall of Weimar Democracy,* trans. Elborg Forster and Larry Eugene Jones (Chapel Hill: University of North Carolina Press, 1996), 51, 67–68; and John A. Leopold, *Alfred Hugenberg: The Radical Nationalist Campaign against the Weimar Republic* (New Haven, Conn.: Yale University Press, 1979).

18. Philipp Haeuser, *Jud und Christ oder Wem gebührt die Weltherrschaft?* (Regensburg: G. J. Manz, 1923). The publisher released *Jud und Christ* in December 1922, though it carried a 1923 copyright date. On this point, see Haeuser, *Mein Werden,* 17. The condensed and slightly revised article is: Philipp Haeuser, "Die Judenfrage vom kirchlichen Standpunkt," *Das Neue Reich* 5 (1923/1924): 442–46.

19. Haeuser, *Jud und Christ,* 15.

20. Ibid., 5–6.

21. Ibid., 6.

22. Ibid., 18–19.

23. Haeuser, "Die Judenfrage," 443.

24. Ibid.

25. Ibid., 442.

26. Ibid., 445.

27. Ibid., 443.

28. Haeuser, *Jud und Christ,* 39.

29. Haeuser, "Die Judenfrage," 445–46.

30. Haeuser, *Mein Werden,* f. 17.

31. Haeuser to Merkt, November 6, 1939, Haueser to Merkt, November 6, 1939, StA Kempten NL Haeuser.

32. Haeuser to Hess, October 17, 1933, Bundesarchiv-Dahlwitz, ZB 1/1411, f. 790.

33. The article also featured profiles of Abbot Alban Schachleiter, O.S.B., and Father Dr. Lorenz Pieper of the archdiocese of Paderborn. *Illustrierter Beobachter,* March 4, 1933. I would like to thank the late Roman Bleistein, S.J., for providing me with this article. On Pieper see Werner Tröster, "'die besondere Eigenart des Herrn Dr. Pieper . . . !' Dr. Lorenz Pieper, Priester der Erzdiözese Paderborn, Mitglied der NSDAP Nr. 9740," in *Das Erzbistum Paderborn in der Zeit des Nationalsozialismus. Beiträge zur regionalen Kirchengeschichte 1933–1945,* ed. Ulrich Wagener (Paderborn: Bonifatius, 1993), 45–91.

34. *Kaufbeurer Nationalzeitung,* May 29, 1934.

35. Ibid.

36. Ibid.

37. Schmid to Augsburg Chancery, July 19, 1936, ABA PA 1410 Haeuser.

38. Father Willibald (Philipp Haeuser), *Der Kämpfer Jesus. Für suchende und ringende deutsche Menschen* (Stuttgart: Wilhelm Schöberl, 1935).

39. Augsburg Chancery to Schmid, July 22, 1936, ABA PA 1410 Haeuser.

40. Augsburg Chancery to Haeuser, July 22, 1936, ABA PA 1410 Haeuser.

41. Augsburg Chancery to Schmid, July 22, 1936, ABA PA 1410 Haeuser.

42. Haeuser to Augsburg Chancery, July 24, 1936, ABA PA 1410 Haeuser.

43. A May 1936 letter from Josefa Boos, an employee of the Landesversicherungsanstalt Schwaben, reported that Haeuser had made similar comments, such as "Adolf Hitler is the light and the life of the world, he is even the greatest soul in the whole world and the best leader of souls," during a recent state-mandated meeting of employees and civil servants. See Boos to Kumpfmüller, May 5, 1936, ABA PA 1410 Haeuser.

44. On the denazification categories see Ordinance No. 79, Table of Categories, Penalties, and Sanctions, US National Archives and Records Administration, OMGUS RG 260 Box 596.

45. Spruchkammer Schwabmünchen Ruling, May 14, 1947, StA Kempten NL Haeuser.

46. Ibid.

47. Haeuser to Frau Oswald, July 11, 1947, Stadtarchiv Bobingen (StA Bobingen) Haeuser Sammlung.

48. Haeuser to Oswald, July 18, 1947, StA Bobingen Haeuser Sammlung.

49. Haeuser to Oswald, August 15, 1947, StA Bobingen Haeuser Sammlung.

50. Haeuser to Oswald, August 29, 1947, StA Bobingen Haeuser Sammlung.

51. Haeuser to Oswald, June 19, 1947, StA Bobingen Haeuser Sammlung.

52. Father Johann Stegmann, administrator of Holy Cross Parish, Straßberg, wrote: "Personally, I have gained the impression that the rebellious spirit that possessed him for so long has left him." Stegmann to Augsburg Chancery, November 8, 1948, ABA PA 1410 Haeuser.

53. Haeuser to Merkt, March 5, 1950, StA Kempten NL Haeuser.

54. Ordinance No. 79, Table of Categories, Penalties, and Sanctions, U.S. National Archives and Records Administration, OMGUS RG 260 Box 596.

55. Haeuser to Oswald, September 1, 1958, StA Bobingen, Haeuser Sammlung.

56. "Mein Weihnachtsansprache 1958 in Oberschönenfeld," StA Bobingen Haeuser Sammlung.

57. Haeuser to Oswald, January 28, 1959, StA Bobingen Haeuser Sammlung.

58. Haeuser to Oswald, December 13, 1947; Haeuser to Oswald, January 28, 1959, StA Bobingen Haeuser Sammlung.

59. Qualification Sheet, 1940, ABA PA 1410 Haeuser.

60. Philipp Haeuser, "Kirche und Entnazifizierung oder War ich Hauptschuldiger?," StA Kempten NL Haeuser.

The Impact of the Spanish Civil War upon Roman Catholic Clergy in Nazi Germany

6

BETH A. GRIECH-POLELLE

On the night of July 17, 1936, civil war broke out in Spain. Soon, many interpreted the events in Spain as an ongoing struggle of the forces of democracy versus the forces of fascism; for others the war represented a struggle between Western Christian civilization and the Bolshevik East. As one historian commented, "Beyond Iberia the civil war embodied and symbolized the conflict between fascism and democracy that ran across the face of Europe."[1]

In 1936, Europe was a land of upheaval and displacement, grappling with the economic depression and a fear of fleeing foreigners. Many Germans, Austrians, and Italians fled Hitler and Mussolini, Romanians hid from the Iron Guard, Poles feared their military dictator, General Pilsudski, and Hungarians suffered under Admiral Horthy's oppressive rule. To many of those who fled their native countries, Spain seemed like the ideal spot to take a stand and fight fascism,[2] while to others Spain seemed to be fertile ground for spreading Bolshevism. In 1936 the Soviet Union doubled its military budget, France ratified an alliance with the Soviet Union, and the populace elected a Popular Front government in Spain.[3] Amid this atmosphere, the events in Spain gripped the imaginations of many people uncertain of their future.

This essay examines the question of how the German government presented the Spanish Civil War to its citizens. I pay particular attention to the Roman Catholic episcopacy's reaction to the portrayal of events in Spain and what impact that portrayal had on the relationship between the Nazi State and the Catholic Church. In the years of 1936–1938, the

Spanish Civil War presented a moment of opportunity whereby German Catholic Church leaders could align themselves more closely to the Nazi State. As part of this alignment, many Church leaders implicitly embraced the idea that behind the Republican forces stood a vast "Judeo-Bolshevik conspiracy" intent on destroying Christian civilization.

Spanish Civil War

The anticlerical fury unleashed by the Republican forces was unavoidable. In the opening months of the Spanish Civil War, these forces murdered more Catholic priests—approximately seven thousand would be dead by 1939—than ever before in modern history. The attacks on clergy, on churches, and on Church-related institutions led the Jesuit superior general in Rome, Wladimir Ledochowski, to advise Pope Pius XI that the Spanish Civil War was "in fact inspired by Soviet Russia as part of a plan to destroy religion everywhere."[4]

As leader of the Roman Catholic Church, Pius XI saw that the majority of the Spanish ruling hierarchy had sided with the Nationalists. He also saw that they were calling for a new crusade to defend Christianity. Pius XI gave his blessing "to those who have assumed the difficult and dangerous task of defending and restoring the rights and honor of God and of religion."[5] Catholics throughout Europe distributed copies of Pius's first papal statement from September 14, 1936, delivered after a meeting with five hundred Spanish pilgrims at Castel Gandolfo, in which the pontiff sympathized with the suffering clergy by using phrases such as "martyrdom in the full . . . satanic preparation similar in kind to those in Russia, China, South America and Mexico."[6] By 1937, Pius drew a distinction between a just and an unjust war by arguing that those who had rebelled were not intrinsically evil. In his encyclical *Divini Redemptoris,* Pius mentioned the Spanish Civil War in only one paragraph, but in that paragraph he wrote, "Communist fury had destroyed churches and clergy, killing people in Spain because they [were] good Christians or at least opposed to atheistic Communism."[7] By May 1938, Pius had formally recognized the Nationalist regime in Spain.

The Ministry of Propaganda and Enlightenment directed by Joseph Goebbels served as the main source of German domestic coverage of the Spanish Civil War. Between July 17 and December 31, 1936, Goebbels recorded in his diary at least seventy entries on the events in Spain. These entries repeatedly mentioned an obsession Goebbels shared with Hitler: the so-called link between "Jewishness" and communism.[8]

In July 1936, the opening salvo began when Goebbels's propaganda ministry issued detailed instructions on how the German press should report the civil war. The ministry informed the press that they must not refer to Franco's troops as "rebels" nor refer to the uprising as a coup or rebellion. Furthermore, they instructed reporters to call the Republican side simply "the Bolshevists" and make no mention of German military involvement.[9] In addition to these instructions, during the September National Socialist Party's Nuremberg Congress, Goebbels spoke publicly about how Europe might possibly never recover its health if Germany allowed international Bolshevism to flourish.[10] Following this, on September 11, 1936, the National Socialist *Völkischer Beobachter* reported that Goebbels described Bolshevism as "pathological criminal nonsense, demonstrably thought up by Jews," and now, under Jewish leadership, it aimed to destroy "civilized European nations" and to create a world dominated by Jews.[11]

On September 14, 1936, during the same Congress, Hitler followed Goebbels's line of argumentation by stressing the impending Bolshevistic threat. In addition, he contrasted the events in Spain with his accomplishments in Germany by stating, "What a difference to another country, where Marxism is attempting to gain power. There the cities burn, there the villages sink into debris and rubble. There people don't know each other anymore. Class fights against class, profession against profession, brother destroys brother. We have chosen the other path: Instead of tearing you apart, I have united you."[12] By using such manipulative language and vivid imagery, Hitler connected every blow leveled against the Republic to a victory in Nazi Germany's war against the "Jewish-Communist International."

National Socialist Propaganda

To ensure the success of his government's and party's anti-Bolshevist goals, Goebbels initiated in his ministry a special section simply called Anti-Comintern. By late 1936, he had appointed Willi Kohn as the German propaganda attaché at the Nationalist headquarters in Salamanca. By December 22, 1936, Kohn had established a National Socialist–controlled radio station. Goebbels urged Kohn to work quickly since he believed that if Spain fell to Bolshevism, Portugal would follow and soon all of South America. Not only would this represent a dramatic ideological loss for Germany, but it would also spell disaster in terms of obtaining raw materials from these countries.[13] Following Goebbels's instructions, Kohn downplayed National Socialist neo-paganism and emphasized a crusade to sweep away Judeo-Bolshevism.[14] Kohn and Goebbels agreed that antisemitism was alive and well in Spain by smugly noting that Spanish publishing houses had reprinted the fictional *Protocols of the Elders of Zion* five times over a six-year period.[15]

Joseph Goebbels's booklet *The Truth about Spain* became one of his best-known publications. In thirty-six pages, he pretended to be an objective agent of truth and reality. He told his German and Spanish readers that they had to make a straightforward choice of either Bolshevism with its "destruction and anarchy" or authority composed of "order and construction." Goebbels easily made the link for the leader between Bolshevism and Judaism by stating that "the internationality of Bolshevism" was mainly "determined by the Jews. As a Bolshevist the Jew becomes indeed the incarnation of all evil." As if this was not enough, Goebbels emphasized how this was not simply a struggle for Spain. Rather, he argued that the Jews were preparing this struggle with all their means since they "need it as the introduction for Bolshevist world rule."[16]

How would the Jews plan to overtake the world as they worked their way through Spain? Goebbels answered this question with biological language and imagery. Repeatedly, he used phrases that would dehumanize Jews by turning the enemy into a faceless, abstract force of evil: "communism poisons the world," "workers are infected," "communist agents are infested," "international carriers of bacilli," "Communist society suggests degeneration and disintegration," "the Reds," "the Red mob," "the red Jewish henchmen," "the sons of chaos," and "the red plague."[17] These left his readers with no doubt about their precarious health situation due to this fast-spreading Jewish-Bolshevistic infection. However, Goebbels did hold out a ray of hope to his readers by stating that there was one man who had the ability to cure this disease: "The Führer comes to us as a savior" who can save "us from the red inundation."[18] By such lines of argumentation, Goebbels forced the link between communism and Judaism and assured his readers that only Hitler could save them from complete and utter ruin.

The German Catholic Church

In 1936, the Spanish Civil War was not the only issue of dominant concern for German Catholics. Rather, they also had to contend with an increase in government-sponsored persecutions of their priests and associations. In addition, the German government had begun to confiscate many of Germany's monasteries and convents through actions that often forced its residents into the streets devoid of any earthly possessions. The government also had begun a steady campaign to defame the Church's clergymen through highly publicized show trials, including notorious foreign currency trials and semi-pornographic morality trials. No less harmful, although slightly less public, were the countless incidents of harassment and arrest of priests for alleged transgression of German state laws. In all of these actions Catholics could see signs of an impending *Kulturkampf* that would ultimately brand Catholics as enemies of the Reich. In view of these numerous contentious issues, many members of the Catholic hierarchy began to search for ways that they might improve their relations with the National Socialist state.

One clear point of convergence was the issue of German patriotism. On March 7, 1936, when Hitler marched German troops into the demilitarized zone of the Rhineland, Catholic priests bestowed blessings on the units as they approached the bridges. In addition, Clemens August Graf von Galen, bishop of Münster, assured German Catholics that they should walk in step with all "true German citizens." He also reminded them that "a large part of National Socialism should be welcomed, especially its anti-Communism and national-aggressive foreign policy." In an effort to prove that Catholics were loyal to the National Socialist state, Galen pointed out the common enemy for both Church and state: communism.[19]

Like so many other Catholic Church leaders, Galen believed that the real threat to Germany's future, if not all of Europe's, was atheistic communism and socialism. Once the civil war broke out in Spain, he dominated his sermons with concerns for Christianity menaced by the spread of Marxism. The only way he could see to combat the spread of radicalism was to maintain the practice of Christianity. He argued, "atheism and Bolshevism go hand in hand."[20] In this respect, Galen wholeheartedly endorsed the National Socialist portrayal of events in Spain. Hitler had told the German people that defeat of Franco's forces would mean victory for Bolshevism over Europe. As the National Socialist government exploited the civil war to gain support for their fight against Bolshevism, Galen encouraged Catholics to fight against the dangers posed by such a godless system.

Quoting 1 Corinthians 12:27, "Now you together are Christ's body, but each of you is a different part of it," Galen preached that destiny had linked Spain's fate with that of Christian Europe's. Only through prayer and vigilance could the "pestilent Communist infection" be overcome.

Telling his parishioners that communism produced estrangement from the teachings of Christianity, hatred of God, and self-destruction, he prayed that the "infection" would not spread to his beloved Germany.[21]

Galen did not confine the expression of his fears to his parishioners and other clergymen. Rather, he drafted a letter to Hitler asking why the chancellor had endorsed the Concordat in one breath and had denounced ultramontanism in another. Quoting from Hitler's *Mein Kampf*, Galen sought to prove to Hitler that Catholics were good and true Germans, unlike the enemy Bolsheviks. The civil war in Spain gave Galen an opportunity to remind all of his various audiences that communism stood in direct opposition to Catholicism. He argued against the state's portrayal of Catholics as being in league with communists, and he pointed out that the Church and Hitler had similar goals: Hitler wanted to destroy communists, and the pope wanted to convert them. Galen believed that ultimately both leaders had the same goal: the complete eradication of communism from European soil.[22]

Did Galen link communism with Judaism? The imagery of the Jews employed by Galen in his sermons leaves one with the feeling that Jews were responsible for their own damnation. His continuing fear of "godless communism," the subtle suggestion that Jews were behind the forces of communism, and his ultranationalism "made him and the whole German episcopacy useful in propping up the Third Reich."[23] The bishop lumped together Bolshevism, communism, Marxism, atheism, and liberalism. To him, all these were foreign, Jewish ideologies that gradually worked to destroy German culture and society. In a draft of a petition to Hitler, Galen agreed with what Hitler had written in *Mein Kampf*: "International Communism is the greatest enemy of the people." Quoting extensively from Hitler's work, Galen claimed that German bishops would continue to fight both old and new enemies, including Freemasons, Marxists, rationalists, and liberals.[24] By emphasizing the shared enemy communism, Galen hoped to solidify Catholicism's place in the state. Similar to Hitler, Galen saw a link between communism and Jewishness.

In a letter to Alfred Meyer, Gauleiter of Münster, Galen again revealed his mastery of *Mein Kampf* by quoting Hitler's concerns about international communism. However, he went one step further in his letter by stating that, according to Hitler, an individual who helped create religious strife, as the communists did, was "whether knowingly or unknowingly . . . a fighter for Jewish interests." The bishop reprimanded Meyer and advised him to stop distributing material that offended "Christian-thinking National Socialists."[25]

In August 1936, the bishops met for their annual conference at Fulda. The discussion of the Spanish Civil War dominated the meetings. Everyone present offered to share in the fight against the spread of Bolshevism. To alert German Catholics about this fear, the German bishops produced a joint pastoral letter in which they fundamentally accepted the National Socialist presentation of the role of Bolsheviks in the Spanish Civil War. In the letter the joint episcopacy stated:

> We start from the obvious fact and conviction that Communism and Bolshevism are at present trying with diabolical determination and toughness to advance into the heart of Europe, putting it in grave danger. Therefore, German unity should not be sacrificed to religious antagonism, quarrels, contempt, and struggles. Rather our national power of resistance must be increased and strengthened so that not only may Europe be freed from Bolshevism by us, but also that the whole civilized world may be indebted to us.[26]

In this section of the pastoral letter, the bishops bargain with the National Socialist regime. In return for the Church's commitment to fight tirelessly against Bolshevism, the bishops expected the National Socialist state to stop its persecution of the Church, its institutions, and associations.[27] The bishops' pastoral letter revealed how they had adopted a one-sided interpretation of the events in Spain with one significant difference: they had replaced Nazism, as the strongest opponent of Bolshevism, with Catholic belief. This was the equivalent of waving a red shirt in front of a bull since Hitler truly believed that he, not the Catholic Church, was the leader in the fight against Bolshevism. Naively, the bishops thought that their support in the fight against Bolshevism would result in a lessening of state persecution of the Church. This maneuver did not pay off. As Gerhard Besier concluded, "Neither its loyalty to the state nor its support for anti-Bolshevism could persuade the Nazi state to accept protest or criticism of its own actions."[28] As a result of the incorporation of a fairly poorly worded protest of state mistreatment of Catholic interests, the state forbade the publication of the pastoral letter.[29]

During the September 1936 Nuremberg Congress, Hitler attacked the Bolshevik danger, as did many other Nazi Party functionaries. Coincidentally, the same day Hitler made his speech, Pope Pius XI had his meeting with the five hundred Spanish refugees. In a publication from the Trier diocese a chancery official wrote, "The coincidence that these two great speeches were delivered on the same day and the congruence of their main ideas appear to us as convincing demonstration of what the hour demands; to wit, a sympathetic cooperation of state and church in Germany for the combined fight against the common enemy."[30] Soon thereafter, Simon Konrad Landersdorfer, O.S.B., at his enthronement as bishop of Passau, declared, "Bolshevism . . . today was the fiercest enemy of the Catholic Church, as events in Soviet Russia, Mexico and Spain sufficiently proved. If nothing else, the need to repel this mutual foe dictated the harmonious collaboration of Church and State."[31] Through the statements, the German hierarchy seemingly embraced the interpretation of the *Völkischer Beobachter* on the Spanish Civil War. According to its editor, the disaster in Spain was due to "Jewish-Bolshevist revolution," something the Church should realize was a consequence of a "Jewish-Marxist invasion of Germany and Europe and, therefore, the destruction of Western Christian culture."[32]

The Turning Point

Because of the growing atmosphere for potential collaboration between the German Catholic Church and the German state, Nuncio Cesare Orsenigo arranged for Cardinal Michael von Faulhaber, bishop of the archdiocese of Munich and Freising, to have a private meeting with Hitler. On November 4, 1936, Faulhaber traveled to Hitler's mountain retreat near Berchtesgaden. During their encounter, Hitler pulled out all the stops and played the part of the gracious host. He impressed the cardinal immensely by his reasonableness. As a result of this three-hour meeting, the German bishops agreed to mend their disagreements with the National Socialist state.

According to Faulhaber's account of the meeting, the atmosphere during the first hour was quite tense as Hitler dominated the conversation. The topic on the agenda was the possible success of Bolshevism in Spain. Gradually, over the course of the three hours, Faulhaber remarked that there was an easing of tension between the two powerful men. Eventually, this led Hitler to invite Faulhaber to dine with him.[33] How did the men reach such a congenial conclusion at the end of their day?

Hitler told Faulhaber that religion was critical for the state, for society, and for the soldier, stating: "Man cannot exist without belief in God. The soldier who for three or four days lies under intense bombardment needs a religious prop."[34] While this was not exactly a ringing

endorsement on the value of religion, Hitler told the cardinal that prag-
matically speaking, the Church had to join in the fight against Bolshevism or "the Church and Christianity in Europe too are finished. Bolshevism is the mortal enemy of the Church as much as it is of Fascism."[35] In
reply, Faulhaber explained that the Church had traditionally and consistently spoken out against the threat of Bolshevism. The cardinal was
eager to remind Hitler of the pope's words against Bolshevism and its
dangers. To Faulhaber's mind, much like Bishop Galen's, the two approaches of pontiff and Führer were not incompatible. As Besier concluded, at this point "the Rubicon was crossed. While the Episcopal
conference at Fulda had carefully avoided explicitly accepting the antisemitic element in Nazi anti-Bolshevism, it now accepted it, implicitly
and tacitly."[36] By choosing to agree with the National Socialist portrayal
of the war, the Catholic hierarchy gave further legitimacy to fears of a
"Judeo-Bolshevik conspiracy."

Toward the close of the meeting, Hitler argued that his goal was to
protect the German people from "congenitally afflicted criminals such
as now wreak havoc in Spain." Faulhaber immediately replied, "The
Church, Mr. Chancellor, will not refuse the state the right to keep these
pests away from the national community within the framework of moral
law."[37] Pleased with this response, Hitler commented:

> Think about all this, Cardinal, and consult with the other leaders of the
> Church how you can support the great undertaking of National Social-
> ism to prevent the victory of Bolshevism and how you can achieve a
> peaceful relationship to the state. Either National Socialism and the
> Church are both victorious or they perish together. Rest assured, I shall
> do away with all those small things that stand in the way of a harmo-
> nious cooperation. . . . I do not wish to engage in horse trading.
> You know that I am opposed to compromises, but let this be a last
> attempt.[38]

Once Cardinal Faulhaber left his meeting with Hitler, on November
18, he met with leading members of the German hierarchy of cardinals to
ask them to warn their parishioners against the errors of communism.
On November 19, Pius XI announced that communism had moved to
the head of the list of "errors" and that a clear statement was needed.[39]
Then, on November 25, Faulhaber informed the Bavarian bishops that he
had promised Hitler that the bishops would issue a new pastoral letter in
which they condemned "Bolshevism which represents the greatest danger for the peace of Europe and the Christian civilization of our country."

In addition, he stated, the pastoral letter "will once again affirm our loyalty and positive attitude, demanded by the Fourth Commandment, toward today's form of government and the *Führer*."[40] The original time-table set for this announcement was December 13; however, before the bishops released it, the German government suppressed it because of its reference to state violations against the Reich-Vatican Concordat.[41]

This did not deter Cardinal Faulhaber. He immediately set to work on another draft of the letter that he submitted to the German bishops. On December 24, 1936, the bishops gave German Catholics a unique Christmas present. The German joint hierarchy ordered its priests to read the pastoral letter, entitled "On the Defense against Bolshevism," from all their pulpits on January 3, 1937.[42] The pastoral letter's text revealed the capitulation of Faulhaber to Hitler's wishes:

> Bolshevism has begun its march from Russia to the countries of Europe, especially to our country, and its aim is to overthrow here as everywhere every social system and every system of government, to destroy economic affluence and to annihilate religious life. Russian Bolshevism controls a large number of able-bodied men and raw material in abundance as in no other European nation. . . . The fateful hour has come for our nation and for the Christian culture of the Western world. . . . The *Führer* and Chancellor Adolf Hitler saw the march of Bolshevism from afar and turned his mind and energies towards averting this enormous danger from the German people and the whole Western world. The German bishops consider it their duty to do their utmost to support the leader of the Reich with every available means in this defense. Since Bolshevism is the mortal enemy of the system of government, since it is primarily the gravedigger of religious culture, and always attacks the servants and sacred places of church life, as the Spanish events recently proved, since it is the question of the survival of church order, so it is clear that support for the struggle against this diabolical power must become an important task of the contemporary Church.[43]

The bishops also warned Catholics that, as they mobilized their spiritual and moral forces to combat diabolical Bolshevism, they should not fall into discontent, as "such a mood has always provided fertile soil for Bolshevik sentiments."[44]

Through this letter, Faulhaber had lived up to his promise to Hitler. The German Catholic Church now publicly endorsed the German government's interpretation of the Spanish Civil War and confirmed the Church's willingness to fight against the spread of Bolshevism. Although the letter did not contain any outwardly antisemitic statements, it did reinforce the National Socialist interpretation of the events in Spain, namely that the Nationalists fought a valiant battle against Bolshevism that was a "product of Jewry intent on destroying Christian European culture."[45]

Hitler's promise to Faulhaber, to clear up "small" problems between the Catholic Church and the Nazi State, never did materialize. Nevertheless, Faulhaber, together with Galen and Pope Pius XI, continued to preach against Bolshevism. They could not understand why the National Socialist state and party continued to persecute their Church, especially since their fight against Bolshevism made them natural allies.

A few Catholic priests, including a Jesuit, Father Friedrich Muckermann, originally from Münster but living in exile in the Netherlands, did voice their disapproval of the hierarchy's stance. For example, when the pastoral letter against Bolshevism reached Muckermann, the exiled priest was dumbstruck. He commented, "despite the inhuman brutalities perpetrated in the concentration camps, despite the currency and defamation trials, despite the personal insults against individual princes of the Church, against the Holy Father, and the entire Church, and in spite of all hostile measures amounting to another Kulturkampf . . . the bishops find words of appreciation for what (next to Bolshevism) is their worst enemy."[46] Muckermann tried to reach a wider audience by publishing *Der Deutsche Weg* each week with his anti-Nazi positions. In these endeavors he was not totally alone as there was an anonymous person(s) in Paris publishing *Kulturkampf* three times a month. Yet even in *Kulturkampf*, an article ran alleging that "if the Nazis would only stop their attacks against the Church, National Socialism and the German Catholics could again become allies."[47] This was truly in keeping with the attitudes of most of the members of the German Catholic hierarchy: if the Nazi government would halt its anti-Catholic attacks, Germany could be made stronger with the full weight of the force of Catholic ideology there to join in the state's battle against the Bolshevik threat.

The obstinate behavior of Hitler's regime, demanding total subordination to Nazi worldviews, led many in the Catholic episcopacy to narrow their criticisms of National Socialism rather than condemn their own government. However, they did not remain silent when the state disbanded and outlawed Catholic unions, workers' associations, and other organizations. Nor were they afraid to speak out when the Gestapo censured and closed down Catholic presses and newspapers. They were not silent when the Gestapo and SS confiscated cloisters, seminaries, and convents or when the state removed crucifixes from school classrooms. They were not silent on the issue of divorce or euthanasia. Nor were they silent on what they perceived to be the greatest threat of all, world domination by a Bolshevik International. What they were silent about was persecution of minorities, the general assault on human rights, and the deadly issue of Jewish persecution.

In the spring of 1939, General Franco, suffering with the flu in bed, declared the Spanish Civil War over. Bishop Galen joyfully exclaimed that the outcome had proved God's power over atheistic communism. Noting again how his Church had fought communism for decades, Galen warned Catholics that godless communism was still a threat, because of Moscow and its desire to defeat Christianity.[48] By this time, the Nazi propaganda machine had slowed down its attacks on world-Bolshevism as the foreign office was preparing the groundwork for the German-Soviet nonaggression pact. Instead, the National Socialist government decided to focus its attack on Western liberal democracies, further disappointing the leaders of the German Catholic Church. Many Church leaders had compromised themselves many times over to appease the German government, yet the expected rewards had not come. The most positive of Catholic leaders believed that Hitler's annexation of Austria and the Sudetenland, which bolstered the German Catholic population to nearly 43 percent, was enough of a reward that it led Cardinal Adolf Bertram to exclaim, "Now we are truly a People's Church."[49] However, in June 1941, there would be much greater rejoicing among the leaders of the German Catholic Church when another fight against Bolshevism began with the German army invading the Soviet Union. Then, once again, Catholic Church leaders believed they could move closer to Hitler's government, united in their fear and hatred of the common foe.

Conclusion

The Spanish Civil War aroused intense passions in Europe and abroad. The fighting seemed to speak to an entire generation. Historian Keith Watkins, writing on the worldwide impact of the Spanish Civil War, said it was "a mirror into which men gazed and cast back at them not a picture of reality, but the image of the hopes and fears of their generation."[50] Jose M. Sanchez argued that the mirror reflected the issues that divided their own nations, as foreigners came to superimpose their own religious tensions and relations upon the Spanish war. It was easier for Protestants in Anglo-Saxon countries and anti-clericals everywhere to support the Republicans because—aside from the political and social issues—the Republicans were anti-Catholic or anticlerical. Catholics came to support the Nationalists, not because they favored the Nationalists' authoritarian political views, but because Nationalists supported the Church, an institution under attack in their own countries.[51]

As for the members of the Catholic Church in Nazi Germany, they certainly felt that they were under attack in their own country. They desired to have a working relationship with their government and found it difficult to believe when Hitler used them for his own propaganda purposes and then abandoned them with empty promises.

On January 30, 1939, a successful Hitler, enjoying his foreign policy achievements, spoke before the Reichstag. He answered the charge that Germany was an antireligious state by arguing that the government had not closed any churches, had not cut off church subsidies, and had not stopped any church services. He then boldly challenged Western governments, "If certain democratic statesmen interceded on behalf of a few German priests, they remained silent when hundreds of thousands of priests and nuns were cut down in Russia and Spain. These were facts that could not be denied, yet the democratic statesmen remained silent while numerous National Socialist and Fascist volunteers had put themselves at the disposal of General Franco to prevent the bloody persecution of Bolshevism from overspreading Europe."[52]

The imagery of the Spanish Civil War fell easily into the black and white categories of "Fascism versus Democracy" and "Catholicism versus Communism" for many people, including members of the Roman Catholic Church in National Socialist Germany. Ignoring the complexity of the war, the German Catholic episcopacy supported the fight against the forces of Bolshevism wholeheartedly, and by doing so, they implicitly accepted the National Socialist definition of what was supposedly behind the atheistic system. They accepted Hitler's portrayal of the "Judeo-Bolshevik conspiracy," aimed at world conquest: "We German National Socialists were never afraid of Communism. We alone recognized this shameful Jewish doctrine of world aggression, we studied its diabolic methods and warned of its consequences." The Catholic Church hierarchy believed that Hitler had missed the point that the Catholic Church and the state could align themselves in the battle against their common enemy of Judeo-Bolshevism.

NOTES

1. Michael Jackson, *Fallen Sparrows: The International Brigades in the Spanish Civil War* (Philadelphia: American Philosophical Society, 1994), 12.

2. Ibid., 42–43.

3. Gerhard Besier, "Bolshevism and Antisemitism: The Catholic Church in Germany and National Socialist Ideology, 1936–37," *Ecclesiastical History* 43 (1992): 448.

4. Jose M. Sanchez, *The Spanish Civil War as a Religious Tragedy* (Notre Dame, Ind.: University of Notre Dame Press, 1987), 123.

5. Guenter Lewy, *The Catholic Church in Nazi Germany* (New York: McGraw-Hill, 1964), 312.

6. Sanchez, 123.

7. Ibid., 126–27.

8. Robert H. Whealey, "Nazi Propagandist Joseph Goebbels Looks at the Spanish Civil War," *Historian* 61 (1999): 1.

9. Christoph Eykman, "The Spanish Civil War in German Publications during the Nazi Years," in *German and International Perspectives on the Spanish Civil War: The Aesthetics of Partisanship*, ed. Luis Costa et al. (Columbia, S.C.: Camden House, 1992), 166.

10. Zbynek A. B. Zeman, *Nazi Propaganda* (London: Oxford University Press, 1964), 94.

11. Ibid., 94.

12. Eykman, 168.

13. Whealey, "Nazi Propagandist Joseph Goebbels," 3.

14. Ibid., 4.

15. Ibid., 8.

16. Peter Monteath, "The Nazi Literature of the Spanish Civil War," in L. Costa, et al., 131–32.

17. Eykman, 174–75.

18. Monteath, 133.

19. *Kirchliches Amtsblatt für die Diozese Münster,* March 7, 1936; Stefan Rahner et al., *Treu deutsch sind wir—wir sind auch treu katholisch: Kardinal von Galen und das Dritte Reich* (Münster: Wurf, 1987), 30; "Predigt v. Galens," February 23, 1936," *Bischof Clemens August Graf von Galen: Akten, Briefe und Predigten, 1933–46*, vol. 1, ed. Peter Loeffler (Mainz: Matthias Grünewald, 1988), 350.

20. "Hirtenbrief v. Galens," October 1, 1936, Loeffler, 1:451.

21. "Hirtenbrief v. Galens," August 14, 1936, Loeffler, 1:424.

22. "Predigt v. Galens," March 6, 1938, Loeffler, 1:609 and 612.

23. Rahner et al., *Treu deutsch sind wir,* 48.

24. "Entwurf v. Galens für eine Denkschrift an Hitler," May 1935, Loeffler, 1:206–21, here 206.

25. "Galen to Meyer," June 3, 1935, Loeffler, 1:228–29.

26. Cited in Besier, 451.

27. Ibid., 452.

28. Ibid., 453.

29. Lewy, 206–207.

30. Ibid., 207.

31. Ibid.

32. Besier, 449.

33. Ludwig Volk, S.J., ed., *Akten Kardinal Michael Faulhabers, 1917–1945*, vol. 2 (Mainz: Matthias Grünewald, 1978), 184–94.

34. Ibid., 236.

35. Ibid., 207.

36. Besier, 453.

37. Ibid.

38. Lewy, 208.

39. Peter Godman, *Hitler and the Vatican: Inside the Secret Archives that Reveal the New Story of the Nazis and the Church* (New York: Free Press, 2004), 128.

40. Lewy, 208.

41. Godman, 131.

42. Ernst C. Helmreich, *The German Churches under Hitler: Background, Struggle, and Epilogue* (Detroit, Mich.: Wayne State University Press, 1979), 279.

43. Besier, 454–55.

44. Lewy, 210.

45. Besier, 456.

46. Lewy, 211.

47. Ibid.

48. "Hirtenbrief v. Galens," April 1, 1939, Loeffler, 1:713–14.

49. Richard Grunberger, *The Twelve Year Reich: A Social History of the Third Reich* (New York: Da Capo, 1971), 449.

50. Sanchez, 159.

51. Ibid.

52. Cited in Helmreich, 299.

7 Faith, Murder, Resurrection

THE IRON GUARD AND THE ROMANIAN ORTHODOX CHURCH

PAUL A. SHAPIRO

Romanian antisemitism had deep roots in the teachings of the Romanian Orthodox Church. In the first half of the twentieth century, unschooled local priests in rural areas, theology faculty at the country's universities, and the national leadership of the Church hierarchy, including the Patriarch himself, openly professed antisemitic views and preached antisemitic stereotypes. They spread intolerance and hatred in language of greater or lesser sophistication, according to the audience being addressed. The antisemitic political parties and fascist movements that emerged in the first half of the twentieth century, including the Legion of the Archangel Michael, or Iron Guard, relied heavily on this Church-disseminated antisemitism in order to establish their rapport with the population at large.[1]

Even as Romania's fascist movements—from the late 1920s dominated by the Iron Guard—moved beyond traditional religious antisemitism to promote economic, cultural, and racial antisemitism and violence against Jews and what they perceived to be a "Judaized" establishment, they did not abandon religious belief, Orthodox symbolism, and spirituality as key components of their dogma. Religious language and symbolism permeated the speeches, poetry, and songs of the Iron Guard. The youth movement of the Iron Guard had its stronghold in the Faculty of Theology of the University of Bucharest. After the assassination in 1938 of Corneliu Zelea Codreanu, the movement's founder, ceremonies and writings replete with the symbolism of resurrection and eternal life clearly raised the question of whether Codreanu, suspected by many of seeking to replace Romania's King Carol II in life, might not—in the minds of his followers at least—have been destined to replace Jesus himself in death.

The Iron Guard did not hold a monopoly on the intertwining of religion and extreme right-wing politics. Other extremist movements that emerged following World War I, such as the League of National Christian Defense and the Crusade of Romanianism, embraced anti-semitism and Romanian Orthodoxy as fundamental elements of their political creeds. Later, the Patriarch of the Romanian Orthodox Church promulgated the country's first explicitly racial antisemitic laws, while he was serving as the first prime minister of King Carol II's dictatorship in 1938–39. After Carol II was forced from the throne, and following the short-lived National Legionary State in which the Iron Guard held a share of power (September 1940–January 1941), wartime dictator Ion Antonescu postured himself as the defender of Christianity against god-less Judeo-Bolshevism.

In the concluding months of the war and following the final defeat of Nazi Germany, the leadership of the Iron Guard (which had lived under protective detention in Germany since a failed coup attempt against Antonescu in January 1941) recognized that it would not soon return to Romania. It was no surprise, given the movement's intimate iden-tification with Romanian Orthodoxy and the large number of priests who had supported the Iron Guard, that Codreanu's successor, Horia Sima, established a Church structure subordinate to the short-lived "Na-tional Government" he headed in Vienna during the final months of the war. At war's end, the Iron Guard leadership consciously pursued a plan to retain a measure of its influence by taking over Romanian Ortho-dox Church organizations outside of Romania. In the 1960s and 1970s, investigations revealed that the Romanian Orthodox archbishops of France and the United States and the Romanian Orthodox parish priest in Washington, D.C., as well as a number of other Orthodox clergy in the Romanian diaspora, had been members and leadership cadres of the Iron Guard in the 1930s. In their postwar exile, émigré intellectuals such as the Romanian-American icon of Eastern religions, Mircea Eliade, and French literary colossus, Emil Cioran, among others, who had been advocates of Romanian spirituality (*Românism*, or "Romanianism"), were shown to have been Iron Guard ideologues in their youth.[2] All of these developments were reminders that Romanian fascism and Roma-nian Orthodoxy were not adversarial but tightly intertwined.

Foundations on the Pre-fascist Extreme Right

Before the emergence of the Legion of the Archangel Michael, or Iron Guard, as the predominant movement of the radical Right, a number of smaller, sometimes short-lived, but still noteworthy ultranationalist and xenophobic movements appeared on the Romanian political scene, each seeking to establish itself in the turbulent decades that immediately preceded and followed World War I.[3] Each movement was typically built around one or two charismatic individuals. Each frequently borrowed ideas, approaches, and members from the others and, in turn, merged or separated and cooperated or competed according to personal as well as political factors that developed over time.

What is striking is that virtually all of these movements included strong identification with Romanian Orthodoxy and vehement antisemitism as fundamental principles of their political credos. Given the decades-long pre–World War I debate over the issue of granting citizenship rights to non-Christians, Jews in particular, and the role that had been played by the Romanian Orthodox Church in sustaining Romanian cultural identity during more than three centuries of Ottoman suzerainty, this was not particularly surprising. The forced granting of citizenship to Jews, as a condition of national territorial aggrandizement, under terms of the minorities stipulations imposed on Romania at the end of World War I, reinforced preexisting antisemitic prejudices. Meanwhile, the inclusion in Greater Romania of significant non-Orthodox Christian minorities (Hungarian Catholics and Lutherans, German Protestants, as well as Romanian and Ukrainian Uniates) appeared to heighten fears that Orthodoxy itself might come under siege. The uniformity of approach in tying Right radicalism and antisemitism to Romanian Orthodoxy—a common feature greater than any other among the precursors of full-fledged Romanian fascism—certainly influenced the identification with the Orthodox Church that became a central part of Codreanu's thinking and the Iron Guard's legacy. As Leon Volovici has pointed out, Romania's new nationalists "sought to define the Romanian ethnic spirit as an element of Orthodoxy, which was incompatible with the model of the existing liberal state. Only a totalitarian state could secure ethnic creativity and the promotion of Christian values."[4]

A comparison of the pre- and postwar political activity of Alexandru C. Cuza illustrates the point. First elected to the Romania's Chamber of Deputies in 1892, Cuza maintained his seat there (with a single hiatus between 1927 and 1931) until the beginning of King Carol II's royal dictatorship in 1938, at which point he became a member of the Crown Council. Between 1895 and 1923, Cuza helped establish six different political movements, all with strong antisemitic platforms.[5] In 1910, Cuza joined with Nicolae Iorga, Romania's leading intellectual figure of the day and a staunch nationalist, to found the National Democratic Party (Partidul Național Democrat). The party platform advocated extreme measures, including violence, to reduce the influence of the Jews, but did not emphasize the role of religion per se or the Orthodox Church within either party or state.[6] Following World War I, Cuza and Iorga parted ways, with Iorga accepting the treatment-of-minorities stipulations of the postwar settlements and Cuza vehemently rejecting them. In 1919, Cuza founded the Christian National Democratic Party and then, in 1922, together with N. C. Paulescu, established the National Christian Union. That same year, the National Christian Union adopted the swastika as its official symbol. In 1923, Cuza established the League of National Christian Defense (Liga Apărării Național Creștine or LANC). Finally, in 1935, he joined forces with the nationalist poet Octavian Goga to form the National Christian Party. When the National Christian Party came to power in late 1937, it implemented decrees that would be used to strip hundreds of thousands of Jews of their citizenship and civil rights.

In the series of "Christian" political movements that he established after World War I, Cuza conscientiously wove more traditional themes of religious antisemitism into his long-established antisemitic rhetoric. The shift in emphasis was clear. Prior to the war, Cuza had expressed his antisemitism principally in cultural, social, and economic terms. The titles of his published works make the point: *The Peasantry and the Ruling Classes* (1895); *On Population: Statistics, Theory and Politics* (1899); *The Decline of the Christian Population and Increase of the Kikes in Romania's Cities* (1910); *Nationality in Art: Statement of Nationalist Doctrine* (1908); *The Kikes in the Press* (1911); and *What is Alcoholism?* (1897).[7] After the war, Cuza focused on more religious themes. His new books bore such titles as *The Teachings of Jesus: Judaism or Christian Theology* (1925) and *Cuzist Doctrine: The Struggle for Faith and the Problem of Religious Education with Examples from the Torah* (1928) and sought to cordon off Christianity's Jewish heritage and draw clear lines of separation between the Hebrews of the Old Testament and modern "kikes" (*jidani*).[8] Cuza's newspaper, *Apărarea Națională*, published in partnership with N. C. Paulescu, disseminated the mythology of Jewish ritual murder by stressing that Jews subjected their victims to "the same torment that Jesus endured before the crucifixion."[9]

Nicolae C. Paulescu, a professor of physiology at the Medical Faculty in Bucharest and a world-renowned specialist in biochemistry, influenced Cuza to incorporate religion into his doctrine. Joining Cuza in the National Christian Union, Paulescu was self-trained in philosophy and the author of pseudoscientific works that served as vehicles for racial and religious hatred. Paulescu sought to merge theology, medicine, and science into what he called "philosophical physiology," through which he expressed his own brand of obsessive antisemitism. Paulescu identified the origins of Jewish perfidy in the Talmud, which he called a tool for the extermination of other nations, and in the kehillah, which he argued secretly plotted the destruction of nations and the disasters that afflicted the rest of humanity. According to Paulescu, history could be defined as a conflict between "Godly Christianity" and "Satanic" Judaism. This battle could only be won by invoking the power of the Church: "In this monumental battle, the Synagogue, united and powerful, cannot be defeated except by a united Church, which must serve as a school for all of Christendom, under the leadership of a Supreme leader—infallible, one and universal."[10]

Paulescu propagated his views through Cuza's newspaper, *Apărarea Națională,* and through published volumes such as *The Kike-Francmasonic Plot against the Romanian People; The Degeneracy of the Kike Race; The Kikes and Alcoholism; The Debauchery of the Kikes;* and *Interpreting the Apocalypse: The Future Fate of the Kikes.*[11] Paulescu advocated a total elimination of the Jews and suggested "exterminating" the "infesting evil parasites" the same way "bedbugs are killed." He concluded, "That would be the simplest, easiest and fastest way to get rid of them."[12]

Not only did Paulescu influence Cuza, but the young Corneliu Zelea Codreanu, future founder of the Iron Guard, specifically acknowledged the powerful impact of Paulescu's ideas on his own development. Codreanu quoted at length from Paulescu's tractate on "Philosophical Physiology: The Talmud, the Kehillah, Freemasonry" in his *For My Legionaries:*

> In other words, the lie is the system used by the Jews, to whom one can say, "You speak, therefore you lie." But the lie has a mortal enemy, namely the truth. And truth is the distinctive trait of Christianity. Christ said, "I am the truth" and that is why His doctrine is in execration by Israel. The lie, on the contrary, characterizes what is called the spirit of evil or of the Devil. Thus Jesus, speaking to the Hebrews, said to them: "You are of your father the devil and the lusts of your father it

is your will to do. He was a murderer from the beginning, and standeth not in the truth because there is no truth in him. When he speaketh a lie he speaketh of his own for he is a liar and the father thereof."[13]

Other pre-fascist movements also laid stress on the religious, Orthodox basis of their doctrine. Codreanu was familiar with all of these movements and associated with some during his own development. He dedicated several pages of *For My Legionaries* to the Guard of National Conscience of Constantin Pancu, a "tradesman, plumber and electrician," with only primary school education, and "a good Christian." In 1919, Codreanu joined the Guard of National Conscience and participated in its 1920 transformation from an anti-Bolshevik "fighting organization" into a nascent political organization that charged the Romanian ruling class with betrayal of God, the Church, and the army. Codreanu quoted in its entirety the "Creed of National Christian Socialism" penned by Pancu, including the following prayerful passage: "I believe in one Sacred Christian Church with priests living in the Gospel and for the Gospel, and who would, like the apostles, sacrifice themselves for the enlightenment of the many. . . . I await the resurrection of national conscience even in the most humble shepherd and the descent of the educated into the midst of the tired, to strengthen and help them in true brotherhood, the foundation of Romania of tomorrow. Amen."[14]

The Romanian National Fascia (Fascia Naţională Română) led by Titus P. Vifor, which borrowed much of its doctrine from Italian fascism, was an exception to the rule. Antisemitism did not figure prominently in its platform, nor did the embrace of religion. The movement lasted only from 1923 to 1925, however, when it merged into LANC. Finally, Romanian Action (Acţiunea Română), also short-lived, left little mark on the political scene, but provided a launching pad for Ion Moţa, later an Iron Guard martyr in the Spanish Civil War. Moţa headed the Romanian Action's youth wing, but was in no position to contest the spiritual leadership role of Codreanu, who had founded the Association of Christian Students in Iaşi and would later become the youth leader of LANC. Nevertheless, before Romanian Action merged into LANC in 1925, Moţa translated *The Protocols of the Elders of Zion* for the first time into Romanian, feeding the religious intolerance against Jews that was escalating exponentially among Romanian youth.[15]

With this as background, it is hardly surprising that as Codreanu assumed the leadership of his own movement, he incorporated religious nationalism—dedication to the Romanian Orthodox Church—as a central element of Iron Guard doctrine. Totalitarian, nationalistic, and anti-semitic, with goals that included social reform to improve the lot of the peasantry and immersion in Romanian culture to combat the influence of Western capitalism, the Iron Guard also idolized iconic, irrational, religious mysticism, and even organized itself at first along the lines of a clerical order.[16] Under Codreanu's leadership, the Iron Guard aspired to bring about not only political change, but also the moral and spiritual rebirth of the Romanian nation, by returning it to Orthodox Christian values that the Iron Guard believed the country's elites had abandoned.

The Legionary Movement

Iorga, Cuza, and other right-leaning political leaders in inter-war Romania were the products of the traditional political regime established in the mid-nineteenth century and inherited by Greater Romania after World War I. They functioned within it, conceived their political strategies based on it, rose to power through it, and clung to it as their power evaporated. This was not the case with Corneliu Zelea Codreanu and the movement he founded, the Legion of the Archangel Michael, also known as the Iron Guard. The Iron Guard was not unequivocally pro-monarchic, and was certainly not pro–King Carol II. The Iron Guard defined itself differently, not as a party, but as a "movement," and was not committed to parliamentarism. Eschewing relationships with the cultural and religious establishments at the top of Romania's social pyramid, the Legion was antiestablishment, embracing youthful "action," peasantist populism, and mystical religiosity as exemplified by the frequently illiterate local clergy.[17]

At the University of Iași, where he studied law, Codreanu imbibed the raw antisemitic outpourings and pseudoscientific theories of Cuza and Paulescu. He became politically active under Cuza's tutelage, becoming president of the Law Students' Association at the university where Cuza taught, and founding the Association of Christian Students there, based on the principles of antidemocracy, discipline, and leadership.[18] When he founded LANC in March 1923, Cuza entrusted Codreanu with the task of expanding Cuza's political reach beyond Moldavia—something that Cuza himself, by this time sixty-six years old, had never managed. Codreanu organized a party youth corps—something new in Romanian politics, began operating outside of Cuza's traditional regional stronghold, and expanded his own personal aspirations. While Cuza wanted to run LANC along the lines of a traditional political party, albeit an extremist and sometimes violent one, Codreanu soon pressed to make the League a revolutionary "movement of moral rejuvenation," in which organized violence, not only against Jews but against the establishment as well, was an acceptable, even preferred, method of advancing the movement's goals. On June 24, 1927, Codreanu and his followers resigned from LANC. They founded their own movement, first called the Legion of the Archangel Michael, then the Iron Guard.[19]

The religious spark—and parallels to the Gospel—that inspired the new movement were clear from the outset. Codreanu described the defining moments in *For My Legionaries.* In 1923, while imprisoned in Văcăreşti monastery for plotting assassination attempts against six cabinet ministers who had been entrusted with the task of organizing the grant of citizenship to Jews, Codreanu prayerfully offered his personal suffering to redeem his nation: "Lord! We take upon ourselves all the sins of this nation. Receive this our suffering now. See that a better day for this people be forthcoming through this suffering."[20] Entering the monastery's church on November 8, the feast of Saint Michael, after weeks of solitary confinement, Codreanu and his comrades prayed before an icon of the saint: "The icon appeared to us of unsurpassed beauty. I was never attracted by the beauty of any icon. But now I felt bound to this one with all my soul, and I had the feeling the Archangel was alive." Codreanu decided that day to name his movement the Legion of the Archangel Michael. Codreanu further noted in *For My Legionaries* that there were thirteen men imprisoned in his group in Văcăreşti —he, the leader, and twelve others, his disciples. How had they been caught and imprisoned? Codreanu's response made the analogy to the Gospel inescapable: "One thought preoccupied us constantly: 'Who betrayed us?' Night after night we sought to solve this enigma. . . . One morning I went to church to pray before the icon to reveal to us the traitor. That evening as we sat down to dinner I spoke to my comrades: 'I am compelled to bring you sad news. The betrayer has been identified. He is in our midst sitting at the table with us.' "[21] Codreanu identifies the betrayer, then forgives him. If after Codreanu's death Iron Guardists progressively portrayed him in a Christlike role, it is clear from these passages that Codreanu himself had sought to establish the parallel.[22]

Codreanu wove together "saintly purity" and "the sword" as the weaponry with which the Legion of the Archangel Michael would pursue its "battle against Satan." Renouncing interest in material, or earthly, concerns, he declared: "We killed in ourselves one world in order to raise another. . . . The absolute rule of matter was overthrown so it could be replaced by the rule of the spirit, of moral values." He declared the first precept of the movement to be "faith in God," even as he introduced what would become a Legionary fascination with death: "All of us believed in God. . . . The more we were alone and surrounded, the more our preoccupations were directed to God and toward contact with our own dead and those of the nation. This gave us an invincible strength and a bright serenity in the face of all blows." Codreanu embellished the icon of Archangel Michael in the movement's headquarters with slogans that mingled notions of faith, violence, death, and resurrection.[23]

The cover of the first issue of the new movement's publication, *Pământul Strămoşesc* (Ancestral Land), displayed the icon of Archangel Michael, with sword outstretched to menace "the unclean hearts who come into the house of the Lord." Proclaiming, in a line borrowed from the poet Gheorghe Coşbuc, "Though descended from the Gods we still owe the debt of death," the cover also showed a map purporting to highlight in darkened colors areas of "Jewish infestation." Descended from the Gods and brandishing the sword stood the Legion, prepared to die if necessary; the house of the Lord was Romania; the infesting unclean hearts were the Jews and "Judaized" Romanians. In the same issue, Ion Moţa's article "By the Icon" spelled out the connections for anyone who had failed to grasp them: "It is from the Icon and the Altar that we started. . . . Now, with heavy hearts, dispersed, torn, we gather . . . at the feet of Jesus Christ, on the threshold of heaven's blinding brilliancy, at the Icon. We have not been engaged in politics. . . . We have a religion, we are the slaves of a faith. We consume ourselves in its fire and, totally subjected to it, serve it to the limit of our strength."[24] The oath of the new movement, also appearing in *Pământul Strămoşesc*, was to "serve the cause of the Romanian Nation and the Cross."[25]

Codreanu defined his battle against the Jews in universal religious and racial, as well as economic, terms. Declaring that the Jewish enemy throughout "the entire world" formed a "great collectivity bound together by blood and by the Talmudic religion,"[26] Codreanu predicted an assault by Jews to destroy Romania and create a "Judaic State": "They will try to break the spiritual ties of the Romanian people to heaven and to earth. To break our ties with heaven they will engage in widespread dissemination of atheistic theories in order to separate the Romanian people or at least some of [its] leaders from God; separating them from God and their dead they can destroy them, not by sword but by severing the roots of their spiritual life."[27]

To oppose this threat, Codreanu organized the Legion on the basis of secret cells, called "nests," and a youth movement dubbed the "Brotherhood of the Cross." He expected Legionaries to treat their participation in Guardist activity as a holy and spiritual religious experience immersed in the Orthodox faith. In his *Guidebook for the Chief of the Nest*, Codreanu declared that the nest constituted "a church." Linking Legionary and religious observance, he instructed Legionaries, who were required to attend regular nest meetings on Saturday evenings, to go to church the next day. Every meeting of a nest began with a prayer, for prayer, according to Codreanu, enlisted both the dead and God on the Legion's side:

> Let it not be forgotten that we, the Romanian people, have been placed on this earth by the will of God and the blessing of the Christian Church. It is around the altars of the Church that the entirety of Romanians on earth—with women, children and the elderly—have gathered thousands of times in periods of exile and sadness, with perfect awareness of this ultimate refuge. . . . Wars are won by those who have summoned from the firmament, from the sky, the mysterious forces of the unseen world and to gain their help. These mysterious forces include the souls of our dead. . . . But even more important than the souls of our dead is God![28]

Beyond faith in God, Codreanu made it clear that the path to be traveled by Legionaries was analogous to Christ's ascent of Calvary. He described the journey up "the mountain of suffering" this way:

> At first it is easy, but later the incline is steeper, the suffering is greater, and the first drops of sweat appear. . . . Then an unclean spirit . . . asks for the first time, "Wouldn't it be better to turn back?" . . . But the Legionary does not listen, goes on, and the climb is hard . . . he begins to tire, his strength begins to leave him. . . . He gets halfway there, then the real climb starts, without water, without grass, without shade, only stone and rock. And the Legionary sees this and prays, "I have already suffered a lot just to get here; help me God to reach the top." . . . With his faith as his strength, he continues to climb the bare rock. But now he is tired, he stumbles. He wounds his hands and his knees, and he can see his own blood flowing. He gets up and sets off again. There is not far to go. But the rock has become steep and sharp, and blood is flowing from his chest and splashing on the pitiless rock. From the devil again, "Wouldn't it be better to turn back?" . . . One final effort. The heroic figure reaches the top, victorious, at the peak of the mountain of suffering, with his Romanian Christian soul full of happiness and joy.[29]

It is not surprising, given this description, that the Legionaries who died for the movement were dubbed "the crucified ones."[30] The Legionary youth movement, the Brotherhood of the Cross, was explicitly organized to prepare young people for the path—and the end—just described.[31]

A number of Codreanu's early followers served as the Legion's theoreticians. All followed Codreanu's lead in identifying the Legion with Romanian Orthodoxy. Vasile Marin, in his *Crisis of a Generation,* identified Romanianism and Romanian nationalism with Orthodoxy: "Orthodoxy was the shield of Romanian nationalism when the nation was formed. Nationalism existed to the extent that we were Orthodox. . . . History would have been written differently if we had embraced Catholicism. . . . We might have been more civilized, . . . but our national essence would have emerged, after dangerous and extended contact, much diminished. . . . Even more than our language, Orthodoxy created the Romanian nation."[32] Ion Banea, one of the original members of the Legion in 1927, wrote in a brochure prepared for the Legionary Propaganda Service that "Christian faith and love of nation" sustained the Romanians and the Iron Guard.[33] But Banea went further, hinting that the Legion might improve on Orthodoxy, when he argued that Codreanu, through his effort to "reestablish the collective Romanian soul," had founded a "new faith."[34] Alexandru Cantacuzino repeated the theme when he affirmed that Christianity sown in a Legionary milieu produces new outcomes:

> The same two thousand year old teachings, the same faith of our ancestors, inspire in our Legionary soul a new and truly superior experience. We are cultivating this Christian seed planted in the Legion's spiritual furrow. . . . But let it be clear, by Christianity we mean our revealed Orthodox faith. . . . We are crafting a superior type of humanity according to Christian concepts and a new philosophy of life, conceived as an irrational yet persistent impulse to free ourselves from material concerns, in order to serve God and a Legionary nation.[35]

Ion Moța pursued similar thinking in his articles "By the Icon" and "The Measure of Our Christianity."[36] This line of thinking naturally raised questions about the Legion's relationship with other interpreters of Romanian Orthodoxy—the established Church hierarchy.

The Legion, the Clergy, and the Church Hierarchy

Codreanu's declaration of his faith and the identification of Legionary nationalism with Orthodoxy was such an integral part of the Legion's image that on occasion he had to draw a distinction between his movement and the Church itself. On some occasions he did so by elevating the Church and adopting a submissive posture: "I have been asked whether our activity so far has followed along the same lines as those of the Christian Church. I answer: We make a great distinction between the line that we follow and the line of the Christian Church. The Church rules us from on high. It reaches perfection and the sublime. . . . It remains to be seen how much we can elevate ourselves toward this line through our worldly efforts."[37] However, on other occasions, and increasingly as he perceived the hierarchy of the Church to be lending its political support to King Carol and to be cooperating with the king's efforts to halt the growth of the Legion, he portrayed the Church as failing the Romanian people by blindly upholding what he considered an illegitimate established order.[38] He was particularly critical of the Patriarch himself, Miron Cristea.[39]

The issues that separated Codreanu and Cristea were certainly not nationalism or antisemitism. The Romanian Orthodox Church had a long history of both. Like Codreanu, Cristea viewed the external threats of communism from the East and encroaching modernism and capitalism from the West with animosity. He feared that Romanian ethnic domination and Orthodox spiritual exclusivism in Romania were at serious risk in the multinational, multireligious state that emerged as a result of the post–World War I territorial settlements. Transylvanian-born and appointed the first Patriarch of Greater Romania in 1925, Cristea wished to preserve for his Church the privileged position Orthodoxy had enjoyed in the prewar kingdom, the nearly homogeneous Romanian Orthodox Regat (Wallachia, Moldavia, and Dobrogea). He believed that the Christian religious denominations of Romania's new non-Romanian minorities, the Romano-Catholic Uniate Church in Transylvania, and the Jews all threatened this position of dominance. He was thus true to the traditional policy of the Romanian Orthodox hierarchy, which upheld the state's authority and favored "any movement, even extremist, whose program included loyalty to Orthodoxism."[40]

While serving on the Council of Regents during the first reign of child-king Michael, Cristea did nothing to challenge the antisemitic propaganda of the Iron Guard or curb its considerable appeal with lower- and mid-level Orthodox clergy. Many priests joined the Legion, dramatically increasing its influence in the countryside, and it was not uncommon for the banners of Romania's principal right-wing antisemitic movements—both LANC and the Legion—to be blessed by Orthodox clergy inside their churches. When alarmed state authorities sought to ban the display of fascist banners in public, the Holy Synod sought to have the banners removed from the churches also, but the Legion's attraction for most clergy was not diminished.[41]

With the inauguration of King Carol II, the Church's official relationship with the Legion changed dramatically. Carol quickly came to view the Iron Guard as a potential threat to his policies, his throne, and possibly the royal dynasty. Having been forced in 1927 to give up his rights to the throne, Carol was particularly sensitive to Codreanu's public appeal and his direct assault in *For My Legionaries* on the principle of hereditary leadership.[42] He also resented Codreanu's refusal to accept in silence the king's long-term extramarital relationship with Elena Lupescu, a woman of Jewish origin. Following the assassination of Prime Minister Ion Duca by the Iron Guard in 1931, and in the wake of its increasingly violent public behavior, in the 1930s the Legion was banned by three separate governments (1931, 1932, and 1938). The Liberal Party government of Gheorghe Tătărescu (1933–37) surveilled it aggressively, as did the governments of the royal dictatorship (1938–40).

As a political player loyal to King Carol, the Patriarch sought to limit the Iron Guard's influence on lower clergy. He wrote pastoral letters in 1934 that urged local clergy to avoid involvement in politics and to keep political activities out of their churches. Codreanu retained his appeal by creating "work camps" and Legionary teams that performed good deeds such as repairing roads, digging wells, and restoring and building churches throughout the countryside. In 1935, at government request, the Orthodox Holy Synod responded by ordering local clergy not to accept any free services without approval in advance from the local bishop or another member of the Church hierarchy. Not all of the upper-level clergy agreed with these restrictions, however, and many disregarded them. As Arnim Heinen has pointed out: "In the months that followed, the Church and the Guard worked together in a way that was useful for both. The Orthodox clergy saw in the Legionary youth a source of religious rediscovery, worthy of recognition; for the Legionaries, social recognition and confirmation were tied to the goodwill of the Church."[43]

In February 1937, the growing strength and appeal of the Legionary movement became even more visible as the funeral train bearing the bodies of Legionaries Ion Moța and Vasile Marin, who had been killed in the Spanish Civil War, passed through the countryside. Crowds gathered all along the route. In Cernăuți, men took the coffins to the cathedral where, over the objections of the mayor, they were blessed by the Metropolitan.

In Cluj, Orăştie, Sibiu, and Roman, large crowds and clergy participated in greeting rituals. Sixty priests accompanied the train, and at every station, crowds knelt in prayer before the bodies. In Bucharest, two Orthodox metropolitans, surrounded by dozens of clergymen, officiated at the funeral service. The cortege included sixteen thousand Legionaries in uniform, who marched through the city in the formation of a "living cross." Representatives from Nazi Germany, fascist Italy, Portugal, Japan, and Spain attended the funeral. The impact on the Legion was enormous, and the symbolism of Moţa and Marin became central to Iron Guard iconography. The event emboldened Codreanu, alarmed the king and government, and left the Church leadership unsettled.[44]

In March 1937, at the urgent request of the government, the Patriarch assembled the Orthodox Holy Synod again. On March 10 and 11, the synod issued two edicts that forbade local clergy to join Iron Guard nests, attend political demonstrations, decorate churches with political symbols, or preach on political subjects. The synod, however, also appeared to endorse nationalist stances of the political Right. While condemning violence, the Church hierarchy upheld a "Christian point of view" against "the spirit of secularism" in politics. It declared that the Church would not take sides among political parties, but specifically endorsed the withdrawal of citizenship and other rights from "citizens of other languages and laws."[45]

The synod's action fell short of what the government had hoped for. On March 13, Codreanu issued a special circular (Number 64) that praised the synod's action and ordered the edicts to be read in all Legionary nests.[46] Nae Ionescu, who by this time had become a principal intellectual force within the Legion, declared, "Responding as it has, the Holy Synod has assured a victory for the Orthodox Church, and also for Romanian nationalism."[47] The mutual attraction between the Legion and the Orthodox clergy remained unchanged, and now had the apparent blessing of the Orthodox Church's leadership. Some Iron Guard priests became vocal advocates of radical steps, including imprisonment in labor camps and execution, to cleanse the country of Jews.[48]

In August 1937, with national elections approaching and the antisemitic rhetoric of LANC and the Iron Guard resonating broadly with the public, Patriarch Cristea realized that the loyalty of the Orthodox clergy was in play. Seeking to redirect the appeal of an ascendant Codreanu and Iron Guard to himself, Cristea drew upon the deep reservoir of Romanian antisemitism and attacked the Jews publicly:

One has to be sorry for the poor Romanian people, whose very marrow is [being] sucked out by the Jews. Not to react against the Jews means that we go open-eyed to our destruction. . . . To defend ourselves is a national and patriotic duty, not "antisemitism." Where does it say that only you Jews have the privilege of living on the backs of other peoples, and on our back, the back of the Romanians, like parasites? . . . [E]xploit one another, but not us and other peoples whose entire wealth you are taking away with your ethnic and talmudic sophistry.[49]

A few months later, in February 1938, King Carol appointed Cristea the first prime minister of his royal dictatorship. Cristea advocated policies that would translate his August antisemitic diatribe into action:

Repair of the historical injustices of all sorts done to the dominant Romanian element. . . . Reexamination of the acquisition of citizenship after the war and annulment of all naturalizations made fraudulently and contrary to the vital interests of the Romanians. . . . The organization of the departure from the country of foreign elements that, recently established in the country, damage and weaken our Romanian ethnic national character. Romania will cooperate . . . with other states that have an excess of Jewish population, helping [the Jews] find their own country.[50]

If the Patriarch viewed Codreanu as a potential rival for the loyalty of the clergy, the advent of the Royal Dictatorship must have seemed to him providential. On February 17, the king ordered the dissolution of all political parties and formed a Crown Council made up of the Patriarch and all of the country's living interwar prime ministers. This eliminated Codreanu from access to the reins of power. Codreanu responded in an open letter addressed to former prime minister Alexandru Vaida-Voievod. He labeled the new regime illegal and its members "criminals" and "perjurers."[51] A few months later, in June, writing from a cell in Jilava Prison, Codreanu heaped scorn on Cristea for his attacks on the Legion, declaring: "The Orthodox Church has taken an attitude openly hostile to Romania's youth. It is painful, very painful. . . . The Church of our fathers, the Church of our ancestors strikes us down. The Patriarch is also Prime Minister, and everything that causes us so much pain is done in his name. God! Oh, God! What a tragedy! How tortured are our souls!" In these notes from his prison cell, Codreanu returned to the theme with which he had begun in *For My Legionaries*—Jesus' suffering, especially emphasizing his willingness to be condemned to die for the sins of others, and his resurrection. Embracing his destiny, Codreanu echoed an earlier savior, declaring, "Father, into thy hands I commend my spirit," and "We will rise from the dead in the name of Christ and only through Christ."[52]

In November 1938, at age thirty-nine, Codreanu was killed while in police custody. Patriarch Miron Cristea died the following March, at age seventy-one, while still serving as prime minister. Their competition for the loyalty of Romanian Orthodox clergy and their rival claims to represent the "true" Church outlived the two men. There were priests among the Legionaries accused of the assassination of Prime Minister Duca in 1931. And there were 33 priests among the 103 parliamentary candidates of the Iron Guard's "All for the Fatherland" political party in the national elections of 1937. When King Carol organized mass arrests of Legionaries in 1938–39 and sought to eliminate the movement's leadership cadres, there were Legionary priests among those arrested and Legionary priests among those killed by government authorities. During the Antonescu-Sima government of September 1940–January 1941, more than 40 priests openly assumed high-level Iron Guard positions. Priests participated in the Iron Guard rebellion against Antonescu in January 1941, not only in the capital, but in locations as widespread as Vântul de Jos, Mihalţ, Galda de Jos, Câmpulung-Muscel, Iaşi, Târgu Nou, Putna, and numerous others. Two hundred and eighteen priests were arrested for their involvement in the rebellion, and arms caches for use in the rebellion were later discovered hidden in Orthodox monasteries. There were priests among the Iron Guardists spirited out of the country by SS and SD operatives to wartime refuge in Nazi Germany following the rebellion.[53] Following World War II, the Romanian Orthodox Church outside Romania provided a comfortable refuge for Legionaries who could not return home, and Iron Guardists assumed leadership positions in the Church outside Romania during the period of communist rule inside the country. As refugees from communism made their way to the West, the churches frequently served as mechanisms to guide them toward a belief in the Legionary movement as the only viable political force for ultimate salvation of the country.

The Legion, Orthodoxy, and "New Generation" Intellectuals

Codreanu's critics within the Romanian establishment often accused him of seeking to emulate Mussolini and Hitler. And yet, in contrast to the fascist movements in Italy and Germany, which were areligious or antireligious in nature, the Iron Guard was "a movement of religious rebirth or, perhaps more precisely, a movement of regeneration with religious overtones."[54] Codreanu and his followers took pains to spell out what distinguished their movement from Nazism and Italian fascism, claiming, with much justification, to have created a specifically Romanian nationalist movement—original, anti-Western, and steeped in Orthodoxy and Eastern mystery.[55]

Codreanu and other Iron Guard authors were fixated on the language and symbolism of sacrifice, crucifixion, and resurrection. The names of fallen Guardist comrades were read out at meetings and demonstrations, and the living in unison responded "present" on their behalf. After Codreanu's death, it was not uncommon for members of the Legion to use the phrase "The Captain is with us!" or to refer to Codreanu's "resurrection" as an affirmation that he still lived. Referring to the Legion's ascent to power in late 1940 in partnership with Ion Antonescu, Horia Cosmovici penned the lines "Behold a great resurrection. . . . It is the resurrection of the Captain."[56] The passage of time did not diminish the Legionaries' commitment to such imagery. The final page of a memorial volume published twenty years after Codreanu's death bears a drawing of an unidentified figure carrying a cross on his back. A poem proclaims, "Your grave is only resurrection." And the resonating message is announced to all: "Corneliu Zelea Codreanu: Present!"[57]

The Legion's call for spiritual renewal, immersion in the mystical, violent battle against Satan, restoration of the Romanian Orthodox faith, "leadership" by an anointed individual, and overthrow of the established, "Judaized" order had immense appeal for the generation of young Romanian intellectuals that reached maturity during the interwar period. The Iron Guard appeared to offer an integrated, purposeful philosophy of life and of death. This "new generation" of intellectuals were not pseudo-scholars of the Cuza or Paulescu type. Nor were they out of the mainstream. On the contrary, they included the principal protagonists of Romanian cultural and intellectual identity in the mid-twentieth century. Some of them who survived World War II, such as Mircea Eliade and Emil Cioran, living outside Romania, hid or renounced their Iron Guard pasts and became internationally recognized intellectual icons. Others who survived inside Romania, such as Nichifor Crainic and Constantin Noica, faded into Romanian prison life, but saw the power of their thinking affect a postwar, post-Holocaust generation of Romanian youth that was also seeking, as they themselves had done earlier, to pursue a destiny better than that offered by the country's established (by then, communist) order. Still others, such as the writers Vintilă Horia and Horia Stamatu, of lesser distinction but of national significance nonetheless, continued their Iron Guard affiliation in exile, seeking to maintain the movement's vitality and hoping for a final resurrection of the Legion before their own days ended.

None of Codreanu's early followers (e.g., Marin, Banea, Cantacuzino, Moța) were as influential intellectually as Crainic, Nae Ionescu, Eliade, Cioran, or Noica. These latter did not emerge from within the Iron Guard. Rather, in the early 1930s they discovered in the Legion the appealing promise of a "national revolution" that corresponded to their own worldviews. To all of them, Greater Romania's promise, so glittering in the aftermath of World War I, appeared to be slipping away. Disillusioned by the failure of the establishment generation to address the country's woes, the "new generation" of intellectuals turned to the Legionary movement in pursuit of a national "resurrection."[58] Their work filled literary journals, bookstore shelves, and the newspapers of the political Right. Their quest for spiritual and political renewal inclined them toward fascist doctrines, while their ethnic, nationalist, Romanian Orthodox focus impelled them and their readers toward the Legionary movement.[59] There is a considerable literature regarding each of these major Romanian intellectuals.[60] The following briefly addresses only their approach to Orthodoxy and the Legion.

Nichifor Crainic, the eldest of the group, was professor of theology at the University of Bucharest and a theoretician of mystical Orthodoxy. A longtime associate of A. C. Cuza, Crainic edited the influential nationalist cultural journal *Gîndirea* (Thought) and published extensively on contemporary politics and philosophy. He hailed N. C. Paulescu as the founder of "Christian nationalism," and placed Orthodoxy at the center of Romanian being: "For whoever writes a philosophy of our history, Orthodoxy will provide the key to understanding that history."[61] Crainic applied his theological expertise to an effort to break the Judeo-Christian relationship, arguing in publication after publication that the Old Testament was not a Jewish document; that Jesus had not been Jewish; and that the Talmud, which Crainic considered to be the defining element of modern Jewry, was nothing more than a Jewish weapon to undermine the Gospel and destroy Christian society.[62] Combating the Talmud was the defining issue of the day: "The Talmud is the obscurantist organization of the most tremendous hatred against the Savior Jesus Christ and against Christians. . . . Europe today is not stirred by a simple social war, nor by an ideological war. Europe is stirred by the war of the Talmud against the Gospel of Christ."[63] The weapons Crainic advocated to win the battle were "autochthonous spirit," Romanian Orthodox "spirituality," and totalitarianism.[64]

While apparently he was never actually a member of the Legion, Crainic's powerful advocacy for the establishment of an Orthodox ethnocratic state organized along fascist lines enhanced the legitimacy of the Iron Guard in Romanian intellectual circles and transformed the Faculty of Theology at the University of Bucharest into a center of student support for the Legion.[65] Crainic served as minister of national propaganda in the pro-Nazi government of Ion Gigurtu (July 4–September 3, 1940), the first Romanian government in which a number of Legionaries held ministerial portfolios. Days after King Carol's forced abdication on September 6, 1940, Crainic hailed the establishment of the "National Legionary State" as a passage from "death to resurrection."[66]

Nae Ionescu was professor of logic and metaphysics at the University of Bucharest. His influence on the "new generation" philosophers was immense, and his influence is often credited with the "Guardist conversion" of Cioran, Eliade, and Noica.[67] Ionescu emphatically rejected Western values and argued the centrality of Eastern Orthodoxy in the intellectual framework of "Romanianism": "The formula of our Romanian civilization and culture is not Western. If we set aside everything that has been added to this civilization in the last 100 years, which in all respects must be considered an unsuccessful addition, Romanian culture is an Eastern reality. . . . What is Latin in us? Our concept of law? . . . Probably Thracian. Of state? Byzantine. Concept of God? Orthodox, thus categorically Eastern."[68]

Ionescu's fixation on Orthodoxy led him to question publicly whether Romanians who belonged to the Uniate (Greco-Catholic) Church could be considered true Romanians and to spell out the bottom line of the "new generation" regarding exclusivist Orthodoxy:

> To be Romanian . . . means to also be Orthodox. . . . The question is, "The moment I become a Catholic, am I still also a Romanian?" . . . Or, more generally, is religion an essential component of a nation or not? . . . Catholicism and Orthodoxy are not simply religions that have some differences of dogma and culture, but two fundamentally different understandings of existence in general. . . . We are Orthodox because we are Romanians, and we are Romanians because we are Orthodox. . . . Become Catholic? . . . To do so would mean to turn our

backs on our history and on our spiritual structures. In other words, to turn our backs on "Romania."[69]

Ionescu was just as categorical regarding the Jews: "Christians and Jews, two bodies alien to one another, which cannot fuse into a synthesis, between which there can only be peace . . . if one of them disappears."[70] Already a powerful protagonist of the radical Right, Ionescu was arrested (then released without trial) following the assassination of Prime Minister Duca in 1933. In spite of—or perhaps because of—the experience, it was at this time that he openly embraced the Iron Guard. He threw the full weight of his influential newspaper, *Cuvântul* (The Word), behind the Legion and added Iron Guardist Vasile Marin to its editorial board.[71] Shortly thereafter, Cioran, Noica, and Eliade followed their mentor into the Legion.

Emil Cioran had studied literature and philosophy at the University of Bucharest, and from 1933 to 1935 studied philosophy on fellowship in Berlin. Witnessing the "making of history" through ruthless action there, Cioran was completely won over by Nazism. At age twenty-two, he expressed his admiration for "Hitlerism" openly in a series of letters published in the newspaper *Vremea*: "Any person with even the least bit of understanding of history has to recognize the irrefutable fact that Hitlerism is Germany's destiny. . . . What pleases me in Hitlerism is the culture of the irrational, the exaltation of vitality per se, the virile use of force, without critical spirit, without reservation and without control."[72] Cioran became a powerful advocate for the radical "transfiguration" and "purification" of Romania—through uncontrolled delirium and violence: "Romania needs exaltation bordering on fanaticism. A fanatical Romania is a transfigured Romania. The fanaticization of Romania is the transfiguration of Romania. . . . Our people are too kind-hearted, too decent, too quiet. I can only love a delirious Romania. . . . We have lived under foreigners for 1,000 years; not to hate them and not to eliminate them would demonstrate an absence of national instinct."[73]

Seeing national revolution and dictatorship as Romania's salvation, Cioran despaired over King Carol's effort to salvage the old regime by placing the National Christian Party of Octavian Goga and A. C. Cuza in power and then installing a royal dictatorship. Cioran sought refuge from his despair in France, once again on fellowship. With the installation of the National Legionary State, however, he returned to Bucharest. The Legionary publication *Cuvântul Strămoșesc* invited Cioran to formally join the movement, and in November 1940 he was asked to deliver a radio address to mark the second anniversary of Codreanu's murder and his reinterment in front of the Iron Guard's headquarters in Bucharest.[74] In that address, entitled "The Interior Profile of the Captain" and published on Christmas Day, Cioran revealed the full extent of his near-religious conversion to faith in the new, resurrected Messiah:

> Before Corneliu Codreanu, Romania was a populated Sahara. Between heaven and earth there was no content, only waiting. Waiting for someone who had to come. . . . This pitiful country was just a vast pause between an inglorious beginning and a vague possibility. The future groaned within us. But in *One* it was seething. He broke the bland silence of our existence and obliged us *to be.* The virtues of the nation took human form in him. . . . The Captain gave Romanians a purpose. . . . The Iron Guard is a fanatical forest. . . . In the presence of the Captain no one could remain lukewarm. A new thrill descended on the country. . . . And after his death each of us felt alone. . . . With the exception of Jesus, no one who has died has remained more alive among the living. Henceforth our country will be led by a dead man . . . [but a] dead man who spread the perfume of eternity over our human wasteland and returned [light to] the sky above Romania.[75]

Following the unsuccessful Iron Guard rebellion against Antonescu, Cioran returned to France and, over time, became one of that country's most appreciated writers and philosophers. He renounced his Iron Guard past as a mistake, but the themes he addressed in his work remained those that had carried him into the Legion—alienation, boredom, futility, decay, the tyranny of history, the disease of reason, despair in need of salvation.[76]

Constantin Noica, another "new generation" philosopher of Romanian spirituality, did not share Cioran's youthful admiration of Hitlerian violence, but he did share the religious and apocalyptic intensity of commitment to the Legion that was evident in Cioran's radio address. In a long series of articles, Noica made it clear that, for him, the Legion was "an object of mystic ecstasy," which revealed "the transcendental significance of Codreanu's death."[77] Noica was so consumed by the messianic mission of the Legion that he claimed to pity the Jews, not because they would be among the movement's victims, but because it was their fate not to be able to share in the glory of the times: "And if there is something we regret as far as our Jewish friends are concerned, it is not so much the fact that the Legionary movement will inflict suffering upon them. . . . What we regret is that they are unable to see and understand everything that is good and truthful in Legionarism. We regret their suffering at not being able to participate in any way—not even a hope, not even with an illusion—in the Romania of tomorrow."[78] In the National Legionary State, Noica served as editor of the Legion's newspaper *Buna Vestire* (Good Tiding) and published regular commentaries justifying the growing violence of Guardist street gangs as "purifying the soul of the nation."[79]

Mircea Eliade, whose reputation after the war as distinguished professor of the history of religions at the University of Chicago was iconic, also experienced conversion to the Iron Guard. Eliade received a doctorate in philosophy from the University of Bucharest and taught there from 1933 to 1939. Even as a twenty-one-year-old student publishing in Nae Ionescu's newspaper, Eliade placed emphasis in his search for a new spirituality on "Orthodoxism" and "Eastern Orthodox living."[80] More politically engaged by the mid-1930s, he praised Codreanu for leading a movement "to reconcile Romania with God," and eulogized Moţa and Marin for laying down their lives voluntarily in Spain in a mystical act of self-sacrifice that was destined to strengthen Christianity and "mobilize a whole generation."[81] In December 1937, on the eve of the last national elections before the collapse of the Romanian interwar parliamentary system, Eliade published in *Buna Vestire* his definitive personal statement of identification with the Legion. In an article entitled "Why I Believe in the Triumph of the Legionary Movement," he communicated as much spiritual Christian Orthodox revelation as political calculation:

> I believe in this triumph, above all, because I believe in the victory of the Christian spirit. . . . [This] is a Christian revolution. While other peoples experience revolution in the name of class struggle and economic primacy (communism) or of the state (fascism) or of race (Hitlerism), the Legionary movement was born under the sign of the Archangel Michael and will triumph through God's grace. . . . Never before has an entire people experienced a revolution with all its being, never before has the word of the Savior been understood as a revolution of the forces of the soul against the sins and weaknesses of the flesh. . . . That is why, whilst all revolutions are political, the Legionary revolution is spiritual and Christian. . . . [T]he supreme target of the Legionary revolution is . . . the salvation of the people, the reconciliation of the Romanian people with God. I believe in the destiny of

our nation. . . . Therefore I believe in the victory of the Legionary movement . . . that will transform the riches of the Romanian soul into universal spiritual values.[82]

Like Codreanu himself, the intellectual base of the Legionary movement fully incorporated a primitive, purifying, yet revolutionary concept of Orthodoxism into the Iron Guard's credo. Romania's influential "new generation" philosophers saw a future Legionary state as an appropriate political vehicle for instrumentalization of their beliefs. The overlapping, often interwoven fabric of approaches and ideas created by the Legionary movement, Romanian Orthodoxy, and the "new generation" philosophers appeared to offer an integrated vision for Romania's place in an emerging new Europe. How well or poorly the fabric would have held together if the Iron Guard had actually come to control the Romanian state and Romanian society cannot be known, however. The National Legionary State collapsed and the Iron Guard was outlawed following the January 1941 rebellion against Antonescu. The movement's leadership spent the war years in protective detention in Nazi Germany. Nevertheless, some aspects of the relationship between the Iron Guard, the Orthodox Church, and the Antonescu regime during World War II are worth exploring, as are some elements of the relationship between the Iron Guard and Orthodoxy in the postwar, post-Holocaust period.

The Romanian Orthodox Church in Transnistria

With the Legion officially banned, the Orthodox Church hierarchy and most of the clergy worked harmoniously with the Antonescu regime throughout the war. Antonescu, for his part, made use of the Church's popular appeal to bolster support for his policies. He referred repeatedly to the war that Romania was waging against the USSR and communism as a "holy war," and when Romanian forces occupied the territory between the Dniester and Bug rivers, administratively dubbed "Transnistria," Antonescu erected a massive monument on the Ukrainian side of the Dniester with the inscription "Through Cross and Sword We Have Been Victorious."[83] The Romanian Orthodox leadership, for its part, endorsed Antonescu's "holy war," and left little doubt as to the true identity of the enemy. Metropolitan Ireneu Mihalcescu of Moldavia and Suceava harangued against "the sick ideas of Lenin, Trotsky and the gang infected with the Judeo-masonic virus that surrounds the seminary deserter Stalin." "Bolshevism," he continued, "is the product of international Judeo-masonic finance, led by the kike bankers of England and the United States."[84]

The Orthodox Church participated eagerly in Antonescu's effort to enhance Romania's long-term claim to Transnistria by re-Christianizing its population, which had lived under Soviet rule for over two decades. In August 1941, even before the military conquest of Transnistria was completed, the Antonescu government approached Patriarch Nicodim, Miron Cristea's successor, who agreed to the establishment of a "Romanian Orthodox Mission to Transnistria." Archimandrite Iuliu Scriban was appointed to head the mission, and in the first eighteen months of its operation, 250 Orthodox priests were sent from Romania to Transnistria. While between 280,000 and 380,000 Romanian and local Ukrainian Jews were being systematically murdered or worked and starved to death in Transnistria—the local Jews having been isolated in ghettos in towns and villages throughout the territory—the priests of the Romanian Orthodox Mission claimed to be reestablishing Christian values in the province. They enlisted 219 local priests in the effort, and in just a few months built or refurbished 309 churches and prayer houses, many in the same towns and villages where the ghettoization and mass murder of Jews were occurring.[85]

Beyond their apparent blindness or lack of concern for the Jews, the Church's effort in Transnistria reflected the nationalist particularism toward other Christian denominations that had been evident in Miron Cristea's immediate post–World War I concerns about the potential loss of exclusive status for the Romanian Orthodox Church in Greater Romania. The Romanian Orthodox Mission went to Transnistria not simply to assist the local communities, but to ensure the affiliation of the local clergy and Ukrainian believers in the province with the Romanian Orthodox Church. The mission also received the government's support in its efforts to suppress Innocentist and small Baptist sects in Transnistria.[86]

While the principal concern of the Romanian Orthodox Mission was the Christian population of Transnistria, the mission inevitably became involved in matters pertaining to Jews. The victory monument that Antonescu had erected was located between Mogilev and Şargorod, on the forced march deportation route of Romanian Jews from Bukovina to Transnistria, and the mission was operating in the midst of a mass killing zone where forced marches of Jews from one holding site to another were commonplace. To date, no documentation has surfaced to implicate the mission directly in Holocaust-related crimes. But humanitarian consideration for the fate of the Jews does not appear to have been voiced at any level. Romania's nationality laws defined Romanian-ness in terms of "blood" and "Christian faith," while Jewish-ness was a factor of parentage and religious faith.[87] Romanian priests became involved in decisions regarding who was a Christian and who was a Jew, and such decisions were often matters of life and death. During months when mass killings were at their peak, some local Ukrainian priests wanted to baptize Jewish children so that they could be adopted by local Christian families and survive. Archimandrite Scriban raised the issue with Patriarch Nicodim, who referred it to the government. The response from the Patriarch was that the conversion and baptism of Jews were not spiritual, ecclesiastical matters, but were ruled by the government's decree regarding the protection of the Romanian "race." Whether that decree, which was valid throughout Romania, was valid in Transnistria also, wrote the Patriarch, was a government decision. The government in Bucharest and the governor of Transnistria followed up with orders to the Romanian Orthodox Mission to halt the baptism of Jewish children. Orders forbidding the conversion of Jews to any other religion followed. The baptism of children of mixed marriages, which had been common in Ukrainian parishes in Transnistria, was also banned.[88]

The Romanian Orthodox Mission filed regular reports with the provincial governor and functioned as part of Antonescu's administration there. Service to the state and pursuit of the exclusivist interests of the Romanian Orthodox Church predominated over any concern with the Jews being murdered within the confines of the small territory they shared. In September 1942, former Metropolitan of Bukovina Visarion Puiu, who would play a role in the Iron Guard's attempted comeback in the last months of the war, replaced Archimandrite Scriban as head of the mission. The mission's work ended with the Romanian retreat from the province in the first half of 1944.[89]

Life after Death: The Church in the Postwar Plans of the Iron Guard

The end of the Antonescu regime and the arrival of the Red Army in Bucharest posed new challenges for the Iron Guard and for the Orthodox Church. Communist rule in Bucharest meant prolonged exile for the Legionary elite. Would the centrality of the movement's commitment to Orthodoxy endure in Western countries of refuge, where

Catholicism and Protestantism, and not Eastern Orthodoxy, were the majority religions?

The answer began to play out as soon as King Michael arrested Ion Antonescu on August 23, 1944. The Nazis released the hundreds of Legionaries they had held under privileged detention throughout the war, and in the hope of encouraging resistance inside Romania, called for the establishment of a Romanian "National Government" in Vienna. Internal divisions had emerged during the Guardist leaders' three and a half year in detention, however, and it was unclear whether Horia Sima's leadership of such a "government" would be accepted by the entire group of Legionaries. With the apparent support of Sima rival Constantin Papanace, General Ion Gheorghe, Antonescu's ambassador to Berlin, considered taking on the job. He argued that his relationships in the Romanian military might help change the course of events. But German foreign minister Joachim von Ribbentrop, who had been charged with organizing the Vienna "government," recognized that Antonescu's man would never get the support of most Legionaries.

The second candidate proposed by Papanace was former Metropolitan of Bukovina and former head of the Romanian Orthodox Mission to Transnistria Visarion Puiu. Visarion was in Zagreb when Antonescu was removed from power, and had taken refuge in Vienna. The Legionary leadership identified closely with Orthodoxy and understood the influence of the Orthodox clergy in Romania. Thus, a leader of the Church represented a viable candidate to lead Romanians inside and outside Romania, and could be expected to stimulate enthusiasm for a new battle against "godless communism." Sima worked hard to undermine Visarion's candidacy, which resulted in considerable tension between the two men.[90]

In the end, the Nazis anointed Sima to lead the prospective National Government. The candidacy of Visarion Puiu, however, had focused some Legionaries on the fact that, just as it had been in the 1930s, the Orthodox Church was a significant potential asset for the Iron Guard, both in the immediate circumstances of winter 1944 and for the long term. Metropolitan Visarion and Father Stefan Palaghiţa, with others who had supported the Visarion option, proposed to Sima and to the Nazis that they establish an episcopate of the Romanian Orthodox Church, independent of Bucharest's authority and headed by Visarion, in Nazi Germany. The plan envisioned the creation of independent episcopates, under Nazi protection, for all of the Orthodox churches of

Southeastern Europe, which by this time seemed destined to fall under Soviet control. An Orthodox Synod of the newly created national episcopates would lay claim to representing all Orthodox faithful outside the borders of the countries involved.

Not prepared to risk the primacy he had just achieved, and concerned at the prospect of a disgruntled rival at the head of a religious body beyond the control of his new "government," Sima countered with a proposal to make Visarion minister of culture in the National Government. When Nazi officials, already impatient with their squabbling Romanian clients, pressured Visarion, he wavered, first agreeing and then declining to accept the government appointment.[91] With dissension among the Romanians gathered in Vienna and conflicting advice coming from his supporters, under pressure from the Nazis, with limited information about events in Romania, and unclear about developments on the battlefield, deciding whether the brightest future lay with the new National Government or in a newly created episcopate was not an easy choice to make.

When the National Government was announced on December 10, 1944, Visarion was not among its members. A "Romanian Orthodox Episcopate of the West" was formed shortly afterward, with its own organizational chart and with Visarion at its head. Visarion's secretary was former Iron Guard youth leader Viorel Trifa. Trifa was a product of the Faculty of Theology at the University of Bucharest and an SS favorite before, during, and after the Iron Guard rebellion. It was Trifa's manifesto and the street demonstration he headed that had ignited the Iron Guard rebellion and associated pogrom in Bucharest in 1941. During the war, while his Legionary comrades languished in protective detention in SS facilities near Buchenwald, Rostock, Berkenbruck, and other concentration camps, Trifa had spent much of his time "taking the cure" at Bad Kissingen, Bad Mergentheim, and other German spas. In late 1944 in Vienna, Trifa aligned himself with Visarion rather than Sima, and moved with Visarion to Kitzbühel in the Tyrol to set up the new episcopate.[92] Very soon, however, the Nazi defeat and events in Romania forced every prominent personality in the exile establishment to hide or flee, seek a safe haven, and hope for a change of fortune. The church was a natural destination.

Visarion was condemned to death in absentia in Romania for his role in Transnistria and his involvement with the Iron Guard and the Nazis in the last months of the war. He took refuge in Italy and then in Switzerland. By 1949, he had reconciled with Sima, who remained "Commandant" of the Iron Guard. Sima recognized that infiltrating Romanian émigré Church structures could provide the Legion, and him personally, with influence they otherwise no longer had. The new Church body, planned to function in fortress Nazi Germany, was moved to Paris, where Visarion was installed as head of the "Romanian Orthodox Episcopate of the West."[93]

By 1950, Viorel Trifa had made his way from Kitzbühel to Italy, where he took up residence in a monastery, and then to America. In 1952, after having been ordained a priest and consecrated a bishop in ceremonies that were of questionable legitimacy, Trifa was installed as the Romanian Archbishop of the United States. Icons of Codreanu adorned the altar of the episcopal church, and Trifa participated regularly in pseudoacademic gatherings of Legionaries who had made their way to America. In 1984, after years of legal maneuvering to deny his Legionary past, Trifa was stripped of his American citizenship, resigned from his position, and was deported to Portugal.[94]

Meanwhile, in France, another well-known Legionary priest rose to the top of that country's Romanian Orthodox Church hierarchy. Father Vasile Boldeanu had joined the Legion early. He had held a number of mid- and upper-middle-level positions within the movement, serving as deputy to Nicolae Pătrașcu in charge of party organization, as a Legionary commandant in the National Legionary State, and as leader of the Legionary underground immediately following the Iron Guard rebellion. He was sufficiently well known to have been selected to officiate at the graveside service during the exhumation of Codreanu's body in November 1940. Arrested by Antonescu's police following the rebellion, Boldeanu spent two years in prison, then escaped and fled to the Serbian Banat, which was under German administration. He engaged in Legionary underground activity there until the Germans arrested him in June 1944 and sent him to join the group of Legionaries being held at Buchenwald. After involvement in Sima's short-lived National Government in Vienna, Boldeanu settled in Paris. With the help of the Legionary exile community there he became Superior at the Romanian Orthodox Church in 1958.[95]

Numerous additional Legionaries removed their green shirts and reappeared in priestly garb after World War II. Throughout the Cold War, Sima continued to stress the centrality of Orthodoxy for the Legionary movement and to criticize the West for failing to appreciate sufficiently the fundamental linkage of Christianity, nationalism, and anticommunism. Faust Bradescu, Sima's heir apparent and the principal

ideologist of the Legion by the 1970s, emphasized the religious spirituality of the movement in his writings.[96] The Legion had a divine mission. In painful exile, the Church had become a natural vehicle through
which to pursue it.

Conclusion

Romanian fascism and Romanian Orthodoxy engaged in a
reciprocal embrace when Right radicalism was ascendant in Europe. The
Legionary movement defined itself as a Christian Orthodox movement,
increased its political power, and elevated its leader to near-divine status
through association with and reliance on the imagery, mysticism, and
appeal of Eastern Orthodoxy. Clergy, illiterate peasant believers, Romanian intellectuals of the "new generation," and many members of
the Orthodox Church hierarchy could not resist—and did not want to
resist—the Legion's appeal. The Legionary-Orthodox identity of credo
and of interests sustained their mutual embrace through crisis after crisis, through the death of leaders, through exile, through communism,
across continents, over oceans, and through more than half a century of
exile and despair after the glory ended.

Normally the staying power of such a powerful bond would inspire
positive comment. In this case, however, the consequences were suffer-
ing, murder, national humiliation, disorientation, and eternal calumny.
Far from experiencing purification and salvation through the Legion,
Romania was "crucified," to borrow a term used as frequently by Iron
Guardists as by Orthodox priests.[97] And the crucifixion was self-inflicted.
The Legion, the Orthodox Church, Ion Antonescu, and many others
took part in raising the cross and wielding the hammer.

Far from heroic, such tragic history has lasting implications. At the
beginning of the twenty-first century, it was credible to many observers
when an allegation surfaced that the then Romanian Orthodox Patriarch
Teoctist Arăpaşu had a Legionary past. Orthodox priests continued to
lead memorial processions and services at the site of Codreanu's death.
The Romanian Orthodox Church continued to harbor extremist political tendencies and exclusivist theological aspirations.[98] And the Legionary thinking and political activism that reappeared after the fall of
communism proved appealing to significant segments of Romania's intelligentsia, Orthodox faithful, and general population. Under these circumstances, it was clear that the true national renewal and spiritual
resurrection of Romania still lay somewhere in the future.

NOTES

1. See the author's chapter "Background and Precursors to the Holocaust," in *International Commission on the Holocaust in Romania: Final Report* (Iaşi: Polirom, 2005), 19–55.

2. The revelation of Eliade's Legionary past diminished the luster of his reputation after his death. On this, see "Eliade, Mircea," a 2005 emendation of the original entry on Eliade, in *Encyclopedia of Religion*, 2nd ed., ed. Lindsay Jones (New York: Macmillan, 2005), 2757–63. On Cioran's acknowledgment and repudiation of his Iron Guard past, see Marta Petreu, *An Infamous Past: E. M. Cioran and the Rise of Fascism in Romania* (Chicago: Ivan R. Dee, 2005).

3. See Henry L. Roberts, *Rumania: Political Problems of an Agrarian State* (New Haven, Conn.: Yale University Press, 1951); Keith Hitchens, *Rumania 1866–1947* (Oxford: Oxford University Press, 1994); and Paul A. Shapiro, "Romania's Past as Challenge for the Future," in *Romania in the 1980s*, ed. Daniel N. Nelson (Boulder, Colo.: Westview Press, 1981), 17–67.

4. Leon Volovici, *Nationalist Ideology and Antisemitism: The Case of Romanian Intellectuals in the 1930s* (Oxford: Pergamon Press, 1991), 59.

5. On Cuza, see Jean Ancel, *Contribuţii la istoria României: Problema evreiască, 1933–1944* (Bucharest: Hasefer, 2001), 23–30; Carol Iancu, *Les Juifs en Roumanie, 1919–1938* (Paris-Louvain: Peeters, 1996), 185–94; and Paul A. Shapiro, "Prelude to Dictatorship in Romania: The National Christian Party in Power, December 1937–February 1938," *Canadian-American Slavic Studies* 8 (Spring 1974): 45–88. For a sympathetic description, see Pamfil Şeicaru, *Un junimist antisemit: A.C. Cuza* (Madrid: Carpaţii, 1956).

6. On the National Democratic Party, see Radu Ioanid, *The Sword of the Archangel: Fascist Ideology in Romania* (Boulder, Colo.: East European Monographs, 1990), 34; William O. Oldson, *The Historical and Nationalistic Thought of Nicolae Iorga* (Boulder, Colo.: East European Monographs, 1973), 8; and Nicolae Iorga, *Problema Evreiască în Cameră: O înterpelare* (Vălenii de Munte: Tipografia Neamului Românesc, 1910).

7. A. C. Cuza, *Ţăranii şi Clasele Dirigente* (Iaşi: Tipografia Naţională, 1895); *Despre Poporaţie: Statistica, Teoria şi Politica Ei*, 2nd ed. (Bucharest: Imp. Independenţa, 1929); *Scăderea Poporaţiei Creştine şi Înmulţirea Jidanilor* (Vălenii de Munte: Tiporafia Neamul Românesc, 1910); *Naţionalitatea în Artă: Expunerea Doctrinei Naţionaliste* (Bucharest: Minerva, 1908); *Jidanii în Presă* (Vălenii de Munte: Neamul Românesc, 1911); and *Ce-i Alcoolismul?* (Iaşi: Tipografia Naţională, 1897).

8. A. C. Cuza, *Învăţătura lui Isus: Judaismul ori teologia creştină* (Iaşi: Ed. LANC, 1925); and *Doctrina cuzistă: Lupta pentru credinţa şi problema învăţământului religios cu ilustraţii din Thora* (Iaşi, 1928). Efforts by Jewish writers to counter such arguments, as in Horia Carp, *Străinii în Biblie şi Talmud* (Bucharest: n.p., 1924) and I. Ludo, *În jurul unei obsesii: Precizările unui evreu pentru Românii de bună credinţă* (Bucharest: Adam, 1936), had little effect.

9. *Apărarea Naţională*, August 15, 1922.

10. N. C. Paulescu, *Fiziologia filozofică: Sinagoga şi Biserica faţă de Pacificarea omenirii* (Bucharest: Apărarea Naţională, 1925), 87–88.

11. N. C. Paulescu, *Complot jidano-francmasonic împotriva neamului Românesc* (Bucharest: Apărarea Naţionala, 1924); *Degenararea Rasei jidăneşti* (Bucharest: n.p., 1928); *Jidanii şi Alcoolismul* (Bucharest: Tipografia Cultura, 1927); *Desfrâul jidanilor* (Bucharest: n.p., 1928); *Tălmăcirea apocalipsului: soarta viitoare a jidănimii* (Bucharest: n.p., 1928).

12. N. C. Paulescu, *Fiziologia filozofică: Talmudul, Cahalul, Francmasoneria* (Bucharest: n.p., 1913), 55. On Paulescu, see Volovici, 28–30; and the introduction by V. Trifu to the 1944 edition of Paulescu's *Fiziologie filozofică: Noțiunile "Suflet" și "Dumnezeu"* in *Fiziologie* (Bucharest: Fundația Regală pentru Literatură și Artă, 1944).

13. Originally published in Romanian in 1936 as *Pentru Legionari;* all citations are to the English edition, Corneliu Z. Codreanu, *For My Legionaries: The Iron Guard* (Madrid: Libertatea, 1976), 36.

14. Ibid., 16–17.

15. Ibid., 84–85. Also, Titus P. Vifor, *Doctrina fascismului românesc și anteproiectul de program* (Bucharest: Ed. F.N.R., 1924).

16. Emanuel Turczynski, "The Background of Romanian Fascism," in *Native Fascism in the Successor States, 1918–1945,* ed. Peter F. Sugar (Santa Barbara, Calif.: ABC Clio, 1971), 111.

17. Important studies of the Iron Guard include Armin Heinen, *Die Legion Erzengel Michael in Rumänien: Soziale Bewegung und politische Organisation* (Munich: R. Oldenbourg Verlag, 1986); Ioanid, *The Sword of the Archangel;* Francisco Viega, *La Mistica del Ultranacionalismo: Historia de la Guardia de Hierro* (Barcelona: Bellaterra, 1989); Eugen Weber, "The Men of the Archangel," in *International Fascism,* ed. George L. Mosse (London: Sage, 1979), 317–43; Eugen Weber, "Romania" in *The European Right,* ed. Hans Rogger and Eugen Weber (Los Angeles: University of California Press, 1966); and Nicholas M. Nagy-Talavera, *The Green Shirts and the Others: A History of Fascism in Hungary and Romania* (Stanford, Calif.: Hoover Institution Press, 1970).

18. Codreanu, *For My Legionaries,* 45 and 48.

19. Codreanu describes his relationship with Cuza in *Pentru Legionari.* The terms Iron Guard, Legion, and Legionary movement are used interchangeably in this chapter, recognizing that the official name of the movement changed over time (e.g., Legion of the Archangel Michael, Iron Guard, All for the Fatherland, etc.).

20. Codreanu, *For My Legionaries,* 124.

21. Ibid., 125–27.

22. Continuing to flirt with "divinity," Codreanu even issued "Ten Commandments" for Legionaries. See C. Z. Codreanu, *Cărticica șefului de cuib* (Munich: Colecția Omul Nou, 1971), 135–37.

23. Ibid., 213–18.

24. Ibid., 227–28.

25. Ibid., 249.

26. Ibid., 103.

27. Ibid., 106.

28. Codreanu, *Cărticica șefului de cuib,* 11, 13, 54–56. On the importance of the nest, see Faust Brădescu, *Le Nid: Unité de base du Mouvement Légionnaire* (Madrid: Editions Carpații, 1973).

29. Codreanu, *Cărticica sefului de cuib,* 58–59.

30. See Bănica Dobre, *Crucificații* (Munich: Colecția Omul Nou, 1951), first published in 1937.

31. See the manual prepared in 1935 by Codreanu's appointee to lead the Brotherhood of the Cross, Gh. Istrate, *Frăția de Cruce* (Munich: Colecția Omul Nou, 1952).

32. Vasile Marin, *Crez de generație,* 2nd ed. (Bucharest: Editura Bucovina, 1937), 50–51.

33. Ion Banea, *Ce este și ce vrea Miscarea Legionară: Cărticica pentru săteni,* 3rd ed. (Sibiu: Tipografia Vestemean, n.d.), 6, 12–13.

34. Ion Banea, *Căpitanul,* 3rd ed. (Sibiu: Tipografia Vestemean, n.d.),141.

35. Alexandru Cantacuzino, *Românul de mâine: Românismul nostru* (1936), in *Opere Complete* (Munich: Colecţia Omul Nou, 1969), 44–45, 48.

36. Both articles can be found in Ion Moţa, *Cranii de lemn–Articole 1922–1936,* 3rd ed. (Bucharest: Editura Totul Pentru Ţară, 1937).

37. Codreanu, *For My Legionaries,* 311.

38. For Codreanu's views on self-perpetuating or hereditary elites, see ibid., 302–11.

39. On Cristea, see Ancel, *Contribuţii la istoria României: Problema evreiască, 1933–1944* (Bucharest: Hasefer, 2001), vol. 1, part 1, 160–68.

40. Volovici, *Nationalist Ideology and Antisemitism,* 40.

41. Ancel, *Contribuţii la istoria României,* vol.1, part 1, 159.

42. Codreanu, *For My Legionaries,* 310.

43. Heinen, *Die Legion Erzengel Michael in Rumänien,* 302–303; Ancel, *Contribuţii la istoria României,* vol.1, part 1, 160; and Z. Ornea, *Anii Treizeci: Extrema dreaptă românească* (Bucharest: Editura Fundaţiei Culturale Române, 1995), 358, 362–63, 374–76.

44. Heinen, *Die Legion Erzengel Michael in Rumänien,* 292–95. For descriptions of the event and photographs of the funeral train, cortege, and living cross formations, see *Ion Moţa şi Vasile Marin: 25 Ani dela Moarte* (Madrid: Editura Carpaţii, 1963).

45. Heinen, *Die Legion Erzengel Michael in Rumänien,* 304; Iancu, *Les juifs en Roumanie,* 301.

46. C. Z. Codreanu, *Circulări şi Manifeste* (Madrid: Colecţia Omul Nou, 1951), 117–18.

47. Nae Ionescu, "Biserică, stat şi naţiune," in *Predanie,* April 1, 1937.

48. See Alexandru Răzmeriţă, *Cum să ne apărăm de evrei : Un plan de eliminare totală* (Turnu Severin: Tipografia Minerva, 1938), 65–69.

49. See Cristea's attacks on the Jews in *Apărarea Naţională,* August 24, 1937, and *Curentul,* August 19, 1937. The quotation is from *Curentul,* August 19, 1937, as cited in Volovici, *Nationalist Ideology and Antisemitism,* 55.

50. Cited in Lya Benjamin, ed., *Evreii din România între anii 1940–1944,* vol. 2: *Problema evreiască în stenogramele Consiliului de Miniştri* (Bucharest: Hasefer, 1996), 31.

51. Codreanu, *Circulări şi Manifeste,* 241–44.

52. Codreanu, *Însemnări dela Jilava* (Salzburg: Colecţia Omul Nou, 1951).

53. Heinen, *Die Legion Erzengel Michael in Rumänien,* 373, 376, 438–39; Ioanid, *Sword of the Archangel,* 142; Lucreţiu Patraşcanu, *Sub Trei Dictaturi,* 4th ed. (Bucharest, Forum, 1946), 190. On the Iron Guard rebellion, see Preşedinţia Consiliului de Miniştri, *Pe Marginea Prăpastiei, 21–23 Ianuarie 1941* (Bucharest: Monitorul Oficial şi Imprimeriile Statului, 1942), vol. 2, 102–105; and Matatias Carp, *Cartea Neagră: Suferinţele Evreilor din România, 1940–1944,* vol. 1, Legionarii şi Rebeliunea (Bucharest: Atelierele grafice Socec, 1946). For the documented experience of one Legionary priest, see Adrian Petcu and Gheorghe Vasilescu, "Părintele Ilie Imbrescu, un promotor al României creştine," *Rost,* May 27, 2005.

54. Weber, "Romania," 534.

55. See, for example, Cantacuzino, *Românul de mâine,* 44–49.

56. For examples of Codreanu's use of such language, see Codreanu, *Circulări şi Manifeste.* On resurrection, see Dobre, *Crucificaţii,* 83–89; *Moţa-Marin: Răscumpărarea* (Munich: Colecţia Omul Nou, 1952), 95–99; Horia H. Cosmovici, *Statul şi Elita Legionară* (Munich: Colecţia Omul Nou, 1953), 11–12; and Vasile Posteuca, *Desgroparea Căpitanului* (Madrid: Editura Mişcării Legionare, 1977), 14–15.

57. See the memorial volume *Corneliu Zelea Codreanu: Douăzeci de ani dela moarte* (Madrid: Editura Carpaţii, 1958), 9, 89, 182.

58. On the "new generation," see Ornea, *Anii Treizeci*, 146–220, and Volovici, *Nationalist Ideology and Antisemitism*, 70–94.

59. Each expressed the attraction differently. Nae Ionescu suggested the term "conversion" in his preface to Marin, *Crez de generaţie*. For the professions of Legionary faith of the others, see Mircea Eliade, "De ce cred în biruinţa mişcării legionare," *Buna Vestire*, December 17, 1937; Emil Cioran, *Schimbarea la faţă a României* (Bucharest: Ed. Vremea, 1936); N. Crainic, *Ortodoxie şi etnocraţie* (Bucharest: Ed. Cugetarea, 1937); and C. Noica, "Între parazitul din afară şi parazitul dinăuntru, " *Vremea*, January 30, 1938.

60. In addition to works on each individually, see comparative treatment in Ornea, *Anii Treizeci*; Volovici, *Nationalist Ideology and Antisemitism*; Vladimir Tismaneanu and Dan Pavel, "Romania's Mystical Revolutionaries: The Generation of Angst and Adventure Revisited," *East European Politics and Societies* 8 (1994): 402–38; and Ovidiu Morar, "Intelectualii români şi 'chestia evreiască,' " in *Contemporanul*, June 2005.

61. Nichifor Crainic, "Sensul tradiţiei," in *Punctele cardinale în haos* (Bucharest: Ed. Cugetarea, 1936), 106–25.

62. Separating Christianity from its Jewish roots preoccupied Crainic early in his career, and his effort grew in intensity as the issue took on greater political significance. For an early statement, see Nichofor Crainic, "Problema biblică," in *Icoanele vremii* (Bucharest: Ed. H. Steinberg, 1919), 203–207. For later development of his argumentation, see Crainic, *Punctele cardinale în haos* and *Ortodoxie şi etnocratie*. For presentation in the journal of the Theology Faculty at the University of Bucharest, see Pr. I. Popescu Mălăieşti, "Iudeii şi Românii," *Raze de Lumină* 10: 1–4 (Bucharest, Facultatea de Teologie, 1938), 5–63.

63. Crainic, *Ortodoxie şi etnocraţie*, 161–64.

64. On "autochtonous spirit," see "Spiritul autohton," in *Gîndirea* 17 (April 1938).

65. On Crainic's influence on his students and nonentry into the Legion, see Ornea, *Anii Treizeci*, 250; and Volovici, *Nationalist Ideology and Antisemitism*, 96–99.

66. Nichifor Crainic, "Revoluţia legionară," *Gîndirea* 19 (October 1940). Crainic also published a volume of admiration for the Nazi and Fascist revolutions in Germany and Italy, *Lupta pentru spiritul nou: Germania şi Italia în scrisul meu dela 1932 încoace* (Bucharest: Ed. Cugetarea, 1941).

67. See, for example, Tismaneanu and Pavel, "Romania's Mystical Revolutionaries," 431–35.

68. The quotation is from Nae Ionescu, "România ţara a Răsăritului," *Cuvântul*, March 9, 1930. On "Romanianism," see Volovici, *Nationalist Ideology and Antisemitism*, 75–94. On Ionescu's impact on the others, see Mircea Eliade's postscript to Nae Ionescu, *Roza vânturilor, 1926–1933* (Bucharest: Editura Cultura Naţională, 1937).

69. Nae Ionescu, "A fi 'bun român,'" *Cuvântul*, November 2 and 5, 1930.

70. Nae Ionescu's preface to Mihai Sebastian, *De două mii de ani* (Bucharest: Nationala-Ciornei, 1934), xxviii.

71. See Ionescu's preface to Marin, *Crez de generaţie*.

72. Emil Cioran, "Aspecte Germane" in *Vremea*, November 19, 1933; and "Germania şi Franţa" in *Vremea*, December 18, 1933.

73. Emil Cioran, *Schimbarea la faţa a României*, 39, 46, 127–128, 188. Cioran's *Pe Culmiile disperării* (Bucharest: Fundaţia pentru literatură şi artă, 1934), *Cartea amăgirilor* (Bucharest: Editura Cugetarea, 1936), and *Amurgul Gândurilor* (Sibiu:

Tipografia Dacia Traiana, 1940) expressed the despair of Romania's young generation and Cioran's yearning for radical change.

74. Cioran's speech followed by just a few days the murder by Legionary bands
of 64 leading political personalities of the interwar political order. See Comandantul
Militar al Capitalei, *Asasinatele dela Jilava . . . Snagov și Strejnicul–26–27 Noemvrie
1940* (Bucharest: Monitorul Oficial și Imprimeriile Statului, 1941).

75. Emil Cioran, "Profilul interior al Căpitanului," in *Glasul Strămoșesc,* December 25, 1940.

76. See Cioran's obituary in *The Guardian* (London), June 23, 1995.

77. Volovici, *Nationalist Ideology and Antisemitism,* 134.

78. Noica, "Între parazitul din afară și parazitul dinauntru."

79. C. Noica, "Sufletul cetății," *Buna Vestire,* September 21, 1940.

80. M. Eliade, "Precizări pentru discuție," *Cuvântul,* June 19, 1928; and "Confe-
siuni și semnificații," *Cuvântul,* October 6, 1928.

81. M. Eliade, "Popor fără misiune," *Vremea,* December 1, 1935; and *Vremea,*
January 24, 1937.

82. Mircea Eliade, "De ce cred în biruința mișcării legionare." Eliade left extraordinary diaries, memoirs, and other writings that reflected his relationship with
the radical Right. A good brief summary of his relationship with the Legion is in
Norman Manea, "Felix Culpa," in *On Clowns: The Dictator and the Artist* (New York:
Grove Weidenfeld, 1992), 91–123. A study by a scholar who was close to Eliade is
Mac Linscott Ricketts, *Mircea Eliade, the Romanian Roots, 1907–1945,* 2 vols. (Boulder, Colo.: Eastern European Monographs, 1988).

83. Jean Ancel, *Transnistria,* vol. 3 (Bucharest: Editura Atlas, 1998), 143.

84. Ireneu Mihalcescu, Mitropolitul Moldovei și Sucevei, *Preoțimea și războiul
sfânt contra hidrei bolșevice* (Iași: Editura Pastorală, 1941).

85. See the Governor's report, Guvernâmantul Transnistriei, *Transnistria*
(Odessa, 1943), 75–78.

86. Ancel, *Transnistria,* vol. 3, 212–14, 224.

87. For Romania's racial laws of August 8, 1940, see Lya Benjamin, ed., *Evreii din
România între anii 1940–1944: Legislația Antievreiască,* vol. 1 (Bucharest: Editura
Hasefer, 1993), 37–56.

88. Ancel, *Transnistria,* vol. 3, 227–29; and Ancel, *Contribuții la Istoria României,* vol. 2, part 2, 17–18, 24–25.

89. On the Romanian Orthodox Mission in Transnistria, see Ancel, *Contribuții
la Istoria României,* vol. 2, part 2, 10–33; and Ancel, *Transnistria,* vol. 3, 208–52.

90. On the Gheorghe and Visarion candidacies, see Horia Sima, *Guvernul Na-
țional Român de la Viena* (Madrid: Editura Mișcării Legionare, 1993), chapter 2, part
4.; and Ștefan Palaghiță, *Garda de Fier spre Reînvierea României* (Bucharest: Editura
Roza Vînturilor, 1993), 262–63. On the National Government, see Faust Bradescu,
Guvernul dela Viena, 1944–1945 (Madrid: Editura Carpații, 1989). Extant German
documentation regarding the National Government is limited; see samples at U.S.
National Archives and Records Administration, Captured German Records, Series
T-120, Reel 2961/ E474099-101 and Reel 6362/E474087-102; Series T-175, Reel
58/2573526-543, Reel 62/2578228-240, Reel 120/2645811-820. The full text of all six
volumes of Horia Sima's memoirs, including those cited in this chapter, can be found
online at http://www.fgmanu.net/istorie.htm and http://www.miscarea.com/carti2
.htm.

91. Palaghiță, *Garda de Fier spre Reînvierea României,* 263–68.

92. On Trifa in Vienna, see Sima, *Era Libertății,* chapter 2, part 5, and chapter 3,
part 7. I documented Trifa's privileged treatment during the war during the Arch-

bishop's denaturalization and deportation proceedings, via Trifa's wartime personal correspondence, signed monthly SS living allowance receipts, and both Nazi and Iron Guard archival records.

93. See "Din istoria bisericii mame" on the web site of the Romanian Orthodox Episcopate for Germany and Central Europe, www.mitropolia-ro.de; Florin Tuscanu, "Un nedreptățit al istoriei: Mitropolitul Visarion Puiu," in *Rost* (Bucharest), no. 19 (September 2004); and Palaghiță, *Garda de Fier spre Reînvierea României,* 299.

94. For a sympathetic treatment, see Gerald J. Bobango, *The Romanian Orthodox Episcopate of America: The First Half Century, 1929–1979* (Jackson, Mich.: Romanian-American Heritage Center, 1979); and Gerald J. Bobango, *Religion and Politics: Bishop Valerian Trifa and His Times* (Boulder, Colo.: East European Monographs, 1981). On Trifa's deportation, see *Washington Post,* August 15, 1984.

95. Horia Sima, *Era Libertății: Statul Național Legionar* (Madrid: Editura Mișcării Legionare, 1982), vol. 1, chapter 1, part 3; chapter 2, part 8; chapter 5, part 10; and Horia Sima, *Prizonieri ai puterilor axei* (Madrid: Editura Mișcării Legionare, 1990), chapter 1, parts 3 and 7; chapter 5, part 1; chapter 14, parts 1 and 4.

96. "Naționalism și Creștinism" (1955) in Horia Sima, *Articole Politice, 1950– 1963* (Munich: Colecția Omul Nou, 1967), 55–57; and Faust Bradescu, *Mișcarea legionară și spiritul religios* (Madrid: Editura Carpații, 1974).

97. See, for example, Nicolae Baciu, *Yalta și Crucificarea României* (Rome: Fundația Europeana Dragan, 1990).

98. On Teoctist, see *Monitorul dela Iași,* January 13 and January 17, 2001; *Observatorul Cultural,* January 23–29, 2001; *Libertatea,* March 22, 2001. Codreanu memorial ceremony photographs are regularly posted at www.nouadreapta.org. On continuing extremism and exclusivism, see Gabriel Andreescu, *Right-Wing Extremism in Romania* (Cluj: Ethnocultural Diversity Resource Center, 2003), 35–46; and "Romania," in *International Religious Freedom Report 2005,* ed. U.S. Department of State (Washington, D.C.: 2005).

Postwar
Jewish-Christian
Encounters

The German Protestant Church and Its *Judenmission,* 1945–1950

8

Matthew D. Hockenos

Beginning in the nineteenth-century, German Protestant churches established mission societies that focused specifically on proselytizing Jews in Germany.[1] The raison d'etre of the *Judenmission* (Jewish missions) was to encourage Jews to convert to Christianity. Pointing to passages in the New Testament and to the example of Jesus for justification of their work, missionaries maintained that the Church had an obligation to spread the gospel and draw as many non-Christians, especially Jews, as possible into the Church.[2] Many Protestants, not only in Germany, considered conversion of Jews to be more important than other missionary work. And there were several reasons why they felt it was more likely to succeed than, say, proselytizing efforts in Asia: Jews believed in the same God as Christians, read the Old Testament, were often educated, and resided in Europe. By 1869, Old Testament scholar Franz Delitzsch had created the Evangelical Lutheran Central Society for Missions Among Israel in order to coordinate the work of the various regional mission societies.[3] When the Nazis came to power they shut down the *Judenmission,* maintaining that there was no place in the Fatherland for Jews—baptized or not. This essay examines the debates and discussions over the fate of the Protestant Church's *Judenmission* after the fall of the Nazis regime, from 1945 to 1950.

Despite the horrors of the Nazi-inflicted atrocities against the Jewish people and the Church's failure to forthrightly condemn the policies that led to these atrocities, recognition by Protestant clergymen after the Second World War of the need for a fundamental transformation of the

Church's relationship to Jews and its understanding of Judaism was slow and halting. By portraying Jews for nearly two thousand years as enemies of Christ and in more recent centuries as a subversive force within the German *Volk*, the German Protestant Church (Evangelische Kirche in Deutschland, or EKD) had created a legacy of anti-Judaism and antisemitism that continued to influence the attitude and behavior of the majority within the Church after 1945.[4] The Church's leadership bodies, the EKD council and chancellery, repeatedly brushed aside serious reconsideration of the Church's relationship to Jews and the Jewish faith, citing the need to address more pressing concerns. To be sure, the sheer extent of physical and psychological damage that accompanied the defeat of Germany meant that exhausted churchmen had little time to address the complicated work of rethinking Protestant-Jewish relations. But an equally serious stumbling block to a rethinking of the Church's doctrine and practice was deeply rooted in Church theology and traditions, including the prevalence of anti-Judaism and antisemitism in the Church's leadership, doctrine, and congregations.

An analysis of the ways in which the Protestant Church wrestled with these issues requires both an evaluation of statements by churchmen and a close look at the actual practices of the churches. While it took several years for Church reformers to recognize that even the more independent Confessing Church (Bekennende Kirche) had not done all it could to oppose Nazi antisemitic policies, and for the reformers to see that drastic changes were needed in Protestant doctrine on Jews, the Church, nevertheless, did make progress in addressing its anti-Judaism and antisemitism in written and verbal proclamations. Certain groups within the Church, which strove for friendly and mutually respectful relationships with Jews, aided the process. Yet, many clergymen and laypersons, including some of the most powerful bishops and presidents of regional churches, maintained their ingrained prejudices, doing little to improve Protestant-Jewish relations. Supporting these prejudices were Christian triumphalism and missionary thinking, which continued to permeate the mainstream Church in the immediate postwar years.

Ultimately, the Church struggle from 1933 to 1945, the Holocaust, the founding of the State of Israel in 1948, and the nascent Christian-Jewish dialogue moved a minority of pastors and theologians to question traditional Church doctrine on the relationship between Jews and Christians.[5] Only after the profound political and theological shock of these events had had time to sink in were some reformist pastors and theologians prepared to abandon their adherence to the long-held myth of supersessionism, which asserted that since the crucifixion of Christ the Christian Church had superseded the Jews as God's chosen people. The misguided effort of reform-minded churchmen in 1948 to renounce the Church's antisemitism while reaffirming its traditional anti-Judaism exemplifies the faltering process by which churchmen struggled with these issues. The gradual realization that the Church's widely accepted anti-Judaic myths provided fertile ground for the growth of antisemitism in nineteenth- and twentieth-century Germany culminated in the repudiation of these myths by churchmen in April 1950 in their famous Berlin-Weissensee statement.[6] How this change in the doctrine of the German Protestant Church came about is central to understanding the fate of the *Judenmission.*

Lack of Concern and Denial of Need

Any explanation for the hesitant and cautious nature of the challenges to established Church doctrine and practice on the "Jewish question" must take into account that the number of church leaders in the postwar period who devoted serious time and energy to addressing anti-Judaism and antisemitism within the Church was very small indeed. Most church leaders demonstrated little interest in addressing the Jewish question on either the practical or the theological level. They reluctantly acknowledged the Jewish suffering in their midst, but quickly dismissed the idea that the Church had been in any way responsible or that it should have a role in making amends. Parishioners across Germany were so resentful toward the remaining Jews, whom they perceived as enjoying preferential treatment from the Allies, that they even contested an annual Sunday church collection devoted to aid offices for Christians of Jewish descent and Protestant missions that focused on proselytizing among Jews.

The same few names of mid-level church leaders appear over and over in the archives in connection with their active concern for a new beginning in relations with Jews from 1945 to 1950: Hermann Maas in Heidelberg; Heinrich Grüber in Berlin; Otto Fricke in Frankfurt; Adolf Freudenberg in London, Geneva, and later Heilsberg near Bad Vilbel; Otto von Harling Jr. in the church chancellery; Otto von Harling Sr. in Celle near Hanover; and Karl Heinrich Rengstorf in Münster. Missing from this list are the names of most of the leading figures in the Church, including Bishops Otto Dibelius, Hans Meiser, and Theophil Wurm of Berlin, Bavaria, and Württemberg; Hans Asmussen, president of the church chancellery; and Martin Niemöller, the most prominent leader of the reform-minded council of brethren. Although Niemöller certainly did more than anyone else in the Church to publicly address the Church's share of responsibility for fostering a context in which the Nazis could come to power and initiate a campaign of discrimination and terror against the Jews, he was not at the forefront when it came time for reforming the Church's relationship to Jews. When the council of brethren finally issued its problematic albeit well-intentioned statement on Christian-Jewish relations, "A Message Concerning the Jewish Question," in April 1948, other members of the council, in particular the Reformed pastor Hermann A. Hesse, played the more prominent roles.[7]

Those most experienced with day-to-day Jewish concerns were the low-level pastors and staff who worked in the *Judenmission* and aid offices for Christians of Jewish descent. Concern for the plight of the racially persecuted and the fostering of a spirit of repentance and reconciliation were far from the minds of most Protestants. The majority in the Church directed their antisemitism toward both Jews and Christians of Jewish descent, thus uniting missionary work and aid work in a common struggle against racial prejudice. Both missionaries and aid workers complained frequently of the lack of support by regional and national church leaders. Although they did not explicitly accuse their superiors of antisemitism, the charge of antisemitism was often implicit in their criticisms of the Church's indifference toward the plight of Jews and Christians of Jewish descent. Although the number of Christians of Jewish-German descent was significant—estimates ranged from fifty thousand to sixty thousand[8]—church leaders lost sight of them among the millions of displaced persons, refugees, and German Gentiles who were also living in desperate conditions. The flight from 1946 to 1948 of tens of thousands of Jews to Germany from Eastern Europe, where fervent antisemitism had in some cases led to horrific pogroms, meant that conditions for Jews in Germany remained hopeless. Not only had Jews lost virtually all their material possessions, they were often housed in former SS barracks and concentration camps, and had virtually no hope of finding employment. The vast majority of letters to the Jewish officials in charge of relief efforts were pleas for food, housing, blankets, and medical attention, as well as for help with finding out the condition of family members or relatives from whom they were separated.[9] Although inadequate food and housing was nearly a universal experience in postwar Germany, the mental and emotional anguish resulting from the Nazi racial policies of discrimination, deportation, and extermination was a plight German

Gentiles did not experience. When the mayor of Frankfurt, Walter Kolb, gave a New Year's radio address in January 1947 in which he encouraged Frankfurt's Jewish émigrés to return, he received a flurry of letters from Jews who had remained in Frankfurt, asking how he could make such an absurd statement, considering the miserable conditions in which they lived and the continued signs of antisemitism.[10]

Protestant *Judenmission*

In a letter to church leaders across Germany in October 1945, the provisional leaders of the Evangelical-Lutheran Central Federation for Mission to Israel, Otto von Harling Sr. and Karl Heinrich Rengstorf, announced the reconstitution of the Central Federation and the Institutum Judaicum Delitzschianum (founded by Delitzsch in Leipzig in 1886).[11] They acknowledged that after the Holocaust the context for missionary work had changed, and they made it clear that the task of the Central Federation was not to do traditional missionary work, at least not yet, but rather to study the Jewish question.[12]

> The undersigned are clear that after all that has taken place, immediate evangelical work among the Jews by the German Church is at this time not possible. Thus it appears all the more important to us that the German Lutheran churches again have an office, which considers as its particular task to waken and encourage an understanding of the history and the present internal and external situation of Jewry, and to provide a hearing for and recognition of the words of the Holy Scriptures on the Jewish question and the meaning of Israel in God's plan. In this we see at the same time a contribution, which the Lutheran Church in Germany can make, to redressing the injustices done to Israel.

Significantly, their hesitation over approaching recently liberated Jews with the intention to convince them that the Messiah had come was practical, not theological. The directors of the Central Federation did not question the theological underpinnings of missionary work among Jews, but they were sensitive enough to recognize that given the Church's abandonment of Jews and neglect for Jewish Christians during the Third Reich—and throughout much of the history of the Church, for that matter—it was hypocritical and certainly unproductive to approach them now with the gospel.

For many German Protestants, especially those connected with missionary activities, the overthrow of Hitler's regime offered the possibility of starting again where they had been forced by the Nazis to leave off. It was hardly surprising, therefore, that many of the prewar attitudes reappeared, and were even given institutional form, as could be seen in the renewed activity of several local branches of the *Judenmission*. These local branch offices did not demonstrate the same sensitivity in regard to proselytizing as Rengstorf's Central Federation. They did, to be sure, give lip service to the importance of studying Judaism and fostering a dialogue between Jews and Christians, but conversion was still the primary goal.

In fact, these sentiments were only sharpened following the Second World War by the recognition that after the barbaric treatment of the Jews by the Nazis, the churches had an even greater responsibility to offer the consolation and love of the Christian gospel's message. As one ardent German supporter of *Judenmission* argued: "Just this fact [the murder of six million Jews] should compel us, out of our feelings of shame, to meet the Jews in the consciousness that we owe them our Christian witness, which alone can lead to Christ himself. Only this vital witness of committed Christians can restore the true relationship between synagogue and church, between Judaism and Christianity."[13]

But it was not merely a guilty conscience or the religious kinship between Jew and Christian that led a segment of Protestant missionaries to assign priority to missionary work among Jews. Jews, they argued, were central to God's salvation plan. Since the nineteenth century, Protestant missionaries, including Franz Delitzsch—himself of Jewish descent—argued that preaching the gospel to Jews was essential, since only when Jews accepted Jesus as the Messiah would God's promise of salvation come to fruition. Karl Heinrich Rengstorf, the postwar German director of the Institutum Judaicum Delitzschianum, reasoned that missionary work among the Jews was "occasioned by the fact that through the unbelief of His own people the fulfillment of God's work is delayed and hindered. His eternal purpose of salvation is not attained so long as His own people refuse to receive Him."[14] For Rengstorf the Church remained incomplete until God's chosen people merged with the Church by recognizing the new covenant manifested in Jesus of Nazareth. Jewish acceptance of the Messiah would mark the climax of God's purpose. "The Church is unfaithful to itself . . . when it does not constantly pray for the redemption of the Jewish people as the people of the Old Testament election. Indeed, one must even say that the church rightly understands itself as the one universal Church of the divine salvation *only when it prays for the Jewish people* with deep sorrow and with earnest longing" (emphasis mine).[15] In this passage, written in the early 1950s, Rengstorf did not advocate the use of missionaries to coax Jews to join the Church, but he clearly believed that Jews would find salvation only when they joined the Church. Thus it was the obligation of Christians to pray that Jews would accept their destiny.

Rengstorf was at the forefront of the movement after the war to reshape the goals and methods of the *Judenmission*. Although the definition of missionary work was undergoing a transformation in the decade after the war, thanks in part to Rengstorf, as long as it continued to include the desire to see Jews convert to Christianity, it relied on the anti-Judaic notion that God's covenant with the Church was in some way superior to his covenant with the Jews and that the act of conversion was an act of completion and fulfillment for Jews.

The Bavarian contact to Rengstorf's Central Federation, Pastor Friedrich Wilhelm Hopf of Mühlhausen near Nuremberg, delineated in a letter to Bavarian churchmen five tasks that the *Judenmission* would pursue in postwar Germany, the first of which was the evangelization of Jews.[16] The other four tasks were fostering a spiritual discussion between church and synagogue, studying the problem of modern Judaism, caring for Christians of Jewish descent, and developing a consciousness among Church members of the Church's partial responsibility for the antisemitic injustices during the Third Reich. Nowhere in Hopf's letter was there even the suggestion that the Church had a responsibility to do something *for* Jews *as* Jews. Jews who had converted and Jews who might be converted to Christianity were the Jews that most interested Hopf.

In August 1946, Pastor Hopf and Pastor Martin Wittenberg of Neuendettelsau, southwest of Nuremberg, asked pastors in Bavaria to remember the Jewish mission on the tenth Sunday after Trinity. It was commonplace in many regional churches for pastors and theologians associated with missionary work to present their colleagues with advice on how to conduct this service. Along with the request for financial support, Hopf and Wittenberg provided a ten-point summary on how to conduct the church service.[17] Nearly three pages provided detailed explanations of various biblical passages for the service, with the recommended lead passage coming from Luke 19:41–48. In this passage Jesus enters the temple in Jerusalem and drives out the traders. At the sight of the traders he prophesizes that "For a time will come upon you, when your enemies will set up siege-works against you; they will encircle you and hem you in at every point; they will bring you to the ground, you and your children within your walls, and will not leave you one stone standing on another, because you did not recognize God's moment when he came." The message for mission Sunday was clear: the Jews had rejected the Son of God, in so doing had earned God's wrath, and were suffering as a result. What stands out in the letters and reports by those churchmen actively engaged in the work of the *Judenmission* is their compassion for the plight of the Jews, their forthright recognition of the Church's partial responsibility for the present situation of Jewish suffering, and most important, their conviction that, more than ever, the Church had an obligation to approach Jews, especially those living in displaced persons camps, with the message that Jesus was crucified for the salvation of all people.

The evidence suggests that for the vast majority of Jews in Germany, nothing could have been further from their minds than joining the Protestant Church.[18] According to the missionaries themselves, the missions were not even remotely successful in convincing Jews to join the Church. In fact, the utter failure of the missions in the wake of the Holocaust and the success of the Zionist movement in Palestine played a significant role in the gradual process of undermining support within the Church for the missions. Jews who had converted to Christianity in nineteenth-century Germany or in pre-Nazi Germany did so either to accelerate the process of assimilation or out of conviction. After experiencing twelve years of humiliation and terror by Germans and other Europeans who often professed to be Christians, there was scarcely a Jew alive who would consider converting to Christianity for any reason. Nevertheless, diehard missionaries remained convinced that Jews needed, now more than ever, the hope and joy that came from knowing about Christ's saving grace.

But it was not just the Jews whom missionaries had trouble convincing that there was a place for Jewish converts in the Church. Theo Burgstahler, a pastor who worked in the *Judenmission* in Ulm—where the approximately ten thousand Jewish refugees lived in DP camps—reproached the Church for neglecting its obligation to preach God's word to Jews. "Missionaries by the thousands carry the gospel to the pagan world," he wrote in a short article in the Basel *Judenmission* newsletter, but "Israel remains until today the stepchild of the mission."[19] Many people in the Church, he pointed out, believed that Jews lived under the curse of God and that the Church should wait for Jews to enter the Church before preaching to them. But, Burgstahler insisted, since Jews would not join the Church independently, the Church must reach out to them.[20]

Protestant Theology and the *Judenmission*

Support for *Judenmission* was not limited to professional missionaries alone. Even highly respected scholars and churchmen supported the missions. Hermann Diem, an outspoken critic of the Church establishment, and members of the Württemberg Theological Society issued a statement in April 1946 that severely criticized the Church for antisemitism and racial arrogance during the Third Reich but also scolded the Church for not contesting the Nazis' prohibition of the Church's special mission to the Jews.[21] And when a group of reputable scholars and churchmen, including Pastor Hermann Maas, who had risked arrest in the 1930s for protecting Jews and Christians of Jewish descent, gathered at the behest of the church chancellery in October 1947 in Assenheim to discuss the Church's relationship to the Jews, they issued a nine-point statement that began by recognizing missionary work as an integral part of the Church's service to the Jewish people.[22]

At its April 1948 meeting in Darmstadt, the brethren council (*Bruderrat*), which represented the reform wing of the Church, issued a four-page statement on the Jewish question. It stated that "since Israel crucified the Messiah, it rejected its own election and its own destiny. . . . Through Christ and since Christ, the chosen people is no longer Israel but the Church."[23] Although Church reformers demonstrated in this statement that they understood the disastrous effect of the Church's institutional failure to take active steps to combat racism and antisemitism, they showed no awareness that the Church's anti-Judaic theology was also at fault.

The brethren council continued to rely on the established dogma that the new people of God, the Church, superseded the Jews as God's chosen people. The council's statement explicitly reaffirmed the theology of the nineteenth-century missionary movement by referring to Jews as the "straying children of Israel" who lived under God's judgment and would find salvation only by joining the Church. They cautioned that "the fate of the Jews is a silent sermon, reminding us that God will not allow Himself to be mocked. It is a warning to us, and an admonition to the Jews to be converted to him, who is their sole hope of salvation."

Anti-Judaism was so deeply rooted in Church doctrine and tradition and so widely accepted by clergy and laity that it was virtually unthinkable in April 1948 that it might have played a role in the horrors that were coming to light daily. Issuing their statement one month before the founding of the State of Israel and only three years after the liberation of the camps, the brethren council had not reflected long enough on these momentous events to comprehend their far-reaching significance for Protestant theology. The blindness in the German churches was not unique. Supersessionism, Christian triumphalism, and missionary thinking were orthodoxy in Protestant churches across Europe. The World Council of Churches declared in its 1948 statement, "The Christian Approach to the Jews," that "All of our churches stand under the commission of our common Lord: 'Go ye into the world and preach the gospel to every creature.' The fulfillment of this commission requires that we include the Jewish people in our evangelistic task."[24]

Despite its continued reliance on theological anti-Judaism, the brethren council's message demonstrated that there was a group of churchmen who took seriously their responsibility to speak publicly about the Church's antisemitism and to encourage reform. It read, in part,

> It may rightly be said that after what has happened, after all that we allowed to happen in silence, we have no authority to speak now. We are distressed about what happened in the past, and about the fact that we did not make any joint statement about it. . . . It was a disastrous mistake when the churches of our time adopted the secular attitude of mere humanity, emancipation and antisemitism toward the Jewish question. There was bound to be bitter retribution for the fact that antisemitism rose and flourished not only among the people (who still seemed to be a Christian nation), not only among the intelligentsia, and in governmental and military circles, but also among Christian leaders. And when finally this radical antisemitism, based on racial hatred, destroyed our nation and our churches from within, and released all its brutal force from without, there existed no power to resist it—because the churches forgot what Israel really is, and no longer loved the Jews. Christian circles washed their hands of all responsibility, justifying themselves by saying that there was a curse on the Jewish people. Christians no longer believed that the promise concerning the Jews still held good, they no longer preached it, nor showed it in their attitude to the Jews. In this way we Christians helped to bring about all the injustices and suffering inflicted upon the Jews in our country.

Church conservatives, such as Bishop of Württemberg Theophil Wurm, vehemently disagreed that the Church had played any role in the injustices or suffering that took place in the Nazi era. As chairman of the

EKD's leadership council and the grand old man in the Church, Bishop Wurm had the opportunity to use his prominent position to provide the Church as well as the world with a model of the repentant and reformed German Protestant. Unfortunately Bishop Wurm did not distinguish himself from many of his fellow countrymen. He deeply regretted that more could not have been done to stop the systematic murder of hundreds of thousands of Jews, but nevertheless he and others continued to nurture the basic prejudices that predated the Holocaust. Although the atrocities committed against the Jews appalled Wurm, his image of the Jew as a corruptor of German values carried over from the first half of the century into the second half.[25] Like many in Germany, he held the fundamental belief that Jews and Judaism had a destructive effect on Germany and must be combated.

Perhaps the most damning piece of evidence confirming Wurm's antisemitic attitude was his response to the council of brethren's April 1948 "A Message Concerning the Jewish Question." In his response to a draft of this statement Wurm asked rhetorically,

> Can one issue a statement on the Jewish question in Germany without mentioning the way Jewish literati, since the days of Heinrich Heine, sinned against the German people by mocking all that is sacred and how in many areas the peasants suffered as a result of Jewish profiteers? And if one wants to take action against today's rising antisemitism can one be silent about the misfortune that the occupying powers have handed the reins of power to the Jews who have returned in order to placate their understandable bitter resentment?[26]

That the chairman of the national leadership council of the Church could reproach his reform-minded colleagues for failing to mention Jewish profiteers and opportunists in their long-awaited statement on the Church's inadequate response to the roundup, deportation, and extermination of German Jews demonstrates that antisemitism was not just a problem among parishioners but continued to infect the highest-ranking members of the church leadership. That Wurm authored the 1952 tribute to the antisemitic Wilhelmine court chaplain, Adolf Stöcker, confirms that his conservative antisemitism remained with him until his death in 1953.[27]

Wurm's critique of the brethren council's "A Message Concerning the Jewish Question" made no reference to the statement's blatantly anti-Judaic theology because these were sentiments he and the council shared.

Wurm explained that he had no objection to the council of brethren's theological statements, which included: "since Israel crucified the Messiah, it rejected its own election and its own destiny."[28] Although conservatives and reformers disagreed over the extent and implications of the Church's antisemitism, they concurred—at least in 1948 when the brethren council issued its statement—that since the Jews had rejected Christ as the Messiah, the Church had superseded them as God's chosen people. Until they accepted Christ and joined the Church, Jewish people would continue to live under God's curse and be forced to wander the earth in exile.

Although churchmen were careful to avoid causally linking the Jews' rejection of Jesus as the Messiah with their persecution in the Holocaust or the Jewish plight in postwar Germany, it was common for churchmen to refer to the divine punishment or curse Jews brought on themselves for rejecting Jesus. It is not always clear what churchmen and theologians meant when they referred continually to God's judgment and punishment of Jews. When the council of brethren declared in its 1948 statement that "God's judgment still pursues Israel until today," were they equating God's punishment with the persecution of Jews during the Third Reich and the hardships they continued to experience after the war? And when Rengstorf stated in the early 1950s that "God has always been compelled by the unfaithfulness of His people to punish them in order to train them," is he suggesting that God used the Holocaust to convince Jews that the path they chose was the wrong one?[29]

Doubtless, holding Jews themselves responsible for the Holocaust was not the intent of the members of the brethren council nor Rengstorf. In fact, the brethren council explicitly and repeatedly charged the German people, including church leaders, with succumbing to antisemitism. "Christian circles," admonished the authors, "washed their hands of all responsibility [for the antisemitic atrocities], justifying themselves by saying that there was a curse on the Jewish people." And Rengstorf further chastised Gentiles when he acknowledged that the Holocaust was "connected with the fact that the peoples of the world feel strange and uncomfortable whenever they are confronted with the people of the divine election." Nevertheless, the theology of supersessionism, which the council of brethren, Rengstorf, and many other reputable Church officials and theologians espoused in their statements, implied that the Jews' unfaithfulness was a cause, if not the primary cause, of Jewish suffering. This becomes abundantly clear when Rengstorf states, just a few lines after acknowledging Gentile prejudices, that the suffering of Israel has a further explanation, even more important than the first. . . . This further explanation arises from the fact that God has always been compelled by the unfaithfulness of His people to punish them in order to train them. . . . Thus the Jewish people and suffering belong together. . . . The greater their distress, the more certain they are of God's final victory, which will bring with it the honorable exaltation of His chosen people.[30]

Despite the broad acceptance of the theology underpinning the *Judenmission* there had been increasing signs that not all churchmen supported missionary theology unconditionally. Three months before the brethren council issued its "A Message Concerning the Jewish Question" in 1948, it met in Kassel to hear and discuss lectures on the Jewish question by Reformed pastor Hermann A. Hesse and Lutheran pastor Otto Fricke of Frankfurt.[31] Fricke caused a stir when he expressed the view that the Church could no longer condone missionary work that expressly sought to convert Jews to Christianity. However, unlike Harling Sr. and Rengstorf in their 1945 announcement, Fricke's objections were theological, not practical. Christians, he argued, could behave in model Christian fashion and in so doing perhaps interest some Jews in the Church. But since Jews put their trust and hope in the same God as Christians, the traditional missionary task of coaxing Jews to convert was inappropriate. Although Fricke called for reforming the way Christians thought about and related to Jews, he did not elaborate except to say that Christians should treat Jews as brothers. Hans Iwand, the principal author of the earlier 1947 brethren council statement, "On the Political Course of Our People," agreed, saying that the Church was sorely mistaken if it thought it could solve the Jewish question with the *Judenmission*.[32]

Shocked by these critiques of the *Judenmission*, Harling Jr. reminded the churchmen at Kassel that the missions were victims of antisemitism during the Nazi period, not advocates of it.[33] Niemöller also was in favor of preaching the gospel to the Jews: "Wherever I confront a Jew I must say to him that Jesus of Nazareth is the Christ."[34] Although Fricke and Iwand's opposition to traditional missionary thinking is evidence of the beginning of a theological critique of the mission to the Jews, these reservations did not find their way into the brethren council's "A Message Concerning the Jewish Question" three months later.

The founding of the State of Israel in May 1948 was a crucial factor in motivating further reflection. That the Jews had not only survived the Holocaust and nearly two thousand years of Christian hostility but were now establishing a state in the land God had promised them baffled churchmen, who had been taught that God condemned Jews to wander the earth in exile until they recognized Jesus as the Messiah. Germans were not the only ones perplexed. At the founding meeting of the World Council of Churches in Amsterdam a few weeks after the May 14 founding of the State of Israel, delegates could only say, "we do not undertake to express a judgment," on the creation of this new nation.[35]

The Swiss Calvinist theologian and friend of Martin Niemöller, Karl Barth, was less reticent. What does it mean, Barth asked in his 1949 essay "The Jewish Problem and the Christian Answer," that God has remained faithful to the Jews? "How have they, all things considered, attained this surprising position of historical permanence, a permanence which increases rather than decreases [with the founding of a new state]?" The Christian answer was that the new state was a sign of God's continued love for the Jews. Christians, Barth explained, hated to hear that the Jews continued to be the chosen people because "we do not enjoy being told that the sun of free grace, by which alone we can live, shines not upon us, but upon the Jews, that it is the Jews who are elect and not the Germans, the French or the Swiss, and that in order to be chosen we must, for good or ill, either be Jews or else be heart and soul on the side of the Jews. 'Salvation is of the Jews.'" Barth's insistence that the survival of Jews and the founding of a Jewish state were signs that the Jewish people were still the chosen people found favor with a small group of his supporters in Germany but was rejected by mainstream Lutherans.

German Evangelical Committee for Service to Israel

More influential than Barth, and more representative of the German Lutheran process of grappling with the Church's triumphalist theology, were the conferences organized by the German Evangelical Committee for Service to Israel (Deutsche evangelische Ausschuß für Dienst an Israel).[36] Founded in January 1948 in Hanover by Rengstorf, the Committee for Service to Israel was a branch of the International Missionary Council's Committee on the Christian Approach to the Jews (IMCCAJ). Replacing the word "mission" with "service" indicated the intention of Rengstorf's Committee for Service to Israel to eschew promoting traditional missionary work. This was particularly evident in the regular conferences organized by the committee to address questions related to the Church and the Jews. Between 1948 and 1982 the committee organized twenty-eight conferences in various West German cities, devoted to the general theme "the Church and the Jews."[37] Despite Rengstorf's close relationship to the *Judenmission* through his continued leadership of the Evangelical Lutheran Central Federation for the Mission to Israel, he opposed making the *Judenmission* an explicit theme in the committee's conferences, in part because he wanted the conference to initiate a discussion with Jews, and to this end he hoped to include prominent Jewish speakers such as Rabbi Leo Baeck.[38]

Leo Baeck, an assimilated German Jew who served as a rabbi for the German army on the Eastern and Western fronts in the First World War, attended the committee's first conference in Darmstadt in October 1948, where he spoke about "Judaism on Old and New Paths."[39] Germany's most famous rabbi and a survivor of Theresienstadt concentration camp in Czechoslovakia, Baeck settled in England after the war and from there was a voice for reconciliation with Germany. He returned to Germany for the first time in October 1948. At a press conference a few days before his lecture in Darmstadt, Baeck explained that ever since his liberation from Theresienstadt he had set himself the task of visiting German Jews wherever German Jewish communities had taken root in the aftermath of the Holocaust.[40] He explained that this was his reason for visiting Germany. But he also wished to visit with his Christian friends, with whom he had remained friendly despite all that happened. Although the Jews who remained in Germany deserved the support of Jews from abroad, Baeck believed that the history of Jews in Germany was over. To stay in Germany or emigrate was a decision each individual Jew would have to make for himself or herself; Baeck's decision to settle in London (until his death in 1956) made clear that he, for one, was not comfortable living in Germany.

At the conference Baeck spoke about the confrontation since the seventeenth and eighteenth centuries between the modern rational world and Jewish mysticism.[41] Modern European states emancipated Jews and gave rights to them in the eighteenth and nineteenth centuries, he acknowledged, but the Jewish soul suffered: "As a man of this mystical world it was hard for him [the Jew] to find a place in this rational world where he could understand and be understood. He must, it seemed, decide for one or the other. . . . A spiritual see-saw began, a struggle between the new world and the old religion."[42] With the establishment of the State of Israel the problem was resolved by providing a place where "mysticism and ratio have been joined." Baeck emphasized the importance of the new state for the future of Judaism. "One thing is clear," he concluded, "the Bible has taken on a new life here [in the State of Israel]."

Baeck's only reference to National Socialism or the Holocaust was an opaque reference to "the unfortunate days when the crime was committed against the Jews of Germany and Poland."[43] He explicitly avoided an accusatory tone, although he did discuss the history of the persecution of Jews over the centuries. He emphasized the common roots of Judaism and Christianity and the need for Christians in Germany to rethink their theological attitude toward Jews. "The Christian Church should never forget that there can be no Bible without the Jewish Bible."[44] Christians who attempt to deny their Jewish roots, he warned, risk repeating Germany's recent past. In his only direct reference to the exculpatory statements by German Protestants regarding Jewish persecution, Baeck asserted that Christians who recognize Jews as God's chosen people will not "seek to justify something wrong which has been done or is about to be done by talking about the orders of creation." Nor will the true Christian, he continued, explain crimes against Jews with references to God's rejection of the Jews. Jewish suffering is no more a sign of God's rejection of them than is Christian suffering a sign of God's rejection of Christians. He concluded on the conciliatory note that Jews and Christians both look forward with the same hope and awe to the time of fulfillment. By stressing that Judaism and Christianity were different "ways of piety" and "ways of hope" that sought a common end, he made clear that Protestant missions to the Jews made no sense.

Although the conference itself was groundbreaking in that it brought together Jews and Christians for a dialogue in postwar Germany, Baeck was one of only four Jews present. Many in the audience were employed by or worked in *Judenmission* in the Western zones of occupation.[45] Despite the opportunity, none of the pastors or theologians explicitly condemned missionary work or called on the Church to confess publicly its role for fostering a spirit in which the Nazis could come to power and carry out their antisemitic agenda.[46] Reports on the conference by churchmen emphasized the valuable exchange of information about the present situation of Jews and Christians of Jewish descent in various regions in Germany and the world.[47]

The next conference organized by the German Evangelical Committee for Service to Israel in late February and early March 1950 in Kassel overcame some of these drawbacks. In his invitation to the conference, Otto Dibelius, who took over the chairmanship of the EKD council in 1949 from Wurm, set the tone by expressing his support for the conference because it was one way to encourage Christians in Germany to accept their share of responsibility for the behavior and attitude of the

German people toward the Jews.[48] More important, the voice and presence of the missions was virtually nonexistent, and the conference was more accessible to the public, including an open roundtable discussion between a Protestant (pastor Karl Janssen), a Catholic (Karl Thieme), and a Jew (Hugo Nothmann) as well as exposure to the conference proceedings through extensive media coverage.[49] Among the keynote speakers were well-known Jews and Christians of Jewish descent: Rudolf Pechel, editor of *Deutsche Rundschau* and an inmate from 1942 to 1945 in Sachsenhausen and Ravensbrück concentration camps; Alfred Wiener, a German Jew who fled to Amsterdam when Hitler came to power and eventually founded the Wiener Library in London; and Hans Ehrenberg, a pastor with Jewish ancestry from Westphalia who, after a short imprisonment in Sachsenhausen concentration camp, emigrated to England in 1939 with assistance from Dietrich Bonhoeffer.[50] The conference ended with a public discussion, which the local community was encouraged to attend, on the relationship between Christians and the new State of Israel.

Berlin-Weissensee Synod

Rengstorf's Committee on Service to Israel had a decisive influence on the EKD's famous Berlin-Weissensee synod. Both the Kassel conference and the April 1950 synod took place amidst a wave of desecrations of Jewish cemeteries that received international attention in the press.[51] The committee agreed at its Kassel conference to send a letter to the chairman of the EKD council, Otto Dibelius, requesting that the council take some practical steps toward addressing the continued signs of antisemitism by encouraging Protestant congregations to protect and care for Jewish cemeteries where the Jewish community either was too small or was no longer present to watch over for their cemeteries. Moreover, Adolf Freudenberg, who had been frustrated for years by the EKD council's habit of putting off issuing a statement on the Jewish question, wanted the Committee for Service to Israel to also send the EKD council a draft of a hard-hitting statement by him on the Jewish question. He insisted that the Church could not speak with integrity on the question "What can the church do for peace?"—the designated topic for the April 1950 Berlin-Weissensee synod—without first acknowledging the Church's complacency and complicity in the mistreatment of Jews.[52] Although Rengstorf's committee decided against sending the EKD council Freudenberg's strongly worded draft statement, they did agree to send the president of the upcoming EKD synod, the layman and former West German minister of interior Gustav Heinemann, a letter requesting that the synod make a statement on the Jewish question.[53]

Presumably the committee's letters to the EKD council and synod president, the rash of cemetery desecrations, and the dedication of a monument to the victims of Nazi racial persecution at the Weissensee Jewish cemetery on April 23, 1950, the Sunday that the synod opened,[54] were all factors that prompted churchmen at the synod to address Christian-Jewish relations.[55] Certainly Bishop Dibelius's opening sermon on April 23, when he declared the Church's hope that Protestant congregations would take it upon themselves to protect Jewish cemeteries, suggests the influence of the committee's letter.[56] On the following day, during the discussion on "What can the church do for peace?" the bishop of the Lutheran Church of Hanover, Hanns Lilje, was the first to raise the issue of the need for the Church to address the Jewish question.[57] He said it would be a great step toward peace if the Church would issue a genuine statement of repentance in the name of the German people on the Jewish question. It was left, however, to his colleague Heinrich Vogel, a professor of systematic theology in Berlin and a friend of Karl Barth's, to call explicitly for the synod to issue a confession of guilt for the behavior of the Church toward the Jewish people. The Church in particular, he contended, must confess its guilt because the roots of the recent catastrophe lay within the Church.[58] Vogel criticized the authors of the October 1945 Stuttgart Declaration of Guilt for dodging the issue of the Church's guilt by referring to the Church's "solidarity of guilt" with the German people as if the Church *itself* was not guilty. The afternoon of the same day Martin Niemöller supported Vogel's call for a declaration of guilt, saying it was long overdue and should have been made at Stuttgart five years earlier, but it would be better late than never.[59] He strongly condemned the prevailing attitude among many Protestants that the reprehensible behavior of the occupation powers somehow alleviated the Germans of their obligation to confess their guilt.

At the end of the second day, a committee was formed to draft a statement on "What can the church do for peace," which included Vogel, Niemöller, Joachim Beckmann, Theodore Dipper, and other churchmen actively interested in the Jewish question.[60] During the evening session of the fourth day Dipper introduced the work of the committee. He explained that the committee members quickly came to the conclusion that the unresolved state of the Church's relationship to the Jews, in particular the Church's guilt toward the Jews, was a serious obstacle to completing the committee's primary task of drafting a peace resolution. Thus the committee formed a subcommittee, headed by Heinrich Vogel, that drafted a statement on the Jewish question.

Meeting, ironically, in the Adolf Stoecker Foundation headquarters, Vogel read a draft of the "Statement on the Jewish Question" to the synod, and for the rest of the evening and the next morning, the first official discussion of the Jewish question by a national body of elected church leaders took place. Although some individuals articulated reservations about a public confession being misunderstood by the world, nearly every churchman who spoke praised the statement and expressed deep gratitude and a sense of genuine relief that the Church was finally issuing a statement that addressed the Church's antisemitism _and_ anti-Judaism.

The final version of the Berlin-Weissensee statement read as follows:

For God has consigned all men to disobedience, that he may have mercy upon all (Rom. 11:32).

We believe in the Lord and Savior, who as a person came from the people of Israel.

We Confess the Church which is joined together in one body of Jewish Christians and Gentile Christians and whose peace is Jesus Christ.

We believe God's promise to be valid for his Chosen People even after the crucifixion of Jesus Christ.

We state that by omission and silence we became implicated before the God of mercy in the outrage which has been perpetrated against the Jews by people of our nation.

We caution all Christians not to balance what has come upon us as God's judgment against what we have done to the Jews; for in judgment God's mercy searches the repentant.

We ask all Christians to dissociate themselves from all antisemitism and earnestly to resist it, whenever it stirs again, and to encounter Jews and Jewish Christians in a brotherly spirit.

We ask the Christian congregations to protect Jewish graveyards within their areas if they are unprotected.

We pray to the Lord of mercy that he may bring about the Day of Fulfillment when we will be praising the triumph of Jesus Christ together with the saved Israel.

The most significant area of disagreement was over the third sentence, which addressed the continued validity of God's covenant with the Jews. Julius Jensen, a pastor from Lübeck and leading figure in the Inner

Mission there, asked whether it was appropriate to speak of God's continued loyalty to the Jews without mentioning God's judgment of the Jews for their rejection of Jesus. Bishop Lilje, prelate Karl Hartenstein of Stuttgart, and Erlangen theologian Walter Künneth all raised similar objections. Significantly, they did not challenge the notion that after the crucifixion of Jesus the Jews remained God's chosen people. This in itself was a sign that the reevaluation of the myth of supersessionism had come a long way. What Künneth and others wanted was to reformulate the sentence so that it addressed the "biblical fact" that since the crucifixion the Jews have stood under God's judgment. Künneth considered it an absolute necessity to mention this because, year after year, on the tenth Sunday after Trinity this fact was preached to the congregations and recognized by Christian churches.[61] Vogel agreed that if one were teaching a Bible lesson, God's promise to the Jews and judgment of them would certainly be taught together. But the "Statement on the Jewish Question," was a confession and the mention of God's judgment of the Jews would send the wrong message—the message of Christian self-righteousness.[62] Vogel's argument must have found a sympathetic hearing because the final draft said nothing about God's judgment of his chosen people. In fact, the only mention of God's judgment was his judgment of Gentile Germany: "We caution all Christians not to balance what has come upon us as God's judgment against what we have done to the Jews." That all people, Christians and Jews, stood under God's judgment and mercy was implicit in the quote from Romans 11:32, which introduced the statement: "For God has consigned all men to disobedience, that he may have mercy upon all."

The decision to avoid explicit mention of God's judgment of the Jews and the subsequent need for Jewish repentance did not mean that the statement had no remnants of missionary thinking. In the final sentence the Church prayed that the God of Mercy might "bring about the Day of Fulfillment when we will be praising the triumph of Jesus Christ together with the saved Israel." Presumably in reference to this sentence Vogel said that he wanted to assuage the pro-missionary critics and assure them that "it is a missionary statement."[63] But it was not a traditional missionary statement. The Church, to be sure, still had an obligation to pray that the Jewish people would one day join the Church and recognize Jesus as the Messiah, but as a prayer it did not involve coercion, pressure, threats, or even coaxing. Nevertheless the sense of superiority and self-righteousness that undergird missionary thinking was clearly present in this last sentence.

Of course the Church's antipathy toward Jews was a consequence of both its anti-Judaism *and* antisemitism. The two were inextricably linked. To address one and not the other was to miss the undeniable link between teaching contempt for the people of the old covenant and violence against Jews. This had been the problem with the brethren council's 1948 statement. The Berlin-Weissensee synod did not make the same mistake; it addressed both the Church's anti-Judaism and its antisemitism, although its repudiation of antisemitism was milder than the brethren council's. The Berlin-Weissensee synod declared:

> We state that *by omission and silence we became implicated* before the God of mercy in the outrage which has been perpetrated against the Jews by people of our nation. . . . We ask all Christians to disassociate themselves from all antisemitism and earnestly to resist it, wherever it stirs again, and to encounter Jews and Jewish Christians in a brotherly spirit. [emphasis mine]

Indeed these sentences could be criticized for using the passive voice and for admitting to complacency and not complicity. The significance of the Berlin-Weissensee statement, however, is that the issuing body was an all-German synod. Unlike the council of brethren, which consisted of reform-minded churchmen from the old Dahlem wing of the Confessing Church, the synod was a broad coalition of churchmen and lay people of all theological persuasions. For such a group to admit to wrongdoing in their treatment of Jews was a vast improvement over previous official Church statements.

Novel too in the Berlin-Weissensee statement was its call for action. In an attempt to curb the growing number of attacks on Jewish cemeteries and to encourage Protestant congregations to take responsibility for the nation's murderous past, the authors of the statement called on Protestant congregations to protect and care for Jewish cemeteries. Although some congregations took up this challenge energetically, others ignored it or did very little. In May 1950 the church chancellery sent out a circular to regional church leaders stating that the words of the Berlin-Weissensee statement needed to be matched by deeds and that churches should not wait any longer to adopt a Jewish cemetery. Of the 715 Jewish cemeteries in Germany, the church chancellery reported 43 were entirely or partly in the care of Protestant communities in 1951.[64] Under the title "An Act of Atonement," the Jewish-German press applauded the efforts of the Church in the Rhineland to protect and care for Jewish cemeteries there as an indication that the Church intended to practice what it preached in Berlin.[65] It is one thing for the Church to publicly proclaim an interest in Protestant-Jewish reconciliation, the reporter wrote, but the integrity of the Church will stand or fall on the degree to which churchmen put into practice the lofty words spoken in Berlin. Although the protection of Jewish cemeteries was a good start, the newspaper called on the Church to do more in terms of teaching and preaching respect and tolerance for all human beings.

The Berlin-Weissensee synod's rejection of supersessionism was unprecedented and momentous. Although church leaders never explicitly tied the Church's anti-Judaism to the Holocaust, they rejected the central tenet of Christian anti-Judaism and brought about a transformation in German Protestant theology. The unanimous acceptance of the Berlin-Weissensee statement by the synod brought to an end the Church's shameful silence on the Jewish question.

The Berlin-Weissensee statement could have been more critical and explicit about the Church's complicity in the discrimination against Jews in the Third Reich. It could have addressed the centuries-long history of anti-Judaism and antisemitism in the Church. And it could have avoided altogether the notion that the Jews would remain lost sheep until they joined the Church. Nevertheless it was a momentous victory for the small group of churchmen who had tirelessly and courageously struggled, some since 1933, for the Church to rethink its historical, practical, and theological relationship to Jews and Judaism. And most important, it was the first step in a process that continues in the twenty-first century of reforming the Church's understanding of and relationship to German Judaism.

The process of challenging established doctrine on the Jewish question and institutionalizing reformed practices in the parishes was slow and intermittent. Missionary thinking and practices continued in the 1950s and afterward, although not always in the same manner as in the nineteenth and early twentieth centuries. The Berlin-Weissensee statement should be understood as a first step in challenging anti-Judaic theology in the German Protestant Church. By the 1960s and 1970s churchmen such as Günther Harder, Karl Heinrich Rengstorf, and Heinrich Vogel, all of whom favored a new relationship with Jews based on dialogue and mutual respect, had succeeded in fostering a public debate within the Church over the question "mission or dialogue?"[66] They all rejected traditional missionary work—defined as the conversion of Jews to Christianity through the efforts of trained missionaries—which sought to resolve the Jewish question through the elimination of Jews by baptizing them. As we have seen, the objection to traditional missionary work did not entail a complete break with the theology that undergirded missionary thinking. Nevertheless the Church did take steps to promote dialogue between Protestant and Jewish theologians and to encourage a relationship based on mutual respect and learning. This new direction was especially evident in 1961 when the tenth postwar German Evangelical Church Rally (Deutsche Evangelische Kirchentag) met in Berlin and thousands of Protestants attended lectures and engaged in discussion on Christian-Jewish relations and Judaism.[67] But it was not until 1980 that the regional Synod of the Evangelical Church in the Rhineland explicitly repudiated the Church's mission to Israel.[68] The Rhineland Synod declared, "We believe that in their respective calling Jews and Christians are witnesses of God before the world and before each other. Therefore we are convinced that the church may not express its witness toward the Jewish people as it does its mission to the peoples of the world." In the two decades since 1980 a number of regional churches, although not all, have published similar documents repudiating the mission to Israel.

NOTES

Significant portions of this essay draw on chapters 7 and 8 of my book *A Church Divided: German Protestants Confront the Nazi Past* (Bloomington: Indiana University Press, 2004).

1. See Paul Aring, *Christliche Judenmission* (Neukirchen-Vluyn: Neukirchener, 1980); John Conway, "Protestant Missions to the Jews 1810–1980: Ecclesiastical Imperialism or Theological Aberration?" *Holocaust and Genocide Studies* 1, no. 1 (1986): 127–46; and Eva Fleischner, *Judaism in German Christian Theology since 1945: Christianity and Israel Considered in Terms of Mission* (Metuchen, N.J.: Scarecrow Press and American Theological Library Association, 1975).

2. Some missionaries cited passages from Matthew and Romans to make the point that missionary work among the Jews should be prioritized, e.g., "Do not take the road to gentile lands, and do not enter an Samaritan town; but go rather to the lost sheep of the house of Israel. As you go proclaim the message: 'The kingdom of heaven is upon you' " (Mt 10:5–7). And from Romans 1:16 they cite, "For I am not ashamed of the gospel. It is the saving power of God for everyone who has the faith—the Jew first, but the Greek also."

3. Following the practice in the Bible, churchmen used the term "Israel" to refer to the Jewish people. In order to avoid confusion I refer to the country of Israel as the State of Israel.

4. Although I recognize that antisemitism and anti-Judaism overlap in significant ways and that antisemitism in the second half of the nineteenth century and the first half of the twentieth century found widespread approval, in part, because of the

Christian churches' centuries-old acceptance of anti-Judaism, there are important distinctions between the two forms of prejudice. Let me be clear, both forms of prejudice are reprehensible, but for different reasons. Antisemitism is a racially driven form of hatred toward Jews. For antisemites a Jew's (bad) character is immutable because it is directly tied to his or her race, which by definition is immutable. Anti-Judaism, in contrast, is theologically based and originates from the Christian belief that Judaism has been superseded by Christianity.

5. Paul van Buren, a former professor of religion at Temple University and author of the three-volume *Theology of the Jewish-Christian Reality* (Lanham: University Press of America, 1980–95), argues persuasively that the Holocaust and the foundation of the Israeli state brought about a "repudiation . . . of what the Church has said and taught [regarding Jews] from the second century until the twentieth." See his essay, "Changes in Christian Theology," in *The Holocaust: Ideology, Bureaucracy, and Genocide,* ed. Henry Friedlander and Sybil Milton (Millwood, N.Y.: Kraus International Publications, 1980), 285–93.

6. The Berlin Weissensee statement, "Wort an die Judenfrage," is translated as "Statement on the Jewish Question" in *The Theology of the Churches and the Jewish People, Statements by the World Council of Churches and Its Member Churches* (Geneva: WCC Publications, 1988), 47–48. The reform-minded brethren council's 1948 statement, "Ein Wort zur Judenfrage," is translated by the World Council of Churches (WCC) as "A Message Concerning the Jewish Question," in *The Relationship of the Church to the Jewish People,* edited by the WCC (Geneva: WCC Publications, 1964), 48–52.

7. The brethren council's 1948 statement on the Jewish question is analyzed in some detail later in this chapter.

8. See *Der Freund Israels,* the Swiss newsletter of the Basel *Judenmission,* 74, no. 6 (Dec. 1947). Also see H. L. Ellison's report, "The Racially Persecuted Christians in Germany: Report on a Journey—May 5 to June 25, 1948," ZEKHN-Darmstadt 36/81.

9. One of President Truman's own aides, Earl G. Harrison, came to the conclusion after visiting DP camps in Germany in late summer 1945, "many Jewish displaced persons . . . are living under guard behind barbed-wire fences, including some of the most notorious concentration camps, amidst crowded, frequently unsanitary and generally grim conditions, in complete idleness, with no opportunity, except surreptitiously, to communicate with the outside world, waiting, hoping for some word of encouragement and action on their behalf." Harrison's report goes on for several pages describing the dismal conditions in which Jews lived in the months immediately following the end of the war. Also see Angelika Königseder and Juliane Wetzel, *Waiting for Hope: Jewish Displaced Persons in Post-World War II Germany,* trans. John Broadwin (Evanston: Northwestern University Press, 2001); Michael Brenner, *After the Holocaust: Rebuilding Jewish Lives in Postwar Germany* (Princeton, N.J.: Princeton University Press, 1997), 1–77, and Jael Geis, *Übrig sein—Leben "danach": Juden deutscher Herkunft in der britischen und amerikanischen Zone Deutschlands 1945–1949* (Berlin: Philo, 2000); Frank Stern, "Breaking the 'Cordon Sanitaire' of Memory: The Jewish Encounter with German Society," in *Thinking about the Holocaust: After Half a Century,* ed. Alvin H. Rosenfeld (Bloomington: Indiana University Press, 1997), 213–32; and Atina Grossman, "Home and Displacement in a City of Bordercrossers: Jews in Berlin 1945–1948," in *Unlikely History: The Changing German-Jewish Symbiosis, 1945–2000,* ed. Leslie Morris and Jack Zipes (New York: Palegrave, 2002), 63–99. An excellent archival source on the conditions of Jews in postwar German is the Central Archive of the History of Jews in Germany, Zentralarchiv für die Geschichte der Juden in Deutschland in Heidelberg (ZAJD-Heidelberg), in particular the activity reports and correspondence of the Jewish aid

office (*Betreuungsstelle*) in Frankfurt and the correspondence of Julius Dreifuss, the chairman of the Jewish community in Düsseldorf.

10. ZAJD-Heidelberg 1/13 A. 740.

11. While the Evangelical-Lutheran Central Federation for Mission to Israel acted as an umbrella organization for the Jewish missions tied to Lutheran regional churches, the Berlin Federation for Mission to the Jews provided guidance to the north-German United churches, and the Swiss Basel Jewish Mission was associated with the missionary work in Württemberg, Baden, Pfalz, and Hessen. See, Bericht über die zweite Sitzung der Geschäftsstelle Stuttgart des Vereins der Freunde Israels (November 16, 1948), LKA Stuttgart A126/659, 8.

12. Evangelisch-Lutherischer Zentralverein für Mission unter Israel to Evangelischen Oberkirchenrat, October 24, 1945, LKA Stuttgart A126/658, 132.

13. Quoted in Conway, "Protestant Missions to the Jews," 139.

14. Karl Heinrich Rengstorf, "The Spiritual Basis for Jewish Evangelism," *International Review of Missions* 40 (April 1951): 149. Also see Rengstorf's brief history of the institute, *Das Institutum Judaicum Delitzschianum 1886–1961* (Munster: Achendorff, 1963).

15. Karl Heinrich Rengstorf, "The Jewish Problem and the Church's Understanding of Its Own Mission," in *The Church and the Jewish People*, ed. Göte Hedenquist (London: Edinburgh, 1954), 27–36.

16. Hopf to H. Sasse, G. Schmidt, H. Kressel, K. Krodel, T. Poehlmann, January 3, 1946, LKA Nuremberg V. III/51, 1.

17. Letter from Hopf and Wittenberg to Alle Pfarrämter der Evang.-Luth. Kirche in Bayern, Jan. 1946, LKA Nuremberg V. III/51, 1.

18. See "Bericht des Herrn Pfarrer Grillenberger über die Judenmission in Bayern beim Landesmissionsfest in Nürnberg Juli 1949," LKA Nuremberg V. III/51, 1.

19. Theo Burgstahler in *Der Freund Israels* 74, no. 6 (Dec. 1947): 83.

20. Theo Burgstahler in *Der Freund Israels* 74, no. 3 (July 1947): 40.

21. Wolfgang Gerlach, *And the Witnesses Were Silent: The Confessing Church and the Persecution of the Jews*, trans. Victoria Barnett (Lincoln: University of Nebraska Press, 2000), 227–28; originally published as *Als die Zeugen schwiegen: Bekennende Kirche und die Juden* (Berlin: Institut Kirche und Judentum, 1987).

22. LKA Stuttgart D1/222, 1. In addition to Hermann Maas and Karl Heinrich Rengstorf, the other signatories of the Assenheim statement were Dr. Günther Harder of Berlin's Kirchliche Hochschule, Prof. Jannasch of the University of Mainz, Dr. Med. and missionary Gottfried Frohwein, pastor Theo Burgstahler from Ulm, and Harling Jr.

23. See the WCC translation of "A Message Concerning the Jewish Question," in *The Relationship of the Church to the Jewish People*, edited by the WCC (Geneva: WCC Publications, 1964), 48–52.

24. See *The Theology of the Churches and the Jewish People*, document 2.

25. David Diephouse, "Antisemitism as Moral Discourse: Theophil Wurm and Protestant Opposition to the Holocaust," paper presented at the Thirtieth Annual Scholars' Conference on the Holocaust and the Churches at St. Joseph's University in Philadelphia, March 6, 2000.

26. Wurm to Mochalski, January 17, 1948, LKA Stuttgart D1/222, 1.

27. Wurm's 14-page tribute, "Adolf Stöckers Kampf für Kirche and Volk" is available at the LKA Stuttgart D1/3, 2. Also see Diephouse, "Antisemitism as Moral Discourse."

28. Wurm to Mochalski, January 17, 1948, ZEKHN-Darmstadt 62/1026.

29. The quote comes from Rengstorf's essay, "The Jewish Problem," 34.

30. Ibid., 34–35. Catholics also espoused similar thoughts on Jewish suffering.

Michael Schmaus, a leading Catholic theologian in Germany wrote in 1949 that "God has . . . great plans for the people chosen by him. . . . God's purpose in his judgments upon the chosen people is not destruction, but salvation. . . . Only because God cannot forget his people, only because he is willing to let it be lost, does he punish it hard and frequently." Quoted in Fleischner, *Judaism in German Christian Theology*, 157. For the entire article see Michael Schmaus, "Das Verhältnis der Christen und Juden," *Judaica* 5 (1949): 182–91.

31. Protokoll über die Sitzung des Bruderrates der EKD am 7–8 Jan. 1948 in Kassel, ZEKHN-Darmstadt 62/1026, 3.

32. Kassel Protokoll, ZEKHN-Darmstadt 62/1026, 3.

33. Ibid., 6.

34. On Niemöller's antisemitism and anti-Judaism, see Robert Michael, "Theological Myth, German Antisemitism and the Holocaust: The Case of Martin Niemoeller," *Holocaust and Genocide Studies* 2 (1987): 105–22.

35. See Allan Brockway's essay, "The Theology of the Churches and the Jewish People," at http://www.abrock.com.

36. Hermle covers the founding of the Committee for Service to Israel and the early debates about its purpose very thoroughly. See *Evangelische Kirche und Judentum*, 205–209, and Otto von Harling Jr., "Kirche und Israel," *Kirchliches Jahrbuch für die Evangelische Kirche in Deutschland* (1953): 324–28.

37. Karin Haufler-Musiol, "125 Jahre Zentralverein: Ein historischer Überblick," in *Auf dem Wege zum christlich-jüdischen Gespräch: 125 Jahre Evangelisch-lutherischer Zentralverein für Zeugnis und Dienst unter Juden und Christen*, ed. Arnulf H. Baumann (Münster: Lit, 1998), 36.

38. Hermle, *Evangelische Kirche und Judentum*, 214–15.

39. Leo Baeck, "Das Judentum auf alten und neuen Wegen," *Judaica* 6 (1950): 133–48.

40. "Pressekonferenz mit Herrn Rabbiner Dr. Baeck," October 14, 1948, ZAJD-Heidelberg 1/13, A. 722.

41. In addition to Baeck the speakers included, among others, Martin Niemöller, who welcomed the conference participants, Conrad Hoffmann, the director of the International Committee on the Christian Approach to the Jews, Curt Radlauer from Grüber's Berlin aid office for Christians of Jewish descent, Martin Wittenberg of the Bavarian *Judenmission*, and Rengstorf.

42. Baeck, "Das Judentum," 138–39.

43. Ibid., 144.

44. Ibid., 146.

45. Hermle, *Evangelische Kirche und Judentum*, 221–22.

46. Ibid., 223; Niemöller's brief introductory remarks were a partial exception; he stressed that the present suffering in Germany was a consequence of German guilt for the atrocities committed against Jews.

47. See two reports on the Darmstadt conference by Otto von Harling Jr. and John Witt, a Swiss pastor from Zurich, ZEKHN-Darmstadt 155/792.

48. Otto Dibelius, "Einladung zu einer Studientagung 'Kirche und Judentum,'" January 1950, in *Die Kirchen und das Judentum. Dokumente von 1945 bis 1985*, ed. Rolf Rendtorff and Hans-Hermann Henrix (Munich: Chr. Kaiser, 1988), 545–46.

49. Hermle, *Evangelische Kirche und Judentum*, 224–27. The meeting was also reported on positively by the Jewish press. See E. G. Lowenthal, "Um den Glauben an das Menschliche," *Allgemeine Wochenzeitung der Juden in Deutschland* (March 10, 1950).

50. Grillenberger to Oberkirchenrat Riedel, "Studientagung in Kassel über

'Kirche und Judentum,' " June 21, 1950, LKA Nuremberg LKR XIV, 1608a. Also see Adolf Freudenberg's report, "Studientagung "Kirche und Judentum" in *Bekennende Kirche auf dem Weg* (March 15, 1950), 7–10.

51. The leading German-Jewish newspaper, *Allgemeine Wochenzeitung der Juden in Deutschland,* devoted considerable space to reports on the desecration of Jewish cemeteries.

52. The draft of Freudenberg's statement, "Sätze zur Judenfrage als Friedensfrage," is reprinted at the end of his report, "Studientagung 'Kirche und Judentum' " in *Bekennende Kirche auf dem Weg* (March 15, 1950), 9–10. On the committee's letters to the EKD council and the President of the Berlin-Weissensee synod, see Grillenberger, June 21, 1950, LKA Nuremberg LKR XIV, 1608a; Hermle, *Evangelische Kirche und Judentum,* 233–34; Otto von Harling Jr., "Kirche und Israel," *Kirchliche Jahrbuch* (1953): 305.

53. Harling, "Kirche und Israel," 305.

54. The monument reads: ". . . dedicated to the memory of our murdered brothers and sisters of 1933–45, and to the living who should fulfill the legacy of the dead." Some 115,000 Jews from working- and lower-middle-class families are buried in the Weissensee cemetery, which was founded in 1880.

55. See Heydenreich, "Erklärungen aus der Evangelischen Kirche Deutschlands und der Ökumene zur Judenfrage 1932–1961," 254–55, and Hermle, *Evangelische Kirche und Judentum,* 348–51.

56. Berlin-Weissensee 1950 Bericht, 14.

57. Ibid., 102.

58. Ibid., 116.

59. Ibid., 131–32.

60. Ibid., 158.

61. Ibid., 341.

62. Ibid., 323.

63. Ibid., 327.

64. See Hermle, *Evangelische Kirche und Judentum,* 363–64, and LKA Nuremberg Kreisdekan München/223. Harling Jr. reported in the 1953 *Kirchliches Jahrbuch für die evangelische Kirche in Deutschland* that approximately 70 cemeteries were under the care of church communities.

65. "Ein Akt der Wiedergutmachung," *Allgemeine Wochenzeitung der Juden in Deutschland* 4 (June 30, 1950): 1.

66. See *Der Ungekündigte Bund: Neue Begegnung von Juden und christlicher Gemeinde,* ed. Dietrich Goldschmidt and Hans-Joachim Kraus (Stuttgart: Kreuz, 1962). Günther Harder was a founder of both the Arbeitsgruppe für Juden und Christen and the Institut Kirche und Judentum at the Kirchliche Hochschule in Berlin. His contribution to the above-mentioned collection, "Kirche und Synagoge: Nicht Mission sondern Gespräch," prompted considerable debate. See also Harder's "Christen vor dem Problem der Judenfrage: Evangelisch-jüdisches Gegenüber seit 1945," in *Christen und Juden: Ihr Gegenüber vom Apostelkonzil bis heute,* ed. Wolf-Dieter Marsch and Karl Thieme (Mainz: Matthias-Grünewald, 1961), 251–69. On the differences between Harder and Rengstorf see Fleischner, *Judaism in German Christian Theology since 1945,* 74–78, 101, and 112. Heinrich Vogel was a professor of theology at the Kirchliche Hochschule and Humboldt University in Berlin. He was also the primary author of the 1950 Berlin-Weissensee statement.

67. On the 1961 *Kirchentag* see *Der ungekündigte Bund.* Founded in August 1949, the *Kirchentag* was an annual rally of Protestant laity organized by the layman Dr. Reinhold von Thadden-Trieglaff. Its purpose was to involve everyday Protestants

in discussions about contemporary issues from a Christian perspective. See Franklin Littell, *The German Phoenix: Men and Movements in the Church in Germany,* vol. 2 (Garden City, N.Y.: Doubleday, 1960), chapter 4.

68. See *The Theology of the Churches,* 175, and John Conway, "The Changes in Recent Decades in the Churches' Doctrine and Practice toward Judaism and the Jewish People," in . . . *und über Barmen hinaus: Studien zur Kirchlichen Zeitgeschichte,* ed. Joachim Mehlhausen (Göttingen: Vandenhoeck and Ruprecht, 1995), 552.

9 Shock, Renewal, Crisis

CATHOLIC REFLECTIONS ON THE SHOAH

ELIAS H. FÜLLENBACH

In February 1937, the Austrian magazine *Die Erfüllung* published a *Memorandum* (*Denkschrift*) entitled *Christ's Church and the Jewish Question,* signed by several renowned Catholic theologians and politicians from cities throughout Europe, including Rome, Prague, Paris, and Vienna, and called for outspoken protest against the antisemitic actions of the National Socialists.[1] In the introduction, it stated: "In view of the confusion caused even among Christians . . . over several decades, and particularly in recent years, by a consciously or unconsciously anti-Christian antisemitism with respect to the Jewish question, we consider it to be our obligation as Christians to point out the teachings of Christ's Church regarding these questions, and, from that point of view, respond to the attempts at a solution made and propagated at present—especially in the German-speaking regions."[2]

Among the fourteen signers were Jacques Maritain and his friend Charles Journet, later a cardinal and theologian of the Second Vatican Council, Dietrich von Hildebrand, a philosopher from Austria, and Eduard Pant, a Catholic politician from Poland.[3] Also signing the statement were a significant number of religious leaders such as the Austrian Franciscan Cyrill Fischer, well-known for his numerous articles and pamphlets on the dangers of National Socialism; Basilius Lang, O.S.B., member of the Benedictine Abbey of Emaus in Prague and a leading figure in the liturgical movement; and four Dominican priests, among them Franziskus M. Stratmann, O.P., the former leader of the Peace League of German Catholics who now lived in exile in Rome.[4] However, the *Memorandum*'s initiators, the Catholic priest and publisher of *Die Erfüllung*, Johannes (John M.) Oesterreicher, and several émigrés from Germany, including the former Center Party politician Joseph Wirth, and the two actual authors of the piece, Waldemar Gurian and Karl Thieme,[5] interestingly did not sign the *Memorandum*. A note by the journal's editors offered the following explanation: "In addition to the concurrence of the signatories, it also meets with the approval of important members of domestic and foreign religious orders as well as prominent Catholic politicians. Current terrorism forces the editors to refrain from publishing the names in order to avoid endangering their friends and their families."[6]

Specifically, Thieme was fearful of actions that the Gestapo might take against his mother, who still lived in Nazi Germany. In 1935, he had left the country after converting from Protestantism to Catholicism as a public protest against the "Aryan Paragraph" that the German Christians adopted.[7] While in exile in Switzerland, he sustained himself on a meager salary that he received for writing theological articles for several émigré periodicals such as Gurian's *Deutsche Briefe*. Gurian and Thieme had been friends for years. They already worked together for the Catholic weekly *Junge Front* (later called *Michael*), which began attacking the totalitarian and antisemitic ideology of National Socialism soon after Hitler's appointment as Reich chancellor.[8]

Shock

In the autumn of 1936, Joseph Wirth invited Gurian and Thieme to write a memorandum against antisemitism. Since his emigration from Germany, Wirth had tried to establish an émigré network. As a "traveling salesman in the service of humane thought" who worked "for better understanding between Jews and Catholics,"[9] he met with opponents of the Nazi regime in Italy, France, and Austria, contacted the representatives of Jewish organizations in Great Britain and the United States,[10] and had an expert opinion prepared in Poland to assess anti-Jewish statements made in the Catholic press there. The former Center Party politician most particularly expected the Catholic intellectuals of Europe to speak out candidly against the growing antisemitism, and especially against National Socialist racial policy in Germany, whose brutality had shocked Wirth from the very beginning. Together with Oesterreicher—the editor of *Die Erfüllung*, he therefore conceived, in

1936, the idea of preparing a memorandum on the "Jewish question" and publishing it with the signatures of notable Catholics. Gurian and Thieme readily agreed to write the memorandum, Wirth having assured them that they would receive a generous stipend for their work.

The *Memorandum*, however, took a great deal of time to compose. In September 1936, Thieme wrote to Oesterreicher: "Tomorrow, three weeks will have gone by since our gathering, still I cannot send you the entire text of my portion of our *Memorandum* but only about the first two thirds. As you will see, I have—with G[urian's] approval—broadened the topic a little in order to protect us from the accusation of having polemicized only in one direction."[11] The difficult writing process continued onward into December, causing Oesterreicher to comment: "I am urgently waiting for the second part of the *Memorandum*, about which Gurian wrote to me that he intended to send it to you last Monday. Dr. Wirth is making this very urgent, and I have to do so likewise. After all, multiple copies of the *Memorandum* will have to be made here, and it will have to be sent to each individual signatory before Christmas."[12] Only a few days before Christmas, Gurian managed to complete his portion of the text, although he was "not entirely satisfied with the draft."[13] But both he and Thieme still hoped that the text, or at least "portions of it," would be impressive enough to combat the antisemitic actions of the National Socialists.

Indeed, their criticism of current politics in Germany was markedly pointed: in the completed joint draft, the authors firmly condemned all "special and emergency acts against Jews" since, it argued, they did not, contrary to what the dictators claimed, purify "the public life from harmful phenomena."[14] Rather, these acts led to "the abolition of the conception of government and legality, which are justified by natural law."[15] In addition, by carrying out these actions, the government unjustly condemned and defamed Jews in a false attempt to "unify the state and the nation" as it steered the majority against an alleged enemy. Furthermore, Gurian and Thieme cautioned that the fate of Jews, "namely their identification with any enemy of the state," might consequently also become the fate of Catholics or any other minority in society.[16]

After this general criticism of special emergency acts against an unpopular group, Gurian and Thieme also directly addressed the antisemitic racism of Nazi ideology by stating that the "racial laws and racial tenets do not result from scientific study but are indeed based on intentions entirely different from those invoked."[17] Therefore, the

Church will have to warn its faithful against succumbing to the heresy of racism. This heresy is based on a naturalistic view of humans, irreconcilable with the Christian belief in God. Once this view of humans has penetrated the ideas of a people via the pathways of ostracizing the "Jewish race," then other consequences ensue: . . . Just as racism attempts to destroy people as individuals responsible before God in their conscience, so it also threatens to tear apart the Mystical Body of Christ: Not only does it deny that humankind is one entity of Creation, but it follows that it also denies its oneness in sin and salvation. Racism thus becomes the archenemy of the gospel and the Church.[18]

In using these words, Gurian and Thieme actually did not do more than express the official teaching of the Church, thus reminding their readers of Pope Pius XI's public condemnation of modern racial antisemitism in March 1928;[19] they then declared: "In view of this unequivocal statement by the Church, any attempt of justifying antisemitism as 'Christian' or 'ecclesiastic' must be most firmly rejected."[20]

As compared to the papal decree, however, Thieme and Gurian interpreted the term "antisemitism" in a much broader sense, because they condemned not only racial antisemitism, but also all other forms of modern Judaeophobia, especially a more "moderate" national-conservative (*völkisch-konservativen*) antisemitism that was often embraced by Christians. They stated that though the advocates of this "moderate" form of antisemitism often felt "full sympathy with individual innocent victims of the measures against the Jewry," they still also demonstrated an acceptance of anti-Jewish acts and special provisions, or, at the very least, "found numerous excuses in the latter's favor."[21] They stated that the Christian proponents of this apparently "harmless" national-conservative antisemitism in particular rejected racism in principle while frequently having no objections to it in practice. According to Gurian and Thieme, it was therefore dishonest for these Christian antisemites to keep asserting that they were opponents of race theories and, therefore, could not possibly be "antisemites," and then to spread abstruse legends about ritual murders or to believe in worldwide Jewish conspiracies, even though the infamous *Protocols of the Learned Elders of Zion* had been publicly discredited as a fictional work.[22]

By condemning not only racists, but also so-called moderate antisemites, Thieme and Gurian truly went against a belief that was culturally and religiously acceptable among Roman Catholics. This conviction condemned racial antisemitism as un-Christian and, therefore, banned by the Church, but at the same time, embraced an apparently "good" and "healthy" fight against Jews as reconcilable with Christian social tenets.[23] This distinction had already been propagated by Father Enrico Rosa, S.J., the editor of the Catholic periodical *La Civiltà Cattolica,* after Pius XI's 1928 statement against racial antisemitism,[24] and it was also present in numerous contemporary Catholic encyclopedias.[25] A few of the *Memorandum*'s initiators had experienced firsthand that the boundaries between these two forms of antisemitism could indeed be quite fluid and that "moderate" Christian antisemitism was not quite so "innocuous" and "healthy" as Rosa and others had claimed. For example, in March 1936, a controversy erupted among members of the board of the Viennese Pauluswerk, the publishing house of *Die Erfüllung,* after the well-respected Jesuit Georg Bichlmair, vice president of the Pauluswerk (Vienna Pastoral Institute), publicly stated that Catholic organizations should also be granted permission to include an "Aryan paragraph" in their statutes.[26] Up to this point, Bichlmair had been regarded as a "friend of Jews," especially in Austria. Nevertheless, as another member of the Pauluswerk, the Austrian philosopher Dietrich von Hildebrand charged that Bichlmair's "unfortunate idea" that one should make certain concessions to the racial antisemites in order "to save them from renunciation of the Church" meant an utter "betrayal" of the Christian corporative state in Austria and its opposition to National Socialism.[27] Johannes Oesterreicher reacted with similar indignation. He saw in Bichlmair's explanation "a weak capitulation to the racial hatred" and insisted on the Jesuit's resignation from his office as vice-president of the Pauluswerk.[28]

Thus Thieme, Gurian, and Oesterreicher held that not even a more "moderate" form of antisemitism should exist because they realized that at any moment it could turn radical and—as in the case of Bichlmair—convert into racial antisemitism. For this reason, in their *Memorandum* they strongly warned against making even the smallest concessions to racism because it "would be maliciously irresponsible to think that this heresy, just because it cannot be publicly uttered by Catholic Christians, remains . . . without any influence on these Christians."[29]

Emphasizing the Jewishness of Jesus,[30] the authors of the *Memorandum* were complaining of "the sorrow and disappointment about the attitude of those who call themselves Christians but who, in all their actions," do not show Christ's love to the Jews.[31] Thieme and Gurian realized that even the traditional-conservative antisemites no longer perceived Jews as brothers or sisters but reduced them to political or social objects.[32] This, the authors argued, could not be tolerated. Therefore, the initiators called for an outspoken protest "against ostracizing the Jews and against any special orders directed not only against the Jews but against all of us because their consequences are so ominous, aiming not for protection and justifiable security measures but for defamation and extermination."[33]

While the *Memorandum* addressed all Christians, its authors primarily directed their words toward the Roman Curia and the pope. Therefore, Joseph Wirth sent the *Memorandum* to Cardinal Eugenio Pacelli, the Vatican secretary of state, among others, and requested that he forward it to Pius XI.[34] The *Memorandum*'s initiators hoped that Rome would issue a frank word against the German "Jewish policy." Wirth wrote to Pacelli that it gave him

> great pleasure to submit to you in the enclosure a *Memorandum* written in Vienna, with the humble request that you may read it. The fact that the *Memorandum* was written in Vienna is only an expression of the belief that a part of the destiny of the Christian West is being decided in Vienna in the fight against modern racism. . . . The situation in Poland is different. There, our fears of a breakthrough of racism have unfortunately grown. . . . It is in this context that I present to Your Excellency this *Memorandum,* which I proposed at the time in Vienna, and humbly request that you also kindly present it to our Holy Father Pope Pius XI, with our expression of the most humble devotion.[35]

Wirth and the other initiators of the *Memorandum* maintained contacts with the Vatican over a period of several months.[36] However, the Vatican did not publicly support the Viennese *Memorandum,*[37] which quickly had been translated into several languages.[38] Frustrated by this "wasted effort,"[39] Thieme wrote: "Antisemitism seems to be growing *rapidly* here below the surface. . . . Therefore, I can only say that every single proof of the 'non-silence' on the part of the Church feels to me like mockery. You will be justified in thinking that this is an exaggeration, but for once I had to get this off my chest."[40] Turning to the speech that Pius XI gave to a group of Belgian pilgrims on September 6, 1938, in which the pope stated that Christians were "spiritually all Semites," Thieme then wrote: "Impromptus on the occasion of receptions for pilgrims, no matter how much they are spoken from the heart, they are no substitute for an authoritative word of doctrine."[41] Together with Oesterreicher, Stratmann, and other supporters, Thieme addressed a new letter to the pope: "Your Holiness is implored to lend a favorable ear to the following ardent request submitted on behalf of a small group of Dutch and Swiss Catholics and originally prompted by news regarding the moods and wishes in German Catholic circles."[42] Together they asked Pius XI to mention the persecuted Jews in his Christmas message, because "what moment could be more appropriate to call for such a Samaritan service to the blood brothers of our Savior than the feast of His birth *ex radice Isai*." The writers were of the opinion

> that such a word would be epochal in the history of the Holy Church, in the history of humanity, and not last of all in the history of Israel's conversion. And even if it should be used as an excuse for new persecutions of the Church in Germany and Austria, which are sure to happen anyway, it would be easier to bear them in the knowledge that they are being suffered for a testimonial of merciful love. May God therefore grant that the Vicar of Christ will say such a word of sustenance and clarification to His flock. It would be the most beautiful Christmas present the children could receive from their father today.[43]

It is not clear whether Pius XI actually received this document.[44] Nevertheless, because of their contacts with the Jesuit priests Gustav Gundlach and John La Farge, the group, or at least some members, had been informed of the pope's project of an encyclical against antisemitism.[45] This news offered them hope that the pope had read their *Memorandum* and taken it to heart. Therefore, following the death of Pius XI, they were deeply disappointed when the fervently hoped-for encyclical failed to be published.[46] Even Oesterreicher, who usually defended Pacelli and the politics of the Vatican, claimed: "It is incomprehensible that Pius XII, after having failed in all of his diplomatic attempts while Cardinal Secretary of State, still tries his hand at diplomacy instead of proclaiming the truth."[47]

Renewal

After the Second World War, many members of this group of dedicated Catholics reestablished contacts with one another, now in order to work toward improving the Catholic-Jewish relationship after the Shoah. Together with equally dedicated Protestants and Jews, they supported the establishment of the International Council of Christians and Jews[48] and comparable local organizations. Most particularly, a group under the leadership of Gertrud Luckner and Karl Thieme was formed in the southwestern German city of Freiburg im Breisgau.

As an employee of the Catholic Caritas Association in Freiburg, Luckner had previously devoted herself to the persecuted Jews during the Nazi period and helped some to emigrate.[49] Under National Socialism, she obtained support and assistance from friends in Great Britain and Switzerland and also from the Relief Committee for Catholic Non-Aryans (Hilfsausschuß für katholische Nichtarier), founded in Berlin in 1935, and the Hamburg-based St. Raphael's Association. After the 1938 annexation of Austria, she also closely cooperated with the Archbishop's Relief Committee for Non-Aryan Catholics (Erzbischöfliche Hilfsstelle für nichtarische Katholiken) in Vienna.[50] However, Luckner in no way restricted her help only to Catholics of Jewish descent. She also maintained contacts with the Protestant *Büro Grüber* and members of the Confessing Church, the German Quakers, and the so-called Representation of Jews in the German Reich (Reichsvertretung der Juden in Deutschland). Luckner especially won "the confidence of the outstanding leader of German Jewry, Rabbi Leo Baeck," who gave her "a secret password so that she could visit Jewish circles in cities throughout the country."[51] In June 1941, the president of Caritas, Benedict Kreutz, issued a written certification allowing her to make longer trips "aiming at emigrant advising" and in this way made it possible for her to continue this courier activity during the war.[52] Equipped with this authorization and an official confirmation issued personally by Conrad Gröber, archbishop of Freiburg, she traveled around Germany and the annexed Austria, "secretly trying to organize an underground support network through local Caritas cells. At the same time, she continued her work in Freiburg, smuggling Jews across the nearby borders of Switzerland and France and providing for those who were unable to emigrate."[53] When systematic deportations started in October 1941, she visited Cardinal Michael von Faulhaber in Munich in order to request the support of the German bishops for deported Catholic "Non-Aryans."[54] Despite his attempts to fulfill Luckner's request, Faulhaber was not able to gain the support of Adolf Bertram, the leading prelate of the Fulda Bishops' Conference.[55] Nevertheless, Faulhaber did provide a substantial part of the five thousand Reichsmark found in Luckner's luggage when she was arrested on March 24, 1943, which were probably destined to aid those deported to Theresienstadt.[56]

The Gestapo, which did not notice Luckner's courier activity until September 1942, previously had suspected that espionage activities were taking place in an alleged "Information Center of Archbishop Gröber" (*Nachrichtenzentrale des Erzbischofs Gröber*), which they believed aided persecuted Jews and maintained contacts with the "enemy" abroad. In reality, no such "Information Center" ever existed. After Gestapo agents arrested Luckner on a train to Berlin, they interrogated her for many hours over several weeks. The Gestapo was adamant in their attempt to uncover the existence of a spy ring within the Church. Nevertheless, as Luckner herself later commented during a 1983 interview: "That was something the Gestapo could not understand. They were forever looking for an organization standing behind what I was doing. There were no organizations. These were all private international contacts. Out of this help between person and person I created help between city and city.... That's how it was. That's how it all developed."[57]

Since the Gestapo found out about her contacts with members of the resistance, such as Dietrich Bonhoeffer and Father Alfred Delp, S.J., who both were considered guilty of high treason, the interrogations had been extended to more than a quarter of a year. Finally, Ernst Kalten-brunner, the chief of the Reich Security Main Office, personally ordered protective custody for Luckner: "As a result of the state police findings, it is evident that she endangers through her attitude the existence and the security of people and state. Through her pro-Jewish activity and con-nections to subversive circles, she gives rise to fear that, on release from custody, she will continue to act to the detriment of the Reich."[58] On account of this order, Luckner was finally taken to the concentration camp Ravensbrück in November 1943. There the guards ordered her to carry out heavy forced labor as a political prisoner of barrack block six. She survived several stays in the sick ward only with the help of several Viennese communists, as she later gratefully remembered.[59]

After her liberation by Soviet troops, Luckner returned to Freiburg. However, she found reintegration quite difficult. Apart from physical ailments, she was tormented by remorse: "Perhaps I did not realize the consequences for others, I don't even know—whether some didn't lose their life. But all of us have done much too little, the guilt is immense. And yet gratitude and joy are paramount."[60] Hardly allowing herself any rest, she took over the management of the newly created department Welfare Office for the Persecuted (*Verfolgtenfürsorge*) in the Freiburg Caritas office. There she tried to help the few survivors of the Shoah and particularly to financially support Catholics of Jewish descent, who did not receive any support from the American Jewish Joint Distribution Committee.

However, there was more to Luckner's commitment than providing material relief to victims. As Michael Phayer noted, "Luckner realized that there was a psychological as well as material aspect to restitution, for which reason" she "wanted to tie compensation to the work of eradicating antisemitism" and improving Christian-Jewish relations.[61] Therefore, she not only attended the Seelisberg conference, an international gathering of Christians and Jews that discussed opportunities for combating antisemitism, in August 1947 as an observer,[62] but only a few months later invited Karl Thieme to Freiburg to draft the text for a German bishops' pastoral letter including a confession of guilt. On March 16, 1948, at a subsequent meeting that took place in the house of the pathologist Franz Büchner in Freiburg, the fight against antisemitic prejudices and stereotypes became the central topic of discussion. Besides Luckner and Thieme, a small group of Catholic intellectuals from Freiburg attended this meeting. During the Third Reich, all the participants had more or less taken a critical position against the Nazi government. For example, in 1941, the host, Franz Büchner, had condemned the Nazi crime of euthanasia in a much noted speech on the Oath of Hippocrates.[63] In addition, some of the other participants had given their support to Luckner's relief work as far back as the early 1930s. Now, three years after the end of the Second World War, Luckner gathered all of them in Büchner's house to wrestle with the question: "How can a discussion on the question of Christianity and Judaism be started within the church?"[64]

Karl Thieme, who had a special position among the participants since he was the only one who was not living in Freiburg, began the meeting by stating that already across Germany prejudice against Jews was rising, but that the German bishops would comment on the current political situation only "if there might arise the danger that souls would suffer permanent damage because of misunderstanding the word of God and not carrying out the will of God."[65] The attendees were in agreement that this danger existed and that speedy action was essential. "We know . . . how urgent the problem [i.e., resurging antisemitism] has unfortunately become," Thieme warned.[66] For this reason, he explained, those present had come together to discuss how to proceed "to prevent this threatening damage from happening."

Whereas Luckner and Thieme had at first been in favor of a pastoral epistle by the German bishops to counter a further increase in antisemitism, doubts increasingly arose during the meeting as to whether the draft that Thieme and Luckner had prepared three months before might be comprehensible. Also, the participants were increasingly unsure whether the German bishops would even accept the text at all. After extensive debates, the Freiburg Circle decided instead to publish its own newsletter in which material would be made available to combat anti-semitism for "use in sermon and catechesis" and "in the press," especially for use in the preparation of the 1948 *Katholikentag*.[67] At first, "Old and New Israel News" and "God's People Then and Now" were proposed as suitable titles. At a subsequent meeting, however, the title "Circular Letter for Friends of the Old and New People of God" was adopted.[68]

Thereupon, the first issue of what later became known as the *Freiburger Rundbrief* was actually distributed in Mainz on the occasion of the 1948 *Katholikentag*. However, many members of the preparatory group for the *Katholikentag* severely criticized the Freiburg Circle for its request to address the Jewish question so soon after the end of the war. Whereas Franziskus M. Stratmann, O.P., and others supported the wishes of the Circle, other members of the preparatory group categorically rejected the consideration of this question. Although the Freiburg members prevailed over their critics, numerous reservations continued. It was hardly surprising that in her preface to the first issue of the *Rundbrief*, Luckner called on Christians to mention openly the general "silence" and "indifference . . . regarding the murder of millions," while she also noted with anxiety that in Germany, only a few years after the end of the war, antisemitism was on the rise again.[69]

In theological questions, it was above all Karl Thieme who determined the contents of the *Freiburger Rundbrief* in its formative years. Although he promoted dialogue with Jews, Thieme continued to maintain their conversion as "his hidden agenda as well."[70] However, as Michael Phayer stressed, the "Freiburg Circle underwent a continuous theological evolution, leading them away from viewing Jews as potential converts toward accepting Judaism's permanent validity."[71] One reason for this "important learning experience,"[72] of course, had been the criticism by Jewish correspondents such as Martin Buber and Hans Ornstein. For example, Ornstein wrote that the first *Rundbrief* as such was very nice indeed and that he would of course welcome the "wish to talk to the Jewish brothers" if there was not always the hint of conversion to Christianity written between the lines.[73] Ornstein concluded that this classification of the Jews as "mistaken" and this "devaluation" of the Jews, even if "only in theological terms for the moment," was namely, from his point of view, "one of the reasons, the deep-rooted reasons, for the antisemitic predisposition" of so many Christians. Theodor W. Adorno, with whom Thieme had been in touch since the early 1930s, also made similar comments.[74] Gradually, this discussion with Jewish intellectuals, such as Leo Baeck, Ernst Ludwig Ehrlich, Schalom Ben-Chorin, and Robert Raphael Geis, opened the eyes of the members of the Freiburg Circle. In the meantime, in 1950, Thieme stated that he had become convinced

> that a Jewish person can be "pleasing to God" not only as a pious individual but, in some respect, also and especially "*as a Jew.*" By this I mean that anyone who, in some sense, religiously accepts the revelation of the God of Abraham, Isaac, and Jacob . . . is definitely closer to God than anyone who is a stranger to revelation or even denies revelation; and, moreover, that for the Jews especially, in keeping with the entire biblical revelation, promises made by God are irrevocable in effect and allow the conclusion that the Jewish people are under His special and particularly merciful guidance even in their distance from Christ.[75]

In his book *Kirche und Synagoge,* published in 1945, Thieme had begun his analysis from the principle that Judaism stands in contradiction to Christianity and, therefore, has to be rejected.[76] In the years following, his position changed radically, as he explained in a letter to Johannes Oesterreicher: "Again and again I have pondered this because of my experiences since then with Christian-Jewish dialogue, and have finally arrived at the conclusion that I really would express some things differently in the book today."[77] However, Oesterreicher was not yet able to understand this point of view. Even in 1954, one year after he founded his Institute of Judaeo-Christian Studies at Seton Hall University, he sent a letter to Thieme in which he praised the progress of the *Freiburger Rundbrief,* but also encouraged him to address the importance of mission. In this letter, Oesterreicher wrote:

> The theological treatment of the people whose vast majority has stayed away from Christ over nearly two thousand years assumed, in earlier days, only too often the form of a tractate *Adversus Judaeos.* It is therefore always a happy circumstance to hear a voice which does not settle for zealous pronouncements *against* Israel's "lack of faith" but rather rejoices in its hope and, even better, turns *toward* the children of Israel and speaks *to* them. . . . It is in this sense that I welcome your theses. No-one can fail to recognize the love with which you look upon the mystery of Israel. But love's sister is truth, and I ask myself whether, in your theses, Israel's mystery is always *truly* perceived in its full height and depth.[78]

As a convert from Judaism himself, Oesterreicher was still of the opinion that Christians should actively missionize Jews.[79] In his eyes, even the description of the *Freiburger Rundbrief* as a journal for "the promotion of friendship between the old and the new people of God" was not correct because, according to Oesterreicher, "the Jew is never the Christian's elder brother. For the New and General Covenant not only exceeds the Old and Specific. In certain respects, the New Covenant existed before the Old one." Therefore, he concluded that it would be better to say: "Our brothers, separated from us because they reject Christ but beloved for Christ's sake." It has to be clear, Oesterreicher continued, that "the 'philosemite,' because of his 'tolerance,' becomes the enemy of Jews for he makes it harder for them to achieve redeeming insight and to change, thus depriving them of the bounty of Christ. Therefore, Christians—in order to avoid becoming the enemy of the children of Abraham —must stress again and again that a Jew is no exception but that he, too, cannot avoid making the decision for or against Christ."[80]

After statements like this, it becomes understandable why the Freiburg Circle did not really feel comfortable when Oesterreicher became involved in the preparation of the "Declaration regarding Jews" during the Second Vatican Council.[81] Of course, one does not wish to bring disrepute upon this leading figure of Catholic-Jewish dialogue in the United States. Furthermore, it has to be noted that Oesterreicher likewise eventually changed his theological attitude on the missionary question. However, in the early 1950s, as Michael Phayer noted, most Catholics "who interested themselves in Christian-Jewish relations . . . thought that the enormity of the Holocaust would be so overwhelming and bewildering for Jews that they would be psychologically disposed to accept Christianity."[82] Confronted with anti-Judaism widespread even within the Church and influenced by their experiences during the "Third Reich," these Christians frequently had to go through a painful internal development process in order to rid themselves of their own anti-Jewish stereotypes and theological concepts. Thieme's and Oesterreicher's writing reveals this plainly. But it is thanks to them that a definite change in the Catholic Church's attitude toward all Jews took place in the 1960s—a change that was expressed in the Vatican declaration *Nostra Aetate* in spite of bitter resistance.

In the preceding years, these Catholic "pioneers" of the Jewish-Christian dialogue had already met with enormous incomprehension or even rejection among large sectors of the Catholic population. Even in 1949, the Freiburg Circle—at this time with a strong optimistic view— had asked for support from the pope: "In this work, we do not have to fight enmity, but we do have to fight inertia as well as some lack of appreciation toward this central concern of Christianity. It would therefore be an extraordinary reinforcement and aid to our work if the Holy Father said a word of encouragement and approval. We are convinced that this would awake the sleeping conscience of many."[83] But efforts at persuading Pius XII to support these initiatives were almost entirely unsuccessful. Although a 1948 decree from the Congregation of Rites, which bore the pope's signature, clarified the correct understanding of the famous phrase *iudaica perfidia* in the intercessory prayer on Good Friday as "disbelief,"[84] the pope still did not allow changes in the text.[85] Indeed, some staff members at the Holy See feared that Christian-Jewish dialogue harbored the danger of "indifferentism," and therefore the "theological evolution and the Freiburg Circle's dialogue with Jews aroused the suspicion of Church authorities both in Rome and in Germany."[86] This mistrust arose especially in regard to a Vatican *monitum* of 1950, which warned the German nuncio about syncretistic tendencies resulting from Christian-Jewish dialogue by stating that the

> Holy Office has instructed the Office of the Secretary of State to inform Your Excellency of the following resolutions, requesting you to forward them to Their Excellencies the Bishops of this country. These are resolutions passed by the Holy Office upon thorough examination and deliberation with respect to the organization "International Council of Christians and Jews." . . . The above-named movement, while having the purpose of combating antisemitism and, with the help of Christians, of protecting Jews from unjust persecution, devotes itself in its conferences and meetings to educational questions as well, seeking to promote religious tolerance and even complete equality among various religious denominations. At a Conference in Freiburg, one speaker maintained that youth should be educated to assume an *absolutely indifferent* attitude toward nationality, race, and religion. On the basis of these facts, the Holy Office has decided that *Catholics* who may be attending such conferences convened by the above-named Council *must adhere to the requirement contained in the monitum issued by the Holy Office on June 5, 1948.*[87]

According to Michael Phayer, this admonition "was clearly intended for the Freiburg activists."[88] However, when Thieme and Luckner heard the first rumors about the *monitum,* they were not at all concerned, but instead hoped to use the text in their dispute with the German Coordinating Council of the local Societies for Christian-Jewish Cooperation (Gesellschaften für Christlich-Jüdische Zusammenarbeit) and the World Brotherhood. Although the precise text of the *monitum* was not at that

time in his hands, Thieme wrote: "By the way, I am not especially un-
happy about the step taken by Rome, even though it is a *faux pas* in the
technical sense and, for the moment, entails many stumbling blocks; but
it is likely to have the great advantage that it provides me at last with a
massive tool for stopping the rather strong tendency toward indifferentism in the Societies [for Christian-Jewish Cooperation]."[89]

In 1950, the Freiburg Circle had founded a local Society for
Christian-Jewish Cooperation and joined the Coordinating Council of
the German Societies. Unlike in Munich, Stuttgart, and Berlin, the Frei-
burgers themselves, and not by the insistence of the American occupation forces, took up the initiative.[90] The Freiburg Circle categorically
rejected the introduction of the "Week of Brotherhood" of the Coordinating Council, which attempted to exploit the Christian-Jewish dialogue for political purposes during the Cold War. The Freiburg Circle
solely desired for the Coordinating Council and the other local Societies
to return to their primary work, the dialogue between Christians and
Jews. Initially, the Vatican *monitum* therefore appeared providential to
Thieme and Luckner. Even greater was the dismay when they received
the text of the *monitum,* which mentioned Freiburg directly and made
specific reference to a conference of the International Council of Christians and Jews, in which the participants were alleged to have made
comments that contradicted official Church teaching.

Thieme realized the threat arising from the Vatican document. Immediately after reading the *monitum,* he wrote all Christian-Jewish Societies in Germany and stressed the following:

> As the foregoing reveals, the congregation has been the victim of a
> denouncer, as our Societies most especially do not wish to gather
> religiously indifferent people and educate them in indifferentism; but
> that, on the contrary, they are led by persons who stand firmly on the
> foundations of Catholic and Protestant Christian faith or else of the
> Jewish religion, considering it the exigency of their faith to conduct
> themselves toward those of different faiths in a brotherly way as chil-
> dren of the one God the Father and Creator, to eliminate bias re-
> ciprocally, and to recognize that each person has the same right of
> conscientious conviction as that which they claim for themselves. Since
> this basis of our Societies, as expressed in the by-laws, has never been
> violated in spite of occasional temptations, I have no doubt that it will
> be possible for us to retain the . . . good will of the German bishops—
> who must, of course, have received this admonition as well—which

they have so often demonstrated, toward our efforts, and to receive their authorization for Catholics to participate in those efforts. . . . In this context, I plead with you to proceed with the utmost care, especially in view of the forthcoming Week of Brotherhood, to make sure that the suspicion of indifference, which we must dispel, is not fuelled anew.[91]

That Thieme did not exaggerate the "utmost care" which he called for is indicated by the reactions of the following months: Lorenz Jaeger, archbishop of Paderborn, for example, reinforced the importance of the Vatican document in his February 1951 correspondence with the Freiburg Caritas office, in which he discussed the possible consequences of the *monitum:*

> With sincere thanks, I confirm the receipt of the new *Rundbrief.* . . . Undoubtedly, your work will be rendered much harder by the new resolution by the Holy Office, according to which this collaboration is subject to the qualifying regulations of the *monitum* in the same way as collaboration with other non-Catholics. It will hardly remain possible to hold supra-diocesan meetings since ROME has to give its permission for them. Moreover, since Catholics can only attend such meetings as observers and since prominent Catholics are not supposed to receive permission to do so, your work becomes practically impossible in its previous mode. I, for one, am eager to know how non-Catholic groups will react.[92]

When Luckner learned of this letter, she attempted to explain the situation to Jaeger, "that the recent admonition by the Congregation of the Holy Office . . . does not apply to the German Societies," since they were not members of the mentioned International Council of Christians and Jews.[93] But Jaeger replied:

> It is a mistake to take as lightly as you have done the statement that the German organizations are not affected by the restriction. It may be true that the "International Council" has been dissolved. But that has not rendered Rome's statement irrelevant. It is easy to dissolve organizations and let them reappear under new names. The spirit remains the same. A reliable source has informed me that several remarks made casually during your Freiburg conference were met with displeasure in ROME because they definitely followed the line of religious indifferentism. Don't misunderstand me. I consider it necessary to correct rela-

tions between Christians and Jews for reasons of genuine Christian morality and responsibility. But it is important to acquaint all parties actively engaged in this endeavor most emphatically with Rome's regulations of October 28, 1950, in order to prevent well-meaning but actually erroneous statements from being made at the conferences, which might result in a prohibition that might even extend to the work which you do and which is prompted by a genuine sense of responsibility.[94]

As this letter shows clearly, the German episcopate, even the bishops who had been supportive of the *Freiburger Rundbrief* in the past, such as Jaeger, became irresolute toward how to deal with the Vatican warning. Again, the Freiburg group had to state: "We, too, are of the opinion that no effort should be spared to prevent indifferentism from being spread through any programs of the Societies for Christian-Jewish Cooperation," by clearing up that

> the conference which you mention . . . was held not in Freiburg im Breisgau but in Fribourg, Switzerland, in 1948. We have found out that it was individuals from Belgium who made indifferent remarks there; but they never joined the (now no longer existing) International Council of Christians and Jews because the latter rejected their tendencies. Moreover, as Your Excellency knows well, our Christian-Jewish work is taking place directly within the scope of the Caritas Association, and our *Rundbriefe* are a Catholic effort.[95]

The fact that the conference mentioned in the *monitum* had actually not taken place in Freiburg im Breisgau, but in the Swiss city of Fribourg, enabled Luckner to dispel any further misgivings for the time being, since the Vatican apparently made nothing but a simple error.

Thieme at once traveled to Rome to talk with respected personalities such as Father Robert Leiber, S.J., the pope's secretary, and Augustin Bea, S.J., director of the Papal Bible School, to clarify the misunderstanding and to secure their support.[96] Afterward, the *monitum* had no further effect in Germany. But in other countries, such as Great Britain, the directive caused a "Catholic Withdrawal" from Jewish-Catholic dialogue.[97] For example, immediately after the *monitum* was sent to him, Cardinal Bernard William Griffin asked for an official ruling as to whether the admonition was to be interpreted as applying to his presidency of the British Council of Christians and Jews. Four years later, he was informed that he had to withdraw from the Council and that the Holy See more-over prohibited all Roman Catholics in England from the joining the Council.[98]

Even within Germany, there were still opponents to the Catholic-Jewish dialogue established by the Freiburg Circle. For example, in 1952, Cardinal Josef Frings sent a circular letter that once again warned the other German bishops against "indifferentism" and "syncretism" result-ing from Catholic-Jewish dialogue.[99] In the respected Jesuit periodical *Stimmen der Zeit* there also appeared an article denying the *Freiburger Rundbrief* any right to exist.[100] Still, the Freiburg Circle received sig-nificant support from some Jewish leaders, such as Leo Baeck, who encouraged Luckner in her "meaningful and significant work" by writ-ing: "I can imagine how difficult [your] work is and how you meet not only with indifference or opposition but also with enemies. However, you are working for a future, for a blessing."[101] Later she recalled that it was above all Baeck's support that enabled her not to give up her en-deavors for the *Rundbrief*.[102]

More widespread change was not achieved until the 1960s, in the era immediately preceding the Second Vatican Council. Together with her friends, Gertrud Luckner had already in 1960 "very quietly prepared a statement on Christians-Jews for the Council."[103] In the same summer, Luckner received counsel from Augustin Bea, who kept the Freiburg Circle informed about the Council's development. When conservative theologians and political circles in the Middle East attempted to prevent the passing of the "Declaration regarding Jews," Gertrud Luckner and her Freiburg Circle drafted a petition by "leading German Catholics" to the pope, collected signatures, and presented it to Paul VI.[104] Then, at last, the document *Nostra Aetate,* which was finally achieved by compro-mise, was to bring about a fundamental change in relations between Catholics and Jews, because it expressly rejected any eruptions of "ha-tred, persecutions, and displays of anti-Semitism directed against Jews at any time and from any source."[105] In addition, the decree stressed the unbroken validity of God's covenant with Israel and "the spiritual pa-trimony common to Christians and Jews."

After the Council had ended, the Catholic-Jewish dialogue found it-self on a much more solid basis. This success was not due only to the majority of the Council participants, who, after long debates and violent protests, eventually accepted the statement on the Jews,[106] but was to a significant degree prepared by years of engagement on the part of fre-quently small Christian-Jewish groups, as exemplified by the Freiburg

Circle. It is of interest that the first Catholics who engaged in this dialogue—at least in the German-speaking area—with few exceptions fall into one of two groups: either they had been persecuted by the National Socialists themselves and had survived in exile—such as Johannes Oesterreicher and Waldemar Gurian on account of their Jewish descent or Karl Thieme, Joseph Wirth, and Franziskus M. Stratmann, O.P., on account of their political beliefs—or they were part of the small group of Catholics who had been in the resistance against Hitler and had actively worked on behalf of the persecuted Jews, such as Gertrud Luckner and also the Italian Angelo Giuseppe Roncalli, who would later become Pope John XXIII and who, as apostolic delegate in Greece and Turkey, rescued numerous Jews before they could be deported.[107] Thus Roncalli's personal experience gained during the Second World War had significantly contributed to the fact that he not only had the texts of various anti-Jewish prayers changed after his election as pope, but that he also took decisive measures after a visit from the Jewish historian Jules Isaac and asked Cardinal Bea to draw up a Council statement on the Jews.[108]

Even if the timid beginnings of a Christian-Jewish rapprochement go back to the time before the terrible incidents of the 1930s and early 1940s,[109] it took the shock of the Nazi crimes and the Shoah for a true and sustainable new consciousness of Jewish-Christian relations to arise. As is frequently overlooked, the step taken by the Council was itself "deeply affected by the memory of the persecution and massacre of Jews which took place in Europe" just a few decades before.[110] As an important milestone in the history of Jewish-Christian relations, the declaration *Nostra Aetate* therefore marks both the hard-won result of long-lasting efforts and a peremptory and irreversible new beginning.

Crises and Unresolved Questions

Now, forty years after the end of the Second Vatican Council, Catholic-Jewish dialogue has become firmly and officially established and has already produced remarkable results. Nevertheless, this dialogue remains extremely fragile and susceptible to disruption.[111] Undoubtedly, the main reason for the recurrence of crises is the completely different assessment of National Socialism, and especially of the Holocaust. Notably, nearly all the conflicts in the relationship between Catholics and Jews that have arisen in recent decades concern the Shoah: examples are the Waldheim affair and the Carmelite convent controversy in Auschwitz, the beatification and canonization of Maximilian Kolbe and Edith

Stein, the reactions to the Vatican document *We Remember,* the endless debate about the role of Pius XII in the Second World War, and the failure of the Catholic-Jewish Historians' Commission.[112] These conflicts reveal not only a deep-seated unfamiliarity with each other's approach to symbols and to history, but also a totally different way of handling the burdened past. Many Catholics no longer understand why the Shoah continues to be a challenge to their Church and to their own faith at a personal level. It seems that the shock regarding mass murder in the death camps that the "generation of founders" of Christian-Jewish dialogue experienced and that motivated them decisively has rapidly dwindled on the Catholic side.

There are undoubtedly many different reasons for this problematic development. For example, a "Theology after Auschwitz" is still in its infancy. A few significant impulses in recent years notwithstanding,[113] it has hardly been noticed outside of small groups of academic specialists, even though the disturbing question how Auschwitz was even possible, especially in a Europe characterized for centuries by Christianity, has lost none of its topicality.[114] It may well be that many people have become so used to the stories and pictures from National Socialist annihilation camps, and have become so indifferent, that they no longer recognize the events there as a question to theology and to Christian faith. Others may see the cold precision and advanced technology with which the National Socialists carried out their crimes as nothing more than a throwback to seemingly overcome forms of barbarism, viewing the Shoah merely as one of many Passions; thus, they misperceive the historic singularity of the annihilation of Jews by the National Socialists, which indeed is not based on the simple anthropological assertion that people are capable of torturing and murdering other people in bestial fashion—after all, cruel acts have been committed and horrible torments suffered at all times and in innumerable places.

By contrast, Jewish as well as Christian scholars have pointed out again and again in the past decades that the uniqueness of the Shoah actually derives from the fact that "never before had a state resolved, and publicly announced, that a certain group of people including the aged, the women, the children, and the infants, would be killed as entirely as possible, implementing this decision by means of all available means of state power."[115] In other words: no matter whether the victims considered themselves Jewish, whether they were baptized or even knew of their Jewish origins, this absolute annihilatory will of the National Socialists was directed against human beings, merely because of the fact that they had been born, taking no heed of any kind of ethical constraints in the attainment of its cruel objective. Seen in this light, Hitler's attempt to extinguish the Jewish people was in fact a radical break with civilization and thus also an assault on biblical ethics, which command "Thou shalt not kill," and their concept that every human being was created in God's image.

This perspective—which by no means intends to raise these events to mythic heights but seeks to approach as closely as possible the concrete fact with its specific historical contours—reveals the poignancy of the question how such a crime could be committed by baptized Christians in a Europe still largely characterized by Christianity.[116] For, even if one denies that the perpetrators were Christians or views them merely as "bad Christians," the fundamental problem remains that they were able to commit their crimes "within a nation which traditionally called itself Christian, and within the 'Christian occident.'" It is true enough that there were Christians of various denominations who, as exemplified by Gertrud Luckner and Angelo Giuseppe Roncalli, attempted to rescue Jews.[117] There were also monasteries and Church institutions that hid Jews or helped them emigrate. But the overwhelming majority of Christians remained silent and inactive—in part out of fear of retaliation, in part out of indifference, but also in part out of agreement with the National Socialist laws on Jews. The latter fact was a consequence of the long tradition of Christian anti-Judaism. Modern antisemitism was able to prevail as it did only "because it included the anti-Jewish attitude of Christians in its calculations for achieving its end, and knew how to take advantage of it," in the words of an outstanding study conducted a few years ago by a work group of German theologians.[118] Moreover, the patristic *Adversus Iudaeos* literature, with its theology of supersessionism and its demonizing of Judaism, and the medieval legends of ritual murder and host desecration actually established the negative image of the Jew, his "terrifying otherness," to which the National Socialists were then able to refer in their propaganda.[119]

Some of the pioneers of Jewish-Christian dialogue after the Second World War, such as Luckner and Thieme, still saw this connection between a centuries-old Christian anti-Judaism and modern antisemitism to be an undeniable fact, and they kept working for the fight against anti-Jewish prejudice within the Church for that very reason.[120] But more recent statements by Catholic scholars and the Vatican point toward the opposite opinion. For example, in the controversial document *We Remember* (1998), the opinion is expressed that the roots of antisemitism are to be found "outside of Christianity," and that consequently the Shoah is "the work of a thoroughly modern neo-pagan regime."[121] Those who embrace this view consider it justified by the fact that National Socialism indeed also spread anti-Christian propaganda, especially against Catholicism. In addition, one could argue that the National Socialists murdered a significant number of Catholic priests and laity in concentration camps. Yet this argument pays as little attention to the heterogeneity of National Socialist ideology and its realization as it does to the ambivalence of the Church's self-defense in the "Third Reich."

For, on the one hand, National Socialist church policies were quite contradictory, determined as they were—in a manner comparable to that of other domains—by competition among various agencies of the Reich and the power struggles of rival groups within the party. Even though National Socialism laid claim to a monopoly in questions of *weltanschauung* that, ultimately, could not suffer such ideological opponents as the churches, the perception of properly handling these opponents fluctuated between extreme enmity toward the churches and rather moderate positions. A few National Socialists, such as Hanns Kerrl, minister of church affairs, were even under the illusion that reconciliation with the Christian churches was possible.[122] Even the security arm (SD) of the SS pursued, in its radical religious policies, a contradictory and opaque "dual strategy" of completely unrestrained actions and tactical moderation.[123] At last, during the war, the planned "total demolition of Christianity" was postponed until after the hoped-for "final victory."[124]

On the other hand, at least many of the German Church dignitaries —coming from a tradition of being subservient to the state and inimical to democracy—strove to preserve some measure of loyalty toward the state and its Führer, and therefore distinguished between Hitler, whose allegedly positive attitude toward Christianity they did not normally call into doubt, and malevolent groups within the party, which they considered to be solely responsible for any measures inimical to the Church—a widespread topos even upheld by members of the Curia of Rome.[125] It is a fact that has recently come to our attention from newly released Vatican archival documents that there was intensive and extremely critical assessment of National Socialist ideology regarding state and race early on, once initial hopes for political taming of the German government had been dashed. But many initiatives were discontinued—presumably due to intervention by the secretary of state, Eugenio Pacelli. For example, the extremely antisemitic *Handbuch der Judenfrage* (Handbook on the Jewish Question) by Theodor Fritsch was never placed on the Index,[126] nor was the *Syllabus* of National Socialist heresies—compiled over a number of years by the *Sanctum Officium*—ever published.[127] The aforementioned encyclical against antisemitism and racism initiated by Pius XI shortly before his death never went beyond several drafts.[128] However, the failure to release these statements against National Socialism, which would have attracted great public attention, was—as Dominik Burkard has convincingly shown—due largely to political and diplomatic consideration and to policy issues within the Curia rather than to implicit agreement with National Socialist racial policy.[129] Indeed, by condemning Alfred Rosenberg, *Reichsleiter* of the Foreign Office of the NSDAP and the Führer's appointee for overseeing all spiritual and ideological training and education, whose programmatic work *Myth of the Twentieth Century* was placed on the Roman Index in February 1934, the Vatican had taken an unequivocal stand against the National Socialists' racism. For example, the newspaper *La Civiltà Cattolica* stated in a commentary, "It is a fanatical and excessively violent book, it sows the seed of hatred between races and religions."[130]

It should be mentioned, however, that the most prominent reason for this condemnation was found not so much in Rosenberg's antisemitic statements as, rather, in his idea of a new German national religion of race and blood, which—according to him—needed to cleanse Christianity of its Jewish roots. This latter fact was primarily viewed by the staff of the *Sacrum Officium* as an assault upon the Catholic Church and its tradition, including the undeniable Jewish roots. It does, of course, seem quite ridiculous that the semiofficial commentary in the *Civiltà Cattolica* goes on to claim that Rosenberg had taken possession of "the Jewish hatred of Jesus Christ" by denying the virgin birth, as did the "Jews during the early period of Christianity."[131] Thus, Rosenberg was unmasked as an enemy of the Church, his racism—implicitly including his racial antisemitism—strongly condemned, and the Jewish heritage in Christianity defended; on the other hand, the committed National Socialist was put, of all places, side by side with the Jews, since they had traditionally also been seen as enemies of the Church. The commentary thus fitted into the classic pattern of anti-Jewish polemics. The *Kirchenkampf* raging in Germany at first directed the eyes of the Church and of the Vatican toward their own concerns. It seems that—in contrast with Joseph Wirth and his coauthors of the 1937 *Memorandum*—many of these officials failed to see that the urgent need to champion the rights of others in jeopardy, not to mention openly defending the Jews, was a mandate for the Church.

In concentrating on the threat to its own institutions, the Church thus very rarely included the persecution of Jews in its considerations, and when it did, it sometimes even differentiated between "bad" and "good" types of anti-Jewish actions.[132] Even Cardinal Faulhaber, who had been one of the most committed members of the philosemitic Amici Israel, which Pius XI condemned in 1928,[133] and who branded National Socialist racial policy as an anti-Church "heresy" as early as 1930, still held the opinion in October 1936 that the German state was "justified in proceeding against the excesses of Jewry in society, especially whenever Jews—as Bolshevists and Communists—have endangered public order."[134] On the other hand, when Faulhaber, in 1941, was informed about the deportations, whose brutality he compared with the "transports by African slave traders,"[135] he tried to persuade the president of the Bishops' Conference to issue a protest, and supported Gertrud Luckner's relief efforts. He might therefore be a model of a Catholic who cultivated quite different points of view related to Jews in various periods in his life and hovered between ambivalence, aversion, and positive opinions.

This inconsistency found both in the Church policy of the "Third Reich" and in the reactions of Catholic dignitaries and the Vatican is also a central problem in today's public discourse. The lines between extreme critics such as Cornwell and Goldhagen on the one hand[136] and apologetic champions of the Church on the other[137] have by now become so entrenched that an objective and differentiated discussion of historical facts has nearly become impossible. A fundamental problem, among others, is the different use of the term "antisemitism": while some no longer distinguish at all between Christian hatred of Jews and National Socialist antisemitism, others draw a sharp line between a modern racial and simultaneously anti-Christian antisemitism on the one hand and a traditionally religious anti-Judaism in the Catholic milieu on the other, thereby arriving at the conclusion that committed Catholics could not have been real antisemites at all.

At first glance, the history of the term "antisemitism" seems to validate the second position, as the term was first coined by Wilhelm Marr and other radical propagandists in the German *Antisemiten-Liga* around 1880 in order to become distinguishable from the already existing forms of Judaeophobia, especially from Christian anti-Judaism. They insisted on complete exclusion of Jews—a claim that, while already familiar to German nationalists in the early nineteenth century, now also embraced racial theories, thus becoming significantly more radical. Assimilation or even conversion as possible integration measures, as particularly de-

manded by Christian enemies of Jews, was, by contrast, generally rejected by the representatives of such racial antisemitism.[138] Wolfgang
Altgeld is therefore correct when he states that

> those who use just this notion of antisemitism to refer in retrospec-
> tive to all forms of Judaeophobia [reduce] each past relation of the
> whole Christian environment to Judaism to a mere station on the
> way to a mass murder and to a planned annihilation of all Jewish
> people—and doing so, they certainly also disdain, as unimportant
> marginal notes, the chances of mutual tolerance and civil equality,
> which are an integral part of Christianity itself and were justified dur-
> ing the Enlightenment.[139]

Nevertheless, it should not be overlooked that the term "anti-Judaism"—
which usually denotes a premodern and religiously motivated hatred of
Jews—is no more appropriate for describing all the varieties of modern, that is, secular, anti-Jewish phenomena—not to mention the fluid
boundaries between the various manifestations.[140] In any case, this is one
of the reasons why the broadened meaning of the term "antisemitism"
occurred by the first half of the twentieth century, with the result that it
is no longer used solely in the sense of a racially arguing version of
Judaeophobia.

Finally, the rather complex discussion in the Catholic circles of the
1920s and 1930s is therefore pointed out in this context once more, as
reflected not only in the articles in *Civiltà Cattolica* but also in the *Memorandum* presented above and first published in *Die Erfüllung,* because
contemporary texts clearly distinguish between two types of modern
antisemitism, a racial type and another, "more moderate," type. Usually,
racial antisemitism is consistently rejected as anti-Christian there, and its
dogmatic condemnation by Pius XI in 1928 is mentioned. But the authors are not in agreement on the second type: whereas the staff of the
Civiltà Cattolica regard "moderate" intervention against the Jews—if
necessary even by means of special laws—as advisable, sometimes even
indispensable, Thieme and Gurian consider this form of antisemitism to
be just as harmful as racism. However, this second type is by no means
identical with traditional Christian anti-Judaism. Even the initiators of
the *Memorandum* do not perceive the latter as problematic at all. Their
attitude toward the theology of supersessionism and the Christian mission to Jews changed only as a result of the dialogue with their Jewish
discussion partners after 1945. Thieme's writing provides insight into
this fact.

On the other hand, the proponents of modern nonracial antisemitism criticized by the 1937 *Memorandum* did not argue from a theological point of view, but sociopolitically. They no longer viewed Jews as Christ killers or desecrators of the host, but as Freemasons, liberals, capitalists, communists, or Bolsheviks whose alleged influence upon public policy, economy, and culture needed to be broken. It is against this antisemitism—widespread among Catholics as well—that the initiators of the *Memorandum* spoke out, because, in their opinion, it could easily evolve into racial antisemitism, as they had seen happen in the case of Austrian Jesuit Georg Bichlmair and his call for an "Aryan" stipulation for Catholic associations. But that, of all people, it was this Father Bichlmair who, after the *Anschluß*, established in Vienna a Church-operated relief agency for Jews, who were now also persecuted in Austria on racial grounds,[141] shows clearly that even modern antisemites did not necessarily approve of actually converting National Socialist racism into such cruel reality.

NOTES

I would like to thank Ilse Andrews for translating significant sections of this chapter into English. I would also like to thank Dorota Pawlucka and Kevin P. Spicer for their editorial assistance.

1. "Die Kirche Christi und die Judenfrage," *Die Erfüllung* 2 (1937): 73–101.

2. Ibid., 73.

3. Pant was one of the first signers of the memorandum. Others, however, initially hesitated to support the memorandum. On this point, see Pia Nordblom, *Für Glaube und Volkstum. Die katholische Wochenzeitung "Der Deutsche in Polen" (1934–1939) in der Auseinandersetzung mit dem Nationalsozialismus* (Paderborn: Ferdinand Schöningh, 2000), 486. Further signatories were Edgar De Bruyne, the Flemish expert in medieval philosophy; Charles (Theómir) Devaux, the father superior of the Pères de Notre Dame de Sion in Paris; Stanislas Fumet, a journalist from France; and Alois Wildenauer, a Viennese canon.

4. See Paulus Engelhardt, "Der Friedenskämpfer. Zum 100. Geburtstag von P. Franziskus Maria Stratmann OP (8.9.1883)," *Wort und Antwort* 24 (1983): 111–20. The three other Dominicans who signed the text were Silvester M. Braito, professor for aesthetics and mysticism in Olmouce, Joannes B. Kors, a social ethicist at the Catholic University of Nijmegen, and Benoit Lavaud, professor for moral theology at the University of Fribourg and a close friend of Maritain and Journet.

5. Gurian is frequently mentioned as the sole author of the memorandum. On Thieme's significant contribution, see Heinz Hürten, *Waldemar Gurian. Ein Zeuge der Krise unserer Welt in der ersten Hälfte des 20. Jahrhunderts* (Mainz: Matthias-Grünewald, 1972), 128. There also existed a separate draft by the Austrian chemist

and journalist Otto M. Karpfen, which was nevertheless only partially used. On the latter point see Oesterreicher to Thieme, October 30, 1936. Institut für Zeitgeschichte, Munich (IfZ), Thieme Papers, ED 163/59.

6. Commentary "Zur Denkschrift" by the editorial staff, *Die Erfüllung* 2 (1937): 127.

7. On Thieme's conversion, see Wolf-Friedrich Schäufele, "Emigration und Konversion," in: *Theologen im Exil—Theologie des Exils. Internationales Kolloquium 17. bis 19. November 1999 in Mainz,* ed. Wolf-Friedrich Schäufele and Markus Vinzent (Mandelbachtal: Edition Cicero, 2001), 135–51, here 146–49.

8. See Klaus Gotto, *Die Wochenzeitung Junge Front/Michael. Eine Studie zum katholischen Selbstverständnis und zum Verhalten der jungen Kirche gegenüber dem Nationalsozialismus* (Mainz: Matthias-Grünewald, 1970), 213–20. According to Gotto, Gurian was one of the few friends to whom Thieme said "Du." On this point, see ibid., 220.

9. Wirth to Jaffé, September 29, 1937. Centralnyj Gosudarstvennyj Archiv, Moscow (CGA), Wirth Papers, 600/I/468. I would like to thank Ulrike Hörster-Philipps, who placed this and the other documents from the Moscow archive at my disposal.

10. Wirth was particularly in contact with Morris D. Waldman, the secretary of the American Jewish Committee in New York.

11. Thieme to Oesterreicher, September 8, 1936. IfZ, Thieme Papers, ED 163/59.

12. Oesterreicher to Thieme, December 17, 1936. IfZ, Thieme Papers, ED 163/59.

13. Gurian to Wirth, December 21, 1936. CGA, Wirth Papers, 600/I/447.

14. "Die Kirche Christi und die Judenfrage," 97–98.

15. Ibid., 97.

16. Ibid., 98. The "extermination of the so-called life unworthy of life" (i.e., the killing of the incurable and mentally and physically handicapped) was also regarded as the consequence of power politics and firmly condemned. On this point, see ibid., 83.

17. Ibid., 99.

18. Ibid., 83.

19. Literally, the papal decree stated that the Apostolic See "just as it repudiates all envy and animosity among the nations, it despises all the more so any hatred of the people once chosen by God, which today is generally termed 'antisemitism.' " The complete text that still adhered to ecclesiastical anti-Judaism and the traditional theology of substitution was first published in the *Acta Apostolicae Sedis* 20 (1928): 103–104. On the creation of this text, see Hubert Wolf, "The Good Friday Supplication for the Jews and the Roman Curia (1928–1975). A Case Example for Research Prospects for the Twentieth Century," in *The Roman Inquisition, the Index and the Jews: Contexts, Sources and Perspectives,* ed. Stephan Wendehorst (Leiden: Brill, 2004), 235–57.

20. "Die Kirche Christi und die Judenfrage," 84.

21. Ibid., 92.

22. See ibid., 95–96.

23. See Wolf, "The Good Friday Supplication," 253.

24. See Enrico Rosa, "Il pericolo giudaico e gli 'Amici d'Israele'," *La Civiltà Cattolica* 79 (1928): 335–44.

25. See, for example, Gustav Gundlach, "Antisemitismus," in *Lexikon für Theologie und Kirche,* vol. 1, ed. Michael Buchberger (Freiburg: Herder, 1930), cols. 504–505.

26. See Erika Weinzierl, *Prüfstand. Österreichs Katholiken und der Nationalsozialismus* (Mödling: St. Gabriel, 1988), 266.

27. See Dietrich von Hildebrand, *Memoiren und Aufsätze gegen den Nationalsozialismus 1933–1938,* ed. Ernst Wenisch (Mainz: Matthias-Grünewald, 1994), 147–48 and 324.

28. Oesterreicher to Thieme, April 16, 1936, IfZ, Thieme Papers, ED 163/59.

29. "Die Kirche Christi und die Judenfrage," 74.

30. Ibid., 79: "This fact (i.e., that Jesus was a Jew himself) can neither be called into doubt nor be reinterpreted."

31. Ibid., 81.

32. See ibid., 99.

33. Ibid., 100–101.

34. See Ulrike Hörster-Philipps, *Joseph Wirth 1879–1956. Eine politische Biographie* (Paderborn: Ferdinand Schöningh, 1998), 496. Robert Leiber, S.J., professor at the Gregoriana and close confidant of Pacelli, as well as Friedrich Muckermann, S.J., the publisher of the *Lettres de Rome,* also received a copy of the memorandum.

35. Wirth to Pacelli, March 25, 1937. CGA, Wirth Papers, 600/I/468.

36. Wirth traveled several times to Rome in order to "persuade the Vatican to protect the rights of Jews in a sense of generous humanity." Wirth to Simon, May 6, 1937. CGA, Wirth Papers, 600/I/474. For example, at the beginning of June 1937, in a letter to the secretary of the American Jewish Committee in New York, Wirth states that he had informed Pacelli personally about antisemitic tendencies in South American countries during his stay in Rome: "His Excellency promised to do everything within his power." Wirth to Waldman, June 26, 1937. CGA, Wirth Papers, 600/I/474.

37. Thieme's efforts to persuade the bishops of St. Gallen, Basel, and Lugano to support the memorandum also remained without success. On this point, see Thieme to Oesterreicher, April 28, 1937. IfZ, Thieme Papers, ED 163/60.

38. Translations into French, English, Spanish, Portuguese, and Polish were in preparation. See Hörster-Philipps, *Joseph Wirth,* 497. According to Oesterreicher, at least English and French versions were published: "I hope both are good. They had not been submitted to us for acceptance." Oesterreicher to Thieme, December 22, 1937. IfZ, Thieme Papers, ED 163/60. The English language version of the memorandum that was translated by Gregory Feige and published by the Committee on National Attitudes of the Catholic Peace League in the United States appears as *The Church and the Jews: A Memorial Issued by Catholic European Scholars,* ed. Catholic Association for International Peace (Washington, D.C.: Paulist, n. d. [1937]).

39. Thieme to Oesterreicher, December 9, 1938. IfZ, Thieme Papers, ED 163/60.

40. Thieme to Oesterreicher, December 2, 1938. IfZ, Thieme Papers, ED 163/60.

41. Ibid. Literally, the pope said: "Antisemitism is inadmissible; spiritually, we are all Semites." See *La Documentation Catholique* 39 (1938): cols. 1459–60. For the English translation, see Pinchas E. Lapide, *Three Popes and the Jews* (New York: Souvenir, 1967), 114.

42. Karl Thieme's draft from December 1938. IfZ, Thieme papers, ED 163/60.

43. Ibid. Nevertheless, Thieme had been skeptical from the very beginning. He wrote to Franziskus M. Stratmann, O.P.: "As already expressed in front of Oe[sterreicher], I would be extremely surprised if our petition was successful; but we are in the meantime anyway in a position in which only a hope for a miracle remains." Thieme to Stratmann, December 17, 1938. IfZ, Thieme Papers, ED 163/60.

44. No evidence could be found in the Vatican archive among the papers of Pius XI that are open for research.

45. See Hörster-Philipps, *Joseph Wirth*, 504–506. On the preparation of the encyclical and its various versions, see Johannes Schwarte, *Gustav Gundlach S.J. (1892–1963). Maßgeblicher Repräsentant der katholischen Soziallehre während der Pontifikate Pius' XI. und Pius' XII* (Munich: Ferdinand Schöningh, 1975), 72–100; Georges Passelecq and Bernard Suchecky, *The Hidden Encyclical of Pius XI* (New York: Harcourt Brace, 1997); and *Wider den Rassismus. Entwurf einer nicht erschienenen Enzyklika (1938). Texte aus dem Nachlaß von Gustav Gundlach SJ*, ed. Anton Rauscher (Paderborn: Ferdinand Schöningh, 2001).

46. Whereas Wirth still hoped in vain for the "long awaited" encyclical in the summer of 1939, Thieme already doubted its publication in January 1939. See Thieme to Streicher, January 9, 1939. IfZ, Thieme Papers, ED 163/60.

47. Oesterreicher to Thieme, June 17, 1939. IfZ, Thieme Papers, ED 163/60.

48. See William W. Simpson and Ruth Weyl, *The Story of the International Council of Christians and Jews* (n.p.: ICCJ, 1995), 20–29.

49. See Hans-Josef Wollasch, *"Betrifft: Nachrichtenzentrale des Erzbischofs Gröber in Freiburg." Die Ermittlungsakten der Geheimen Staatspolizei gegen Gertrud Luckner 1942–1944* (Konstanz: Universitäts-Verlag Konstanz, 1999), 25–30.

50. See ibid., 31. On the history of this Viennese organization, also see Weinzierl, *Prüfstand*, 265–72.

51. Michael Phayer, *The Catholic Church and the Holocaust, 1930–1965* (Bloomington: Indiana University Press, 2000), 115.

52. Instruction of the *Kirchliche Kriegshilfestelle* (Church War Relief Committee) for Gertrud Luckner, June 1, 1941. Deutscher Caritasverband, Freiburg (DCV), Luckner Papers, 093.2 N 10.

53. Phayer, *The Catholic Church*, 115. In Luckner's estate at the DCV, two penciled sketches that presumably served as a means of orientation for people fleeing Germany are preserved in an envelope marked *Grenze*. On this point, see Wollasch, *Betrifft: Nachrichtenzentrale des Erzbischofs Gröber*, 28 and 234–35.

54. Luckner did manage to save a few Jews living in Baden from transports to Gurs leaving in October 1940 by asking a doctor who enjoyed her confidence to certify their condition as being "not transportable." On this point, see Wollasch, *Betrifft: Nachrichtenzentrale des Erzbischofs Gröber*, 32.

55. See Faulhaber to Bertram, November 13, 1941, in *Akten Kardinal Michael von Faulhabers (1917–1945)*, vol. 2, ed. Ludwig Volk (Mainz: Matthias-Grünewald, 1978), 824–25. On November 17, Bertram answered Faulhaber that there were "more important and more global concerns from the ecclesiastical point of view." See ibid., 845.

56. See Wollasch, *Betrifft: Nachrichtenzentrale des Erzbischofs Gröber*, 34–35.

57. Quoted in Elizabeth Petuchowsky, "Gertrud Luckner: Resistance and Assistance: A German Women Who Defied Nazis and Aided Jews," in *Ministers of Compassion during the Nazi Period: Gertrud Luckner and Raoul Wallenberg*, Sixth Monsignor John M. Oesterreicher Memorial Lecture, ed. Institute of Judaeo-Christian Studies, Seton Hall University (South Orange, N.J.: Seton Hall University, 1999), 4–19, here 11.

58. Warrant for Gertrud Luckner's protective custody issued by the *RSHA* Berlin, May 26, 1943, quoted in Wollasch, *Betrifft: Nachrichtenzentrale des Erzbischofs Gröber*, 195–96.

59. For example, see the manuscript "Gesprächsabend mit Frau Dr. Gertrud Luckner in der KHG-Freiburg," January 11, 1989, p. 10. DCV, Luckner Papers, 093.2 N 40, box 5.

60. Luckner note, July 14, 1945. DCV, Luckner Papers, 093.2 N 47.

61. Phayer, *The Catholic Church*, 192–93.

62. The Swiss conference adopted ten theses for combating anti-Jewish prejudices in Christian sermons and catechesis. See Simpson and Weyl, *The Story of the International Council*, 24–27 and 117.

63. See Eduard Seidler, "Die Medizinische Fakultät zwischen 1926 und 1948," in *Die Freiburger Universität in der Zeit des Nationalsozialismus*, ed. Eckhard John et al. (Freiburg: Ploetz, 1991), 73–89, here 86.

64. Luckner Report, March 18, 1948. DCV, Luckner Papers, 093.2 N 22, box 1.

65. Ibid.

66. Ibid.

67. Luckner to Preysing, March 26, 1949. DCV, Luckner Papers, 221.91+511, fasc. 01.

68. Memo of April 30, 1948 and June 14, 1948, DCV, Luckner Papers, 183+ 532.11, fasc. 01.

69. Gertrud Luckner, "Geleitwort," *Freiburger Rundbrief* 1 (1948): 1–2, here 1.

70. Phayer, *The Catholic Church*, 186.

71. Ibid., 188.

72. Ibid., 189.

73. Ornstein to Luckner, September 16, 1948. IfZ, Thieme Papers, ED 163/13.

74. Adorno to Thieme, June 1, 1949. IfZ, Thieme Papers, ED 163/1.

75. Thieme to Oesterreicher, Easter 1950. IfZ, Thieme Papers, ED 163/60.

76. Karl Thieme, *Kirche und Synagoge. Die ersten nachbiblischen Zeugnisse ihres Gegensatzes im Offenbarungsverständnis: Der Barnabasbrief und der Dialog Justins des Märtyrers* (Olten: O. Walter, 1945). See also Phayer, *The Catholic Church*, 188–89.

77. Thieme to Oesterreicher, Easter 1950. IfZ, Thieme Papers, ED 163/60.

78. Oesterreicher to Thieme, "Fest der Heimsuchung Mariens," [July 2], 1954. IfZ, Thieme Papers, ED 163/60.

79. Ibid.

80. Ibid.

81. See Thieme to Luckner, July 10, 1960. DCV, Luckner Papers, 221.91.025, fasc. 07. One Jewish observer of the Council also shared similar impressions. On this latter point, see Gerhart M. Riegner, *Niemals verzweifeln. Sechzig Jahre für das jüdische Volk und die Menschenrechte* (Gerlingen: Bleicher, 2001), 338.

82. Phayer, *The Catholic Church*, 186.

83. Luckner to Leiber, March 31, 1949. IfZ, Thieme Papers, ED 163/48.

84. See John M. Oesterreicher, *The New Encounter: Between Christians and Jews* (New York: Philosophical Library, 1985), 52. The original Latin text of the decree was published for the first time in the *Acta Apostolicae Sedis* 40 (1948): 342.

85. The text was changed not earlier than under John XXIII and Paul VI. In November 1955, after a request by the Jewish historian Jules Isaac, Pius XII reintroduced at least the liturgical genuflection, which had been omitted in the course of Church history after the Good Friday intercession for Jews as a sign of scorn for the alleged "murders of God." On this minor change by Pius XII, i.e., the reintroduction of the genuflection, which was nevertheless at that time considered the first important improvement, see Paul Démann, "Das Fürbitten für die Juden in der neuen Karwochen-Liturgie," *Freiburger Rundbrief* 10 (1957/58): 15–17, and Kathryn Sullivan, "Pro Perfidis Judaeis," *The Bridge: A Yearbook of Judaeo-Christian Studies* 2 (1956): 212–23.

86. Phayer, *The Catholic Church*, 189.

87. Vatican Secretary of State to Muench, October 28, 1950, Diözesanarchiv Berlin (DAB), Sommer Papers, I/1–100. The earlier *monitum* from 1948 the letter is referring to forbade nearly all ecumenical meetings with Protestants.

88. Phayer, *The Catholic Church*, 189.

89. Thieme to Schneider, January 6, 1951. DCV, Luckner Papers, 221.91.025, fasc. 03 (earlier 04).

90. See Luckner Report, June 8, 1950. DCV, Luckner Papers, 093.2+284.3. On the history of the other first German Societies for Christian-Jewish Cooperation, see Josef Foschepoth, *Im Schatten der Vergangenheit. Die Anfänge der Gesellschaften für Christlich-Jüdische Zusammenarbeit* (Göttingen: Vandenhoeck and Ruprecht, 1993).

91. Thieme to the *Gesellschaften für christlich-jüdische Zusammenarbeit* and the Coordinating Council, January 8, 1951. DCV, Luckner Papers, 221.91.025, fasc. 03 (earlier 04).

92. Jaeger to Joerger, February 21, 1951. DCV, Luckner Papers, 221.91+511, fasc. 02.

93. Joerger and Luckner to Jaeger, March 19, 1951. DCV, Luckner Papers, 221.91+511, fasc. 02.

94. Jaeger to Luckner, March 28, 1951. DCV, Luckner Papers, 221.91+511, fasc. 02.

95. Joerger and Luckner to Jaeger, April 12, 1951. DCV, Luckner Papers, 221.91+511, fasc. 02.

96. See Thieme's "Bericht über Besprechungen mit römischen Kirchenbehörden über die christlich-jüdische Zusammenarbeit," April 20, 1951. DCV, Luckner Papers, 183+533, fasc. 05.

97. Marcus Braybrooke, *Children of One God: A History of the Council of Christians and Jews* (London: Mitchell, 1991), 33.

98. See ibid., 33–38, and Simpson and Weyl, *The Story of the International Council*, 29–32.

99. See Phayer, *The Catholic Church*, 189.

100. See Rudolf Leder, "Christus und Israel. Franz Werfels Deutung des jüdischen Schicksals," *Stimmen der Zeit* 76 (1950/51): 34–42, here 36.

101. Baeck to Luckner, June 29, 1949. DCV, Luckner Papers, 093.2+284.01, box 2.

102. See Gertrud Luckner, "Zum 100. Geburtstag von Rabbiner Dr. Leo Baeck, 23.5.1873–2.11.1956," in *Freiburger Rundbrief* 25 (1973): 75.

103. See Luckner's "Tätigkeitsbericht des Referats Verfolgtenfürsorge auf der Jahressitzung des Deutschen Caritasverbandes," October 1960. DCV, Luckner Papers, 093.2+284.3.

104. A list of the signers may be found in John M. Oesterreicher, "Declaration of the Church to Non-Christian Religions. Introduction and Commentary," in *Commentary of the Documents of Vatican II*, vol. 3, ed. Herbert Vorgrimler (London: Burns and Oats, 1969), 1–136, here 116.

105. "Nostra Aetate: Declaration on the Relationship of the Church to Non-Christian Religions," in *The Vatican and the Holocaust: The Catholic Church and the Jews during the Nazi Era*, ed. Randolph L. Braham (New York: Columbia University, 2000), 111–12, here 112.

106. The prevailing voting results can be found in Oesterreicher, *The New Encounter*, 275–76.

107. See Alberto Melloni, *Fra Istanbul, Atene e la guerra. La missione di A. G. Roncalli (1935–1944)* (Geneva: Marietti, 1992), 273–97.

108. See Oesterreicher, *The New Encounter*, 108–14.

109. For example, one should consider the 1928 foundations of the Society of Jews and Christians in London and the National Conference of Christians and Jews in the United States. On this point, see Simpson and Weyl, *The Story of the International Council*, 15–17.

110. "Guidelines and Suggestions for Implementing the Conciliar Declaration 'Nostra aetate,' No. 4 (December 1, 1974)," in *The Vatican and the Holocaust*, 115.

111. See Hans Hermann Henrix, "Krisenerprobt und doch bleibend störanfällig. Das aktuelle christlich-jüdische Verhältnis," *Herderkorrespondenz* 56 (2002): 341–46.

112. See especially Wladyslaw T. Bartoszewski, *The Convent at Auschwitz* (London: Bowerdean, 1990); Théo Klein, *L'Affaire du Carmel d'Auschwitz* (Paris: Bertoin, 1991); Reinhard Körner, "'Sag mir, was mich leiden läßt!' Der Streit um das Karmelitinnenkloster in Auschwitz," in *Edith Stein Jahrbuch* 1 (1995), 207–42; Pierre Blet, "La legenda alle prova degli archivi. Le ricorrenti accuse contro Pio XII," *La Civiltà Cattolica* 149 (1998): 531–41; Clemens Thoma, "Vatikanische Reue—mit Einschränkungen. Kommentar zum Dokument 'Wir erinnern uns,'" *Freiburger Rundbrief, Neue Folge* 5 (1998): 161–67; Elias H. Füllenbach, "Die Heiligsprechung Edith Steins. Hemmnis im christlich-jüdischen Dialog?" *Freiburger Rundbrief,* Neue Folge 6 (1999): 3–20; Walter Brandmüller, "Ein neuer Streit um Pius XII. Zum Desaster der katholisch-jüdischen Historikerkommission," *Die Neue Ordnung* 55 (2001): 371–81; Doris L. Bergen, "An Easy Target? The Controversy about Pius XII and the Holocaust," in *Pope Pius XII and the Holocaust,* ed. Carol Ritter and John K. Roth (London: Leicester University, 2002), 105–19; José M. Sanchez, *Pius XII and the Holocaust: Understanding the Controversy* (Washington, D.C.: Catholic University of America, 2002).

113. See the overview by Norbert Reck, "Perspektivenwechsel. Neue Fragen und Sichtweisen in der Theologie nach Auschwitz," in *Theologie nach Auschwitz? Jüdische und christliche Versuche einer Antwort,* ed. Birte Petersen, 3rd ed. (Berlin: Institut Kirche und Judentum, 2004), 141–76.

114. On the following, see also Elias H. Füllenbach, "Auschwitz als Krise christlicher Theologie. Zum Kölner Edith-Stein-Denkmal von Bert Gerresheim," *Edith Stein Jahrbuch* 10 (2004): 175–92, here 186–91.

115. Eberhard Jäckel, "Die elende Praxis der Untersteller. Das Einmalige der nationalsozialistischen Verbrechen läßt sich nicht leugnen," in *"Historikerstreit." Die Dokumentation der Kontroverse um die Einzigartigkeit der nationalsozialistischen Judenvernichtung,* ed. Ernst Reinhard Piper (München: Piper, 1987), 115–22, here 118.

116. Gregor Taxacher, *Nicht endende Endzeit. Nach Auschwitz Gott in der Geschichte denken* (Gütersloh: Kaiser, 1998), 41.

117. See, for example, Martin Gilbert, *The Righteous: The Unsung Heroes of the Holocaust* (New York: Henry Holt, 2003).

118. "Antisemitismus, Schoa und Kirche. Studie eines theologischen Arbeitskreises," *Freiburger Rundbrief, Neue Folge* 6 (1999): 262–79, here 266. This study is a draft—unfortunately not implemented—for the Vatican document *We Remember.*

119. See Steven Theodore Katz, *Kontinuität und Diskontinuität zwischen christlichem und nationalsozialistischem Antisemitismus* (Tübingen: Mohr Siebeck, 2001), 40–43.

120. See Karl Thieme, "Der religiöse Aspekt der Judenfeindschaft (Judentum und Christentum)," *Freiburger Rundbrief* 10 (1957/58): 7–14, especially 13; Gertrud Luckner, "Der Katholizismus und die Juden—Rückblick und Ausblick nach dem Konzil," *Freiburger Rundbrief* 18 (1966): 58–59.

121. "We Remember. A Reflection on the Shoah (March 16, 1998)," in *The Vatican and the Holocaust,* 100–109, here 105.

122. See Heike Kreutzer, *Das Reichskirchenministerium im Gefüge der nationalsozialistischen Herrschaft* (Düsseldorf: Droste, 2000), 100–130 and 321–22.

123. See Wolfgang Dierker, *Himmlers Glaubenskrieger. Der Sicherheitsdienst der SS und seine Religionspolitik 1933–1941,* 2nd ed. (Paderborn: Ferdinand Schöningh, 2003), 499.

124. See ibid., 522–34.

125. See Dominik Burkard, *Häresie und Mythus des 20. Jahrhunderts. Rosenbergs nationalsozialistische Weltanschauung vor dem Tribunal der Römischen Inquisition* (Paderborn: Ferdinand Schöningh, 2005), 253.

126. See ibid., 206–209.

127. See ibid., 182–92. The internal letter from the Vatican Congregation for Education to all Catholic universities and departments dated April 13, 1938, although likewise called *Syllabus,* is not a sequel to this original *Syllabus* project. See ibid., 224–32.

128. See ibid., 232–38.

129. See ibid., 252–62.

130. Mario Barbera, "Mito razzista anticristiano," *La Civiltà Cattolica* 85 (1934): 238–49, here 238.

131. Ibid., 246–47.

132. For example, see the declaration by the Slovak bishops published in the newspaper *Katolícke noviny* on April 26, 1942. This text is an unmistakable protest against the first deportations of the Slovak Jews; however, it also contains blatant antisemitism when it states that special orders against the "bad influence of Jews" in business and cultural life would be quite reconcilable with the social teaching of the Church. For the original text along with a German translation, see Walter Brandmüller, *Holocaust in der Slowakei und katholische Kirche* (Neustadt: Ph.C.W. Schmidt, 2003), 155–63.

133. On this point, see Marcel Poorthuis and Theo Salemink, *Op zoek naar de blauwe ruiter. Sophie van Leer een leven tussen avant-garde, jodendom en christendom (1892–1953)* (Nijmegen: Valkhof, 2000).

134. Faulhaber to Bertram, October 23, 1936, in *Akten Kardinal Michael von Faulhabers (1917–1945),* vol. 2, 179. In the same letter, he also condemned antisemitic actions against baptized Jews by arguing that "the state can have the . . . confidence that they are not Communists or Bolshevists."

135. See Faulhaber to Bertram, November 13, 1941, in ibid., 824–25.

136. See John Cornwell, *Hitler's Pope: The Secret History of Pius XII* (London: Viking, 1999); Daniel Jonah Goldhagen, *A Moral Reckoning: The Role of the Catholic Church in the Holocaust and Its Unfulfilled Duty of Repair* (New York: Knopf, 2002).

137. For example, see Margherita Marchione, *Pope Pius XII: Architect for Peace* (New York: Paulist, 2000); Antonio Gaspari, *Gli ebrei salvati da Pio XII* (Rome: Logos, 2001); Ralph McInery, *The Defamation of Pius XII* (South Bend, Ind.: St. Augustine's Press, 2001); Andrea Tornielli, *Pio XII: Il Papa degli Ebrei* (Casale Monferrato: Piemme, 2001). These more or less apologetic studies have to be strictly differentiated from the book by the right-wing extremist Konrad Löw, *Die Schuld. Christen und Juden im Urteil der Nationalsozialisten und der Gegenwart* (Gräfelfing: Resch, 2002), which was unfortunately praised by several German Catholic Church newspapers.

138. See Uriel Tal, *Christians and Jews in Germany: Religion, Politics, and Ideology in the Second Reich, 1870–1914* (Ithaca: Cornell University, 1975), 259–79.

139. Wolfgang Altgeld, "Katholizismus und Antisemitismus. Kommentar," in *Zeitgeschichtliche Katholizismusforschung. Tatsachen, Deutungen, Fragen. Eine Zwischenbilanz,* ed. Karl-Joseph Hummel (Paderborn: Ferdinand Schöningh, 2004), 49–55, here 52.

140. On this problem, see also the articles by Christhard Hoffmann, "Christlicher Antijudaismus und moderner Antisemitismus. Zusammenhänge und Differenzen als Problem der historischen Antisemitismusforschung," in *Christlicher*

Antijudaismus und Antisemitismus. Theologische und kirchliche Programme Deutscher Christen, ed. Leonore Siegele-Wenschkewitz (Frankfurt: Haag and Herchen, 1994), 293–317, and Johannes Heil, "'Antijudaismus' und 'Antisemitismus.' Begriffe als Bedeutungsträger," *Jahrbuch für Antisemitismusforschung* 6 (1997): 92–114.

141. See Weinzierl, *Prüfstand,* 266–67.

IV

Viewing
Each Other

Wartime Jewish Orthodoxy's Encounter with Holocaust Christianity

10

GERSHON GREENBERG

For the most part, Orthodox Jewish thinkers during the war had either a dualistic conception of Christianity, according to which sacred Israel remained categorically split from Christianity, or a unitive conception, according to which Israel and Christianity were bound together on a humanistic or spiritual level.

There were also some instances of mixture, for example, those in the rabbinic responses of Rabbi Ephraim Oshry of Kovno (and after the war Rome and New York). Oshry was convinced that Judaism (sacred) had nothing in common with Christianity (profane), but the dire circumstances mandated attempts to compromise. In the case of a Jew who attended church and wore a cross (referred to by Oshry as *Ot tumatam, To'evet hagoyim,* and *Ot shekutsam*—their sign of profanity, the Gentile disgrace, their detestable sign) to save his life, Oshry ruled that he could reenter the Jewish community after performing penitent return (*Teshuvah*) and paying a fine.[1] He judged that having "R.C." (for Roman Catholic) stamped on the passport was unacceptable if it allowed the Christian inspector to believe that a Jew was denying God, but acceptable if the inspector believed the passport holder was truly a Christian.[2] When asked about a Jewish corpse found with a cross around its neck and a *Mezuzah* in its pocket, he reasoned that the person might have converted to save his life, might have atoned for the trespass, and should therefore be buried in a Jewish cemetery—although not among the section reserved for pious Jews. When it came to reburying a girl who escaped slaughter by living as a Christian in a Christian home, Oshry stipulated that since she became a Christian under duress her body should be exhumed and buried among Jews.[3] Further, he agreed that the Christian headstone for a Jew who acted as a Christian to survive should be replaced by one with a *Magen David*. In the case of an orphan boy who was hidden by a Christian, converted, and subsequently risked his life to return to the Kovno ghetto in order to live as a Jew, Oshry ruled that he could fully join the Jewish community—and even resume the religious privileges to which he was entitled as one of priestly descent (a *Kohen*).[4] After the war, when asked about praying for a Christian who had hidden a Jewish boy and fell critically ill, he cited the rabbinic sages' opinion that the poor and sick among the heathen were to be supported by Jews just as the poor and sick of Israel, "in the interests of peace."[5] Finally, Oshry absolved an observant Jew who shot a Christian thief to death trying to recover funds stolen from an impoverished Jewish widow—not because the victim was a Christian, but because otherwise the Jew would have been killed.[6]

The dualistic and unitive conceptions were rooted in Jewish tradition through rabbinic, medieval, and early modern periods. At times Christianity was referred to specifically, notably by Maimonides, at other time implicitly with the term "Gentile." In some cases the earlier texts were cited by Holocaust thinkers. In others not—although, given the cohesive character of the tradition from which Orthodox Jewish thinkers during the Holocaust drew, it may be assumed that they were influenced by them.

The Divided Universe: Traditional Views

The rabbinic sages of the Talmudic era drew a metaphysical division between the realm of Israel and the realm of the nations: "Israel had her side, the rest of the world had its side" (*Pesikta Rabbati, Perek 33, Siman 3; Midrash Bereshit Rabbah* 41:6, 42:8). In his deliberations about whether Gentile corpses caused impurity, Simeon bar Yohai (mid-second century) cited "And you My sheep, the sheep of My pasture, are men, and I am your God, saith the Lord God" (Ez 34:31) and concluded that "You [Israelites] are called 'men' while the [Gentile] idolaters are not called men" (*Yevamot* 61[b]).[7] Over time, the alienated relationship became crystallized around Amalek, a figure of scriptural history who assumed mythic status. The Amalekites once attacked the people of Israel in the wilderness, and Moses declared that "The Lord will be at war with Amalek through the ages" [Ex 17:14–16]. As explained by the rabbinic sages, the deepest root of Amalek's assault was planted by the people of Israel themselves:

> Amalek's strength was derived from Israel itself. Because of the heretical ways Israel had fallen into, as evident from the unforgivable question asked at Refidim, "Is the Lord among us?" [Ex 17:7], Amalek was made the instrument by which [the people of] Israel were purged of their sins. "Remember what Amalek did unto thee" [Dt 25:17] is really a round-about way of reminding Israel of their own misconduct. / Indeed Amalek, who was [Haman's ancestor], was the very first to set upon Israel when they went out of Egypt, as is said, "Then came Amalek and fought with Israel at Refidim" [Ex 17:8]. And what did the wicked Amalek do to them? R. Joshua of Siknin said in the name of Rabbi Levi: He severed from the Israelites' bodies their male organs, and threw these skyward saying, "Is this what Thou desirest? Behold, it is given Thee." (*Pesikta Rabbati, Perek* 13, *Siman* 1)

Nevertheless, Amalek came to personify the evil Other. Amalek was identified retroactively with Esau and with Israel's long-time enemy of the biblical period, the Edomites (see, e.g., Am 1:11; Nahmanides *ad Exodus* 17:9; Rashi *ad Ovadiah* 1:21), as well as with Haman and later tyrants who assaulted Israel, such as Bogdan Chmielnitski. As the official religion of Constantine's Roman Empire, Christianity became part of Amalek's metahistorical reality.[8]

In the medieval period the philosopher Yehudah Halevi opined that only the "sons of Jacob" were chosen to inherit the perfect soul and intellect of Adam and transmit it by birth, and this divided them off from all other nations:

> The first man received from the deity a vital soul in all its completeness, and an intellect of the highest possible level for a human being. . . . Now the first man begat many children. Of all of them, however, only Abel was worthy to stand in his place [as recipient of Adam's complete soul and highest intellect] . . . and when he was killed by his brother Cain . . . [God] gave Adam Seth, in place of Abel. Seth resembled Adam and therefore became the chosen among men. . . . The sons of Jacob were all chosen. All of them together were worthy of the divine message. . . . Though there were among them sinners who were hated by the deity, there can be no doubt that they were still chosen in a recognizable sense, since their roots and nature were "chosen" and they were to beget children who would be "chosen." (*Ha-Kuzari* I, 95)

Israel's distinctiveness in terms of chosenness was developed by Maimonides. In the *Epistle to Yemen* (1172) he wrote that in an act of grace responding to the patriarchs' recognition of and obedience to Him, God distinguished Israel from the nations ("Yet it was to your fathers that the Lord was drawn in His love for them, so that He chose you, their linear descendants, from among all the peoples." Dt 10:15). Israel's unique selection and identification through laws and precepts provoked jealousy and enmity: "All the nations, instigated by envy and impiety, rose up against us in anger; and all the kings of the earth, motivated by injustice and enmity, applied themselves to persecute us. They wanted to thwart God, but He will not be thwarted" (Cohen translation, iii).[9] The enmity assumed three different forms. One form started at the revelation on Mt. Sinai (See *Shabbat* 89[a]/[b]) and involved the destruction of Israel's law and religion through physical violence. Its proponents included Amalek, Sisera, Sennacharib, Nebuchadnezzar, Titus, and Hadrian, as well as the Muslim leader Abd al-Nabi ibn Mahdi, whose effort to convert Yemenite Jews by force occasioned the *Epistle*. The second involved the destruction of Israel through arguments with and controversies over its laws; its proponents were Syrians, Persians, and Greeks. The third involved violence and controversy together. Its proponents claimed their own prophecy and new law from God, both of which were contrary to Judaism, with the intention of creating a potentially destructive confusion. Maimonides characterized this as "A remarkable plan, contrived by the type of personality who is envious and malicious, who will strive to kill his enemy and save his own life. And if he cannot achieve this, he will devise a scheme whereby they both will be slain" (Cohen translation, iii). He had Jesus in mind:

> The first to institute this plan was Jesus the Nazarene, may his bones be ground to dust. He was Jewish because his mother was a Jewess, although his father was a Gentile, and our principle is that a child born of a Jewess and a Gentile or a slave, is legitimate [*Yevamot* 45[a]]. Only figuratively do we call him an illegitimate child. He impelled people to believe that he was a prophet sent by God to clarify perplexities in the Torah, and that he was the Messiah predicted by each and every seer. His purpose was to interpret the Torah in a fashion that would lead to its total annulment, to the abolition of its commitments, and to the violation of all its prohibitions. The sages of blessed memory, having become aware of his plans before his reputation spread among our people, meted out fitting punishment to him. . . . / Quite some time

later, a religion which is traced to him by the descendants of Esau [i.e., the Romans] gained popularity [i.e., with Paul and the Apostles]. Although this was the aim he hoped to realize, he had no impact on Israel, as neither groups nor individuals [of Israel] became unsettled in their beliefs. His inconsistencies were transparent to everyone, as was his failure and disappointment. Finally he was overpowered and put a stop to by us when he fell into our hands and his fate is well known. (Halkin translation, 97–99)

The division between Israel and the nations was sharpened by the sixteenth century Kabbalist Samuel Uceda of Safed (born 1540), a student of Isaac Luria and Hayim Vital, who asserted that the people of Israel possessed a divine image of holiness that was unavailable to the rest of humanity. While all humankind was created in the image of God, the image of Israel was holy while the image of others was impure and profane; Israel's image was of the right, that of all others of the left. Referring to the statement of Rabbi Akiva (50–135) that "Beloved is man for he was created in the image of God" (*Pirkei Avot* 3:14), Uceda wrote:

It is possible to say that "image" does not refer to an attribute of man *per se* [as distinct from the animal] such that [all members of] the entire human species, including the children of Noah, are equal. Rather, it refers to the image of holiness which is special to the children of Israel alone. "Image" (*Tselem*) comes from shadow (*Tsel*), as in the shadow over a person's head, which rescues him [from death]. Scripture states that "surely man walketh as an image" [Ps 39:7], meaning that a person has life as long as there is an image. The scholars of the Zohar, Rabbi Simeon bar Yohai and his friends, recognized how the image disappeared when a man—of whom it was said, "Beloved is man for he was created in the image of God" [*Pirkei Avot* 3:14]—was close to death. This image [according to Simeon bar Yohai and his friends] was found only in the nation which is called Israel. In truth, it was found [only] among the pious. The evil ones [i.e., the children of Noah outside Israel] were imprinted with the image of the left, the image of impurity. Man refers to the first man [*Adam*], who was the beginning of creation, formed by the hands of the Holy One Blessed be He. Of him it is said "Beloved is man." This applies properly to the pious [children of Israel] who emerged from the first man. For surely they were created in the image of God. This image is of holiness, and applies [exclusively] to the entire nation of the children of Israel.[10]

Uceda's contemporary Judah Loew of Prague ("Maharal," 1525–1609) drew the distinction between the people of Israel, inherently disposed to accept the Torah, and idolaters of the world, represented by Esau and Ishmael, whose evil-inclined souls were not. The people of Israel possessed a lofty soul that fit divine activities (*Mitsvot*), while idolaters possessed a diminished soul that did not. When God went around to every nation and culture offering the *Mitsvot,* the idolatrous nations declined—more than not being prepared for Torah, they were opposed to it. The people of Israel were ready, because of their sublime soul (*Midrash Shemot Rabbah* 5:9, 27:9). The idolatrous souls of Esau and Ishmael and their descendants tended toward the extreme, and that implied evil. Of Esau it was said, "And by thy sword shalt thou live" (Gn 27:40) and of Ishmael, "His hand against everyone" (Gn 16:12). Both were extremists. The Torah was addressed to the upright, and they took the path of moderation. Further, for Maharal, while the nations were opposed to one another they shared an opposition to Israel whereby Israel's failure meant life to them and Israel's success meant their failure. Their life became complete when Jerusalem became ruins (as in "I shall be filled with her that is laid waste." Ez 26:2). This did not mean, however, that an idolater could not convert: "Now is it possible for a stranger to accept the Torah, if his soul is not good? This is not a problem. The fact that he comes to convert means that he already has the quality [of goodness and moderation inherent to] Israel. Once he converts, [his qualities] enable him to subordinate [himself] to the nation of Israel and become like its people."[11]

The division between sacred Israel and profane nations was also enunciated by the founder of Habad Hasidism, Shneor Zalman of Lyady (1745–1813). Each Jew had two souls, one of positive existence (drawn from the shards of the broken cosmic vessel of divine light, *Kelippot*) and the other from the realm of negative other-being (*Sitra ahra*). The souls of other nations, specifically those which "worshiped reincarnations and the resurrection of the body," were drawn from the *Kelippot,* which were polluted and devoid of goodness (*Likutei Amarim, Helek* I, *Perek* I, p. 5[a] and *Perek* 6, p. 11[a]).

By the modern period, a tradition settled into Judaism according to which the nations were of Amalek, the "other" which was at war with Israel and with which Israel was at war. Israel possessed the exclusive character of divine chosenness. Its people were created in the holy image of God, their natural character made the Torah appropriate to them, and their souls were uniquely sanctified. There was nothing in common with the nations, whose very profane existence was a negation of holy Israel. Any contact, as such, would be destructive for Israel.

The Holocaust

Shlomoh Halevi Faynzilber was the head of the religious court (*Av Beit Din*) in Kedainiai, Lithuania, and the president of Lithuania's rabbinical organization. He and his family were killed by Lithuanians in 1941. In late spring 1940 he sought to offer some consolation to his people, and turned to Maimonides' *Epistle to Yemen* (1172). Years before, Jews had stopped reciting the religious poetry (*Piyyutim*), for the period between Passover and Shavuot. It related the destruction and suffering of the medieval period and offered solace, and they believed it had no relevance in the civilized world.

> But regrettably a time has now come which transcends the medieval era, whose barbarism and lament is unprecedented. We leaf through Jewish history, soaked in blood and tears, and we find no comparison to our bitter time. We should turn back to the old *Piyyutim*. Perhaps we will find words of consolation which could ease the great pain. But the pain is so great, that it is difficult to find any consolation and healing of our wound even in them.

Faynzilber turned to Maimonides' *Epistle*, written in response to Muslim persecution and Islam's quest to spread their faith by fire and sword. The *Epistle*, he said, was written in such a way that all could read, women and children included: "We consider it a sacred obligation to write a summary of Maimonides' holy address in Yiddish, in order that everyone can know what is very necessary to know in our time. So that Maimonides' words of consolation might ease our pain just a little."

Faynzilber believed that there was a hatred of the world toward the eternal nation (*Sinat olam le'am olam*)—for example the torture of Jewish bodies by stretching machines (apparently referring to the Christian Inquisition in Spain) and medieval religious disputations. Maimonides pointed to the predictions of the prophet Amos ("I beseech then: how shall Jacob stand? For he is small." Am 7:5) and Isaiah ("My heart is bewildered, terror hath overwhelmed me." Is 21:4) that the people of Israel would be victims of contempt and assault (Cohen translation, ii). Maimonides attributed it to jealousy and enmity over Israel's having Torah—and Israel alone. But the troubles were also a means designed by God to test and purify the people:

Put your trust in these true texts of Scripture [e.g., "Yet even then, when they are in the land of their enemies, I will not reject or spurn them so as to destroy them, annulling My covenant with them: for I the Lord am their God." Lv 20:44], brethren, and be not dismayed by the succession of persecutions or the enemy's ascendancy over us, or the weakness of our people. These trials are designed to test and purify us so that only the saints and the pious men of the pure and undefiled lineage of Jacob will adhere to our religion and remain within the fold, as has been stated: "Anyone who invokes the name of the Lord shall be among the survivors" [Jl 3:5]. (Halkin translation, 102–103)

Faynzilber affirmed the belief in the divine dimension to the suffering. It would not be effective for all Jews ("Many shall purify themselves and make themselves whole and be refined; but the wicked shall do so wickedly; and none of the wicked shall understand; but the wise shall understand." Dn 12:10), but on the collective level it would serve as an atonement sacrifice that sanctified the nation. Throughout, God's protective presence was assured: "We have continuous divine assurance, that whenever a decree of apostasy is passed against us and wrath breaks out, God will ultimately terminate it." Faynzilber pointed to David's reflection about how the children of Israel went through trials and tribulations since their history began but were not exterminated, and then exclaimed, "Since my youth they have often assailed me, but they have never overcome me" (Ps 129:1). That is, he continued, God would not turn them away, even if the people turned from Him: "God has avowed and assured us that it is unimaginable that He will reject us entirely even if we disobey Him and disregard His behests." In the words of Jeremiah, "If the heavens above could be measured, and the foundations of the earth could be fathomed, only then would I reject the offspring of Israel for all that they have done, declares the Lord" (Jer 35:37). While Faynzilber identified the suffering as an atonement sacrifice, and even compared it to the *Olah* of the Temple ritual in which the sacrificial object was burned completely on the altar (see Ex 20:2), he was convinced that Israel would never be defeated. He cited Maimonides' *Epistle to Yemen:*

The divine assurance was given to Jacob our father, that his descendants would survive the people who degraded and discomfited them. As it is written, "And thy seed shall be like the dust of the earth" [Gn 28:14]. Although the descendents of Jacob will be abased like the dust that is trodden under foot, they will ultimately emerge triumphant and victorious. As the simile implies, just as the dust settles finally upon him

who tramples upon it and remains after him, so will Israel outlive its
oppressors. . . . As it is impossible for God to cease to exist, so is our
destruction and disappearance from the world unthinkable. He declares, "For I am the Lord—I have not changed; and you are the children
of Jacob—you have not ceased to be" [Mal 3:6]. (Halkin translation, 62)

The persecutors, however, would be. Babylon and Greece, for example,
were no more. Employing Maimonides' terminology, Faynzilber declared that the very dust into which Israel was transformed (see "Your
descendants shall be made as the dust of the earth." Gn 18:14), on which
the persecutors trampled, would rise up and then descend upon the
persecutors in their graves.

According to Faynzilber, the world hated Israel, jealous because it
had Torah, and proceeded to persecute its people. But the persecutions
were also means of purification set in place by God. God would also
remain with the people and assure their survival and the demise of the
persecutors. He drew from the *Epistle to Yemen,* where he found explanation and consolation in an era of unprecedented barbarism—when even
the *Piyyutim* addressed to the horrors of the medieval period were not
enough. Faynzilber did not refer specifically to Christians. But given his
reliance on the *Epistle* in which Maimonides did, and the fact that Lithuanian society, which constituted a significant component of the threat,
was Christian, it may be assumed that in his mind the persecutors included Christians—although without knowing if Christians who persecuted did so as Christians or as Lithuanians.[12]

The split between Judaism and Christianity specifically was enunciated at the close of the war, when Shlomoh Yahalomi-Diamant blended
Nazism into Christianity. From Stripow, Poland, Yahalomi-Diamant
survived Siberia and made his way back to Lublin. On May 17, 1946, he
reflected on how the city of great luminaries (Shlomoh ben Yehiel Luria,
Shmuel Edels, Meir ben Gedalyah) and of the great Hakhmei Lublin
yeshiva of Meir Shapira had been turned into the death factory of Maidanek. Then he went to Maidanek:

> I saw the gas chambers into which infants and nurslings were sent.
> Men, women, the elderly, children. I saw the ovens in which they were
> burned. There were bones which had not been burned. More than
> 800,000 pairs of shoes, their soles ripped open in search of gold and
> diamonds of the holy ones. I did lose a piece of my heart [as I knew I
> would]. / But the deepest impression came from a monument in the
> middle of Maidanek, atop the mass grave of hundreds of corpses.

When the Russians came they had not been buried. I can still see the great crucifix in the middle of Maidanek, and I tremble. Why wasn't there a *Magen David*? Weren't the children of David murdered there? Didn't the Jews who were about to be killed cry out *Shema Yisrael*? Why was there a crucifix? Because even the ground which became the grave of our holy ones is not ours. It is Christian (*Si iz ah goyishe*). That is why there is a Christian crucifix (*ah goyisher Tselem*). We have nowhere to live. Nowhere to die. When I was asked what I saw in Maidanek, I answered: I saw a crucifix.

For Yahalomi-Diamant the crucifix, apparently placed there by Russians (presumably Orthodox Christian), was inseparable from the mass murder. The Jews were no more, leaving the murderous world to be Christian.[13]

In November 1948 the themes of Maimonides, with specific reference to Christianity, reappeared. Bentsiyon Firer, head of the She'erit Yisrael yeshiva in the Ulm DP camp outside Munich, revived Maimonides' theme that the nations of the world envied Israel because of its unique possession of Torah's laws and precepts as well as the Maharal's point about intra-Gentile opposition vis-à-vis unified hatred toward Israel:

The Gentiles are not angry with us because we have a religion which is different than [any particular one of] theirs. After all, there are many different religions in the universe of the Gentiles; and there is no overwhelming hatred of any particular one towards the other. [At least] nothing like the collective hatred of the Gentile religions against the religion of Israel in particular. Their collective anger is due solely to the fact that our religion is totally different, in form and substance, from all other religions in the world. All other religions in the world are essentially idolatrous. All the idols are sensibly, visibly, perceptible to the Gentile. No matter whether the idol is Buddha, Mohammad or the Christian one [Jesus].

The jealousy meant persecution:

The history of Israel has a monotone character, that of grievous tragedy. A cry of pain, of the powerless and unfortunate people, is sounded from every page and line of our history. Collectively, the chapters of Israel's history make up a lengthy, continuously bloody narrative. The terrifying tragedy freezes the blood in our veins. There is no real spark of light in our history, no bright star in the cloudy Jewish heaven. Only a black, leaden cloud over the Jewish horizon. This has been so for 2,000 years of exile.

Firer cited Maimonides' point that Israel's identity as God's chosen people was not a matter of physical size or strength: "Not because of numbers will Abraham be famed or celebrated, but by the noted and illustrious scions of Isaac" (Cohen translation, viii). Nor did God choose the people of Israel because of their number: "'The Lord did not set His love upon you, nor choose you, because ye were more in number than any people . . .' [Dt 7:7]" (Cohen translation, iii). Echoing Maimonides ("As it is impossible for God to cease to exist, so is our destruction and disappearance from the world unthinkable." Halkin translation, 62), Firer observed how Israel endured. It did so, physically as well as spiritually in the sense of resisting assimilation into dominant nations. Employing a theme spelled out by the nineteenth-century philosopher Nahman Krokhmal, Firer pointed out that Israel's endurance followed a cyclical pattern of birth, flowering, and decay. Other nations grew and flowered, but once they decayed they left the stage of history:

> This is an authentic miracle of world-scale. It is a phenomenon of world-history without comparison. In the history of every other nation there are ascents and descents, eras and epochs of blossoming and periods of decay, decline and misfortune. The history of the Jewish people for the last thousand years is different. [Despite the relentless persecution], the Jewish people have not been doomed. The pyres and crematoria [of the Holocaust] have shaken the nation of Israel, and torn away large sections of the Jewish-national organism. But they have not completely destroyed Israel. The Jewish people live on. They continue to exist and to be—despite the enemy's fury.

Maimonides had written of the divine assurance that Israel would not be destroyed, and how Israel's disappearance was no more possible than for God to cease to exist: "For I the Lord change not, and ye, O sons of Jacob, will not be consumed" (*Malachi* 3:6) (Cohen translation, v–vi), and Firer spoke of Israel's metahistorical eternity: "Upon Israel's birth, God removed it from the realm of history to which all other peoples belonged, and assured Israel of endless eternity and that it would be forever unconquerable." He cited Maimonides' simile of dust, where the descendants of Jacob, debased like dust trodden under foot, would emerge victorious, the dust settling on those who did the trampling and outlasting them (Halkin translation, 62), and added that like stars, Jews could never be captured. They existed in a perennial state of "nevertheless," "despite" and "contrary" to all. Not only would Israel survive, Firer continued. They would multiply—according to the principle of "The more they afflicted them the more they multiplied" (Ex 1:12). Still, Israel's existence was not to be defined in terms of numbers ("That if a man can number the dust of the earth, then shall thy seed also be numbered." Gn 13:10). He cited the *Epistle:*

> Not because of numbers will Abraham be famed or celebrated, but by the noted and illustrious scions of Israel. The phrase "shall be called" simply means, shall be renowned, as it does in the verse, "Let thy name be called in them, and the name of my fathers Abraham and Isaac" (Gn 45:16). . . . The Divine covenant made with Abraham to grant the sublime Law to his descendants referred exclusively to those who belonged to the stock of both Isaac and Jacob. (Cohen translation, viii–ix)

Islam's greatness lay in its numbers ("I will make thee a great nation." Gn 17:20) (Cohen translation 17:20), not in prophecy or law, as the angel promised Hagar ("I will greatly multiply they seed, that it shall not be numbered for multitude." Gn 16:10). Israel's greatness lay in the blessings of eternity and the spiritual quality to endure the world's hatred to the eternal nation (*Sinat olam le'am olam*).[14]

In an essay written eight years later in the Land of Israel, Firer identified the enemy with Amalek, and this included Christianity. He declared that there was now no more vital concern for Israel than erasing Amalek's name. Hatred of Amalek had the highest priority, and was of such absolute and unconditional character as to be a *Mitsvah* (sacred command):

> The battle between the nation of Israel and Amalek is one of life and death. All that Amalek wants for us is our absolute obliteration. Given this reality, what higher concern could there possibly be, than for us to defend ourselves against this ultimately serious danger. It would be an error to fail to see that antisemitism is the mature fruit of original Amalekism. / The German Fascist government recognized no higher spiritual authority which limited human activity. The reason German Fascism did not fight against Christianity as it did against Judaism was that, from the religious perspective there was little difference between German Fascism and Christianity. While Christianity affirmed that "that man" [Jesus] governed it, Fascism affirmed the right of the *Führer* to govern the generation in which he lived. Both Christianity

and German Fascism affirmed that a human being [Jesus and the *Führer* respectively] was an idol [and divine]. And because of this they hated the people of Israel. For them *Hashem,* not some human being, was God.[15]

For Faynzilber, Yahalomi-Diamant, and Firer, the Israel (sacred)–nations (profane) division, with Christianity belonging implicitly or explicitly to the latter, had to be maintained by Israel. The division and animosity was not resolvable through any common ground. To the contrary, should sacred and profane enter one another and the sacred be compromised, the internal and metaphysical chaos that resulted would reverberate empirically.

For some thinkers, any overture made by Israel that involved common ground spelled disaster. Shlomoh Zalman Ehrenreich, the communal rabbi of Simleul-Silvaniei, Transylvania, was imprisoned with its Jewish citizens in nearby Cehul-Silvaniei, and subsequently murdered in Auschwitz (June 1944). In the sermons he delivered through October 22, 1943, he inveighed against the marriages that took place between Jewish men and Christian women. One (unnamed) rabbi issued divorce decrees to Polish and Russian Jewish women to facilitate the husbands' remarriage to Christian women. Jewish women in Vienna were marrying Polish Catholic men. There were also some Jews who waited expectantly for the war to end so they could convert to Christianity. Such Christian intrusion into Israel's sanctity reverberated in the form of Israel's physical destruction—inner spiritual being determined outer material events. According to Ehrenreich's traditional interpretation of the metahistorical dimension, the destruction took place under divine aegis and was intended to restore Israel's holiness. When Ehrenreich saw Jews from Grosswardein (Oradea Mare) passing through Simleul-Silvaniei, with swastikas branded on their faces and parts of their fingers bitten off, he introduced the explanation of Mosheh Hayim Ephraim of Sudilkov, the grandson of the founder of Hasidism Ba'al Shem Tov:

> "The voice is Jacob's voice but the hands are the hands of Esau" [Gn 27:22]. The rabbinic sages explained, that when Jacob's voice is of Torah, the hands of Esau do not rule the world with harshness. God forbid, that Esau's hands should ever take control of the world. As long as Israel does God's will . . . the evil ones [of Esau] will care for Israel's needs and serve the people of Israel as a servant its master. As long as Jacob's voice is of Torah and Jacob studies Torah with intensity, Esau's hands will remain tied up with other business.[16]

When the people of Israel failed in terms of Torah, Ehrenreich explained, God transferred his indignation over to Esau, with the freedom to act and will and (without his knowing it) force Jews back to Torah.[17]

Shlomoh Zalman Unsdorfer was the last rabbinical leader of the Orthodox Jewish community in Bratislava. He was imprisoned in the city's ghetto in 1944, and murdered in Auschwitz in October of that year. Citing the *Epistle,* he averred that Israel's chosen status incited the nations. Distance had to be kept to keep the incitement under control. The current persecution and suffering were reverberations of internal chaos, consequent to removing the distance through Judaism's self-Christianizing. As an example, Unsdorfer spoke of the calendar:

> The authorities have forbidden us from leaving our homes at the beginning of the Christian year, referred to as *Neu Jahr.* On account of our many sins, in peaceful times we celebrated and rejoiced according to the [Christian] calendar of the nations. What business do we have with their profane (*Tumah*) holidays? People of Israel, do not rejoice on the [Christian] new year of the nations. [We are separate]: "For I the Lord am holy, and have set you apart from the peoples, that ye should be mine." [Lv 20:26]

Unsdorfer remained convinced, however, that the troubles were intended by God to restore Israel to holiness.[18] For Ehrenreich and Unsdorfer, Israel's selective sacred being had metaphysical dimensions. The very order of the world was disturbed when it was not maintained, because of compromise with the profane. Reminiscent of the view portrayed in *Pesikta Rabbati, Perek* 13, *Siman* 1, according to which Amalek attacked due to Israel's misconduct, for these two thinkers Israel's own initiative compromised the separation and resultant troubles reflected the spiritual chaos. The world created by God required Israel's distinctive sanctity, and the troubles were set by God to restore Israel to its sacred self.

Preserving the Divide: Religious Thought

The metaphysical truth of the divide between Israel and the nations (including Christianity) had to be preserved lest the chaos continue to bring catastrophe. Efforts were made to do so, theological and existential. Christianity's attempt to corrupt the suffering servant of Isaiah 53 ("He was wounded for our transgressions, he was bruised for our iniquities . . . and the Lord hath laid on him the iniquity of us all." Is 53:5–6) was rebuffed. In 1939 two religious nationalist thinkers in Palestine, Yeshayahu Wolfsberg-Aviad and Shlomoh Zalman Shraggai, confronted the adaptation. Wolfsberg-Aviad discredited the Christian notion that a single individual could assume all of mankind's sins and atone for them. The correct (and Jewish) view was that one nation could suffer for another, as German and Austrian Jews were doing now. Judaism was smitten of God and afflicted (Is 53:4) for other nations, lest the whole world suffer and all existence be threatened. But this did not mean that the people of Israel, or any single Jew, could or did assume the sins of others and atone for them. Each individual was responsible for his or her sins. Wolfsberg-Aviad added that the passage "wounded for our transgressions, bruised for our iniquities, the chastisement of our peace was upon him, and with his stripes we are healed" (Is 53:5) did not imply that Israel itself was guilty of any crimes. Shlomoh Zalman Shraggai rejected Christianity's principle of vicarious suffering:

> It may be possible to live for the sake of others, and many have identified this as Israel's historical task. To suffer for others was something else entirely. There were special individuals, who were extremely sensitive to [the plight] of others. They were filled with a sublime level of pride when they suffered for others and thought that doing so created a place of such sublimity as to be empty of all despair. But most people of Israel recognized the prophet Ezekiel's bold statement: "The soul that sinneth, it shall die; the soul shall not bear the iniquity of the father with him, neither shall the father bear the iniquity of the son with him; the righteousness of the righteous shall be upon him, and the wickedness of the wicked shall be upon him." (Ez 18:20)

The medieval commentator David Kimhi added, "Let alone one person bear iniquity for another and let alone one nation bear iniquity for another" (David Kimhi *ad Isaiah* 53:4).[19]

In Brooklyn in May 1941 Yosef Yitshak Schneersohn, the rav of Lubavitch Hasidism, fought to co-opt attempts to Christianize redemption. Because mainline Orthodoxy (specifically the world rabbinical organization Agudat Yisrael) failed to explain and proclaim that the suffering meant imminent redemption (the pains preceding the birth of the Messiah), Jews were left to feel that God was distant from their troubles. Christian missionaries stepped into the vacuum and offered their Messiah, one who was imminent, claiming that Jews were drowning in their blood because they did not accept Jesus, the Messiah. Schneersohn referred to thirty-one conversions to Catholicism and thousands to Christian Science in the New York area. He found consolation in the fact that

Christianity itself would disappear completely with the redemption of Israel. In March 1943 his spokesman identified Christianity with Haman ("The sooner all the Jewish masses and classes will perceive the [apocalyptic] truths, the lesser will be the soap [from Jewish corpses] to fill the pockets of Haman (*Haman Tashen*) of the Christians and followers of Mohammed"), and predicted that Christianity would be destroyed just as Haman was. The Jews, despite their obliteration into the millions, would survive to possess the Land of Israel.[20] Three years later, Simhah Elberg, a legal scholar, theologian, and poet who escaped Warsaw for Shanghai, rejected the application of Christian forgiveness to Judaism. Martin Niemöller sought Jewish forgiveness of Germans in exchange for Christian-German collective regret:

> No, and a thousand times no, Pastor Niemöller. The pardon does not rest in our hands. Hitler struck his claws into our stock, into our parents and ancestors. No one had any right to desecrate thousand year-old bodies in their graves. Not I, and not the Torah, will forgive the Germans for desecrating graves. No, Pastor Niemöller, you will not get our forgiveness, not at any price. We shall bear an eternal, incendiary hatred and vengeance in our hearts towards you [Christian-Germans], just as we do towards Amalek.[21]

Preserving the Divide: Existential Activity

Maintaining the religious divide was, for many Orthodox Jews, more important than life itself. Faced with the opportunity to survive by assuming Christian identity, they chose death. Yissakhar Taykhtahl of Munkács, Hungary, author of the now classic work on the implications of the catastrophe for returning to and restoring the Land of Israel, *The Mother of Children Is Happy* (*Em Habanim Semehah*, Budapest 1943), was killed in 1943. As a rabbinical authority, he was called upon to rule on whether or not a baptismal certificate with a Christian name could be used in order to escape. He cited Maimonides:

> In times of a decree, i.e., when a wicked king like Nebuchadnezzar or his like will arise and issue a decree against the Jews to nullify their faith or one of the religious commands (*Mitsvot*), one should sacrifice one's life rather than transgress ("*yehareg ve'al ya'avor*") the *Mitsvot* [prohibiting idolatry, murder, forbidden sexual acts]—whether one is compelled to transgress amid ten Jews or one is compelled to transgress merely amid Gentiles. (*Hilkhot Yesodei Hatorah, Perek* 5, *Halakhah* 3)

Even when the Jew's heart remained pure in terms of faith, transgression was not permissible. He again cited Maimonides:

> The ninth *Mitsvah* is that God commanded us to sanctify the name. And it is said, 'I will be sanctified among the children of Israel' [*Leviticus* 22:52]. We are commanded to publicize the subject of this *Mitsvah* around the world, not fearing injury [for doing so]. Even should a force overwhelm us and demand that we become heretics about the Exalted One, we will pay no heed. We will submit ourselves to death [rather than let the persecutors] think we have become heretics. No matter that in our hearts we continue to believe in the Exalted One, such is the *Mitsvah* of sanctification of God's name (*Kiddush Hashem*) as commanded to all of Israel. It means submitting the soul in death by the hand of the oppressor, out of love for the Blessed One and the belief in His unity. (Maimonides, "*Mitsvah Aseh: Mitsvah Teshi'i*," in *Sefer Hamitsvot*)

He also cited Aharon Halevi of Barcelona, thirteenth century:

> We have been commanded to sanctify the name [in the face of death]. It says, "I will be sanctified among the children of Israel" [Lv 22:52]. That is, in order to keep the *Mitsvot* of religion, we will [even] submit our soul to death. It does state "Live in them" [Lv 18:5], i.e., do not die in them. But according to [oral] and written tradition, this does not apply to all kinds of trespass. [According to *Sanhedrin* 74ᵃ, there are three *Mitsvot* where a person is obliged to be killed rather than trespass (*yehareg ve'al ya'avor*)—idolatry, murder and sexual perversion. If a person is told, "Commit idolatry or we will kill you," the person should [let himself] be killed rather than trespass, the person should be killed even if the heart remains pure with belief of God. . . . There should be no opportunity [for the perpetrator to think that a Jew] denied God. (Aharon Halevi of Barcelona, "*Siman* 296: *Mitsvot Kiddush Hashem*, in *Sefer Hahinukh*)

Taykhtahl added that using a baptismal certificate would send a message that God had less (sacred) power than did the realm of negative other-being (*Sitra-ahra*). His basic conclusion was that death was preferable to assuming Christian identity—which both constituted a transgression (of the *Mitsvah* regarding idolatry) and allowed the persecutor to believe the Jew committed heresy (diminishing the perceived reality of the sacred). In some instances, Taykhtahl rationalized around the dilemma. When he was asked about having "R.C." (for Roman Catholic)

stamped on a passport to enable border crossing (as distinct from ac-
quiring a baptismal certificate), he responded that if it were possible for the Jew to use R.C. as a mnemonic device to remember God—
specifically, indicating *Rak* ("only") which could stand for "Only guard
your soul well lest it forget God" ("*Rak ushemor nafsheha me'od pen
tishkakh et Hashem*")—it would be acceptable. He cited Shlomoh ben
Yitshak's (Rashi, 1040–1105) point that one could bow before Nebuchadnezzar outwardly but remain upright within (Rashi *ad Song of Songs*
7:8). And in the case of a Jew who already converted to Christianity
under force, he ruled not to cut him off from the community and that he
could even be called up to bless the Torah. He again cited Maimonides,
who (apparently reversing the principle to "sacrifice one's life rather than
trespass" in *Hilkhot Yesodei Hatorah, Perek* 5, *Halakhah* 3) stipulated: "If
concerning the worship of false gods, which is the most serious of sins, a
person who is forced to worship is not liable [for the punishment] of
being cut off from the community, let alone of being [condemned] by a
court to be executed, how much more so does this apply to [liability]
with regard to other *Mitsvot* of Torah" (*Hilkhot Yesodei Hatorah, Perek* 5,
Halakhah 4). But these rulings (roundabout and after-the-fact) did not
change his basic disposition, that when the choice was given, death was
preferable to assuming Christian identity, affirming the sacred-profane
divide vis-à-vis Christianity.[22]

In an instance reported by Yehudah Yekutiel Halberstamm, the
rebbe of Klausenberg (Cluj), Transylvania, who survived the Holocaust
and reestablished his Hasidic court in Brooklyn and then Netanya, Israel,
a follower was so afraid to take the chance that his daughters would
convert if sheltered by a certain Christian that he risked having them
killed instead. He recalled:

> An innocent Jew related to me that his Christian neighbor was ready to
> take his three daughters until the fury passed [Is 26:20]. He knew that
> he himself would not return from where he would [certainly] be taken,
> and that he would be burned in an oven. He resolved to take his daugh-
> ters as well, rather than let them change their religion and live like
> Gentiles [i.e., Christians]. In vain I tried to convince him to leave his
> daughters [with the Christian]. It was not self-evident that they would
> not change their religion, even if he would not be fortunate enough to
> return. Especially so, since his daughters were already grown. But he
> remained firm: "Rabbi, I have always listened to everything you have

told me to do. But here I cannot. I could never die with a whole heart, knowing that perhaps, God forbid, my daughters would convert and live like Gentiles." With these words he rushed to leave my house.[23]

When it came to his own life and that of his family, Halberstamm rejected the opportunity to assume Christian names for their identity papers. He cited Maimonides' ruling that "one should sacrifice one's life rather than transgress" (*Hilkhot Yesodei Hatorah, Perek* 5, *Halakhah* 3) along with the rabbinic sages' position that one should love God with all one's soul, even should the soul be taken by God in death (*Berakhot* 61[b]). Nor could the use of a Christian name be split from one's personality. Instead of Rashi's division between without and within (*ad Song of Songs* 7:8), Halberstamm believed that assuming a Christian name made one into a Christian. His wife and eleven children were killed in the Holocaust.[24]

On September 5, 1942, a Warsaw Jew was faced with the choice of handing his daughter over to a monastery (with payment). He spoke directly about the destruction of sacred Israel. In the past, he explained, Jews let their bodies burn as their souls survived. The pages of Torah parchment in which they were wrapped (the body) on the pyre burned but the letters (the soul) ascended to heaven without becoming desecrated (see for example the murder of Hananiyah ben Teradyon, head of the Sikhnin yeshiva in Galilee, second century; *Avodah Zarah* 17[b]–18[a]). Now there was the possibility for the body to survive by conversion to Christianity. But the letters (the soul) would burn and alien (Christian) letters would be written on the empty pages. Nor would the Christians in the monastery refrain from burning the soul:

> Anyone who knows anything about the character and methodology of Catholic priests will understand that they are not receiving youngsters with open arms for its own sake. They have always been out to acquire souls for Christianity. They are now wrapping themselves with talk of compassion and humanity, and how those were the reasons for wanting to educate the children in their institutions. But we are not blind to the real reason, which is to convert the souls (*la'asot nefashot*). . . . They want to bring the children under the Christian wings of their *Shekhinah* (i.e., light of their God). The priests are not motivated to pity our children out of love of the other as "that man" (*oto ish*) of Nazareth preached and taught. Were it so, they would have pity not only on the children, but on the older people who have sought their help as well.[25]

This stance was expressed by the wife of a certain Rabbi Levin in the Lvov ghetto. When faced with placing her youngest son in the home of Ortho-dox Christian metropolitan Sheftitsky, she told her older son:

> The promises of the Metropolitan are very nice, but the possibility of conversion will sooner or later become very real. I am certain that you will remain faithful to Judaism, and that you will make every effort that your brother Natan will [grow up] a Jew. But if I also give over your little brother for protection, still an infant, who will take care that he does not, God forbid, leave the congregation of Israel? I have therefore come to the decision that I and the boy will remain in the ghetto. If we are worthy of staying alive, well and good. If not, wherever your [de-parted] father is, there we shall be also.[26]

In a postwar reflection, Ephraim Oshry echoed the position of the Warsaw Jew on September 5, 1942:

> There were some priests of the supposed [Christian] religion of love, and some monks and nuns, who were not out for revenge against the Jews. They did not identify Jewish misery and destruction as [justified] revenge and payback for the blood of the one "who was hung," who was "crucified"—for which the Jews were [allegedly] guilty. Their com-passion was stirred by Jewish children and infants, as the cursed Ger-mans, may their name be erased, plotted to destroy the Jews, to uproot the Jewish future and hope of the Jewish people, to obliterate the nation and the memory of its name. But even they were concerned primarily with trapping innocent [Jewish] souls in their net; in sever-ing them from their sources and the religion of their fathers; and in having them forget that they ever were Jews.[27]

The Unitive Disposition

The traditional view that Israel (sacred) was split off from nations (profane), including Christianity, that Israel was chosen, that the people of Israel alone were the holy image of God and that the nations were jealous and attacked Israel out of enmity, continued into the Holo-caust. Faynzilber and Firer brought forward Maimonides' *Epistle to Ye-men* with its ingredients of Israel's chosenness, the nations' enmity, God's use thereof to purify Israel, and Israel's survival and inevitable victory over the nations: Yahalomi-Diamant blended Maidanek with the crucifix, and Firer spoke of hatred of Amalek (and Christianity) as a *Mitsvah*. Ehrenreich and Unsdorfer believed that the Holocaust happened because Jews Christianized Israel (sacred). The divide had to be preserved, and efforts were made to do so on the level of religious thought as well as in existential matters of life and death. For these thinkers, the Israel-nations divide was a matter of existence itself. Any intermingling and self-Christianizing inflamed hatred of Israel's chosenness and set off attacks upon Israel. Israel's integrity and life depended upon the separation—even should life mean survival of the sacred nation but death of millions of Jews.

At the very same time, there were Orthodox Jews who found common ground between Israel and the nations, including Christianity, in terms of shared humanity and shared religious values. According to this view, instead of the result of weakening the line between Israel and the nations, the disaster that befell Israel had to do with the failure to establish contact and develop means of harmony.

Traditional Views

The theme of commonality was evident in the second-century sage Rabbi Meir's opinion that a non-Jew who learned Torah should be seen as equivalent to a Jew—even a Jew with the lofty position of high priest: "How do we know that a Gentile who occupies himself in Torah is like a High Priest? Scripture states, 'which a man will do and live by them' [Lv 18:5]. Scripture does not refer to priests, Levites and Israelites but rather to man. Thus you have learned that even a Gentile who occupies himself with Torah is like a High Priest" (*Sanhedrin* 59ª).

The commonality was also to be found in the attitude toward conversion (referred to above in the writings of the Maharal of Prague). While Maimonides drew a divide between chosen Israel and envious nations and anticipated Israel's ultimate victory over the nations, he still supported conversion. In response to a question from Rabbi Ovadyah the proselyte, he explained that many of the children of Israel who left Egypt were themselves idolaters, having integrated into the culture of Egypt. Moses separated them from the Gentiles and brought them under the divine presence (*Shekhinah*). From then on they shared the one law with those who had remained Israelites. According to Maimonides, Jewish identity was a function of the spiritual legacy of the patriarchs and the law, not of physical descent.

Anyone who converts [to Judaism], up to the end of the generations, and everyone who unites the name of the Holy One Blessed be He as written in the Torah, is a student of Abraham our father, may peace be upon him, and members of his household. Abraham turned them all to the right path. As he turned all those of his generation by word and by teaching, he turned all those who would convert in future, by the testament he left to his children and members of his household to come after him. Abraham our patriarch, may peace be upon him, was the father of his seed, all those who are upright and take his path. He is the father of their students and all those who would convert.

Addressing Rabbi Ovadyah directly, Maimonides spoke of the convert's equality with the born Jew in terms of chosenness, Torah, and God:

There is no difference at all between us and you in any matter whatsoever. For sure, you are to recite blessings [which include such phrases as] "Who selected us . . . and gave to us . . . and bequeathed to us . . . and distinguished us." For the sublime creator already chose you and distinguished you for the nations and gave you the Torah. The Torah was given to us and to strangers. . . . You know that our forefathers who left Egypt were for the most part idolaters in Egypt. They assimilated into the Gentiles and learned their ways, until God sent our teacher Moses, may peace be upon him, the head of all the prophets, who distinguished them from the nations and entered them under the wings of the divine presence (*Shekhinah*). There was one law for us and for all the strangers. Your relation should not be taken lightly. If we relate together to Abraham, Isaac and Jacob, you relate to the One who spoke and the world came into being.[28]

The concept of common ground in terms of Torah-study and conversion was extended in the seventeenth century by Yomtov Lipman Heller. He interpreted Rabbi Akiva's principle that "beloved is man for he was created in the divine image" (*Pirkei Avot* 3:14) to mean that all human beings, all the children of Noah and not only the people of Israel, were created in God's one image.[29] Aharon Ibn Hayim (Morocco, d. 1632) held that the passage "This is the book of the generations of man (*Adam*)" (Gn 5:3) was of greater weight even than the injunction to love one's neighbor as oneself and not to hate one's neighbor (*Shabbat* 31[a]). "The book of the generations of man (*Adam*)" meant that all human beings were generated from the one *Adam*; that all were brothers and that none was to overcome the other. It indicated that all human beings were of one and the same image and imprint of God, all were forms of the divine, and that all were to come together through their deeds.[30] The concept of commonality of humankind was brought forward in nineteenth-century Poland by Mordekhai Ettinger and Yosef Shaul Natanzohn, in their commentary on the Jerusalem Talmud (*Nedarim, Perek* 9, *Halakhah* 4). In the passage, "This is the book of the generations of man (*Adam*), in the day that God (*Elohim*) created he them. Male and female created He them; and blessed them, and called their name *Adam* in the day when they were created" (Gn 5:1–3), the term for God, *Elohim*, was plural in a secondary sense, and singular in a primary sense. While several powers branched out of God, He remained one and unique. So it was with the exponential branching out of the first man (*Adam*). All human beings stemmed from a single *Adam*, resembling one body with many limbs. Love and brotherhood followed. When God created *Adam*, he created male and female ("them"); the plurality was implied by the unity. In the image of God, *Adam* and humankind resembled His plurality-in-unity.[31]

Also in the nineteenth century, Yisrael ben Gedalyah Lipschutz introduced the concept of the universality of righteousness. He objected to Simeon bar Yohai's interpretation of Ezekiel 34:31 to mean "You [Israelites] are called 'men' while the [Gentile] idolators are not called men" (*Yevamot* 61[b]). Were the people who belonged to nations other than Israel supposed to be beasts? Then why is it said that "The Lord thy God hath chosen thee to be His own treasure, out of all peoples that are upon the face of the earth" (Dt 7:6)? Should it not have said, "out of all the apes that looked like men upon the face of the earth" instead? And if the other nations were made up of beasts, who certainly could not be subject to reward and punishment, how could the Jews believe that "the righteous among the nations have a portion in the world to come" and that God was "righteous in all His works and gracious in all His deeds" (Ps 145:17)? Beyond the conceptual level, Lipschutz continued, there were Gentiles who were righteous, who believed in the divinity of Torah, who recognized God the creator and were kind to the people of Israel. There were even Gentiles who benefited all of humanity. For example, Edward Jenner, who invented the smallpox vaccine; Francis Drake, who brought the potato to Europe and prevented famine; Johannes Gutenberg, who invented printing; and Johannes Reuchlin, who risked his life and then was persecuted because he tried to prevent a burning of the Talmud. Were they ineligible for reward in the world to come? Gentiles who were righteous and pious were not beasts who impurified the sacred. They were men, created in God's image and had a portion in the world to come. There was but one exception—Gentiles who were evil:

> [The assumption is that] all nations are [like Israel] beloved by God, because they contain the image of God. However, if they become extremely bad it is possible for the image to disappear from them. Israelites, [unlike the nations] are called children [of God] even if they become idolaters [See *Kiddushin* 36ᵃ]. They remain beloved, even if they sin. This is because all Israelites resemble their [divine] father [permanently] and it is impossible for the image [they hold] to become absolutely impure.[32]

The Holocaust

The perception of commonalities between Israel and the Gentiles (which for our seventeenth- and nineteenth-century sources meant Christian) in terms of Torah, potential conversion, descent from Adam, and righteousness, as opposed to the view that any mutuality meant enmity, divinely ordained persecution, and such a serious threat to Israel's sanctity that death was preferable, continued into the Holocaust.

In one stream of thought, authentic Christianity was disassociated from Nazism. Christians did join forces during the Holocaust. But this was the result of pagan inroads into and expressions of Christianity, not the product of Christianity in itself. According to Eliyahu Botschko, founding head of the Emek Halakhah yeshiva in Montreux, Switzerland, when Christianity first began it made efforts to repel paganism, along with its bestial hatred of Israel, and sought to incorporate portions of Torah (Botschko did not offer examples). But the efforts did not succeed, and by the medieval period Christianity assumed a pagan character. That character explained the persecution of Jews, the pyres built for Jews in the name of the Church. Botschko wrote in 1937:

> The paganism [which early Christianity sought to repel] seemed to become permanently dormant in Christianity. Instead it awakened later. It assumed new and powerful forms, with orgies [of persecution]. / The Great Gate of Rome, the [center of the] Church in which so many [Jews] placed their hopes, in which so many thought they would find protection and love, turned out to be a bitter disappointment. The original intimations of a [Christian] messiah would be lost once again.[33]

Gedalyah Bublick, a religious nationalist in New York City, echoed this view. In December 1940 he wrote that the Christian Church sought to undermine racial fanaticism, jingoism, and international hatreds, in the name of unified humanity.[34] In summer 1947 he wrote that over time the effort failed because barbarism infested the Christian world. It finally erupted from within it, and the rest of Christian Europe did not resist.[35] The paganism-Christianity distinction was also drawn by Mosheh Prager, the leading Orthodox Jewish historian of the Holocaust, who escaped Warsaw at the beginning of the war and lived in Bene Beraq, Israel. The *Deutsche Christen* blended Christianity with Nazi pagan racism, and sought to expel the Old Testament from Christianity. Prager referred to the November 13, 1933, rally where Dr. Reinhold Krause demanded that German worship be liberated from the reward-and-punishment morality of the Old Testament and that Christian pastors stop issuing statements such as "We stand with one foot on the ground of the Old Testament and another on correct Christianity."[36] Yehudah Layb Gerst of Łódź also followed this line of thought. He wrote in 1938 how the Church Fathers once attributed the Temple's destruction to Israel's failure to replace Torah with Christ, and Origen, Eusebius, and Hieronymous misinterpreted Jewish history according to Christian principles.[37] But were it not for paganism, Christianity would never have joined with Nazism. Gerst wrote in 1936 that paganism was the real source for the Inquisition and for other Christian assaults against Israel. It lay dormant in Christianity from the beginning (which Botschko said the next year). There it lay, infuriated over Judaism's "colonizing" of Christianity, in its "blood" and "marrow" streaming through Christian religious veins. Paganism erupted, he wrote in 1947, with Nazism. In the nineteenth century the pagan ingredient in Christianity demanded absolute conversion as the price of equal rights for Jews (not the partial concession of Jewish Reformers), he explained, and now the Christians and Nazis together condemned converts because these Jews were becoming Christians to Judaize Christianity from within. In an essay in 1970 in Israel, Gerst wrote that the paganism dormant in Christianity, filled with feelings of vengeance against Judaism's presence, emerged in tandem with the weakening of Christianity in modern times:

> Wherever the light of [true] Christianity suddenly went dim, the metaphysical principles of the Christian faith followed. In the second half of the nineteenth century, streams of [pagan] heresy expanded within

[Christian] nations of Europe. Weakening and hatred came together. The weakening of Christian principles was paralleled by an unprecedented wave of poisonous hatred towards the people of Israel. The hatred developed into the most extreme form possible: Nazism.[38]

For some, the fact that authentic Christianity did not belong together with Nazism left it to share the realm of Israel. In 1933, Gerst wrote that Christianity was rooted in Judaism, that Christianity's very "spinal chord" and "nervous system" were Jewish. Alfred Rosenberg's demand in *Der Mythus des 20. Jahrhunderts* that Christianity extract itself from Judaism was impossible to meet. Indeed, Rosenberg himself "evidently understands that humanistic Judaism has been implanted in Christianity."[39] In 1936 Gerst asserted that Judaism's influence on Christianity was so deep that the Nazi wild idolaters were as frightened of Christianity as they were of Judaism. Thus Rosenberg's intense contempt for Christianity.[40] In February 1940 Jakob Rosenheim of Frankfurt am Main, world president of the Agudat Yisrael organization, then in London, wrote that "Hitler's morbid hatred against Jews and against the Christian church as well is surely no coincidence, but conclusive proof of the metaphysical character of the great struggle of our day."[41] Toward the end of the war he called upon Christians of Germany "in whose heart there is a spark of human feeling" to rise up against the unprecedented inhuman crimes of Hitler against the Jews.[42] Gedalyah Bublick posited fascism in the realm of Esau (and Satan), a realm of hatred against human beings who believed in something beyond the state and of belligerence toward the *Tanakh* as source of faith and Christianity as derived from it. This was the realm of the sword and life as blood. Judaism and Christianity resided together in the realm of justice, humaneness, and emulation of God in terms of morality. Bublick cited the self-described "metahistorian" Christopher Dawson's observation that "modern civilization is not only ceasing to be Christian. It is setting itself up as an anti-religion which will tolerate no rival, and which claims to be sole master of the world."[43]

Some spoke of a common God and common Scripture. In his attempt to stop deportation of Jews from Slovakia, Rabbi Avraham Frieder of Nova Mesto sent a letter on March 6, 1942, to president of the Republic of Slovakia Joseph Tiso, appealing to him in the name of the God they shared. He implored Tiso (a priest), as one who served "Almighty God" and believed in the "supreme judge above him":

Hear our voices and answer us. . . . Did not one God create us? Do we not all owe a final accounting to Him? Have mercy on [those] . . . who pour out their hearts with tears, and pray to our father in heaven for salvation. Hoping for His mercy, we place our fate in your hands. . . . "[And it will be] before the Lord, for He is come to judge the earth. He will judge the world with righteousness and the peoples with equity." [Ps 98:9][44]

In October 1933 German Orthodox leaders (including M. Schlesinger, Esra Munk, Shlomoh Ehrman, Isaac Breuer, Moses Auerbach, and Jakob Rosenheim) wrote to chancellor of the Reich Hitler in response to the Nationalist Socialist Party's attacks against the Jewish race, in the name of common Scripture:

On the spiritual level, the Jewish people (*Volk*) are not some strangers unknown to Germans. The Jewish Bible and New Testament Scripture, [both of which] Jews conceived of and composed, have [together] made an intelligible impression on the German essence for [a period of] a thousand years. In certain instances, the slogan about liberation from the alien Jewish racial influence [has been] applied to the Bible. Observing how the new Germany treasures and protects the Church as a powerful, indispensable bastion in the construction of healthy national life, [we would point out that] no Christian Church, no matter how *völkisch* it may be construed, would be able to demolish the [biblical] bridge to its own history of salvation.[45]

Mosheh Prager drew attention to the June 1945 response of the Catholic anti-Nazi leader, Irene Harand, to Alfred Rosenberg's call to replace the Old Testament with Nordic sagas: "Whoever does injury to the Old Testament expels Christ. The redeemer thought of Himself as being closely bound up with the Old Testament: 'Think not that I am come to destroy the law or the prophets; I am not come to destroy but to fulfill. For verily I say unto you, till heaven and earth pass, one jot or one tittle shall in no wise pass from the law, till all be fulfilled' [Mt 5:17–18]."

Harand attributed the *Nächstenliebe* (love and compassion for one's neighbor) theme of Catholicism to the spirit of Jewish Scripture.[46] Prager observed that German Protestant Christianity was based on Luther's translation of the Old and New Testaments together; that a 1935 Hamburg exhibit displayed a tree representing Hebrew Scripture with branches that represented the art, science, and education of Protestant

Germany; that according to Johannes Scherr in *Wirkt El Schaddai der Judengott noch?* Hebrew Scripture was a source of spiritual nourishment for millions of German Protestant farmers; and that Gerhard Schmidt (in *Der Alte Testament und der evangelische Religionsunterricht*) deemed it impossible to teach the New Testament without the Old. Prager added observations about contemporary German Catholic leadership and Hebrew Scripture. In October 1934 the *Bischöflicher Ordinariat* responded to Rosenberg: "Either we are Christians *with* the *entire* Holy Scripture, New Testament *and* Old Testament, or we are not Christians, period. This is because Jesus Christ is bound together inseparably with the Old Testament in His person, life, word and work. Anyone who rejects the Old Testament . . . rejects Jesus Christ."

Bishop Clemens August von Galen invoked Hebrew Scripture to condemn the execution of the mentally ill (*Hirtenbrief,* August 1941), and Cardinal Faulhaber objected in his Advent Sermon of December 3, 1933, to applying racial research to the Old Testament: "When racial research, in itself religiously neutral, gathers its forces to fight religion and it shakes the foundation of Christianity; when the current aversion towards Jews is carried over to the holy books of the Old Testament, and when Christianity is condemned because of its original connection to pre-Christian Judaism . . . the Bishop cannot be silent."[47]

Conclusion

There have been numerous scholarly studies of Christianity's attitudes toward Jews and Judaism during the war. This initial exploration is intended to begin to shed light on the other side. Ultimately, Christian attitudes and views should be studied in terms of the dialectical relationship that existed during the war, interrelating Judaism and Christianity in terms of each other's perceptions; their separate study creates an independence and an active-passive dichotomy that did not exist historically. On the basis of the data I have been able to gather, it appears that within Jewish Orthodoxy, two parallel schools of thought existed.

One school drew a division between Israel and the nations (including Christianity). The division was of ontological proportions and had to be preserved—even if it meant death to do so. Jews had to remain separate biologically (intermarriage), culturally, theologically (suffering servant, Messiah) and existentially (death instead of conversion). The division was assured by divine intervention in history, in the form of igniting the flames of long-term animosity to overcome Israel's compromising its chosen status. The second school began with commonality in terms of Torah or conversion to Judaism. Some maintained that all humans were created in God's one image, belonged to a single human family, and were one in terms of righteousness. During the Holocaust, this school enunciated a distinction between Christianity and the pagan residue within it that welcomed Nazism; it detailed Christianity's roots in Jewish morality and Scripture and identified the shared God. It implied that Israel's troubles were brought about by separation from Christianity, not association with it.

A study of Jewish perceptions of Christianity during the Holocaust removes Judaism from passive status. It also removes it from monolithic characterization that comes with distance. In this closer look at Judaism in its own terms, it turns out that two diametrically opposed positions coexisted.

NOTES

1. Ephraim Oshry, "She'elah 15," in *Shu"t: Mima'amakim, Helek* V (New York: s.n., 1970), 135–39, and "Siman 21," in *Shu"t, Helek* II (New York: s.n., 1963), 120–30. See Massimo Giuliani, "Introduzione," in *Ephraim Oshry: Responsa. Dilemmi etici e religiosi nella Shoa,* ed. Massimo Giuliani (Brescia: Morcelliano, 2004), 7–41.

2. Oshry, "She'elah 3," in *Shu"t, Helek* V (New York: s.n., 1970), 36–47.

3. Oshry, "She'elah 25," in *Shu"t, Helek* I (New York: s.n., 1959), 135–45.

4. Oshry, "Siman 2," in *Shu"t, Helek* II (New York: s.n., 1963), 16, 24.

5. Oshry, "She'elah 16," in *Shu"t, Helek* IV (New York: s.n., 1976), 99–100.

6. Oshry, "She'elah 24," in *Shu"t, Helek* IV (New York: s.n., 1976), 129–34.

7. On this passage see Joseph S. Bloch, *Israel and the Nations* (Berlin: Benjamin Harz, 1927), 387, as cited by Michael Tsevi Nehorai, "Created in the Image of God: Jews and the Nations," in *Bioethical and Ethical Issues Surrounding the Trials and Code of Nuremburg,* ed. Jacques S. Rosenberg (Lewiston: Mellen, 2003), 229–38.

8. See further Gershon Greenberg, "Amalek in Holocaust-Era Orthodox Jewish Thought," in *Bioethical and Ethical Issues Surrounding the Trials and Code of Nuremberg,* 201–27, and "Amalek Bitekufat Hashoah: Mahshavah Yehudit Ortodoksit," in *Derekh Haruah: Sefer Likhvod Eliezer Schweid,* ed. Yehoyada Amir (Jerusalem: Hebrew University, 2005), 859–81. Also, Editor, "Zekhirat Ma'aseh Amalek," in *Entsiklopedyah Talmudit,* vol. 12, ed. Meir Berlin and Shlomoh Yosef Zevin (Jerusalem: Hotsa'at Entsiklopedyah Talmudit be-siyva Mosad Harav Kook, 1947), 217–23. Drawing from Josippon (tenth century), *Korot Am Yisrael Bitekufat Habayit Hasheni Umilhemet Hayehudim Im Haroma'im,* Gerson Cohen writes that Esau moved from the eagle of Rome to the cross of Christianity. Gerson D. Cohen, "Esau as Symbol in Early Medieval Thought," in *Jewish Medieval and Renaissance Studies,* ed. Alexander Altmann (Cambridge: Harvard University, 1967), 19–48.

9. Translations are from Maimonides, "The Epistle to Yemen," in *Crisis and*

Leadership: Epistles of Maimonides, trans. Abraham Halkin (Philadelphia: JPS, 1985), 91–146 (hereafter "Halkin translation"), and *Moses Maimonides' Epistle to Yemen,* ed. Abraham Halkin and trans. Boaz Cohen (New York: American Academy for Jewish Research, 1952), i–xx (hereafter "Cohen translation").

10. Shmuel Uceda, *Midrash Shemuel: Vehu Beur Nehmad Veyakar al Pirkei Avot* (New York: Shemuel Zanvil Hakohen, 1988), *ad Perek* 3:18. I learned of the positions of Shmuel Uceda, Judah Loew of Prague, Shneour Zalman of Lyady, Aaron Ibn Hayim, and Yisrael Lipschutz from Mosheh Greenberg, "'Atem Keruim Adam . . . ,'" in *Al Hamikra Ve'al Hayahadut* (Tel Aviv: Om Oved, 1985), 55–67.

11. Judah Loew of Prague, *Kitvei Maharal Miprag: Mivhar,* vol. 1 (Jerusalem: Mosad Harav Kook, 1960), 197–98, and vol. 2 (Jerusalem: Mosad Harav Kook, 1960), 158.

12. The role of Lithuanian Christianity during the war and the Jewish perception thereof has yet to be researched. According to Vareikis, some Lithuanian Catholics were antisemitic and regarded Jews as a political and social problem on the eve of World War II, but still did not support the harsh treatment and murder of Jews during the Holocaust. In some instances they even tried to help them, and were inspired to do so by Christian morality. Vygantas Vareikis, "In the Shadow of the Holocaust: Lithuanian-Jewish Relations in the Crucial Years 1940–1944," in *Nazi Europe and the Final Solution,* ed. David Bankier and Israel Gutmann (Jerusalem: Yad Vashem, 2003), 252. Shlomoh Halevi Faynzilber, *Ma'amar Hisna'ari Me'afar* (Kedainiai: s.n., 1940). I am grateful to the staff of the University of Vilnius Library for providing this rare text. The phrase "Hatred of the world towards the eternal nation," a shibboleth among wartime Orthodox Jews, goes back at least to Nahum Sokolow, *Sinat Olam Le'am Olam* (Warsaw: Y. Goldman Printing, 1882).

13. Shlomoh Yahalomi-Diamant, "Ben Hametsarim: Refleksen," *Di Yidishe Shtime* 1, no. 28 (July 4, 1947): 3.

14. Bentsiyon Firer, "Netsah Yisrael," *Di Yidishe Shtime* 3, no. 4 (November 12, 1948): 4. See Nahman Krokhmal, "Am Olam Umo'adov," in *Moreh Nevukhei Hazeman* (Leopoli: Josephi Schnayder Printing, 1851), 32–40.

15. Bentsiyon Firer, "Parashat Zakhor" and "Purim: Vedatehem Mikal Am," in *Yisrael Vehazemanim* (Tel Aviv: B. Ts. Firer, 1956/57), 79–82, 87–89.

16. Mosheh Hayim Ephraim of Sudilkov, *Degel Mahaneh Ephraim* (Yozefof: Barukh Zetser Ptg., 1883 rpt.), 14[a].

17. Shlomoh Zalman Ehrenreich, "Mah Shedarashti Beyom Alef Parashat Tetsaveh [February 20, 1939]"; "Mah Shedarashti Bishemini Atseret [October 21, 1943]"; and "Mah Shedarashti Besimhat Torah [October 22, 1943]," in *Derashot Lehem Shelomoh* (Brooklyn: Y. Kats, 1975/1976), 283–89, 128–29, 151–53.

18. Shlomoh Zalman Unsdorfer, "Parashat Vayehi [January 2, 1942]," in *Siftei Shlomoh* (Brooklyn: Balshon Printing, 1972), 84–89.

19. Yeshayahu Wolfsberg-Aviad, "Penei Hador: Eved Hashem," *Hatsofeh* 3, no. 342 (February 10, 1939): 6. Shlomoh Zalman Shraggai, "Be'aspeklariyah Shelanu: Yesurei Yisrael," *Hatsofeh* 3, no. 36 (March 3, 1939): 6–7. See Havah Eshkoli, "Eved Hashem," in *Bein Hatsalah Ligeulah* (Jerusalem: Yad Vashem, 2004), 205–208.

20. Editor, "Der Emes vegn dem itstigen idishen Hurbn," *Hakeriyah Vehakedushah* 1, no. 9 (May 26, 1941): 2. Ish Yehudi, "Bakent zikh mit di Haman Tashen," *Hakeriyah Vehakedushah* 3, no. 31 (March 6, 1943): 6. I have been unable to verify the numbers of the conversions in New York.

21. Simhah Elberg, *Akedas Treblinka* (Shanghai: North China Press, 1946), 22–24. I have been unable to identify the source for Elberg's attribution to Niemöller. Niemöller was a signatory of the *Stuttgarter Schuldbekenntnis* of the Evangelical

Church, October 18–19, 1945. See H. Michaelis and E. Schrapler, eds., *Ursachen und Folgen. Von deutschen Zusammenbruch 1918 und 1945 bis zur staatlichen Neuordnung Deutschlands in der Gegenwart*, vol. 23 (Berlin: Dokumenten Verlag, 1956–1979), 307f. I am grateful to Katharina von Kellenbach for this reference.

22. Yissakhar Taykhtahl, "Siman 27," in *Yerushat Peleitah: Kovets Teshuvot Migedolei Medinat Hungaryah Asher Rubam Nehergu Al Kiddush Hashem Beshoat Hagezerah* 5704 (Budapest: Ha'ahim Gevirts Printing, 1945/46), 75–77; and *Emunah Tserufah Bekhur Hashoah: Pirkei Zikhronot Me'et Hagaon Hakadosh Rabi Yissakhar Shlomoh Taykhtahl*, vol. 1 (Jerusalem: H. M. Taykhtahl, 1984/1995), 157, 164.

23. Yekutiel Yehudah Halberstamm, as recorded by Sh. Noyvirt, *Yahadut* 10 (1962/63): 4–5, and cited by Esther Farbstein, *Beseter Ra'am* (Jerusalem: Mosad Harav Kook, 2002), 21.

24. Yekutiel Yehudah Halberstamm, "Shabbat Bereshit," in *Shefa Hayim*, vol. 2 (Union City, N.J.: 1983), 260–70 as cited in Yissakhar Taykhtahl, *Emunah Tserufah Bekhur Hashoah*, 169n–170n.

25. A. H. K., "Mukdash Lebiti Ha'ahuvah Miryam Sarah Shenilkehah Mi'iti Beyom [September 5, 1942]." AYV. M-10 AR 2/283 Arkhiyon Ringelblum, as cited by Farbstein, *Beseter Ra'am*, 206–208. See Oshry, "She'elah 9," in *Shu"t, Helek* V, 84–93.

26. Yitshak Levin, *Aliti Mi-Spetsyah* (Tel Aviv: s.n., 1947), 128–29; 149–50, as cited by Farbstein, *Beseter Ra'am*, 11. The child was killed during the January 1943 *Aktion* in Lvov; the mother in September 1943 in Yanovsky camp.

27. Oshry, "Siman 25," in *Shu"t, Helek* II, 142–64.

28. Maimonides, "Siman 42," in *Teshuvot Harambam*, ed. Alfred Freimann (Jerusalem: Mekitsei Nirdamim, 1934), 40–42.

29. Yomtov Lipman Heller, "Ikar Tosfot Yomtov," in *Mishnayot: Im Perush Ovadyah Mibartenura, Ikar Tosfot Yomtov, Perush Tiferet Yisrael* (Jerusalem: Tiferet Yisrael, 1964), *ad Pirkei Avot* 3:14. See Joseph M. Davis, "Humanizing the Non-Jews," in *Yom-Tov Lipmann Heller: Portrait of a Seventeenth Century Rabbi* (Oxford: Littman Library of Jewish Civilization, 2004), 92–97.

30. Aharon Ibn Hayim, *Korban Aharon: Vehu Perush Lesefer Sifra Zeh Torat Kohanim* (Venice: Giovanni di Gara, 1608), *ad Kedoshim, Perek* 4, *Mishnah* 12.

31. Mordekhai Ze'ev Ettinger and Yosef Shaul Natanzohn, *Tsiyon Yerushalayim ad Talmud* Yerushalami Nedarim Perek 9, Halakhah 4, as cited by Mosheh Greenberg, "'Atem Keruyim Adam. . . .'"

32. Yisrael ben Gedalyah Lipschutz, "Yakhin," in *Mishnayot: Im Perush Ovadyah Mibartenura, Ikar Tosfot Yomtov, Perush Tiferet Yisrael* (Jerusalem: Tiferet Yisrael, 1964), *ad Pirkei Avot* 3:15.

33. Eliyahu Botschko, "Rom und Jerusalem," in *Die Spuren des Meßias* (Montreux: s.n., 1937), 9–11.

34. Bublick, "Bay vemn Hitler hat gelernt zayn rasen Teorie," *Idishe Vokhntsaytung* 5 (December 20, 1940): 2.

35. Bublick, "Kamf fun Avodah Zarah gegen di Nevi'im . . . Unser aybiger Kamf gegen der Avodah Zarah," *Idishe Vokhntsaytung* 2, no. 83 (August 27, 1937): 31; 2, no. 84 (September 3, 1937): 3; 2, no. 85 (September 10, 1937): 2.

36. Andreas Duhm, *Der Kampf um die deutsche Kirche* (Gotha: L. Klotz, 1934), 217. Prager, *Hurban Yahadut Be'ayropah* (En Harod: Hakibuts Hameuhad, 1947), 83–84.

37. Gerst, "Die alte Historozafie vegn yidishe Geshikhte," in *Yiddishkayt un Veltishkayt* (Łódź: Mesorah, 1938), 35–37.

38. Gerst, *Peleitat Beit Yehudah* (Jerusalem: Mosad al Shem Y. L. Girsht, 1970/71), 34–36.

39. Yehudah Layb Gerst, "Tsvay Revolutsies," *Beit Ya'akov* 10, no. 106 (June–July 1933): 8–11.

40. Gerst, "Yidn Faynshaft un zayn Haylung [1936]," in *Yiddishkayt un Veltishkayt*, 24–31.

41. Jakob Rosenheim, "The Battle of God against Amalek: The War in the Light of Jewish Tradition," *Moriyah* (February 1940), reprinted in *Comfort, Comfort My People*, ed. Yitshak Levin (New York: Research Institute of Religious Jewry, 1984).

42. Jakob Rosenheim, "Entwurf eines Flugblattes," Agudat Yisrael Archives, New York.

43. Gedalyah Bublick, "Ha'amnam rak tehiah le'umit?" *Hayesod* 16, no. 554 (November 7, 1947): 3; "Zvay Bibel Lender," *Idishe Vokhntsaytung* 6 (January 24, 1941): 2; "Der Kval fun der gute und nobele baym Menshen," *Idishe Vokhntsaytung* 2 (July 9, 1937): 2; Christopher Dawson, *Religion and the Modern State* (London: Sheed and Ward, 1935), 15; Bublick, "Hatsalat Ha'enoshut," *Hayesod* 8, no. 261 (March 29, 1939): 1, 8.

44. The entire letter reads as follows:

Bratislava
March 6, 1942

His Excellency
President of the Republic of Slovakia
Bratislava

In deep distress we, the rabbis of the Jewish communities of Slovakia, turn to you, Mr. President, as the religious leader, as the supreme judge and legislator of this state, in supplication. We have heard the terrible tidings, although not yet officially confirmed, that offices of the government are planning to expel the Jews, men separately and women separately, to countries further east. This decree, which under the law can be given any name and can be accounted for by any motives and justifications, under the present circumstances is tantamount to the physical annihilation of the Jews of Slovakia.

In despair we cry out to you, Mr. President, the supreme judge of this state, confident that His Honor, as well, believes in the Supreme Judge who is above him, and as servants of Almighty God we humbly request in our straits: hear our voices and answer us, for we are in great distress. Did not one God create us? And do we not all owe a final accounting to Him? Have mercy on us, on our families, on our wives, on our men, our children and our elderly, who pour out their hearts with tears and pray to our Father in Heaven for salvation. Hoping for His mercy, we place our fate in your hands.

For many years now we have been persecuted by the heavy hand of the law. Believing ourselves innocent of any crime, for two thousand years we have silently borne our suffering, born the heavy yoke of a life of hardship, of attacks on our honor, our property, our health, without crying out. But such a harsh decree, so unjust and cruel as the one which threatens to descend on us, strikes fear and terror in our hearts; and eighty thousand Jews cry out in mortal dread for aid and deliverance, for such calamity as this has not befallen us in the thousands of years of our existence.

Mr. President, tens of thousands of Jews will make do with the meager bread that they earn by the sweat of their brow and by any hard labor that be required of them, but we entreat you, Mr. President, let these poor people live and remain with their families, in their homes.

"Before the Lord, for He is come to judge the earth; He will judge the world with righteousness, and the peoples with equity" [Ps 98:9], we, too, entreat you, Mr. President, Father and servant of God, please hearken to the voice of the eighty thousand miserable beings who fear for their lives and the lives of their dear ones.
      Most respectfully yours,
      A. Frieder
      In the name of the Rabbis of Slovakia

Emanuel Frieder, *To Deliver Their Souls* (New York: Holocaust Library, 1990), 66, 69. Avraham Frieder's son kindly provided me with a copy of the original letter in Czech, which is now housed in the Yad Vashem Archives.

   45. M. Schlesinger, E. Munk, S. Ehrmann, J. Breuer, M. Auerbach, and Jakob Rosenheim, *Denkschrift an den Herrn Reichskanzler* (October 1937). Agudat Yisrael Archives, London. I am grateful to Yehudah Ben Avner of Bar Ilan University for providing a copy of this letter, which he brought from London to Ramat Gan. It has since been translated and published by Marc Shapiro, "Letter to Hitler," in *Between the Yeshiva World and Modern Orthodoxy: The Life and Works of Rabbi Jehiel Jacob Weinberg* (Oxford: Littman Library, 1999), 225–33.

   46. Alfred Rosenberg, *Der Mythus des 20. Jahrhunderts: Eine Wertung der seelisch geistigen Gestaltenkämpfe unserer Zeit* (Munich: Hoheneichen, 1934), 603–14. Harand, *Sein Kampf: Antwort an Hitler* (Vienna: s.n., 1935), 298, 303–305. Editor, "Frau Harand bei zion. Akademikern," *Gerechtigkeit* 4, no. [125] (December 26, 1935): 2. See also Gershon Greenberg, "Irene Harand's Campaign against Nazi Antisemitism in Vienna, 1933–1938: The Catholic Context," in *Christian Responses to the Holocaust*, ed. Donald J. Dietrich (Syracuse: Syracuse University, 2003), 132–50. Prager, *Hurban Yisrael Be'ayropah*, 98–99.

   47. Prager cited: Rudolf Eucken, *Die geistesgeschichtliche Bedeutung der Bibel* (Leipzig: A. Kröner, 1917), 26; *Deutsches Bibel-Archiv Sechster Bericht*, 4; Johannes Scherr, *Wirkt 'El Schaddai' der Judengott noch? Ein grauenvolles Beispiel induzierten Irreseins, Auszug aus 'Die Gekreuzigte'* (Munich: Ludendorff, 1934), 29; Gerhard Schmidt, *Das Alte Testament und der evangelische Religionsunterricht* (Munich: C. Kaiser, 1934), 17; Bischöflichen Ordinariats Berlin, *Amtsblatt des Bischöflicher Ordinariats Berlin* (Berlin: October 1934), 64; Michael von Faulhaber, "Die religiöse Werte des Alten Testaments und ihre Erfüllung im Christentum," in *Judentum, Christentum, Germanentum. Advents-Predigten gehalten in St. Michael zu München* [1933] (Munich: A. Huber, 1934), and Clemens August von Galen, "Oeffentliche Anklager auf ämtlichen Mord," in Johann Neuhäusler, *Kreuz und Hakenkreuz: Der Kampf des Nationalsozialismus gegen die katholische Kirche und der kirchliche Widerstand*, vol. 2 (Munich: Katholische Kirche Bayern, 1946), 364–69. Prager, "Ha'olam Hanotsri Lo Hifkir Et Hatanakh, Aval Et Hayehudim, Yotsrei Hatanakh, Hifkir," in *Hurban Yisrael Be'ayropah*, 82–85.

11 Confronting Antisemitism

**RABBI PHILIP SIDNEY BERNSTEIN AND
THE ROMAN CATHOLIC HIERARCHY**

SUZANNE BROWN-FLEMING

On July 13, 1946, Rabbi Philip Bernstein, advisor on Jewish affairs to General Joseph T. McNarney, theater commander, U.S. Forces, European Theater (USFET), wrote a letter home to Rochester, New York. That week, he had attended the International Military Tribunal (IMT) in Nuremberg and afterward recorded:

> There before me, only a few feet away, were the arch criminals of history.
>
> [Hermann] Goering has become much thinner but remains the strong man of the group. He has an outgoing personality and remains an unregenerate Nazi. The notorious [Julius] Streicher was chewing gum and looks like a crude busybody. [Rudolf] Hess has an intense, far-away look, and appears unbalanced. [Alfred] Rosenberg might be anything. He seems phony. At the session which I attended, the attorney for [Joachim von] Ribbentrop was summing up. It was craven. They were blaming everything on Hitler. Ribbentrop claimed that Hitler even treated him rudely when he tried to influence his policy. The attorney tried to give the impression that Ribbentrop himself was the victim of Hitler's fanaticism. From what I was told, I judge that the only one in the group who really stood up and took full responsibility was Goering. The rest, like rats, deserted the sinking ship.[1]

Rabbi Bernstein's Roman Catholic counterpart, whose task it was to care for Catholic displaced persons, was Cardinal Aloisius Muench.[2] Muench held five key positions in Germany between the years 1946 and

1959. He was the Catholic liaison representative between the U.S. Office of Military Government and the German Catholic Church in the American zone of occupied Germany (1946–49), Pope Pius XII's apostolic visitor to Germany (1946–47),[3] and later Vatican relief officer in Kronberg, near Frankfurt am Main (1947–49). He was Vatican regent in Kronberg (1949–51),[4] and, later, Vatican nuncio, or papal diplomat, from the nunciature's new seat in the suburb of Bad Godesberg, outside of Bonn (1951–59).[5]

These two Americans, who arrived in Frankfurt within months of one another in the summer of 1946 and worked with many of the same American officials and offices, viewed those men indicted and sentenced at the IMT in Nuremberg very differently. In a diary entry dated April 21, 1953, Muench noted that according to his sources, Konstantin von Neurath, Erich Räder, Karl Dönitz, Walther Funk, Baldur von Schirach, Albert Speer, and Rudolf Hess had "no bed during the day, chairs without a back, lights [remained on] at night . . . [and they were given] poor meals" while incarcerated in Spandau prison. Cardinal (then Archbishop) Muench called the imprisonment of these leading Third Reich personalities "another terrible blotch on our record for decent, humane treatment toward war criminals." Referring to these men, Muench wrote, "mercy toward criminals—if they were that—is still a Christian virtue."[6]

The differences in the perspectives of Rabbi Bernstein and Cardinal Muench are quite striking. This chapter examines key historical moments juxtaposing Rabbi Philip Sidney Bernstein's thoughts and actions against those of four powerful contemporaries in the Catholic Church: Cardinal August Hlond, primate of Poland; Cardinal Edward Mooney, archbishop of Detroit; Cardinal Samuel Stritch, archbishop of Chicago; and Pope Pius XII. In the study of the Holocaust and the role of Christian antisemitism therein, it is instructive to look not only at Christian thought patterns and actions, but, in tandem, at Jewish responses. What emerges is a fuller picture of the dynamic of antisemitism—one that recognizes that Jews were not passive, lifeless repositories of discrimination, but, rather, acted concretely and strategically to confront antisemitism. Bernstein's activism, coupled with his ability to grasp the magnitude and unprecedented nature of the Holocaust as it was happening and afterward, marked him as an important example of Jewish leadership counterbalancing the prejudices and dangers their communities faced.

Rabbi Philip S. Bernstein of Rochester, New York, was the second American civilian to assume the position of advisor on Jewish affairs in occupied Germany.[7] The position was first created in 1945. On August 3, 1945, General of the Army George C. Marshall sent an urgent cable to General Dwight D. Eisenhower, theater commander, USFET. The cable summarized the conclusions of the now infamous Harrison Report and asked General Eisenhower to verify "the accuracy of Mr. Harrison's conclusions."[8] On August 7, Rabbi Stephen S. Wise, president of the American Jewish Congress, sent a message to General Eisenhower as well, requesting that a "liaison officer to [headquarters] G-5 for purpose of coordinating activity of Jewish displaced persons" be created.[9] These and other events resulted in a August 10 cable from General Eisenhower to Secretary of War Henry L. Stimson acknowledging the need to appoint a "Special Advisor on affairs dealing with displaced Jewish persons."[10] The first "Special Consultant on Jewish Problems," defined as such in a memorandum dated August 29, 1945, was Major Judah Nadich.[11] The first civilian adviser to theater commander Eisenhower on Jewish affairs, Simon H. Rifkind, federal judge for the southern district of the state of New York, arrived in Frankfurt on October 20, 1945.[12] Major Nadich would continue in his separate post of military adviser until November 10.[13] Bernstein was Judge Rifkind's successor.

"Even the pigs seem to grunt in Hebrew," Philip Bernstein wrote with some satisfaction when describing Nili Kibutz in the vicinity of Fürth, Germany, upon his arrival in Germany in July 1946. Established on a farm that formerly belonged to Julius Streicher, Nili Kibutz was the site of training in agriculture for young Jews planning to emigrate to Palestine. Bernstein's remark reflected a pride in those young Jews who had "done a magnificent job with the farm" against such odds, and often in a hostile environment. Bernstein was concerned about the continuing manifestation of antisemitism in postwar Germany. In July 1946, he wrote, "I have seen little or no evidence of a change of heart among the Germans."[14]

Rabbi Bernstein arrived in Germany as someone with a history of engagement in the Jewish fight against antisemitism. In a letter dated July 30, 1938, he wrote to his close acquaintance, Cardinal Edward Mooney, archbishop of Rochester and subsequently Detroit, for aid in combating Father Charles Coughlin, founder of the National Union for Social Justice (NUSJ) and of the Christian Front. On Sundays, from 1928 to 1942, Father Coughlin broadcast his radio program, "The Golden Hour of the Shrine of the Little Flower" (Father Coughlin's church) from Royal Oak, Michigan. He also published the incendiary tabloid newspaper *Social*

Justice. Father Coughlin was "a right-wing antisemitic extremist" who blamed the Depression, and later World War II, on "banksters, plutocrats, atheistic Marxists, and international financiers," code words for Jews. By 1938, forty-six radio stations in major cities across the United States carried his Sunday program.[15]

According to Donald Warren, neither the Vatican nor the American Catholic hierarchy supported Father Coughlin, with the exception of Bishop Michael Gallagher of Detroit. Warren credits Cardinal Mooney with support for the "long-standing efforts of Vatican officials, including then-Secretary of State Pacelli and Pope Pius XI, to curb Father Coughlin."[16] Writing with regard to use of the fictitious *Protocols of the Elders of Zion* in Father Coughlin's magazine, *Social Justice,* Bernstein asked his close acquaintance, Cardinal Mooney, whether there was not "some Christian way by which Father Coughlin can be asked on what Christian basis he spreads such slanders about a helpless, persecuted minority people."[17]

Cardinal Mooney addressed his response to "my dear Rabbi Bernstein," writing that he:

> ought to answer it in the frankest terms. If you have read the articles in question, you will agree they are written in such a way as to make it extremely difficult for anyone, and particularly for me, to bring to bear upon the writer the high-minded considerations you urge. For I am confident that the author would join us in deploring the stirring up of race antagonism in this country—or in any country, for that matter. But I feel that what you have in mind is the possible effect on indiscriminating readers. In this regard I see no reason why you should hesitate to put that view directly before the writer of the articles in question. In fact I know this will be no surprise to him from what I said in bringing your letter to his attention.[18]

Cardinal Mooney did not reference Coughlin by name in his written reply to Rabbi Bernstein, referring instead to "the writer of the articles in question." He pointed out that Coughlin's use of code language—references to banksters, plutocrats, atheistic Marxists, and international financiers, but not to Jews specifically—made it "difficult" for Catholics, and members of the hierarchy, to criticize him.

The only hint of potential disapproval of Father Coughlin's writings on Cardinal Mooney's part was his reference to having shared Bernstein's letter with Coughlin. Had Cardinal Mooney agreed with Coughlin's writings, he would likely not have bothered to share Bernstein's critique with the "radio priest." That Cardinal Mooney did not feel he could openly disagree with Coughlin, and say so in his response to his friend, Rabbi Bernstein, demonstrated the significant limitations the cardinal believed to exist with regard to his freedom to criticize one of his own. Cardinal Mooney concluded his letter to the rabbi with a further suggestion:

> I wonder is this a practical thought on what we might do in a situation that might become dangerously muddled. The Catholic Church is victim number one of communistic totalitarianism; the Jewish race is victim number one of an opposite type of totalitarianism. Might we not set ourselves to have prominent Catholic groups publicly condemn antisemitism and to have prominent Jewish groups publicly condemn Communism? In both cases we would be making a real contribution to better Americanism—as well as defending the principles of Christian charity and the spiritual heritage of Judaism.[19]

Cardinal Mooney's response confirms that in the minds of the Catholic hierarchy, communism was the most important enemy against which the Church needed to defend itself.

Bernstein was not satisfied with Cardinal Mooney's lukewarm response. Following a late November 1938 Sunday broadcast by Coughlin, Bernstein wrote Mooney again: "It is true that Father Coughlin made no open avowal of antisemitism, but everyone who heard his address knew exactly what he meant. . . . Scores of people in Rochester talked to me about this broadcast, most of them with indignation and some, especially Catholics, with a sense of shame." Bernstein acknowledged that the American Catholic response to *Reichskristallnacht* (November 9–10, 1938) had been one of disapproval. He commented, "When the whole nation, including the distinguished leaders of your Church, was publicly protesting against the wicked persecutions in Germany, only two voices were lifted up in America to give comfort to the persecutors, that of Fritz Kuhn, leader of the [German American] Bund, and that of Father Coughlin." Then Bernstein took each of Coughlin's accusations—Jews as communists, international bankers, and disproportionately wealthy—and presented facts belying these anti-Jewish stereotypes. He ended his letter with a heartfelt plea: "In the name of Americanism, in the name of a tragic, persecuted minority, in the name of the friendly relations we have enjoyed in Rochester, I beg you to remind Father Coughlin that Jesus said: 'by this shall men know that you are my disciples—if you have love for one another.' "[20]

Cardinal Mooney declined to respond personally to this strong letter.

Instead, Rabbi Bernstein received a reply from the archbishop's secretary, noting that "Archbishop Mooney has asked me to acknowledge receipt of your letter of November 25 because he has been away for six or seven weeks, and resultant efforts to catch up with the work of the Chancery are taking almost all of his time." Whereas Mooney had been evasive in his response, his secretary was not: "Those who request more decisive action in such matters by Church superiors are evidently not fully informed on the absolute character of ecclesiastical authority in situations of this kind. . . . I feel there is very little to be said in reply to your letter of the above date except to refer you to the recent letter of the archbishop to you." He noted also the enclosure of an interview with Archbishop Mooney, published in the November 24 edition of the *Detroit News,* which "should do much to dispel the misunderstanding in many minds concerning the attitude of Church authorities to utterances such as those in question."[21] The secretary's response (which also failed to reference Father Coughlin specifically) indicated that the archbishop did not wish to issue a clear condemnation of one of his own priests without approval from a higher authority, meaning, presumably, from Pope Pius XI in Rome.

In 1943, Rabbi Bernstein demonstrated an astounding level of awareness of the Holocaust when writing a brave series of articles published in *The Nation.*[22] In the first of four articles, entitled "The Jews of Europe: The Remnants of a People,"[23] Bernstein quoted an April 8, 1942, letter "from a responsible person in Germany" whom he did not name, vividly describing 1,200 suicides by German Jews and transports of Jews toŁódź, Poland, "each consisting of 1,500 souls." This letter even referred specifically to a January 25, 1942, transport which "surpassed all previous transports for the bestial treatment accorded the Jews."[24] In his own analysis of the situation, writing in January 1943, Bernstein noted that "it is in Poland that the Nazis have given the fullest implementation to their policy. . . . Something was happening which even they, inured to suffering, could not believe. It was heralded by the suicide of [Warsaw *Judenrat* chairman] Adam Czerniakow, the full import of which was not immediately understood."[25]

Adam Czerniakow chose to kill himself rather than comply with German orders to assist in the roundup of Warsaw Jews for the "great deportation" (July 22 to September 6, 1942) to the gas chambers of the Treblinka death camp. Bernstein quoted a report by the deputy prime minister of the Polish government-in-exile, Stanislaw Mikolajczyk:

> In the Warsaw ghetto, behind walls cutting them off from the world, hundreds of thousands of doomed are awaiting death. . . . On the pavements lie unburied bodies. Daily a described number of victims amounts from eight thousand to ten thousand. . . . Children who cannot walk by themselves are put into trucks. This is carried out in such a brutal manner that very few reach the ramparts alive. . . . At the ramparts railway cars wait. People are packed so tightly that those who die cannot fall but remain standing side by side with those still living or dying slowly from fumes of lime and chlorine, from being deprived of air, water and food. . . . Wherever and whenever death trains arrive they contain only corpses. . . . What has been going on in the Warsaw ghetto has been going on in hundreds of the larger and smaller Polish places. . . . All are perishing.[26]

To this detailed description he added statistics for estimated numbers of murdered Jews in Yugoslavia, Slovakia, Romania, and Belgium, citing a December 19, 1942, Allied declaration.[27]

Bernstein also detailed what he understood to be the Christian response to the murder of European Jewry: "European Christendom, at first confused or silent before the Nazi assault, has more recently reasserted its righteous indignation and its humanity." He cited specifically, "Catholic denunciations of the expulsion of French Jews," the "voluntary wearing of the yellow badge of David" by Dutch Protestants, and the "conduct of German men and women who quietly take their places in shopping lines with Jews." Bernstein called such acts a "reaffirmation of Christian principles. . . . What a pity that this reaction comes so late. A clearer perception ten years ago [in 1933] of the meaning and intent of Hitlerism might have spared the world this holocaust."[28]

As the vast majority of Christians in Europe did not protest actions against European Jewry, one can interpret Bernstein's generous comments as a recognition that he could not afford to alienate *The Nation*'s predominantly Christian readership. Harsh criticism would not have served his ultimate purpose, which he stated in the first few sentences of "The Jews of Europe: The Remnants of a People": "There is the hope to impress on the conscience of freemen the vastness and ghastliness of the Jewish tragedy in Europe . . . then perhaps when occasions arise to help . . . their decisions may be influenced by compassion, not by self-interest alone."[29]

On July 4, 1946, in Kielce, Poland, nine-year old Henryk Blaszczyk "led a crowd of townspeople" to the community center building where "200 Jews were living. . . . There he repeated the centuries-old antisemitic canard of ritual murder by Jews of Christian children," claiming to have been "imprisoned by Jews for two days in the cellar of a building where there were, he said, corpses of fifteen children."[30] In the pogrom that followed, local Poles murdered forty-one of their Jewish neighbors, including women, children, and a seven-month-old fetus.[31] On July 11, Cardinal August Hlond, primate of Poland, issued the following statement:

> The Catholic Church has always condemned killings, and done so immediately. It condemns them in Poland as well, irrespective of whether they have been committed by Poles or Jews, in Kielce or in any other part of the Polish Republic. The course taken by the unfortunate and grievous events in Kielce shows that racism cannot be attributed to them. They developed against a wholly different background, a painful and tragic one. These are a great calamity that fills me with grief and regret. When Jews were being annihilated in Poland, Poles though themselves persecuted, supported and hid Jews at the risk of their own lives. Many are the Jews who owe their lives to Poles and Polish priests. Blame for the breakdown in these good relations is borne to a great extent by the Jews. In Poland they occupy positions in the first line of the nation's political existence, and their attempt to impose forms of government completely rejected by the great majority of people is a pernicious game, for it is the cause of dangerous tensions. Unfortunately, in the fateful armed clashes taking place on the front line of the political struggle in Poland, not merely Jews but incomparably more Poles are losing their lives.[32]

Cardinal Hlond, then, alleged that the Kielce pogrom was a reaction against Jewish bureaucrats serving the Communist regime's attempts to restructure Polish life.[33]

In an October 26, 1946, letter to papal nuncio to the United States Amleto Cicognani, Cardinal Samuel Stritch of Chicago wrote:

> It is true that not knowing all the facts in the Polish situation, the first accounts of the statement of the Cardinal [Hlond] were a bit surprising. But the facts have been made known, and every fair mind knows now that the Cardinal was not in any way antisemitic. Look at what the Polish priests and the Polish Catholics did in sympathy for the Jew during the Nazi occupation of Poland. When anyone dares to write to express his indignation regarding the present policy of the Catholic Church towards the Jew, he simply isn't looking at the facts.[34]

Bernstein visited Poland from July 23 through July 30, in order to "make a realistic evaluation of the situation" and to report on its impact on the U.S. zone of occupied Germany.[35] He reported that by the accounts he received, "the police and local militia lent themselves to the pogrom. . . . The Church authorities declined to intervene."[36] Regarding the allegation of Jewish involvement in the communist movement government, Bernstein's report noted that "of the fifty top members of government [in Poland], three are Jews. It should be added that they are of Jewish descent only and are not identified with Jewish religious or communal life."[37] Cardinal Hlond, he wrote, had "in effect condoned the Kielce pogrom by attributing as its root cause the presence and the program of these [three] Jews in the government."[38]

Of the many important Catholic figures Rabbi Bernstein met with, none ranked higher than the Holy Father himself. On September 11, 1946, Pope Pius XII granted Rabbi Bernstein an audience at Castel Gandolfo, the pope's summer residence. Bernstein wished to speak to him regarding two subjects specifically: first, rampant antisemitism in Poland, as evidenced by the recent pogrom in Kielce, and second, temporary placement for twenty-five thousand Polish Jewish refugees in Italy. On September 14, he subsequently wrote to General McNarney about his forty-minute audience.[39]

Bernstein believed he had reason to be optimistic about the pope's receptiveness. During the war, Rabbi Bernstein had served as executive director of the National Jewish Welfare Board's (NJWB) Committee on Army and Navy Religious Activities (CANRA), the body responsible for recruiting and training rabbis for military service, providing them with support materials, and maintaining oversight of Jewish chapel facilities at military installations.[40] As such, he was privy to an interesting written exchange between Frank L. Weil, President of the NJWB, and Louis Kraft, executive director, NJWB, regarding the role of the Catholic Church in Italy during German occupation (September 8, 1943, to June 4, 1944).

Frank Weil had consulted Louis Kraft on the wording of a letter from himself and David de Sola Pool, chairman of CANRA, to Pope Pius XII in Rome. In the draft letter, dated July 19, 1944, Weil and de Sola Pool wrote that "word comes to us from our army chaplains in Italy telling of the aid and protection given to so many Italian Jews by the Vatican and by priests and institutions of the Church during the Nazi occupation of the land." The purpose of the letter was twofold: first, to transmit "gratitude for this noble expression of religious and brotherly love," and, second, to offer a "fervent prayer" that "your example, your influence and your intervention may yet save some of the remnant of the Jews in other lands who are marked down by the Germans for murder and extinction."[41]

In a separate, handwritten note to Frank Weil, Louis Kraft wrote the following: "I see no objection [to the letter]. The circumstances have already been reported in the press. Anything that can be done to encourage the Pope to use his influence with the church in Hungary and Romania, etc. is worth the effort. What do you think?"[42] At a time when the fate of Jews in Romania and Hungary still hung in the balance, an emphasis on the positive actions of some Italian bishops, clerics, and lay Catholics made much sense. Here emerges a pattern that would continue during the postwar period: that of Jewish leaders' emphasis of the positive, motivated by the hope that such an emphasis might help enlist papal support for the needs and causes of the Jewish community, present and future.

Privy to the exchange of correspondence between Frank Weil and Louis Kraft, Bernstein also heard positive reports about the role of the papacy in 1946 and noted in his memorandum to General McNarney that two Jewish kibbutzim awaiting emigration to Palestine were temporarily settled on the outskirts of Castel Gandolfo. Bernstein reported, "The villas they occupy were made available to them by the Vatican, practically without charge. I was informed that this was typical of the attitude of helpfulness on the part of the Pope in relation to Jewish refugees now in Italy."[43] Despite the positive impressions and assumptions held by Weil, Kraft, and Rabbi Bernstein in 1944–1946, no evidence of a written or oral order from Pius XII to shelter Italian Jews has surfaced to this day.[44]

Bernstein began the audience with the pope much as the Weil-de Sola Pool letter had begun: with thanks for "the great assistance the Church had rendered in saving persecuted Jews during the period of Nazi domination, particularly in Italy, France and Belgium . . . on the basis of reports from [Jewish] chaplains during the war."[45] This is Bernstein's account of Pope Pius XII's response:

> At this point he [Pius XII] said the persecution of the Jews "was dreadful." He used that word "dreadful" again and again in the conversation, as he referred to the martyrdom of the Jews. The word seemed to have special significance to him, as if connoting something vile and unholy. He also used the word "pity" often in referring to what happened to the Jews; i.e., "It was a great pity."

Bernstein's response mirrored the pattern seen in the draft letter by Weil and de Sola Pool to the pope in July 1944: words of thanks for past good deeds, followed by a request for future concrete action. Bernstein wrote to McNarney:

> At this point I reminded him that the persecution had not ended. I told him that I was particularly concerned about what was happening in Poland. I briefly recapitulated the sad story of current Polish antisemitism, culminating in the Kielce pogrom. He [Pius XII] said that the pogrom was "dreadful," that the church had condemned such "violence." *I replied that a general condemnation of violence would not meet the urgent needs of the crucial situation in Poland, that there ought to be issued, on the part of the church, and particularly the Polish hierarchy, a specific condemnation of antisemitism.* I told him that Polish Jewry, and especially some of the survivors of the Kielce pogrom, had urged me to appeal to him on this score. For it was their conviction that the Catholic Church could be the most influential factor in counteracting antisemitism in Poland, if it chose to do so. (emphasis mine)

In reply, the universal head of the Catholic Church stated, "They [Polish Catholics], too, do not have freedom from fear." Bernstein's full account of Pius XII's response is as follows:

> He [Pius XII] responded that the Church itself is in difficulty in Poland and that Catholics are being persecuted by the present government. "They, too, do not have freedom from fear," he said, in the words of the Atlantic Charter. At this point, he commented on the hostile attitude of the Soviet government and of its satellites. He deplored the unrelenting attacks on the universal church and universal values. He felt that there had been a recrudescence of primitive nationalism in Russia, which was very dangerous to the world and against which freedom loving nations would have to stand guard. "As you know," he said, using Mr. Churchill's phrase, "there is an iron curtain around Poland, and communication with the hierarchy is very difficult." Nevertheless, he assured me that he would find a way to communicate with the Catholic authorities in Poland, instructing them to take positive action against antisemitism in that country.

As had Cardinal Mooney in 1938, Pope Pius XII responded to Rabbi Bernstein's request for a clear statement condemning antisemitism by immediately citing the dangers of communism to the Catholic Church. The Pope tried to impress upon Bernstein the challenges Catholics themselves faced, challenges that seemed equivalent to both Cardinal Mooney and Pope Pius XII. The pope did not mention specifically, nor did he condemn, Cardinal Hlond's July 11, 1946, statement, indicating (perhaps disingenuously) that he was not in communication with the Polish hierarchy, and, by implication, had no control over their response to the Kielce pogrom.

Following this exchange, Rabbi Bernstein moved to his second item of business: that of the temporary resettlement of twenty-five thousand Polish Jewish refugees in Italy. He briefed the pope as to the efforts of the U.S. Army to find shelter for Jewish displaced persons in Germany, Austria, and elsewhere. Pope Pius XII responded that according to one recent newspaper report, the Italian government had agreed to accept ten thousand Jewish displaced persons. Bernstein commented that this report was "unconfirmed," and "took the liberty of suggesting that he [the pope] might be helpful in influencing the Italian government toward a favorable consideration of this project." According to Rabbi Bernstein, the pope "then agreed to get in touch with the Italian government for this purpose." Moving to a general discussion of Jewish displaced persons, the pope suggested that the United States "was best equipped to absorb them." Most, countered Rabbi Bernstein, did not wish to emigrate to the United States, but to Palestine. The pope responded, "Yes, I recognize that as their desire."

Bernstein viewed the audience as successful. In his report to General McNarney, Bernstein concluded that Pius XII "had made a deep and favorable impression on me which, I trust, will be confirmed by implementation of his promises." In his cover letter to General McNarney, Bernstein wrote that Franklin C. Gowen, assistant to Myron Taylor, the personal representative of the president to Pope Pius XII, discussed "the subject of the conversation with the acting papal secretary of state [Monsignor Giovanni Battista Montini, the future Pope Paul VI]." Montini offered the advice that "no publicity be given to the two specific commitments of the Pope, on the ground that, both in Italy and Poland, premature announcements of the Pope's intentions would militate against the effectiveness of his efforts." Rabbi Bernstein then added, "of course I agree."

In exchanges with his Catholic counterparts, Rabbi Bernstein was quite frank with regard to the problem of antisemitism, as evidenced by his very pointed request that his close acquaintance Cardinal Mooney curb Father Coughlin and his specific request that Pope Pius XII mandate a clear condemnation of antisemitism in Poland—this during his first audience with the pope, whom he had never before met personally. This frankness indicates a comfort level and also a belief on Bernstein's part that his Catholic counterparts might be willing to help mitigate the problem of antisemitism. Bernstein's published remark, "there is the hope to impress on the conscience of freemen the vastness and ghastliness of the Jewish tragedy in Europe . . . then perhaps when occasions arise to help . . . their decisions may be influenced by compassion, not by self-interest alone," reflects this pattern. The responses by Cardinal Mooney and Pope Pius XII to Rabbi Bernstein's requests were disappointing. Cardinals Hlond and Stritch demonstrated their own antisemitism as well as their unwillingness to recognize antisemitism among their own countrymen.

NOTES

The views expressed are the author's alone and do not necessarily represent those of the United States Holocaust Memorial Museum or any other organization. This chapter is dedicated to Theodore Zev Weiss, president and founder of the Holocaust Educational Foundation, who knew Rabbi Bernstein. I wish to thank the United States Holocaust Memorial Museum's Center for Advanced Holocaust Studies, and particularly Robert M. Ehrenreich, director of University Programs, and Paul Shapiro, director of the Center, for supporting my research in the Rabbi Philip S. Bernstein Collection in September 2003. Special thanks goes also to Professor Michael Berkowitz in the department of Hebrew and Jewish Studies at University College London. During his tenure as 2002 Charles H. Revson Foundation Fellow at the Center, Professor Berkowitz made me aware of this collection. Finally, I thank Nancy Martin, John M. and Barbara Keil University Archivist and Rochester Collections Librarian, for her smooth facilitation of my research.

1. Bernstein to Friends, July 13, 1946, Rabbi Philip S. Bernstein Collection (hereafter PSB), Advisor on Jewish Affairs, Box 1, Folder 6 (hereafter AJA 1/6), Rush Rhees Library, Rare Books, Special Collections & Preservation, University of Rochester, New York.

2. For a full treatment of Muench's relief efforts and work with Catholic displaced persons, see Colman Barry, O.S.B., *American Nuncio: Cardinal Aloisius Muench* (Collegeville, Minn.: Saint John's University Press, 1969).

3. An apostolic visitor, also referred to as a "papal visitor," is a papal representative to a particular church, government, or internationally accredited council. Apostolic visitors differ from other papal legates in that the pope summons them for special emergencies only, and their missions are generally of short duration.

4. The role of the Vatican regent was in practice that of a nuncio, but due to the Federal Republic of Germany's lack of full autonomy in 1949, no diplomats could, in principle, operate there. This changed in 1951, when the Federal Republic established an independently operating foreign ministry and received foreign diplomats for the first time.

5. The Holy See employs its own ambassadors, called nuncios, to represent the

pope to hundreds of civil governments. Nuncios hold the rank of ambassador and also hold the honorary title "dean of diplomatic corps" in nation-states adhering to the Congress of Vienna (1815).

6. Suzanne Brown-Fleming, *The Holocaust and Catholic Conscience: Cardinal Aloisius Muench and the Guilt Question in Germany* (Notre Dame, Ind.: University of Notre Dame Press in association with the United States Holocaust Memorial Museum, 2006), 5.

7. Bernstein' successors were Judge Louis E. Levinthal of the Court of Common Pleas, Philadelphia; Dr. William C. Haber of the University of Michigan, Ann Arbor; and Harry Greenstein, executive director of the Jewish Charities and Jewish Welfare Fund in Baltimore, Maryland. Major Abraham S. Hyman, acting adviser on Jewish affairs to U.S. occupation authorities in Germany and Austria from October 1949 to December 1949, served in the position of deputy to Rabbi Bernstein, Judge Levinthal, Dr. Haber, and Mr. Greenstein before becoming acting adviser. "Army Releases Its Final Report on Jewish Affairs in Germany and Austria," Memorandum No. 303–50 dated Sunday, March 12, 1950, Department of Defense Office of Public Information, Washington, D.C. In PSB: Correspondence 3/18.

8. Judah Nadich, *Eisenhower and the Jews* (New York: Twayne Publishers, 1953), 33–35. In a letter dated June 22, 1945, U.S. President Harry Truman requested that Earl G. Harrison, dean of the University of Pennsylvania's law school, "investigate the conditions under which displaced persons were living, especially in Germany and Austria; the needs of such persons; how those needs were being met by military authorities; the governments of residence and international and private relief bodies; and the views of the non-repatriable persons as to their future destinations." With authorization from the State Department, Dr. Joseph Schwartz, European director of the American Jewish Joint Distribution Committee, joined Mr. Harrison on the mission. At other points in the trip, Mr. Patrick M. Malin, vice-director of the Inter-Governmental Committee of Refugees, and M. Herbert Katzki of the War Refugee Board also assisted.

9. Nadich, *Eisenhower and the Jews*, 36. The message, sent by way of the U.S. Embassy in London, read in part as follows: "MA London transmits following message to General Eisenhower from Rabbi Stephen S. Wise, President American Jewish Congress, Grosvenor House, London. There is urgent necessity to assign liaison officer to HQ G-5 for purpose of coordinating activity of Jewish displaced persons. Such officer would aid in establishment of all-Jewish camps, including religious program for same, prepare pertinent data and help frame policy covering these people. Immediate action advisable."

10. Nadich, *Eisenhower and the Jews*, 38–40.

11. Ibid., 48–49.

12. Ibid., 235.

13. Ibid., 258–59.

14. Bernstein to Friends, July 13, 1946. PSB: AJA 1/6.

15. Ronald H. Carpenter, *Father Charles Coughlin: Surrogate Spokesman for the Disaffected* (Westport, Conn.: Greenwood Press, 1998), 13.

16. Donald Warren, *Radio Priest: Charles Coughlin, the Father of Hate Radio* (New York: Free Press, 1996), 204–207.

17. Bernstein to Mooney, July 30, 1938. PSB: AJA 4/50.

18. Mooney to Bernstein, August 4, 1938. PSB: AJA 4/50.

19. Ibid.

20. Bernstein to Mooney, November 25, 1938. PSB: Correspondence 4/50.

21. Donovan to Bernstein, November 29, 1938. PSB: Correspondence 4/50.

22. During the 1930s and 1940s, *The Nation,* one of the longest surviving American liberal journals, had a small circulation (roughly 25,000) but held tremen-

dous influence in political and intellectual circles. Freda Kirchwey, a journalist with *The Nation* from 1918 to 1955, used her position to campaign against the fascist regimes in Europe. After the outbreak of war, *The Nation* campaigned for the United States to give more help to Jews trying to escape persecution in Germany and the occupied territories. By January 1942 over half a million Jews had been exterminated in Europe. This received little coverage in newspapers in the United States. Constituting a rare exception, *The Nation* published a series of articles by Philip Bernstein detailing what was happening in the concentration camps, reprinted in 1943 by Nation Associates as *The Jews of Europe*. See Sara Alpern, *Freda Kirchwey: A Woman of* The Nation (Cambridge, Mass.: Harvard University Press, 1987).

23. *The Nation,* 156 (January 2, 1943).

24. Philip Sidney Bernstein, *The Jews of Europe* (New York: Nation Associates, 1943), 7.

25. Ibid., 8–9.

26. Ibid., 9.

27. Ibid., 10.

28. Ibid., 11–12.

29. Ibid., 5.

30. "Polish-Jewish Survey," July 1946. PSB: AJA 1/50.

31. Ibid.

32. Israel Gutman and Shmuel Krakowski, *Unequal Victims: Poles and Jews during World War Two,* trans. Ted Gorelick and Witold Jedlicki (New York: Holocaust Library, 1986), 373–74.

33. Michael Phayer, *The Catholic Church and the Holocaust* (Bloomington, Ind.: Indiana University Press, 2000), 181.

34. Brown-Fleming, *The Holocaust and Catholic Conscience,* 113–14.

35. "Report on Poland," in Bernstein to McNarney, August 2, 1946. PSB: AJA 1/47.

36. Ibid.

37. Ibid.

38. Ibid.

39. Bernstein to McNarney, September 14, 1946. PSB: AJA 1/67.

40. The National Jewish Welfare Board (JWB) was formed on April 9, 1917, three days after the United States declared war on Germany. The organization was charged with recruiting and training rabbis for military service, as well as providing support materials to these newly commissioned chaplains. The JWB also maintained oversight of Jewish chapel facilities at military installations. In 1941, in a response to a mandate from President Franklin D. Roosevelt, six private organizations—the YMCA, YWCA, National Catholic Community Service, National Jewish Welfare Board, Traveler's Aid Association, and Salvation Army were challenged to handle the on-leave morale and recreational needs for members of the Armed Forces. On February 4, 1941, after the six organizations pooled their resources, they incorporated in New York into the United Service Organizations (USO).

41. Weil and de Sola Pool to Pius XII, July 19, 1944. PSB: AJA 1/5.

42. Kraft to Weil, no date. PSB: AJA 1/5.

43. Bernstein to McNarney, September 14, 1946, PSB: AJA 1/5.

44. See Susan Zuccotti, *Under His Very Windows: The Vatican and the Holocaust in Italy* (New Haven, Conn.: Yale University Press, 2000).

45. Bernstein to McNarney, September 14, 1946, PSB: AJA 1/5. All subsequent quotations are from this source.

12 Old Wine in New Bottles?

RELIGION AND RACE IN NAZI ANTISEMITISM

Richard Steigmann-Gall

On September 7, 2000, more than 170 rabbis and Jewish scholars signed a statement on Christians and Christianity titled *Dabru Emet* (Hebrew for "speak the truth"). The Institute for Christian and Jewish Studies in Baltimore provided the impetus for crafting the document. Among other things, it represents an important element of the increasingly public dialogue between Christians and Jews about what precisely contributed to the worst instance of antisemitic violence in world history, the Holocaust. In the years immediately preceding its release, the Vatican had increasingly scrutinized itself (and continues to do so) with regard to the Catholic Church's possible contributions to an exclusionary, violent past: *Dabru Emet* represented something of a response and encouragement from prominent American Jews to this new wave of Christian self-scrutiny. Seeking to acknowledge and esteem these latest moves, *Dabru Emet* took stock of progress in mutual understanding and respect and pointed to future paths of development. As a statement of ethics—with among other things a thanks for Christian renunciations of triumphalism and supersessionism—it was received warmly.

However, as a statement of history, it garnered some degree of controversy. The pivotal moment came when the document maintained that, in spite of whatever affinities may have existed between Nazi antisemitism and preexisting Christian varieties, "Nazism was not a Christian phenomenon." While more than 170 rabbis and Jewish scholars chose to sign the statement, a substantial number of those invited to add their signature refused to do so, specifically over this particular passage, even though the very next sentence stated: "Without the long history of Christian anti-Judaism and Christian violence against Jews, Nazi ideology could not have taken hold nor could it have been carried out." One scholar in particular, A. James Rudin, expressed puzzlement that two such sentences could be found right next to each other. Equally unacceptable to him, as to others, was the assertion in *Dabru Emet* that "If the Nazi extermination of the Jews had been fully successful, it would have turned its murderous rage more directly to Christians." This statement reflects a widely shared presumption, among laypeople as well as some historians, that Nazism was antithetical to the multiple messages of humanity and kindness reflected and originating in Christianity. In this understanding, whatever guilt the churches carried in the face of such a hostile regime was that of inaction, of passivity in the face of immoral behavior. The question of how actively the churches or their traditions contributed to Nazism through the *longue durée* of antisemitism is in this conception not considered. In other words, the sins of the churches in the Third Reich were those of omission, not commission.

Such a position does indeed seem to be confusing. On the one hand, the statement plainly declares the prior existence of Christian traditions of Jew-hatred as a necessary precondition for the growth of Nazi antisemitism. This would seem to suggest an ideological continuity, or at least confluence of some kind. On the other hand, that same connection seems to be denied in the rather unambiguous opening line of the paragraph under scrutiny. This tension is what critics like Rudin apparently find hard to relieve. It would seem that Rudin seeks to place Christianity more squarely at the core of Nazism than the statement allows, and rightfully shows that many ecclesiastical bodies have themselves been less reticent to make the kind of statement he felt should have been included. However, after explicating the nature of his concern, Rudin seems to replicate this tension himself when he suggests that "Christianity was an anathema to many Nazi leaders, and there were attempts to co-opt the *authentic* Church by creating a Nazi-based Christian puppet church."[1] At this point, a new tension arises; Rudin demands a more forthright ethical statement about the proximity of Nazism to Christianity, regardless of the discomfort this might induce among some of the signatories, but then proceeds to assure his reader that indeed the Nazis were not truly Christian. As a result, it becomes all the harder to detect for what exactly Rudin is taking *Dabru Emet* to task. On the one hand, he is dissatisfied that the statement seems to exonerate Christianity of the greater charge of ideological commission in the crimes of Nazism, in favor of the lesser charge of omission of Christian brotherly love toward the Jews. But on the other hand he undermines his own claim that questions of commission should be more closely interrogated.

On one level, of course, Rudin's predicament is in no way unusual. Within the realm of a putatively positivist, ethics-free historical profession, scholars of the history of antisemitism have long debated the logical necessity of Christian antisemitism for the Holocaust. Some have argued against such a connection, arguing that the unprecedented brutality of Nazi antisemitism made it qualitatively as well as quantitatively different from prior expressions of Jew-hatred and, therefore, not rooted in them. Other scholars of antisemitism have drawn rather different conclusions, insisting that the connection was there, and was strong. But like Rudin, they at some point find themselves confronting a Gordian knot: Nazi antisemitism is rooted in Christianity, but the Nazis themselves apparently were un- or even anti-Christian. How to accommodate this dialectic has been one of the most enduring problems scholars of Christian antisemitism have had to face. Some, such as Richard Rubenstein, contend that the Nazis were "anti-Christian Christians," a rather confusing appellation that, while acknowledging the paradoxes with which certain moments in history confront us, does not necessarily synthesize the dialectic.

However in this field in particular, where the moral baggage can be particularly heavy to carry, historians of religion and the Third Reich often find themselves committed to a strong ethical position, not only on behalf of their readership but also on behalf of themselves. Their desire to expose the harm that past religious practices have caused is often entangled with a need to nonetheless preserve something positive and essential from the original faith that spawned such prejudice. They conceive of their role as twofold—to instruct both historically and morally. Whereas any kind of religious history can test the skill of those who seek to walk this dividing line with any sense of objective distancing, the challenge is much greater when it comes to the Nazi period. It is therefore no surprise that particularly early works on church and state in the Third Reich, while generally painting a picture of ecclesiastical resistance to the movement, simultaneously drew a picture of almost unqualified Nazi opposition to Christian institutions and teachings.[2] Such a view was in part a result of the war: the histories of the churches during the Third Reich tended to emphasize those clergymen on the "winning side" of events. Whereas former German Christians understandably remained silent, the flood of books on the Confessing Church (Bekennende Kirche), often written by the protagonists themselves, led to the impression that the position of the churches toward the Nazi state was one of resistance or opposition.[3] This view was reinforced by the dominance of totalitarianism theory in the immediate postwar period. With the suggestion that Nazism was totalitarian—that it made a "total claim" on the society it ruled and forbade "institutional space for any alternative"[4]—church histories presented a picture of Christian resistance by virtue of simple existence. In fact, the strongest supporters of totalitarianism theory could be found among church historians, who saw in this theory an explanation for the general lack of resistance by the churches regarding Nazi activity outside the direct sphere of the Church.

With the passing of time, more critical works emerged examining churches and prominent theologians who were supportive of the Nazi movement.[5] Several scholars have demonstrated the ambivalent and often positive stand that even members of the Confessing Church took toward the regime.[6] Particularly with regard to Jew-hatred, the literature has been very probing. Whereas some church historians remained convinced that the Nazis were as anti-Christian as they were antisemitic, others took a dissenting position. One was the theologian Franklin Littell, who rejected the view of the churches as victims of Nazism, instead showing how they contributed to the prevalent antisemitism of the period: "The record of most theologians and churchmen, in England and America as well as in the Third Reich, was confused and weak where not outright wicked."[7] Littell cast a critical eye on the churches, and for many years exposed himself to sharp criticism from other Christians as a result. Recent years have seen Littell's ideas gain wider currency, certainly within academic circles. However, in spite of his unapologetic approach, he finds it somewhat more difficult to cast his gaze on the belief system these churchmen stood for: "The conduct of the masses of baptized Christians covered the scale from enthusiastic *apostasy* to accommodation."[8] A clear ethical point about the need for Christians to recognize evil is being made here. But another argument is also present: had these Christians remained Christian, their eyes would have been open to the evils of Nazism.

Scholars of antisemitism proper have, on the whole, been less reticent in pointing to the influence of particular strands of Christian thought, though there has been broad disagreement on how essential these were to later racial antisemitism. Conventionally, the line separating racial from religious antisemitism is deemed to be the sanctity of baptism, which in the latter saves the individual Jew by removing him from Judaism, but which in the former is deemed ineffectual against the alleged immutability of Jewish "biology." A growing number of scholars have rethought earlier assumptions that religious antisemitism played no part in the formation of its racialist counterpart. Saul Friedländer is the most recent prominent voice to argue in this direction. Even though he sees certain of Jacob Katz's arguments concerning religion and Nazi antisemitism as "excessive," he nonetheless agrees with Katz that Christian antisemitism played a central role in shaping Nazi antisemitism. Citing the chimerical nature of the Nazis' antisemitism, its ascription of demonic and supernatural powers to the Jews, Friedländer argues: "The centrality of the Jews in this phantasmic universe can be explained only by its roots in the Christian tradition."[9] A wider circle of public intellectuals mirror this development, arguing that Nazi antisemitism was essentially a branch on the tree of Christianity. As George Steiner has put it: "We will not . . . be capable of 'thinking the Shoah,' albeit inadequately, if we divorce its genesis and its radical enormity from theological origins."[10] This line of argument has been more frequently associated with Hyam Maccoby. A religious-literary scholar known for his many points of difference with Steiner, Maccoby nonetheless similarly seeks the larger metaphysical sources of Nazism in Christianity, but without relying on the Nazis' own views to make his argument.[11] Suggestions that Nazism was "indebted" in this way to Christianity would not have been uttered publicly at that time. But the question remains: Were the Nazis cognizant of this debt? How did they articulate such an ideological connection? Is it possible they even considered their movement itself to be a Christian one? In what follows we will explore what the Nazis themselves had to say about Christianity, in terms of both explaining their antisemitism, and also explaining their movement as a whole.

Beyond the plain political advantages of doing so, many Nazis simultaneously embraced religious and racialist ideologies when describing their hatred of Jews. Their prejudices relied not just upon notions of racial inferiority, which could allegedly be measured by objective means, but also upon older notions of Jews as religious enemies of Christianity, supposedly responsible for the death of Christ. Contrary to Detlev Peukert's analysis,[12] they did not rely primarily upon a scientist discourse of modernity, a social-darwinistic language of biology, to justify their antisemitism—even as they insisted that Jewishness was inherited and immutable.

One way in which the Nazis attempted to reconcile the inherent contraction between race, which claimed that Jewishness was an immutable category, and religion, which via conversion nominally allows for Jewish mutability, was to insist that race was God's law. In a theological formulation that bears striking resemblance to the religious arguments of the KKK and the "Christian Identity" movement in the United States, as well as the particular Reformed theology underpinning apartheid ideology in South Africa, many leading Nazis—significantly, most of them Protestant—claimed that they were not creating a new race cult, but rather preserving preexisting divine ordinances for racial separation. As David Goldenberg has recently reminded us, the "Curse of Ham" theology has had a long history among racialist societies, a history that extends well beyond the radical fringe or even the slave-holding classes.[13] While the Nazis never relied upon this particular religious construction in their antisemitism, the notion that racial separation begat racial subordination was certainly present.

The leader of the Nazi Teachers' League, Hans Schemm, spoke frequently of what he believed was the inherently religious quality of Nazi racialism:

> When one puts steel into fire, the steel will glow and shine in its own distinctive way. . . . When I put the German *Volk* into the fire of Christianity, the German *Volk* will react in its racially distinctive way. It will build German cathedrals and create a German hymn. . . . We want to preserve, not subvert, what God has created, just as the oak tree and the fir tree retain their difference in a forest. Why should our concept of race suddenly turn into the Marxist concept of a single type of human? We are accused of wanting to deify the idea of race. But since race is willed by God, we want nothing else but to keep the race pure, in order to fulfill God's law.[14]

Schemm contended that this sublimation of race into religion had been a part of the Christian past—in particular, the culmination of a particularly Protestant trajectory. Like many Nazis, Schemm explicitly compared Hitler with Martin Luther—both for public consumption and behind closed doors. One very public instance of this was the official state celebration of the 450th anniversary of Luther's birth, on November 19, 1933, in Berlin. Here, Schemm made the connection explicit, especially with regard to the sanctification of antisemitism: "The older and more experienced [Luther] became, the less he could understand one particular type of person: this was the Jew. His engagement against the decomposing Jewish spirit is clearly evident not only from his writing against the Jews; his life too was idealistically, philosophically antisemitic. Now we Germans of today have the duty to recognize and acknowledge this."[15] Aside from Schemm, in attendance on this occasion were Reich President Hindenburg, the (non-Nazi) foreign minister Konstantin von Neurath, the historian Gerhard Ritter, and the Erlangen theologian Werner Elert.

Even when not addressing explicitly the synthesis of racial and religious categories, Nazi ideologues employed a strongly Christian language when describing their enmity for the Jews. Dietrich Eckart, one of the movement's most important ideological articulators early on, and Hitler's most important mentor in postwar Munich, set much of the Christian tone that was to follow in Nazi ideology: "Wonders never cease; from the deluge is born a new world, while the Pharisees whine about their miserable pennies! The liberation of humanity from the curse of gold stands before us! But for that our collapse, but for that our Golgotha!"[16] The antisemitism implicit in the use of such phrases as "Pharisees" and "curse of gold," and the belief that Christianity served as the antipode to the Jew, is made more explicit on other occasions: "[The] Jewish conception of God is of no interest to us Germans! We seek God nowhere but in ourselves. For us the soul is divine, of which the Jew, on the other hand, knows nothing: 'The Kingdom of Heaven is within you' (Luke 17:21), thus God also, who belongs to the Kingdom of Heaven. We feel our soul is immortal, eternal from the beginning, and therefore we refuse to be told that we are created from nothingness."[17] Jews, on the other hand, did originate "out of nothingness."[18]

We see in Eckart's antisemitism a clear racial element: Christ is cast as the representative of a preexisting Aryan spirit. As important as race belief is in this passage, no less important is Christ's rejection of the Jews. This is further revealed in one of Eckart's poems, called "The Riddle": "The New Testament broke away from the Old / as you once released yourself from the world/ And as you are freed from your past delusions / so did Jesus Christ reject his Jewishness."[19] Eckart here suggests that the Old Testament is to be not only superseded by the New Testament, but totally detached from it. The Old Testament's Jewishness, and the call to effectively remove it from the canon of Christianity, would be a theme echoed by others in the Nazi leadership. Eckart's overlapping of racial and religious categories was further revealed when he maintained: "To be an Aryan and to sense transcendence are one and the same thing."[20] Eckart showed that his religion was not a naturalist pantheism, but a transcendent supernatural faith—one so important that in its absence one could not be considered Aryan. But Eckart went further than this, demonstrating an underlying assumption that his struggle against the Jews was ontologically bound with the struggle for Christianity. The racial duality between Aryan and Semite was coterminous with a religious duality between Christian and Jew. Eckart made the interchangeability of these categories clear when describing a conversation he had about Freemasonry with Alfred Rosenberg: "In light of the indisputable facts, together with Rosenberg I showed the anti-German or rather anti-Christian, or—what amounts to the same thing—Jewish character of Freemasonry."[21]

The dualism of Christian-Aryan and Jew-Semite was also exhibited in the work of Artur Dinter, *Gauleiter* of Thuringia and one of the Nazi movement's most vituperative antisemites. Inspired by Houston Stewart Chamberlain's *Foundations of the Nineteenth Century,* which he maintained led to his "total spiritual rebirth," Dinter turned from an ambition in the theater to the writing of novels. His most famous, *The Sin against the Blood,* was published in 1918 and sold 235,000 copies by 1927, making it the most popular novel written by a National Socialist. Two subsequent novels further expounded his world view: *The Sin against the Spirit,* published in 1921, which sold 100,000 copies in its first year; and *The Sin against Love,* published in 1922, which sold 30,000 copies by 1928. A projected fourth novel on Jesus was never completed.[22] *The Sin against the Blood* was a perfect expression of the Nazis' racialist topos, and "stood at the summit of an enormous production of antisemitic publication."[23] The protagonist of the novel, Hermann Kämpfer, marries a half-Jew who is torn between the "noble and profound" influence of her mother's German blood and the "licentious, pleasure seeking" influence of her father's Jewish blood, and hence personifies the "curse of the sin against the blood to which she owes her existence."[24] They have a child, whose appearance represents the triumph of her father's inheritance. Outraged by this racial contamination, Kämpfer commits himself to the antisemitic cause, founding a society for "race research and hygiene" that is restricted to those who can prove Aryan status up to three generations.[25] Awakened to the malignance of Jewish blood, he remarries, this time to a fully Aryan woman. But amazingly, their child is born with fully Jewish features. As Kämpfer later discovers, his second wife had permanently contaminated herself by having born a child fathered by a Jew years before. Though fully Aryan herself, this one encounter with Jewish blood was enough to destroy her racial purity. Outraged at this act of defilement, Kämpfer kills the Jewish seducer. He is tried for murder, and proclaims before the court: "To lead the spirit to victory over matter, and struggling humanity to its divine destiny: that was the goal God created for himself when he created the Germans! . . . In the Jewish race are found, since time immemorial, those hellish powers which lead man away from God."[26] The jury acquits Kämpfer; racial separation and purity is affirmed as a divine ordinance.

Just as with Eckart, for Dinter the question of the German-Jewish duality was as much religious as it was racial. The struggle between Christ and Antichrist was the archetype of the eternal battle between the Aryan and the Semite, between good and evil.[27] According to Dinter, Jesus was the perfect Aryan, who was born among the Jews only to emphasize their polar opposition. Dinter followed Houston Stewart Chamberlain's argument that Galilee was inhabited by Aryans, and that Jesus could not have been racially Jewish. Similarly, all the apostles save Judas were Aryan.[28] In *The Sin against the Blood*, Dinter unveiled an admiration for Jesus that went beyond a mere political appropriation: "Jesus is the only spirit created by God and incarnated on earth who never misused his free will to sin."[29] He also suggested the removal of the Old Testament from the Christian canon: it was too "materialistic" for Christians, a monument to "the religious thinking of the Jews, which is based upon lies and betrayal, business and profit."[30] The expurgation of the Old Testament would bring about a "return" to the unadulterated teachings of Jesus.

The religious dimension of Nazi antisemitism was evident as well in Joseph Goebbels. Like Eckart and Dinter, Goebbels had literary pretensions. He was one of the most prolific writers of the movement, in both number of published works and quantity of unpublished, private material.[31] Goebbels's diary entries revealed not just that religious antisemitism lingered in the Nazi mind, but that the Nazi *weltanschauung* as a whole was cast in a religious light: "Money is the power of evil and the Jew its servant. Aryan, Semite, positive, negative, constructive, destructive. The Jew has his fateful mission to once more dominate the sick Aryan race. Our salvation or our ruin is dependent upon us."[32] Such religious imagery ("salvation," "mission") was not simply detached from its originating context. The eternal quality of the struggle was intimately connected with God and with Hitler as "an instrument of divine will shaped by history. . . . Nothing exists outside of God."[33] Here we see reference to the interventionist God of history on which certain Christian theologians in Germany had long ruminated. For Goebbels, the Nazi struggle was innately religious; it was a struggle against the Devil himself: "Whoever cannot hate the Devil cannot love God. Whoever loves his *Volk* must hate the destroyer of his *Volk*, hate him from the depths of his soul."[34]

In his novel *Michael*, written before 1933 and based loosely on his own diary entries, Goebbels revealed the same duality evident in Eckart and Dinter. More than just vaguely religious, this language was an explicitly Christian one. Goebbels's fascination with the person of Christ bordered on a type of evangelism: "I converse with Christ. I believed I had overcome him, but I have only overcome his idolatrous priests and false servants. Christ is harsh and relentless."[35] As Dinter had done in his novel, Goebbels created a fictional protagonist, Michael Vormann, through whom he voiced this view: "Christ is the genius of love, as such the most diametrical opposite of Judaism, which is the incarnation of hate. The Jew is a non-race among the races of the earth. . . . Christ is the first great enemy of the Jews. . . . That is why Judaism had to get rid of him. For he was shaking the very foundations of its future international power. The Jew is the lie personified. When he crucified Christ, he crucified everlasting truth for the first time in history."[36] In his reference to Jews as a "non-race," Goebbels seemed to question the very scientific or biological nature of the struggle—if only they *were* a race, he suggested. This is also brought out in his reference to Jesus, whom Goebbels insisted was not Jewish: "Christ cannot have been a Jew. I do not need to prove this with *science* or scholarship. It is so!"[37] The evangelical reverence for Jesus that Goebbels revealed pertained especially to antisemitism: "He drives the Jewish money-changers out of the temple. A declaration of war against money. If a man said that today, he would wind up in prison or a madhouse."[38] This reference to John 2:15 was to appear repeatedly in the Nazis' antisemitic ideology. As Julius Streicher insisted in 1924: "[We] relentlessly fight the shady mixing of religion and Jewish party politics, and fight to keep religion pure, as did the Lord when he threw the hagglers and usurers out of the Temple."[39]

In Goebbels, we see not only a cohabitation of racial and religious tropes for describing the Jew, as is the case with other Nazis, but an ontology that actually gave priority to religion over science. The Jewish threat is primarily spiritual; Jesus' Aryanhood is a matter of faith. We see much the same conceptualization in Dietrich Klagges, a friend of Goebbels who had the distinction of being one of the first Nazis to attain ministerial office, being appointed state interior and education minister of Braunschweig in 1931. He gained notoriety for providing Hitler with his German citizenship (by making him an official in the Braunschweig government), thereby allowing him to run in the presidential elections of 1932.[40] Klagges also turned his attention to Christianity. As a member of the German-Christian Working Group, a precursor to the German Christians, he wrote a work entitled *The Original Gospel of Jesus,* in which he expounded on the meaning of Christ to the Nazi movement. Goebbels took note of his friend's book, writing in his dairy: "Klagges' 'The original gospel of Jesus', perhaps an epoch-making book. . . . A fabulous book."[41] Klagges closely followed the same ideological pattern laid out by his fellow party-members: "Christianity—Judaism, creation—destruction, good—evil, God—Satan, and in the last consequence, re-demption—annihilation."[42] But more than just a model antisemite, Jesus was the son of God.[43] Whereas Nazis tended to emphasize Christ's hu-manity, Klagges confirmed his divinity. He also revealed a conviction that the Jews were not simply a harmful race, but possessors of a "satanic spirit" that sought to control the world. And in Christ they found their greatest enemy.[44] Christ was in Klagges's conception an Aryan; despite having belonged to the Jewish "faith-community," he was never a Jew in-wardly. Christ fought on behalf of his fellow Galileans against the domi-nant Jews and was to be regarded not just as one antisemite among many, but as nothing less than the world's "greatest opponent of Judaism."

Even more than Eckart or Dinter, Klagges and Goebbels placed a special emphasis on Christ. Walter Buch also emphasized the inspiration of Jesus as a person. As chairman of the party's Investigation and Concili-ation Committee and president of the party's supreme court, he held one of the most powerful positions in Nazism.[45] Martin Bormann, who would achieve infamy near the end of the party's life, was Buch's son-in-law: according to his biographer, Bormann married Buch's daughter to gain entry to Hitler's inner circle.[46] Like other ideological leaders of the movement, Buch related Nazism as a movement to Christ's own "struggle," sounding a distinct note of triumphalism. Unlike Goebbels or Eckart, Buch was not given to literary flourishes, choosing instead to speak in a more straightforward manner on the relevance of Christ and Christianity for Nazism. To an assembly of the National Socialist Student League he declared: "When Point 24 of our program says the party stands for a positive Christianity, here above all is the cornerstone of our thinking. Christ preached struggle as did no other. His life was struggle for his beliefs, for which he went to his death. From everyone he de-manded a decision between yes or no. . . . That is the necessity: that man find the power to decide between yes and no."[47] This stark black-or-white vision makes clear the dualism of the Nazi worldview. In addition, Buch drew direct comparisons not only between Christ's struggle and the Nazis', but between Christ's followers and members of the NSDAP: "Just as Christianity only prevailed through the fanatical belief of its followers, so too shall it be with the spiritual movement of National Socialism."[48]

Whereas Eckart, Dinter, and Goebbels were all brought up Catholics, Buch was a Lutheran. Unlike his Catholic colleagues, however, Buch held his childhood faith in high esteem. His antisemitism, according to one authority, "he had learned as a young boy from his rigid Lutheran parents."[49] Buch's antisemitism displayed a more equal reliance on racial and religious tropes than did Goebbels's. "The Jew," according to Buch, "is not a human being: he is a manifestation of decay." He supposed that the nefarious influence of the Jew was especially notable in the state of German family life. As he said in a speech from 1932: "Never more than in the last ten years has the truth behind Luther's words been more evident: 'The family is the source of everyone's blessing and misfortune.'" The Jew caused the breakdown of the German family, since for him marriage was simply a means to an end, a contract concluded for material benefit. The German, on the other hand, entered into marriage to produce children and imbue them with values such as honor, obedience, and national feeling. As with Eckart, Dinter, and Goebbels, for Buch the antithesis of the Jew was the Christian as well as the German: "The idea of eternal life, of which the Jew knows nothing, is just as characteristic of our Germanic forefathers as it was of Christ."[50] Buch's reference to life after death, as with Eckart, revealed belief in a supernatural faith rather than a pantheistic religion of nature.

Buch insisted that any mixing of Jews and Germans, whether biological or social, was a violation of the "divine world order."[51] This state of affairs Buch blamed on the liberalism of the previous century: "The heresies and enticements of the French Revolution allowed the pious German to totally forget that the guest in his house comes from the *Volk* who nailed the Savior to the cross.... In the nineteenth century the lie of the rabbis' sons, that the Holy Scripture made the Savior into a Jew, finally bore fruit." It was under auspices of Europe's liberal regimes that Jews were allowed their emancipation, to the detriment of Christian Europe. The nineteenth century debate over Jesus' Jewishness, exemplified in the debates surrounding biblical criticism, to Buch's mind only facilitated the Jews' hegemony. The truth was that Jesus' "entire character and learning betrayed Germanic blood."[52] In his antisemitic cause Buch was able to appropriate the legacy of Martin Luther: "When Luther turned his attention to the Jews, after he completed his translation of the

Bible, he left behind 'On the Jews and their Lies' for posterity."[53] His language was unmistakably racialist, but he nonetheless maintained Christian references to the Jews as "Christ-killers."

Hitler himself spoke of the religious underpinning that he believed was intrinsic to his type of racialism: "Peoples that bastardize themselves, or let themselves be bastardized, sin against the will of eternal Providence."[54] Whereas reference to a vague providential force bears little resemblance to belief in the biblical God, elsewhere in *Mein Kampf* Hitler intones more than a naturalist pantheism devoid of Christian content. Again, it was in the question of race and race purity where Hitler most frequently intoned such a God: it was, in his view, the duty of Germans "to put an end to the constant and continuous original sin of racial poisoning, and to give the Almighty Creator beings such as He Himself created."[55] Even as Hitler elsewhere made reference to an anthropomorphized "Nature," and the laws of Nature that humanity must follow, he also revealed his belief that these were divine laws ordained by God: "The folkish-minded man, in particular, has the sacred duty, each in his own denomination, of making *people stop just talking superficially of God's will, and actually fulfill God's will, and not let God's word be desecrated.* For God's will gave men their form, their essence and their abilities. Anyone who destroys His work is declaring war on the Lord's creation, the divine will."[56] The reference to God as the Lord of Creation, and the necessity of obeying "His" will, reveals a more recognizably Christian conception. Hitler's insistence on another occasion that Jesus was "the true God" and simultaneously "our greatest Aryan leader" only confirms his belief that race was a religious trope.[57]

Hitler's explicit references to the Jews reveal further this racial-religious sublimation. In *Mein Kampf,* Hitler spoke of the Jewish "problem" in racial, economic, political, and even eugenic terms, but he frequently concluded on a religious basis: "Hence today I believe that I am acting in accordance with the will of the Almighty Creator: by defending myself against the Jew, I am fighting for the work of the Lord."[58] As did his mentor Eckart, Hitler emphasized the Aryan belief in the afterlife over against Jewish belief, which according to Hitler could not even be called religion: "Due to his own original special nature, the Jew cannot possess a religious institution, if for no other reason because he lacks idealism in any form, and hence belief in a hereafter is absolutely foreign to him. And a religion in the Aryan sense cannot be imagined which lacks the conviction of survival after death in some form."[59] While emphasizing again his belief in a supernatural religion instead of a religion of nature, here Hitler speaks of the Aryan rather than the Christian. But there is an implicit equating of the two, made explicit on other occasions. Consistent with his party comrades, Hitler regarded the antithesis of the Jew to be not only the Aryan, but the Christian—in this case Christ himself:

> [The Jew's] life is only of this world, and his spirit is inwardly as alien to true Christianity as his nature two thousand years previous was to the great founder of the new doctrine. Of course, the latter made no secret of his attitude toward the Jewish people, and when necessary he even took to the whip to drive from the temple of the Lord this adversary of all humanity, who then as always saw in religion nothing but an instrument for his business existence.[60]

Here again we see reference to John 2:15. Elsewhere in *Mein Kampf*, the Jew took on the satanic proportions of the Antichrist: "in his vileness he becomes so gigantic that no one need be surprised if among our people the personification of the devil as the symbol of all evil assumes the living shape of the Jew."[61]

Even before his adaptation of a new electoral strategy and the writing of *Mein Kampf*, Hitler had been enunciating these basic themes. At the founding of the NSDAP local office in Rosenheim, in April 1921, Hitler displayed the same dualistic thinking that marked other Nazi leaders surveyed so far, overlapping categories of the Christian and the Aryan on the one hand, the Antichrist and the Semite on the other: "I can imagine Christ as nothing other than blond and with blue eyes, the devil however only with a Jewish grimace."[62] In a party gathering at Munich's Bürgerbräukeller in April 1922, Hitler dealt with the question of whether one could be both antisemitic and Christian: "My Christian feelings point me to my Lord and Savior as a fighter (tumultuous, prolonged applause). They point me toward the man who, once lonely and surrounded by only a few followers, recognized these Jews and called for battle against them, and who, as the true God, was not only the greatest as a sufferer but also the greatest as a warrior."[63]

The acquisition of power did not lead the Nazis to jettison this Christian language. After the seizure of power as before it, in private as in public, such themes continued to be enunciated. In a reception for the Catholic Bishop Berning on 26 April, Hitler freely conceded: "I have been attacked because of my handling of the Jewish question." But he immediately tied his attitude toward the Jews with the Church's historical position: "The Catholic Church considered the Jews pestilent for fifteen hundred years, put them in ghettos, etc., because it recognized the Jews for what they were." Hitler suggested antisemitic legislation being taken was in line with Christian principle: "I recognize the representatives of this race as pestilent for the state and for the church and perhaps I am thereby doing Christianity a great service by pushing them out of schools and public functions."[64] The strategic usefulness of such a statement—to disarm possible criticism of Nazi antisemitism from Catholic quarters—is self-evident. However, there is again no direct evidence that Hitler did not believe what he said. In 1937, Goebbels took note of Hitler's religious views: "The *Führer* on Christianity and Christ. [Christ] was also against Jewish world domination. Jewry had him crucified. But Paul falsified his doctrine and undermined ancient Rome. The Jew in Christianity. Marx did the same with the German sense of community, with socialism. That must not prevent us from being socialists."[65] Nor, Goebbels implies, must Paul prevent them from being Christian. Just as a "pure" socialism could be redeemed from a "Jewish" or Marxist corruption, so could a pure Christianity be redeemed from a Jewish or Pauline corruption. For Hitler, Nazism represented not only the antithesis of these later defilements, but the defense of the original forms.

Even during the war, when Hitler's ranting against the churches grew increasingly vituperative, he retained the religious dimension of his antisemitism. According to the *Table Talk,* on one such occasion he proclaimed: "The Galilean, who later was called the Christ, intended something quite different. He must be regarded as a popular leader who took up his position against Jewry. . . . He set Himself against Jewish capitalism, and that is why the Jews liquidated Him."[66] This interpretation of Jesus—as the messenger of a new belief who had been betrayed by a corrupt establishment—was remarkably consistent with the remarks Hitler made about the churches before he came to power.[67] Hitler showed no willingness to give up on the figure of Jesus, whose status as an Aryan remained unquestioned: "It is certain that Jesus was not a Jew."[68] As late as November 1944, just a few months before his death, he stated: "Jesus was most certainly not a Jew. . . . Jesus fought against the materialism of His age, and, therefore, against the Jews."[69]

The continued inspiration Hitler professed to gain from Christ as the "original antisemite" points to an ongoing Christian element in Hitler's Jew-hatred. In *Table Talk,* Hitler makes no direct declaration that his antisemitism was religious rather than racial. But his political testament, written just a few days before his death, contains a highly relevant passage about the nature of his hatred: "We speak of the Jewish race only as a linguistic convenience, for in the true sense of the word, and from a genetic standpoint, *there is no Jewish race.* . . . The Jewish race is above all a community of the spirit. Anthropologically the Jews do not exhibit those common characteristics that would identify them as a uniform race. . . . A spiritual race is harder and more lasting than a natural race."[70] With one stroke Hitler apparently discarded the flimsy biologistic apparatus he and his movement had used with such regularity to prove that Nazi antisemitism, unlike previous forms of Jew-hatred, was "scientific." Rejecting the notion that the Jews were a biological race implicitly meant that the idea of biological antisemitism—never a clean category in the first place—was also to be rejected.[71] In this instance, at least, we see not an interweaving or cohabitation of racial and religious categories of the Jew, but a simple denial of the racial category altogether. As Hitler stated in his secret conversations, Christ understood the danger of the Jews, and led an inspired struggle against them. If Hitler made no explicit statement that killing the Jews was revenge for the death of Christ, or for the refusal of Jews to recognize Christ as the Lord, he nonetheless believed that Christ "fought" the Jews, and that they "liquidated" him. Christ's affirmative example was returned to again and again, throughout the period of the Final Solution.

Even among the so-called neo-pagans of the Nazi movement, those who strenuously professed their hatred and rejection of Christianity in all its forms, we see a similar use of Christian rhetoric and logic to explain Nazi antisemitism. The most important exponent of this strand of Nazi ideology was Alfred Rosenberg. And of his many books, the most important for elaborating upon these ideas is *Der Mythus des 20. Jahrhunderts* (The Myth of the Twentieth Century). Speaking of the need to create a new religion, Rosenberg proclaimed: "Today a new faith is awakening: the myth of blood, the faith that the divine essence of mankind is to be defended through blood; the faith embodied by the fullest realization that Nordic blood represents the mystery which has supplanted and surmounted the old sacraments."[72] This new religion would place the highest value in the idea of racial honor: "The idea of honor—national honor—is for us the beginning and end of all our thoughts and deeds. It can endure no equivalent center of power of any type, neither Christian love nor freemasonic humanism nor Roman dogmatism."[73] This Christian "brotherhood of man" was nothing more than an attempt to allow Jew and "Turk" to take precedence over the European. In the name of Christian love, Europe was besieged by unrest and chaos: "Thanks to preaching on humanity and the equality of all peoples, every

Jew, Negro and Mulatto can be a full citizen of a European state."[74] When the Nordic states of Europe were overwhelmed by the Roman south, the concept of honor was overtaken by that of Christian love: "Christianity . . . did not know the idea of race and nationality, because it represented a violent fusion of different elements; it also knew nothing of the idea of honor, because in pursuance of the late Roman quest for power it subdued not only the body, but also the soul."[75] This emphasis on love brought Christianity in alliance with Marxism. If the concept of national honor was once again to be dominant, it could only happen when the "true workers" of the German *Volk* formed a united front against all forces associated with economy, profit, and money, "regardless of whether these forces were hidden under the cloak of democracy, Christianity, internationalism [or] humanism."[76]

Rosenberg also rejected the Christian doctrine of original sin: "The sense of sin always goes together with physical and racial cross-breeding. The abominable mixing of races creates . . . inner uncertainty and the feeling that our whole existence is sinful."[77] The Romans had been racially aware, according to Rosenberg, and so could only reject this Christian cross-breeding: "Everything still imbued with the Roman character sought to defend itself against the rise of Christianity, all the more because it represented, next to its religious teaching, a completely proletarian-nihilistic political trend."[78] Rosenberg was also opposed to the Trinity, which he believed overlooked the spirituality of racial nationalism and lead to the "nihilism" implicit in the biblical expression of Paul: "Here is neither Jew nor Greek, neither bond nor free, neither man nor woman." This nihilism led to the purposeful destruction of Greek and Roman civilizations as culturally worthless. Another Christian doctrine, this time explicitly Catholic, rejected by Rosenberg was the "dogmatization" of the virgin birth of Jesus, which was regarded as a negation of nature. In addition, he also attacked the biblical emphasis on the resurrection.[79]

Hence we have a near total denunciation of Christian doctrines. Unlike other Nazis, who for the most part left doctrinal questions unexamined, Rosenberg actively rejected them. Where other Nazis referred to "positive Christianity" as a fundament of party ideology, in *Mythus* Rosenberg made no mention of it. Where other Nazis believed that racialism could be subsumed into Christianity, apparently Rosenberg believed that only a new, anti-Christian or non-Christian religion could arrive at such a synthesis. However, in spite of Rosenberg's denunciation of Christianity's history and his desire to build a new racialist faith, time and again he excluded the most prominent figures of the Christian faith—Jesus most importantly—from his attacks, and upheld another Christian—the medieval mystic Meister Eckhart—as the inspiration of his new belief system. Indeed, in *Mythus* Rosenberg ultimately argued that Christianity itself could be reformed and saved from the "Judeo-Roman" infections of its clerical representatives.

Like all the other Nazis surveyed here, Rosenberg believed that Jesus had been an Aryan. Here he followed his greatest mentor, Houston Stewart Chamberlain, who had maintained that "in all probability" Jesus had not been a Jew.[80] Rosenberg affirmed his belief that whereas Jesus was born into a Jewish culture, "there was not the slightest reason" to assume that Jesus was Jewish. Christ's teaching that the Kingdom of Heaven is within us was a "thoroughly un-Jewish, mystical teaching."[81] The traditional, ecclesiastical picture of Jesus had been a distortion of the Roman Church to present a picture of submission and meekness, in order to create an ideal that would foster servility. In its place Rosenberg called for a new, manly image of Christ: "Today Jesus appears to us as the self-confident Lord in the best and highest sense of the word. It is his *life* which holds meaning for the Germanic people, not his agonizing death, which is the image of him among the Alpine and Mediterranean peoples. The mighty preacher and wrathful one in the temple, the man who swept along his followers, is the ideal which today shines forth from the Gospels, not the sacrificial lamb of the Jewish prophets, not the crucified."[82] Instead of the conventional image of Jesus as the sufferer, an old-new picture had to emerge: Jesus the *hero*.[83] Jesus was not the "hook-nosed, flat-footed savior" of southern European depiction, but the "slim, tall, blond" savior of northern European portrayals.[84] His entire being was a fiery resistance: for *that* reason he had to die.[85]

Although Rosenberg emphasized Jesus' human, temporal acts over his divine transcendence, this did not necessarily mean that Jesus had lost his divinity altogether. "In *spite* of all the Christian churches, Jesus is a linchpin of our history. He became the God of the Europeans."[86] Rosenberg made many other references of Christ's divinity. In the context of the "Nordic" Meister Eckhart, whom he regarded as both the ultimate Germanic religious hero and the "poet of the Savior," Rosenberg suggested that humankind should be independent of the clergy, be made aware of the individual's own spiritual uniqueness, and follow the example of Christ's own "holy union of divine and human natures."[87] Rosenberg even adhered to conventional Christology when discussing Chamberlain's religious views: "A totally free man, who inwardly disposed with the total culture of our time, demonstrated the finest feeling for the great superhuman simplicity of Christ . . . as the mediator between man and God."[88]

As with other Nazi leaders, Rosenberg also believed the Old Testament had to be removed from Christianity's corpus: "As a religious book the so-called Old Testament must be abolished for all time. With it will end the failed attempt of the last fifteen hundred years to spiritually make us Jews."[89] However, while other Nazis were largely content to stop at the Old Testament, Rosenberg went a step further, calling as well for the removal of "obviously distorted" portions of the New Testament. In addition, a new "Fifth Gospel" should be introduced.[90] Rejecting so much of Christianity and suggesting alternatives clearly prohibits Rosenberg from being considered Christian. But his agenda did not amount to a total negation of preexisting gospel. Rosenberg approved of two in particular, those of John and Mark. John held out the "first ingenious interpretation, the experience of the eternal polarity between good and evil," and stood "against the Old Testament delusion that God created good and evil out of nothing."[91] The Gospel of Mark signified "the real heart of the message of kinship with God, against the semitic teaching of God's tyranny."[92] Even the Christian notion of love, while it had wrought racial contamination in Nordic Europe, could in some instances be salvaged: "Love, humility, charity, prayer, good works, mercy and repentance are all good and useful, but only under one condition: if they strengthen the power of the soul, elevate it and make it more God-like."[93]

In Rosenberg's other writings, an element favorable to Christianity (albeit radically reformist) is found. In his 1920 book *Immorality in the Talmud,* Rosenberg attempted to show that the Jews' "rise to power" had come by way of lies and treachery motivated by a hatred of Christianity, which "has reached its summit in the systematic persecution of Christians by the Jewish Bolshevik rulers in Russia."[94] In the second book he wrote that year, *The Tracks of the Jew in the Change of Time,* Rosenberg called for an attack on Jewish materialism. A sharp distinction was to be made between it and Christian spirituality. The antimaterialist, Nordic religious renascence was to take place by purging the Old Testament from Christianity, which would raise Christian belief above the "Jewish slag."[95]

While it might be supposed that such utterances typify the Nazi ability to improvise an ideological mumbo-jumbo to suit their immediate purposes (obtaining the votes of church-goers in this case), many Nazis spoke repeatedly and systematically in such terms—and not solely for public consumption. Nor was the Nazi understanding of Christianity as a race religion simply an external "infection" of a formally pristine faith: all of their racial-religious formulations found expression within one of the varieties of Christian theology current in Germany before the Nazis even existed. The Nazi call for a theology of race; the rejection of the Old Testament as "Jewish"; even in the denial of Jewishness of the person of Jesus; all these seemingly heretical aspects of Nazi religious thinking could find their counterparts in some form or another of preexisting Christian theology—significantly, usually Protestant.

The ontological priority given in the Nazi worldview to race is undeniable. And among the many targets of Nazi racism, or racialism, the Jews stood squarely in the middle and qualitatively apart. However, the same antisemitism that is usually regarded as a function of racialism was for many Nazis conceived within a Christian frame of reference. Even as they argued that race was the supreme law of life, they did not argue that it overrode religion, since in their view race was God's law. Rather, they commingled racial and religious categories of the Jew, and conversely used "Aryan" and "Christian" as interchangeable categories as well. Some went even further by subsuming racialism within religion. As we have seen, the two categories did not constitute an "either-or" choice for Nazi ideologues. To the contrary: some of the most vituperative racialists also displayed a keen identity as Christians, and furthermore imparted a Christian identity to their movement. In the process, they revealed that their antisemitism was far from a secular or scientific replacement for Christian forms of Jew-hatred.

NOTES

1. http://www.jcrelations.net/articl1/rudin.htm, accessed June 2004 (emphasis added).

2. The most prominent works in this vein are John Conway, *The Nazi Persecution of the Churches* (London: Weidenfeld and Nicolson, 1968), and Hans Buchheim, *Glaubenskrise im Dritten Reich: Drei Kapitel nationalsozialistischer Religionspolitik* (Stuttgart: Deutsche Verlags-Anstalt, 1953).

3. Besides the works cited above, there is Hubert Locke, ed., *The Church Confronts the Nazis: Barmen Then and Now* (Lewiston, N.Y.: Edwin Mellon Press, 1984), and more recently Theodore Thomas, *Women against Hitler: Christian Resistance in the Third Reich* (Westport, Conn.: Praeger, 1995).

4. Ian Kershaw, "Totalitarianism Revisited: Nazism and Stalinism in Comparative Perspective," *Tel Aviver Jahrbuch für deutsche Geschichte* 23 (1994): 32.

5. For example, see Doris Bergen, *Twisted Cross: The German Christian Move-

ment in the Third Reich (Chapel Hill: University of North Carolina Press,1996);
Robert Ericksen, *Theologians under Hitler: Gerhard Kittel, Paul Althaus and Em-
manuel Hirsch* (New Haven, Conn.: Yale University Press, 1985); Ernst Klee, 'Die SA
Jesu Christi': Die Kirche im Banne Hitlers (Frankfurt: Fischer, 1989). An excellent
overview can be found in Robert Ericksen and Susannah Heschel, "The German
Churches Face Hitler." The collection of essays Ericksen and Heschel have edited,
Betrayal: German Churches and the Holocaust (Minneapolis: Fortress Press, 1999),
provides the best overview of current research on the topic.

6. Shelley Baranowski, *The Confessing Church, Conservative Elites, and the Nazi
State* (Lewiston, N.Y.: Edwin Mellen Press,1986); Victoria Barnett, *For the Soul of the
People: Protestant Protest against Hitler* (New York: Oxford University Press, 1992);
Wolfgang Gerlach, *Als die Zeugen schwiegen: Bekennende Kirche und die Juden* (Ber-
lin: Institut Kirche und Judentum, 1987).

7. Franklin Littell, *The Crucifixion of the Jews* (New York: Harper and Row,
1975), 45.

8. Ibid. (emphasis mine).

9. Saul Friedländer, *Nazi Germany and the Jews: The Years of Persecution, 1933–
1939* (New York: HarperCollins, 1997), 85.

10. George Steiner, "Through that Glass Darkly," reprinted in *No Passion Spent:
Essays 1978–1996*, (London: Faber and Faber, 1996), 336. He continues: "More
specifically, we will not achieve penetration into the persistent psychosis of Christianity which is that of Jew-hatred (even where there are no or hardly any Jews left)
unless we come to discern in this dynamic pathology the unhealed scars left by the
Jew's 'No' to the crucified Messiah."

11. A good introduction to the frequently sharp disagreements between Steiner
and Maccoby is found in Ron Rosenbaum, *Explaining Hitler: The Search for the
Origins of his Evil* (New York: Random House, 1998), 320–21, 330–31.

12. Detlev Peukert, "The Genesis of the 'Final Solution' from the Spirit of
Science," in *Reevaluating the Third Reich,* ed. Thomas Childers and Jane Caplan (New
York: Holmes and Meier, 1993), 247.

13. David Goldenberg, *The Curse of Ham: Race and Slavery in Early Judaism,
Christianity and Islam* (Princeton, N.J.: Princeton University Press, 2003).

14. Walter Künneth, Werner Wilm, and Hans Schemm, *Was haben wir als
evangelische Christen zum Rufe des Nationalsozialismus zu sagen?* (Dresden: Land-
esverein für Innere Mission, 1931), 19–20.

15. "Luther und das Deutschtum," Bundesarchiv Berlin (hereafter BArch B)
NS12/808, reprinted in *Hans Schemm spricht: Seine Reden und sein Werk,* ed. Ger-
trud Kahl-Furthmann (Bayreuth: Gauverlag Bayerische Ostmark 1935), 126. This
reference confirms that Nazis were aware of Luther's notorious "On the Jews and
Their Lies" and seem to have gained inspiration from it. Portions of this tract also
found their way onto the pages of the *Völkischer Beobachter* (hereafter *VB*): see
"Luther und die Juden," *VB*, September 8, 1933; "Luther und die Judenfrage," *VB*,
November 18, 1933.

16. *Auf gut deutsch* 3 (1919): 297.

17. Ibid., 38.

18. *Auf gut deutsch* 1 (1919): 199.

19. Quoted in Alfred Rosenberg, *Dietrich Eckart: Ein Vermächtnis* (Munich:
Franz Eher, 1935), 112.

20. Margarete Plewnia, *Auf dem Weg zu Hitler: Der 'völkische' Publizist Dietrich
Eckart* (Bremen: Schünemann 1970), 46.

21. *Auf gut deutsch* 3 (1919): 36.

22. D. R. Tracey, "The Development of the National Socialist Party in Thuringia,
1924–1930," *Central European History* 8 (1975): 26n13; George Kren and Rodler

Morris, "Race and Spirituality: Arthur Dinter's Theosophical Antisemitism," *Holocaust and Genocide Studies* 6 (1991): 238.

23. Uwe Lohalm, *Völkischer Radikalismus: Die Geschichte des deutschvölkischen Schutz- und Trutz-Bundes, 1919–1923* (Hamburg: Leibniz, 1970), 126.

24. Arthur Dinter, *Die Sünde wider das Blut* (Leipzig: Matthes und Thost, 1918), 187.

25. Ibid., 296.

26. Ibid., 369.

27. Arthur Dinter, *Die Sünde wider die Liebe* (Leipzig: Matthes und Thost, 1922), 169.

28. Dinter, *Blut*, 172.

29. Arthur Dinter, *Die Sünde wider den Geist* (Leipzig: Matthes und Thost, 1921), 60.

30. As quoted in Kren and Morris, "Spirituality," 242.

31. See, among others, Helmut Heiber, *Joseph Goebbels* (Munich: Colloquium, 1988); Ulrich Höver, *Joseph Goebbels, ein nationaler Sozialist* (Bonn: Bouvier, 1992); Ulrich Nill, *Die 'geniale Vereinfachung': Anti-Intellektualismus in Ideologie und Sprachgebrauch bei Joseph Goebbels* (Frankfurt: Peter Lang, 1991); Ralf Georg Reuth, *Goebbels* (Munich: Piper, 1990). None of these works address Goebbels's Christian preoccupations: the only one not to overlook this is Claus-Ekkehard Bärsch, *Erlösung und Vernichtung, Joseph Goebbels: Zur Psyche und Ideologie eines jungen Nationalsozialisten* (Munich: Boer, 1987). See also the very important collection of Goebbels's diaries: Elke Fröhlich, ed., *Die Tagebücher von Joseph Goebbels: Sämtliche Fragmente* (Munich: K. G. Saur, 1987).

32. Fröhlich, ed., *Tagebücher,* entry for August 6, 1924.

33. Joseph Goebbels, "Die Revolution als Ding an sich," in *Wege ins Dritte Reich: Briefe und Aufsätze für Zeitgenossen* (Munich: Franz Eher, 1927), 48.

34. Joseph Goebbels, *Michael: Ein deutsches Schicksal in Tagebuchblättern* (Munich: Franz Eher, 1929) (English translation hereafter: *Michael: A Novel,* trans. Joachim Neugroschel [New York: Amok Press, 1987], 45). Helmut Heiber for one believes that the manuscript was written as early as 1923. It went through seventeen printings by 1945.

35. Ibid., 38.

36. Ibid., 65.

37. Ibid., 45 (emphasis added).

38. Ibid., 38–39.

39. "Kulturkampf!" March 10, 1924, Institut für Zeitgeschichte (hereafter IfZ), MA 740.

40. Holger Germann, *Die politische Religion des Nationalsozialisten Dietrich Klagges: Ein Beitrag zur Phänomenologie der NS-Ideologie* (Frankfurt: Peter Lang, 1995), 16.

41. Fröhlich, *Tagebücher,* entry for May 29, 1926.

42. Dietrich Klagges, *Das Urevangelium Jesu: Der Deutsche Glaube* (Wilster: Meister Ekkehart Verlag, 1925), 265.

43. Ibid., 46.

44. Ibid., 57–58.

45. See Donald M. McKale, *The Nazi Party Courts: Hitler's Management of Conflict in His Movement, 1921–1945* (Lawrence: University Press of Kansas, 1974).

46. Jochen von Lang, *The Secretary, Martin Bormann: The Man Who Manipulated Hitler* (New York: Random House, 1979), 47–48.

47. "Geist und Kampf," n.d., BArch NS 26/1375.

48. *Der Aufmärsch, Blätter der deutschen Jugend* 2 (January 1931), in BArch B NS26/1375.

49. McKale, *Courts,* 54.

50. *Der Aufmarsch* 2. Based on this evidence we can argue against McKale's assertion that Buch "despised Jews not so much for religious or cultural reasons" (*Courts,* 55).

51. McKale, *Courts,* 57.

52. "Niedergang und Aufstieg der deutschen Familie," *Der Schlesische Erzieher,* May 18–25, 1935 (transcript of 1932 speech): in BArch B Personalakte Buch.

53. "On the Jews and Their Lies" is one of the most notorious antisemitic tracts ever written, especially for someone of Luther's esteem. The rising tide of violence in the work finds its climax in the following passages: "If I had power over the Jews, as our princes and cities have, I would deal severely with their lying mouths. . . . For a usurer is an arch-thief and a robber who should rightly be hanged on the gallows seven times higher than other thieves. . . . We are at fault in not avenging all this innocent blood of our Lord and of the Christians which they shed for three hundred years after the destruction of Jerusalem, and the blood of the children they have shed since then (which still shines forth from their eyes and their skin). We are at fault in not slaying them." Martin Luther, "On the Jews and Their Lies," in *Luther's Works,* trans. Franklin Sherman (Philadelphia, Pa.: Fortress Press, 1971), 267 and 289. At one point, Luther anticipates the medical and scientific metaphors used by racialist antisemites later: "I wish and I ask that our rulers who have Jewish subjects exercise a sharp mercy towards these wretched people. . . . They must act like a good physician who, when gangrene has set in, proceeds without mercy to cut, saw, and burn flesh, veins, bone and marrow. Such a procedure must also be followed in this instance" (ibid., 292).

54. Hitler, *Mein Kampf,* trans. Ralph Manheim (Boston: Houghton Mifflin, 1962), 214, 327.

55. Ibid., 405.

56. Ibid., 562 (emphasis in the original).

57. Eberhard Jäckel, ed., *Hitler: Sämtliche Aufzeichnungen 1905–1924* (Stuttgart: Deutsche Verlags-Anstalt, 1980), 635. Speech of May 26, 1922, originally reported in the *NSDAP-Mitteilungsblatt,* Nr. 14.

58. Hitler, *Mein Kampf,* 65. Saul Friedländer suggests that this passage got to the heart of the Nazis' antisemitism: *Nazi Germany and the Jews,* 98. He contends that the Nazis subscribed to a "Redemptive" antisemitism, "born from the fear of racial degeneration and the religious belief in redemption" (ibid., 87).

59. Hitler, *Mein Kampf,* 306.

60. Ibid., 307.

61. Ibid., 324.

62. *VB,* April 28, 1921.

63. *VB,* April 22, 1922.

64. Quoted in Friedländer, *Nazi Germany and the Jews,* 47.

65. Fröhlich, *Tagebücher,* entry for February 23, 1937.

66. Entry of October 21, 1941. *Hitler's Table Talk 1941–1944: His Private Conversations,* trans. Norman Cameron and R. H. Stevens (London: Weidenfeld and Nicolson, 1953), 76.

67. Otto Wagener, *Hitler: Memoirs of a Confidant,* ed. Henry Ashby Turner (New Haven, Conn.: Yale University Press, 1985), 139–40.

68. Entry of October 21, 1941, *Hitler's Table Talk,* 76.

69. Ibid., 721 (November 29–30, 1944).

70. Adolf Hitler, *Politisches Testament: Die Bormann-Diktate vom Februar und April 1945* (Hamburg: A. Knaus, 1981), 68–69 (emphasis added).

71. This goes against the argument of many scholars of antisemitism who contend, as Gavin Langmuir puts it, that "[w]hen Hitler thought of 'Jews,' he thought

about an imaginary race whose members' horrifyingly evil moral and social ideas and characteristics could not be changed because they were inescapably determined by biological characteristics that might be diluted but could not be changed." Gavin Langmuir, "Continuities, Discontinuities and Contingencies of the Holocaust," in *The Fate of the European Jews, 1939–1945: Continuity or Contingency?* ed. Jonathan Frankel (Oxford: Oxford University Press, 1997), 25.

72. Alfred Rosenberg, *Der Mythus des 20. Jahrhunderts: Eine Wertung der seelisch-geistigen Gestaltenkämpfe unserer Zeit* (Munich: Hoheneichen, 1931), 114.

73. Ibid., 514.

74. Ibid., 203.

75. Ibid., 155–56.

76. Ibid., 204–205.

77. Ibid., 71.

78. Ibid.

79. Ibid., 77–78.

80. The very title "Myth of the Twentieth Century" was a tribute to Chamberlain's "Foundations of the Nineteenth Century" of 1899, a work which Rosenberg adored and for which *Mythus* was designed as a type of sequel.

81. Rosenberg, *Mythus*, 76.

82. Ibid., 604 (emphasis in the original).

83. Ibid., 414.

84. Ibid., 616.

85. Ibid., 607.

86. Ibid., 391 (emphasis in the original).

87. Ibid., 230.

88. Ibid., 623–34.

89. Ibid., 603.

90. Ibid. Rosenberg made no mention of what this new gospel would look like.

91. Ibid., 604.

92. Ibid.

93. Ibid., 238.

94. Alfred Rosenberg, *Unmoral im Talmud,* as quoted in Robert Cecil, *The Myth of the Master Race: Alfred Rosenberg and Nazi Ideology* (London: Batsford, 1972), 74. The reference to Christian Russians was not simply a feigned sympathy for Slavs. As would become evident during his failed career as Reich minister for the occupied eastern territories, Rosenberg was perhaps the most sympathetic of any Nazi to the conditions of the Slavic population, and often fought with his nominal underlings to lessen the brutality of their rule (Cecil, *Master Race,* 189–216, esp. 200). Whereas Rosenberg had envisioned a system of Slavic satellite states under German suzerainty, most other Nazis preferred a simpler system of direct German administration and exploitation.

95. Alfred Rosenberg, *Die Spur des Juden im Wandel der Zeiten* (Munich: Dt. Volks-Verlag, 1920), 321–22.

CONTRIBUTORS

SUZANNE BROWN-FLEMING is Senior Program Officer in the University Programs Division, Center for Advanced Holocaust Studies, United States Holocaust Memorial Museum, and a 2000–2001 Center for Advanced Holocaust Studies Fellow. She is author of *The Holocaust and Catholic Conscience: Cardinal Aloisius Muench and the Guilt Question in Germany*. Dr. Brown-Fleming's current research project, "The Vatican-German Relationship Re-Examined, 1922–1939," is a study of the Vatican nunciature in Munich and Berlin during the Weimar Republic and the period of Eugenio Pacelli's tenure as Vatican secretary of state (1930–39).

DONALD J. DIETRICH, Professor of Theology at Boston College, has focused his research and publications on German Catholic experiences ranging from the Tübingen School of Theology to the Third Reich. He has recently edited *Christian Responses to the Holocaust: Moral and Ethical Issues* and is completing his next book, *From Hitler to Human Rights: The Contributions of the German Catholic Experiences*. He is a member of the Church Relations Committee of the Center for Advanced Holocaust Studies, United States Holocaust Memorial Museum.

ELIAS H. FÜLLENBACH, O.P., is a doctoral student at the University of Bonn and a member of the Dominican Order. Currently, he is writing his dissertation on the life and work of Gertrud Luckner and editing a volume of essays that examines the relationship between Jews and Dominicans from the foundation of the order to the end of the Second World War. Füllenbach has published articles in the area of Catholic-Jewish relations and ecclesiastical history in a variety of German journals such as *Freiburger Rundbrief* and *Zeitschrift für Geschichtswissenschaft*. He is a member of the Rhineland Evangelical Church's Christen und Juden Committee and the Institute for Research of the History of the Dominican Order in the German-Speaking Lands. Together with Rabbi Walter Homolka he is the author of *Leo Baeck— Eine Skizze seines Lebens*.

GERSHON GREENBERG has served as Visiting Professor of Jewish Thought at Hebrew, Tel Aviv, Bar Ilan, and Haifa universities in Israel, and is Professor of Philosophy and Religion at American University in Washington, D.C. His research centers on the history of Jewish and Christian religious thought through the Holocaust. Publications include a three-volume bibliography, in Hebrew and Yiddish, of wartime Orthodox Jewish religious thought in response to the catastrophe; *Wrestling with God: Jewish Theological Responses during and after the Holocaust: A Source Reader,* with Steven T. Katz; and numerous articles and essays published in English-language, Hebrew, and German journals including *Yad Vashem Studies, Holocaust and Genocide Studies,* and *Journal of Jewish Thought and Philosophy.* Greenberg serves on the Lithuanian Commission for the Evaluation of the Crimes of the Nazi and Soviet Occupation Regimes, in the area of religious losses.

BETH A. GRIECH-POLELLE is Associate Professor of Modern European History at Bowling Green State University, Ohio. She earned her Ph.D. from Rutgers, The State University of New Jersey, New Brunswick. She has written *Bishop von Galen: German Catholicism and National Socialism* as well as articles and reviews for *Kirchliche Zeitgeschichte, The Journal of Contemporary History, The Journal of Modern European History, Holocaust and Genocide Studies, Social History, Catholic Historical Review,* and H-German (online).

MATTHEW D. HOCKENOS is Associate Professor of History at Skidmore College in upstate New York. His book *A Church Divided: German Protestants Confront the Nazi Past* (Indiana University Press, 2004) examines how Protestant church leaders, theologians, pastors, and parishioners struggled to explain and come to terms with the church's complacency toward and complicity under Nazi rule. He is presently engaged in researching and writing a study on Protestant-Jewish relations in postwar Germany.

ROBERT A. KRIEG is Professor of Theology at the University of Notre Dame. Krieg is author of *Catholic Theologians in Nazi Germany; Story-Shaped Christology; Karl Adam: Catholicism in German Culture;* and *Romano Guardini: A Precursor of Vatican II.* He has also edited *Romano Guardini: Spiritual Writings* and *Romano Guardini: Proclaiming the Sacred in a Modern World.* Krieg's articles have appeared in *The Heythrop Journal, The Irish Theological Quarterly, The Journal of Religious Thought, Theologische Quartalschrift, Theological Studies,* and *Worship.* Currently, he serves on the editorial board of *Theological Studies.*

ANNA ŁYSIAK is a Ph.D. candidate at Jagiellonian University, Department of Philosophy, Institute for the Study of Religion, Kraków, Poland. Her doctoral dissertation examines the perception of Judaism in the writings of Polish Catholic theologians in the interwar period (1918–39). She is also actively involved with the Pontifical Academy of Theology in Kraków and with interfaith dialogue.

JOHN T. PAWLIKOWSKI, O.S.M., is Professor of Ethics and Director of the Catholic-Jewish Studies Program at the Catholic Theological Union. Pawlikowski is a preeminent figure in the area of Jewish-Christian relations and is author of numerous books and articles on interfaith dialogue and the Holocaust. Involved with the work of the United States Holocaust Memorial

Museum since its creation, he currently serves as chair of its Church Relations Committee and as a member of its Committee on Conscience and Academic Committee. Pawlikowski is a priest of the Servite order.

PAUL A. SHAPIRO is Director of the Center for Advanced Holocaust Studies, United States Holocaust Memorial Museum. Shapiro has served as a consultant to the Office of Special Investigations (OSI), United States Department of Justice. In the 1970s, he provided the historical research that led to the denaturalization and deportation of the Romanian Archbishop of the United States, a former leader of the Romanian fascist Iron Guard. This was the first case brought to successful conclusion by the OSI. Currently, Shapiro is a member of the congressionally mandated Interagency Working Group on Nazi War Crimes and Japanese Imperial Government Records that is overseeing the declassification of Holocaust-related materials in the archives of U.S. federal government agencies; serves as a specialist on the U.S. delegation to the International Commission of the International Tracing Service of the Red Cross; and is on the Academic Advisory Committee of the Center for Jewish History in New York. In 2003–2004, he served as a member of the International Commission on the Holocaust in Romania, chaired by Nobel Laureate Elie Wiesel, and wrote, among other sections, the chapter on Romanian antisemitism before the Holocaust.

KEVIN P. SPICER, C.S.C., is Associate Professor of History at Stonehill College, Easton, Massachusetts. He is author of *Resisting the Third Reich: The Catholic Clergy in Hitler's Berlin.* He has also published articles in a variety of journals, including *Church History* and *Historisches Jahrbuch,* and in several edited volumes. Currently he is writing a collective biographical study of Catholic priests who openly supported Hitler and the Nazi Party. Spicer is a member of the Church Relations Committee of the Center for Advanced Holocaust Studies, United States Holocaust Memorial Museum, a 2005–2006 Center for Advanced Holocaust Studies Fellow, and a priest of the Congregation of Holy Cross.

RICHARD STEIGMANN-GALL is Associate Professor of History and Director of the Jewish Studies Program at Kent State University. He received his Ph.D. in history at the University of Toronto in 1999, specializing in Nazi Germany. He has published *The Holy Reich: Nazi Conceptions of Christianity, 1919–1945* and articles, on various aspects of the relationship between Christianity and Nazism, in the journals *German History, Kirchliche Zeitgeschichte, Social History, Central European History,* and *Totalitarian Movements and Political Religions.* He will contribute the chapter on "Religion and the Churches" to the forthcoming *Oxford Short History of the Third Reich.* His current research project, tentatively titled "Neither Aryan nor Semite," concerns the construction of racial identity in the Nazi state.

Thorsten Wagner is a doctoral student at the Technical University of Berlin, Germany. His dissertation addresses the emancipation and acculturation of Danish Jewry between 1780 and 1849 through a comparative European perspective. He is author of numerous scholarly articles that have appeared journals such as *Nyt fra Historien, Tidsskrift for Historie, Kirchliche Zeitgeschichte, Noter,* and *Scandinavian Jewish Studies.*

INDEX

KEVIN P. SPICER, C.S.C., is Associate Professor of History at Stonehill College in Easton, Massachusetts. He is author of *Resisting the Third Reich: The Catholic Clergy in Hitler's Berlin*.